GLOBAL VALUE CHAINS IN A POSTCRISIS WORLD

GLOBAL VALUE CHAINS IN A POSTCRISIS WORLD

A DEVELOPMENT PERSPECTIVE

Olivier Cattaneo, Gary Gereffi, and Cornelia Staritz
Editors

THE WORLD BANK
Washington, D.C.

1818 H Street, NW
Washington, DC 20433
Telephone: 202-473-1000
Internet: www.worldbank.org

1 2 3 4 13 12 11 10

ISBN: 978-0-8213-8499-2
eISBN: 978-0-8213-8503-6
DOI: 10.1596/978-0-8213-8499-2

Library of Congress Cataloging-in-Publication Data

Global value chains in a postcrisis world : a development perspective / Olivier Cattaneo, Gary Gereffi, and Cornelia Staritz, editors.

p. cm.

Includes bibliographical references and index.

ISBN 978-0-8213-8499-2 — ISBN 978-0-8213-8503-6 (electronic)

1. International trade. 2. International economic relations. 3. Global Financial Crisis, 2008–2009. I. Cattaneo, Olivier. II. Gereffi, Gary. III. Staritz, Cornelia.

HF1379.G587 2010

337—dc22

2010031476

Cover images: © iStockphoto.com/Devonyu (Trade War); © iStockphoto.com/Wrangel (Golden Coins Texture)
Cover design by Tomoko Hirata/World Bank

CONTENTS

Boxes

Figures

Maps

Tables

CONTRIBUTORS

Olivier Cattaneo, Trade and Integration team in the Development Research Group at the World Bank, Washington, D.C.

Hubert Escaith, Economic Research and Statistics Division at the World Trade Organization, Geneva

Masuma Farooki, Development Policy and Practice Department at the Open University, Milton Keynes, U.K.

Karina Fernandez-Stark, Center on Globalization, Governance, and Competitiveness at Duke University, Durham, N.C.

Stacey Frederick, Center on Globalization, Governance, and Competitiveness at Duke University, Durham, N.C.

Gary Gereffi, Center on Globalization, Governance, and Competitiveness at Duke University, Durham, N.C.

Raphael Kaplinsky, Development Policy and Practice Department at the Open University, Milton Keynes, U.K.

Momoko Kawakami, Institute of Developing Economies at the Japan External Trade Organization, Chiba, Japan

Nannette Lindenberg, Institute of Empirical Economic Research at the University of Osnabrück, Germany

William Milberg, Department of Economics at the New School for Social Research, New York, N.Y.

Sébastien Miroudot, Trade and Policy Linkages and Services Division in the Trade and Agriculture Directorate at the Organisation for Economic Co-operation and Development, Paris

Cornelia Staritz, International Trade Department in the Poverty Reduction and Economic Management Network at the World Bank, Washington, D.C.

Timothy J. Sturgeon, Industrial Performance Center at the Massachusetts Institute of Technology, Cambridge, Mass.

Anne Terheggen, Development Policy and Practice at the Open University, Milton Keynes, U.K.

Julia Tijaja, Development Policy and Practice at the Open University, Milton Keynes, U.K.

Johannes Van Biesebroeck, Center for Economic Studies at Katholieke Universiteit Leuven, Belgium

Deborah Winkler, International Trade Department in the Poverty Reduction and Economic Management Network at the World Bank, Washington, D.C.

FOREWORD

The global economic crisis of 2008–09 has revealed the interdependence of the world economy. The financial crisis originated in the United States, but the resulting economic downturn quickly spread to the rest of the world. Trade, along with finance, was one of the main vectors of transmission of the crisis. In 2009, there was a massive contraction in global trade—minus 13 percent. The contraction was largely a reflection of a drop in demand, especially for durable goods.

The fact that the shock was transmitted very rapidly reflects the increasing reliance by businesses on so-called global value chains (GVCs)—the process of ever-finer specialization and geographic fragmentation of production, with the more labor-intensive parts of the production process transferred to developing countries. In a world where GVCs are the prevalent business model for multinational corporations, a reduction in demand for final products by global buyers implies that demand shocks are immediately transmitted "upstream" to subcontractors in developing countries.

The studies that are collected in this volume analyze the operation and likely implications of the ongoing "rebalancing" of the world economy for global value chains. The studies suggest that the crisis will not reverse globalization; instead, in the postcrisis period, it is likely that there will be faster consolidation of GVCs and a shift in demand from the traditional high-income markets in the North to the rising economic powers in the South.

As discussed in the contributions, the shift in the center of gravity of global demand and the growth in South-South trade create a number of challenges. These include the need to adjust production to satisfy different consumer preferences in emerging markets, a greater emphasis on price competitiveness, as well as possibly greater hurdles for low-income countries to move up the value chain given the structure of demand for—and supply of—exports by high-growth emerging markets.

The chapters collected in this book offer a comprehensive, in-depth analysis of one of the major drivers of global integration, shedding new light on recent developments and likely trends in the prospects for global production sharing going forward.

I am very grateful to the volume editors—Olivier Cattaneo, Gary Gereffi, and Cornelia Staritz—for their initiative in organizing the contributed chapters and to the Global Trade and Financial Architecture project (supported by the U.K. Department for International Development) that provided financial support for the effort.

Bernard Hoekman
Director, International Trade Department
Poverty Reduction and Economic Management Network
World Bank

ACKNOWLEDGMENTS

After the May 2009 London Summit, where leaders of the Group of Twenty designed a global plan for recovery and reform, the World Bank brought together researchers and trade policy practitioners to analyze responses to the global economic crisis of 2008–09 and their impact on trade and development. This work led to the 2009 publication of a first volume on the responses of national governments to the crisis—*Effective Crisis Response and Openness: Implications for the Trading System*, edited by Simon J. Evenett, Bernard Hoekman, and Olivier Cattaneo. This second volume focuses on business responses to the recent economic crisis.

The editors are grateful for the dedicated way in which the authors delivered, under serious time constraints, far more than we could have reasonably expected. The fast and constant evolution of the economic situation, from crisis to recovery, increased the difficulty, but also the value, of their task. At the time this volume was edited, the fate of the world economy was still uncertain, and the timid signs of recovery should not distract us from the revealed problems and changes prompted by the crisis.

The editors thank Bernard Hoekman, Director of the International Trade Department at the World Bank, for his guidance and support throughout the project. Michelle Chester and Rebecca Martin provided outstanding administrative support. They also acknowledge the impetus of the BIS-DFID (Department for Business Innovation and Skills—Department for International Development) Joint Trade Policy Unit that has been decisive in the launch of the project.

Analysis of the reactions to the crisis was part of the Global Trade and Financial Architecture (GTFA) project. Designed to build on the findings of the U.N. Millennium Task Force report on *Trade for Development*, GTFA is led by a steering committee of leading researchers and policy makers and cochaired by Ernesto Zedillo, Yale Center for the Study of Globalization, and Patrick Messerlin, Groupe d'Economie Mondiale de SciencesPo. GTFA's objectives are to identify and promote concrete policy options for reinvigorating and strengthening the multilateral economic system and institutions that have supported the process of globalization. A particular focus of the work, sponsored by DFID and managed by the World Bank, is on making the globalization process more sustainable and inclusive.

The views expressed in this volume are those of the authors and do not represent a position, official or unofficial, of the World Bank, GTFA, or the authors' organizations of affiliation.

Reference

Evenett, Simon J., Bernard Hoekman, and Olivier Cattaneo, eds. 2009. *Effective Crisis Response and Openness: Implications for the Trading System.* London: Centre for Economic Policy Research (CEPR) and World Bank.

ABBREVIATIONS

$	All dollar amounts are U.S. dollars unless otherwise indicated
ARDL	autoregressive distributed lag
ASEAN	Association of Southeast Asian Nations
ASICS	application-specific integrated circuits
ATC	Agreement on Textiles and Clothing
BCG	Boston Consulting Group
BEC	Broad Economic Category
BIOS	board-level operating system (also basic input-output system)
BPO	business process outsourcing
BRIC	Brazil, Russia, India, and China (economies)
CAD	computer-aided design
CAFTA	Central American Free Trade Agreement
CAGR	compound annual growth rate
CAP	Common Agricultural Policy (European Union)
CEEC	Central and Eastern European Countries
CGE	computable general equilibrium
CGGC	Center on Globalization, Governance, and Competitiveness
CMT	cut, make, and trim
CNC	computer numerical control (also computer-controlled)
CPU	central processing unit
CSF	critical success factor
CSR	corporate social responsibility
DR-CAFTA	Dominican Republic and Costa Rica, El Salvador, Guatemala, Honduras, and Nicaragua, member countries in the Central American Free Trade Agreement
ECM	error correction model
EIU	Economist Intelligence Unit
EMS	electronics manufacturing services

EPZ	export processing zone
EU 15	European Union 15 members (before 2004) (Austria, Belgium, Denmark, Finland, France, Germany, Greece, Ireland, Italy, Luxembourg, Netherlands, Portugal, Spain, Sweden, and the United Kingdom)
EU 27	European Union 27 members (Austria, Belgium, Bulgaria, Cyprus [Greek part], Czech Republic, Denmark, Estonia, Finland, France, Germany, Greece, Hungary, Ireland, Italy, Latvia, Lithuania, Luxembourg, Malta, Netherlands, Poland, Portugal, Romania, Slovakia, Slovenia, Spain, Sweden, and the United Kingdom)
FDI	foreign direct investment
FLEGT	Forest Law Enforcement, Governance and Trade Programme (European Union)
FOB	free-on-board
FSC	Forest Stewardship Council
FTA	Free Trade Agreement
GDP	gross domestic product
GMP	Good Manufacturing Practice
GSP	Generalized System of Preferences
GTAP	Global Trade Analysis Project
GVC	global value chain
HACCP	Hazard Analysis and Critical Control Point certification
HHI	Herfindahl-Hirschman Index
IC	integrated circuit
ICT	information and communication technology
IDE-JETRO	Institute of Developing Economies–Japan External Trade Organization
IDH	independent design house
IDM	integrated device manufacturer
IMF	International Monetary Fund
IMVP	International Motor Vehicle Program
I-O	input-output
IRF	impulse response function
ISO	International Organization for Standardization
JV	joint venture
KPO	knowledge process outsourcing
LDC	less developed country
MDG	Millennium Development Goal
MFA	Multi-Fibre Arrangement
MIG	manufactured intermediate goods

MNC	multinational corporation
MNE	multinational enterprise
NAFTA	North American Free Trade Agreement
NBER	National Bureau of Economic Research
n.e.s.	not elsewhere specified
OBM	original brand manufacturing
ODM	original design manufacturing
OECD	Organisation for Economic Co-operation and Development
OEM	original equipment manufacturing
OLB	Origine et Légalité des Bois
OPT	outward processing trade arrangement (European Union)
PND	portable navigation device
PPP	purchasing power parity
QCD	quality, cost, delivery
R&D	research and development
RMG	ready-made garments
ROW	rest of the world
SAFTA	South Asian Free Trade Area
SITC	Standard International Trade Classification
SOC	system-on-chip technology
UNCTAD	United Nations Conference on Trade and Development
UNIDO	United Nations Industrial Development Organization
USITC	United States International Trade Commission
WDI	World Development Indicators
WEO	*World Economic Outlook*
WITS	World Integrated Trade Solution
WOS	wholly owned foreign subsidiary
WTO	World Trade Organization
YTY	year-to-year

PART I

INTRODUCTION AND OVERVIEW

1

GLOBAL VALUE CHAINS IN A POSTCRISIS WORLD: RESILIENCE, CONSOLIDATION, AND SHIFTING END MARKETS

Olivier Cattaneo, Gary Gereffi, and Cornelia Staritz

Setting the Scene

The world is recovering in a painful and halting manner from one of the most severe economic crises of modern history. There is no room for complacency or triumphalism: surging public debts and deficits, increasing global imbalances, and tensions in the monetary system are just a few of the challenges facing the postcrisis world economy. As the recovery unfolds, unemployment continues to rise in many countries, suggesting that the human chapter of the crisis is not closed. It is time, however, to draw some lessons from the turmoil of the past two years and take stock of changes that may profoundly affect the world economy for years to come. Was the recent crisis the first global recession of the 21st century or a more structural breakdown of globalization? Will global trade, demand, and production look the same as before, or has the crisis triggered or entrenched fundamental shifts?

This volume attempts to answer these questions by analyzing reactions to the global economic crisis of 2008–09 at the firm and industry levels through the lens of global value chains (GVCs). GVCs encompass the full range of activities that are required to bring a good or service from conception through the different phases of production—provision of raw materials; the input of various components, subassemblies, and producer services; the assembly of finished goods—to delivery to final consumers, as well as disposal after use. In the context of globalization, the activities that constitute a value chain are generally carried out in interfirm networks on a global scale. While the expansion of international trade since the 1970s is typically cited as evidence of economic globalization, much of this trade is not arm's length in nature. Indeed, a large and growing percentage of international trade occurs within various kinds of coordinated networks, which are economic structures that lie *between* the conceptual poles of markets and hierarchies (see, for instance, Gereffi 1999; Gereffi, Humphrey, and Sturgeon 2005).[1]

The GVC framework has been developed over the past decade by a diverse interdisciplinary and international group of researchers who have tracked the global spread of industries and studied the implications for both corporations and countries. By focusing on the sequences of value-added, from conception and production to end use, GVC analysis provides a holistic view of global industries—both from the top down (for example, examining how lead firms "govern" their global-scale affiliate and supplier networks) and from the bottom up (for example, asking how these business decisions affect the trajectories of economic and social "upgrading" or "downgrading" in specific countries and regions).

This volume analyzes GVC dynamics in the postcrisis environment with a particular focus on the opportunities and challenges faced by developing countries seeking to enter and upgrade their positions within GVCs. It also suggests measures countries might take to facilitate a more sustainable recovery from the economic crisis. After a discussion of general trends in GVCs, the chapters in this volume assess industry-specific dynamics in diverse global industries: apparel, automobiles, electronics, information technology (IT)-enabled services, and two specific agricultural commodities (timber and cassava). These industries were chosen to include the three main sectors in the global economy—extractive/agriculture, manufacturing, and services—and within manufacturing to cover industries with varied levels of technological sophistication.

Responses to the Crisis: Shifting from a Policy to a Business Focus

Since the April 2009 London Summit, where the Group of Twenty[2] leaders committed to "not repeat the historic mistakes of protectionism of previous eras,"[3] governments have made significant efforts to monitor and analyze policy responses to the crisis. Less is known about business responses to the crisis, even though the primary objective of policy interventions is to support economic activity through measures such as fiscal stimuli, bailouts, or large infrastructure projects—and sometimes to influence the location of business activity for the benefit of local production and employment. While it is impossible to examine every transaction in global industries, much can be learned from the actions of "lead firms," which include brand-name manufacturers, global marketers and traders, and large retailers that place orders with affiliate and supplier networks worldwide. How have lead firms responded to the crisis, the drop in demand, and policy interventions in major markets? Have they changed their supply chain strategies? Have they increased offshoring or outsourcing of production? Have they consolidated their supply chains?

Although economists have given considerable attention to measuring the effects of the crisis on industries in major developed countries, less is known about policy and business responses in developing countries, despite widespread recognition of their central role in the crisis and recovery. If major policy and business changes occurred during the crisis, what are the implications for developing countries that want to enter and upgrade within GVCs? What policy responses are appropriate?

At the Pittsburgh Summit in September 2009, the Group of Twenty leaders congratulated themselves and declared that the worst of the crisis was over: "It worked. Our forceful response helped stop the dangerous, sharp decline in global activity and [helped] stabilize financial markets. Industrial output is now rising in nearly all our economies. International trade is starting to recover."[4] It is unclear, however, whether there will be symmetry in recovery: Does a global crisis necessarily lead to a global recovery? Are there winners and losers emerging from the crisis and the recovery? Developing countries face opportunities and challenges as global growth returns. Now is the time to design policies that best prepare them for recovery and sustainable integration into GVCs in the postcrisis world.

The First Global Recession of the 21st Century or a Crisis of Globalization?

The economic downturn started with the bursting of the U.S. housing bubble in 2007, but quickly spread to the rest of the world through financial and trade channels. The crisis has clearly been the first global recession of the 21st century, often compared in its magnitude to the 1930s Great Depression. Some observers have suggested the crisis was not cyclical, however, but structural, calling it "a crisis of globalization."[5] There are diverse drivers and hence varied conceptions of globalization. In the 1970s and 1980s, globalization was driven to a large degree by the outsourcing of production by transnational manufacturers to low-wage countries and the corresponding expansion of international trade of both intermediate and finished goods However, events in the last two decades, most notably the Asian financial crisis of the late 1990s and the economic crisis of 2008–09, suggest that the key component of the most recent wave of globalization has not been trade, but rather financial globalization. How has the face of globalization changed as a result of this crisis? Is the current crisis of globalization likely to lead to a repudiation of the policies of openness and export-led growth, with drastic and permanent changes in global production, demand, and trade patterns? Will international firms continue to use business strategies centered on GVCs?

This volume concludes that GVCs have proven resilient. They have become crucial and enduring structural features of the world economy. In the aftermath of the Asian financial crisis in the late 1990s, similar discussions about "the end of globalization" and the "retrenchment of global production arrangements" in the Asian context arose, but global supply chains bounced back more quickly than expected. The research collected in this volume suggests that the crisis has not reversed globalization, but accelerated two long-term trends in the global economy: the consolidation of GVCs and the growing salience of markets in the South. Not all developing countries face similar options in the context of these changes: The shift to Southern markets and the growth in South-South trade has created more possibilities for entry and upgrading in GVCs, but also has resulted in new challenges, in particular for the least-developed countries. GVC consolidation poses significant opportunities as well, especially for countries and firms with rising capabilities, but it threatens to leave many countries on the periphery. This volume suggests that international production and consumption have remained global. The role of the South has grown, but inequalities among developing countries threaten to rise, which could generate additional sources of instability and potential crises in the future.

The Crisis, Trade, and Global Value Chains

In recent decades, the world economy has been shaken by several financial crises, but most tended to remain regional in scope (for example, Asia in 1997 and South America in 2002). In this most recent crisis, major trade and financial imbalances, a liquidity problem, and a collapse of demand in the United States quickly spread to the rest of the world through financial and trade channels, resulting in a global slowdown of unprecedented scale. This crisis was felt globally (rather than in just some regions), and it spread as the result of the globalized nature of financial markets (see, for instance, Reinhart and Felton 2008). But this is also true for the trade and production side of the economy.

The crisis of 2008–09 is the first that clearly reflects the pervasive and sophisticated globalization of production. For example, the postponement of new auto purchases by U.S. consumers affected not only the U.S. automobile industry, but also the Liberian rubber sector that produces the material for the tires, and so on through the global automotive supply chain (Jansen and von Uexkull 2010). In the electronics industry, Ferrantino and Larsen (2009) observe that "the drop in U.S. imports for computers and cell phones leads indirectly to a drop in U.S. exports of semiconductors and components." This is because cell phone assembly plants in China and elsewhere in the developing world depend on parts and components manufactured in the United States and other industrialized countries. An analysis of the recent export decline in Japan suggests that the fall in U.S. demand for Japanese final goods was accompanied by a drop in demand for intermediate goods destined for final assembly in China and Southeast Asia for shipment to the United States (Fukao and Yuan 2009). Ma and Van Assche (2009, 35) find that "[D]ue to China's heavy reliance on imported inputs from within the East Asian region, China's economy is actually less export-dependent than is traditionally thought. . . China effectively transfers a large portion of its negative export demand shocks to its East Asian neighbors by reducing its demand for their processing imports."

These examples illustrate a number of lessons. First, the world economies are increasingly integrated, interdependent, and specialized: when the largest supermarkets of the world or other large companies have sudden and severe declines in sales, foreign suppliers have to close down factories, and these shocks are transmitted throughout entire regions. Second, trade openness is a double-edged sword: while it can help to buffer against domestic and regional shocks, it increases exposure to external shocks. Third, given that production processes in many industries have been fragmented and moved around on a global scale, GVCs have become the world economy's backbone and central nervous system (see, for instance, Gereffi 1994; Gereffi, Humphrey, and Sturgeon 2005). As Milberg and Winkler (chapter 2) contend, GVCs, which only recently have entered the purview of economists, have suddenly moved to the core of debates over the causes and consequences of the 2009 collapse of global trade (see, for instance, Baldwin 2009).

Trade as Both a Casualty and a Transmission Channel of Economic Crises

International trade has been a casualty of the financial crisis. According to the World Bank, for the first time since the Great Depression, the world's gross domestic product (GDP) dropped by 2.2 percent in 2009, with a sharp 3.3 percent decline in the rich countries and a deceleration in developing countries as well from 5.6 percent growth of GDP in 2008 to 1.2 percent in 2009 (World Bank 2010). Net private capital flows fell by nearly 70 percent from their record high in 2007. The International Labour Office (ILO) estimates that unemployment increased by more than 30 million in 2009 to a total of 200 million unemployed (ILO 2010). On the poverty front, it is claimed that an additional 64 million people lived in extreme poverty at the end of 2009 as a result of the crisis (World Bank 2010).

The effect of the crisis on trade has been even more pronounced. According to the World Trade Organization (WTO 2010), trade volumes dropped by over 12 percent in 2009—the sharpest contraction in world trade ever recorded. Only services trade seemed to be relatively resilient to the crisis, as documented by Borchert and Mattoo (2009) and Gereffi and Fernandez-Stark (chapter 9). The sharp contraction in demand, which was larger and more widespread than in past crises, was identified by economists as the primary cause of the trade collapse. The magnitude of the overshooting of trade that occurred during the 2008–09 crisis has surprised economists, however, and a number of explanations have been put forward, including the shortage of trade finance and the amplification of intermediate goods trade in GVCs, a topic explored in detail in the first part of this volume (chapters 2, 3, and 4).

International trade was not only a casualty of the crisis, but also one of its main transmission channels. In recent decades, an increasing number of developing countries have relied on exports to sustain growth. This shift from import-substituting industrialization to export-oriented development strategies translated into a higher reliance on export revenues and greater exposure to external shocks. As documented by Milberg and Winkler (chapter 2), exports as a share of low- and middle-income countries' GDP grew from just 10 percent in 1970 to 33 percent in 2007. For China, the reliance on exports jumped from 3 to 43 percent of GDP over the same period. Similar patterns were observed in most emerging economies, including Argentina, India, Mexico, and the Republic of Korea. This increasing reliance on exports translates into a rising share of low- and middle-income countries in world exports of goods from 16 percent in 1986 to over 30 percent in 2008; in services the share grew from 13 percent in 1986 to 20 percent in 2007.

Many countries are still highly dependent on exports to the United States and the European Union (EU), which represented 13.4 percent and 14.2 percent (or 42.4 percent if one includes intra-EU trade), respectively, of world imports in 2008. At the onset of the crisis, Europe and North America still captured 60 percent of African manufactured exports (down from about 70 percent in 2000). By comparison, Asia and South America represented only 13 percent and 2 percent, respectively, of African manufactured exports (WTO 2009). These differences help explain the magnitude and geographical diffusion of the 2008–09 crisis: countries less dependent on imports from high-income economies were buffered from the crisis. In Asia, for example, regional trade and large emerging markets like China fared relatively well.

GVCs: From Macroeconomic to Industry Level of Analysis

The economic crisis underscored the importance of GVCs in the world economy. It is now widely recognized that the role of trade in the transmission of the economic crisis was heightened by the predominance of business models based on global production and trade networks. According to Escaith, Lindenberg, and Miroudot (chapter 3), GVCs introduce new microeconomic dimensions to the traditional macroeconomic mechanisms used to understand the transmission of economic shocks. Specifically, GVCs can partially explain the apparent overreaction of international trade to the financial crisis. Because of GVCs, adverse shocks affect firms not only through their sales of finished goods (final demand), but also through fluctuations in the supply and demand of intermediate goods via forward and backward linkages in GVCs. Thus, the globalization of production has raised the ratio of global imports and exports per unit of output. Sturgeon and Kawakami (chapter 7) document a 10-fold increase of world imports of intermediate goods in the last four decades (constant price data), which represented more than 56 percent of total world imports in 2006.

Using historical data, Escaith, Lindenberg, and Miroudot (chapter 3) show that the elasticity of global trade volumes to real world GDP has increased gradually from around 2 in the 1960s to above 3 in recent years, driven by production sharing arrangements in GVCs (see also Freund 2009). Milberg and Winkler (chapter 2) confirm that economic globalization has resulted in a steady increase in the income elasticity of world trade, and provide further explanations of the role of GVCs in the trade collapse. The magnitude and speed of adjustment have increased as GVCs have become a larger conduit for both real and financial shocks. Today, downturns in GDP result in not only larger but also more rapid declines in trade than previously because GVCs enable lead firms to make faster adjustments to changes in market demand.[6]

Shortage of trade finance is another factor contributing to the trade collapse. A series of surveys conducted in 2009 by the World Bank and others confirmed that trade finance was more expensive and less available than prior to the crisis, with banks becoming more risk averse and selective in their supply of credit. A recent update suggests that small exporters were the principal victims of this shortage and lost their credit lines when demand for their products declined (Malouche 2009). Milberg and Winkler (chapter 2) observe that a trade credit crunch has a more severe impact on international trade when such trade is organized in GVCs because of the interrelationship of firms and the rapid transmission of financial shocks. Credit market problems can cascade through GVCs as the denial of credit to importers in one country leads to credit problems for sellers in others, reducing their access to credit and in turn affecting their ability to import.

On the other hand, support from lead firms and large intermediaries within GVCs has in some cases helped to remedy trade finance shortages and to mitigate the credit crisis. According to Gereffi and Frederick (chapter 5), a number of retailers and buyers in the apparel sector offered financial support to their suppliers: Kohl's provided 41 percent of its suppliers a Supply Chain Finance program, and Walmart offered about 1,000 suppliers an alternative to their traditional means of financing and launched a Supplier Alliance Program for expediting payments. Li & Fung, a trading company based in Hong Kong, China, that serves as an intermediary between large retailers and sewing contractors in the apparel industry, became a lender of last resort to factories and small importers whose credit was cut off during the crisis.

Not all effects of the crisis on trade are necessarily negative. A fall in GDP in major markets has two main concurrent effects on trade: first, a drop in demand, where consumers postpone their purchases, and second, a search for cheaper goods, where consumers cannot postpone their purchases. The first effect translates into a contraction of imports. The second effect is one of substitution and its net impact on trade is less obvious: trade in certain higher-end goods drops when imports of lower-priced products increase. The overall net effect of the crisis on trade varies according to the relative weight of these substitution and demand effects for a specific country, industry, or firm. For example, the substitution effect could explain the record sales of Walmart and the vitality of Chinese and Bangladeshi exports during the crisis.

Lead firms that face declining profits and uncertain demand may also try to reduce costs and increase flexibility through additional offshoring and outsourcing to low-cost countries. Van Biesebroeck and Sturgeon (chapter 6) suggest that lead firms in the automobile sector in the United States and Western Europe will increase sourcing in Mexico and Central and Eastern Europe in the wake of the crisis. In the services sector, Gereffi and Fernandez-Stark (chapter 9) observe two opposing effects: some companies froze offshore contracts, while others outsourced additional services in order to lower their costs and remain competitive. The overall sharp decline in the volume of trade in 2009 suggests that thus far the demand effect has swamped the substitution effect.

The awareness of the role of trade and GVCs in the transmission of the crisis could have resulted in the rejection of export-led growth models and global production business strategies. Some murky protectionism and "buy national" stipulations to crisis-related legislation have surfaced, but governments by and large have respected regional and multilateral trade rules (Evenett, Hoekman, and Cattaneo 2009). The resilience and increased interdependence of the global economy probably played a key role in containing protectionism: governments quickly realized the futility of discriminatory stimuli and the cost of raising barriers on intermediate goods on which whole segments of domestic industries depend.

The Recovery: Its Opportunities and Challenges

Trade is not just a transmission channel for the crisis; it could also be central to the recovery. According to the World Bank (2010), global GDP is expected to grow 2.7 percent in 2010 and 3.2 percent in 2011. Recovery will be led by developing countries, with a projected 5.2 percent growth in 2010, and 5.8 percent growth in 2011. In wealthy countries, the pace of recovery is likely to be slower, with 1.8 percent and 2.3 percent growth rates projected for 2010 and 2011, respectively. While investment is expected to rebound, medium-term foreign direct investment inflows will probably remain at 2.8 to 3 percent of developing country GDP, compared to 3.7 percent in 2007.

On the trade front, the WTO estimates that the volume of world exports will grow by 9.5 percent in 2010, with developed-country exports expanding by 7.5 percent and the rest of the world's, by 11 percent (WTO 2010). Developing countries are therefore expected to be the main driving force of the recovery. If these estimates are correct and growth proceeds apace, it will take another two or three years to surpass precrisis trade levels.

A key question is whether the recovery is likely to be as globally pervasive as the crisis that preceded it. Should a symmetrical rebound of world trade and growth be expected, or will there be hysteresis effects and uneven recoveries across countries and firms? High trade elasticity implies a faster recovery of world trade compared to GDP as the recession ends. The WTO trade statistics for 2010 suggest a quick rebound of world trade. There is, however, an ongoing debate among economists on the shape of the recovery curve, which is summarized in Kaplinsky and Farooki (chapter 4).

Chapter 4 presents a number of possible outcomes to the current crisis. The first is the "V scenario"—a rapid downturn followed by a fairly rapid upturn. The "U scenario" suggests a similar outcome but with a more protracted dip. Less comfortable is the "W scenario"—a double-dip growth path but with a subsequent revival to past growth trajectories. The most pessimistic potential outcome is that the financial crisis will follow the same path as that experienced by Japan after its financial bubble burst in the early 1990s, that is, a sharp downturn followed by a protracted period of stagnation. This is the "L scenario." Somewhere between the L and the W scenarios is a "square root scenario" ($\sqrt{}$), that is, a sharp downturn followed by a small rise followed by a period of protracted stagnation. A recent study supports this last outcome for member countries of the Organisation for Economic Co-operation and Development (OECD) stating that "we expect growth to resume by the end of [2009] in most countries, [but] the level of output in the OECD will remain permanently lower" (Holland et al. 2009, 9). Milberg and Winkler (chapter 2) suggest that because the recent downturn is deeper and different from previous downturns, there is a greater likelihood of a lag in the recovery of world trade—that is, the V-curve appears to be shifting to the right.

Change in Continuity: Accelerated Shifts in Global Demand and Production

Globalization after the 2008–09 crisis will not look the same as before. The observers who characterized it as a "crisis of globalization" had a reversal of global economic integration in mind, for example, through the abandonment of export-led strategies, the return of import substitution strategies, or the reinstatement of protectionism. In fact, Sturgeon and Kawakami (chapter 7) claim that globalization, measured by the rate of increase in intermediate goods trade, has increased its pace after every major recession and crisis in the past 30 years.

However, the research in this volume reveals that important shifts in global production and demand have taken place during the crisis that accelerated preexisting trends. On the demand side, the trend is toward diversification: South-South trade has increased along with the collapse of demand in the North, and emerging markets have become more attractive to domestic and foreign producers, both from the North and the South. On the production side, the trend is toward consolidation at the country and firm levels. These changes create opportunities for development, along with challenges.

Shifts in Global Demand

Excessive dependence on exports to the United States and the EU has long been identified as a problem for developing countries. Product and market diversification should be part of any trade or development strategy. The fall in demand in the United States and the EU triggered by the crisis made this problem even more acute, and made rapid adjustment a requirement. In an effort to lessen their dependence on traditional export markets, many companies have paid more attention to emerging markets during the crisis. For large emerging economies, this has translated into a greater focus on domestic markets. For smaller economies, it has meant a focus on exporting regionally. For the poorest countries, the shift in demand has resulted in the arrival of new brands and new investors from emerging countries. Kaplinsky and Farooki (chapter 4) put this into a historical perspective, detailing a major shift in demand from Europe, North America, and Japan to China, India, and other emerging countries.

Shifting markets to the South

The shift in markets to the South has two components: the growth of South-South trade, including a greater focus on domestic markets in large emerging economies; and the increased interest of exporters in the North in emerging markets in the South.

Local producers in emerging economies, particularly in Brazil, China, India, and South Africa, have tried and increasingly succeeded in competing with foreign producers at home. As illustrated by Sturgeon and Kawakami (chapter 7) in the mobile phone sector, the lack of variety in low-end product lines, higher prices, incompatible standards, and restrictive regulatory requirements all contributed to the shift in demand from foreign to local handsets in China. The 2008–09 crisis has accelerated these trends.[7] In the apparel sector as well, leading suppliers like China, India, and Turkey, concerned about a slowdown in global exports, have begun to focus more on sales to their domestic markets. Gereffi and Frederick (chapter 5) show that, in 2007, the estimated value of sales of Chinese apparel producers to the domestic market totaled US$93 billion, with 56 percent of overall apparel production activities in China destined for local consumers (Clothesource 2008).

The crisis in advanced country markets has inspired export strategies to other developing countries. Milberg and Winkler (chapter 2) observe that the crisis has boosted South-South trade, which can be seen in the case of intermediate goods where South-South trade jumped to 50 percent of world intermediate goods trade in 2009 compared to about 25 percent in 2000. In the apparel sector, Gereffi and Frederick (chapter 5) find that China is lessening its dependence on traditional export markets while adding important new ones, such as the Russian Federation and countries of the former Soviet Union. These examples show that South-South trade involves trade in final products that are designated for end markets in the South, as well as trade in intermediaries where the final products may still end up in traditional end markets in the North.

Exporters in the North are also aware of these new opportunities, as they face the same drop in demand at home. As a result, the share of North-North trade in global trade has declined. The apparel sector provides an interesting illustration. The Spanish group Inditex (Zara) improved its performance in 2009 amidst the financial crisis by opening new retail outlets in emerging countries such as Bulgaria, China, Kazakhstan, the Republic of Korea, Poland, and Russia. India is next in line, and the share of Asia in the group's sales is expected to double between 2008

(10.5 percent) and 2012 (20 percent), rising to 40 percent of new store openings (*Les Echos* 2010).

Challenges for development

The shift in the center of gravity of global demand and the increasing share of South-South trade have major implications for GVCs. Kaplinsky and Farooki (chapter 4) state that although GVC-centered economic growth has largely been a story of rising supplier capabilities, there has been a growing recognition of the key role that final markets play in this process. While market size and growth are part of the story, the nature of final markets and the role of buyers in guiding the direction of supplier capabilities have been crucial.

The shift of end markets to the South presents several major challenges for firms in developing countries, which are discussed in chapter 4. First, consumer preferences in emerging countries are different from those in industrialized economies. While both emerging market firms and consumers are moving up-market, price remains an overwhelming consideration in developing countries. As a result, product differentiation based on variety and quality matters less. Exporters to these markets, therefore, need to "commodify" or standardize established products by dramatically reducing costs without sacrificing quality. Van Biesebroeck and Sturgeon (chapter 6) and Sturgeon and Kawakami (chapter 7) illustrate this process for the automotive and electronics sectors, respectively, with the growing importance of products like the $3,000 car and the $300 notebook computer.

Second, the importance of product and process standards can be significantly lower when the demand comes from developing countries—for both final and intermediate goods in GVCs. This could have significant consequences for developing countries that invest in complying with higher standards set by developed countries. Also, it has a potentially important impact on the negative externalities of global production on social and environment compliance and other public goods.

Third, emerging economies like China have a preference for relatively unprocessed products. This trend could affect less-developed countries trying to improve their position in value chains. Localization of value-added, such as processing at the source, has been an important strategy for developing countries trying to move up the value chain, and it has often been the first step in industrial upgrading. However, there is no guarantee of a win-win division of labor among emerging countries at different stages of development. By restricting imports to unprocessed products, a lead firm can confine its suppliers to the low end of the value chain and limit their upgrading path: in other words, the buyer has the power to either create a path to upgrading or kick away the development ladder.

Kaplinsky, Terheggen, and Tijaja (chapter 8) illustrate these challenges to developing countries caused by the North-South shift in the case studies of Thai cassava and Gabon timber. In the case of cassava, the shift in demand from the EU to China coincided with changes in the product composition of Thai cassava exports and a move down the technological chain, pushing Thai producers backwards into agriculture and away from manufacturing (a clear illustration of economic downgrading). A further consequence of this shift in demand was a reduced role of standards in production processes and in products. The story of Gabon's timber products is quite similar. While China's demand for wood has grown rapidly, its competencies in wood-using industries have also expanded, and the shortfall in supply has led to China importing logs rather than processed wood products. The shift in the end market from the EU to China also led to a collapse of standards. The authors of chapter 8 suggest that greater demands for quality require the capacity to improve quality and skill levels over time. With the market shifting to China, Gabonese timber suppliers can sell timber products to China irrespective of the quality, as long as the price is low and volumes are large. Virtually none of the environmental or labor standards required for export to the EU apply to products exported to China.

The shift of demand from the North to the South, at least when it comes to China, creates a bind for suppliers in the developing world. On the one hand, China and other emerging economies can boost the volume of exports to other developing countries in the short run, compensating for falling exports to industrial countries and opening up export opportunities for small-scale firms or firms with limited capabilities. On the other hand, the shift to more basic products and processes with lower standards could stall industrial upgrading in the medium run and long run. As chapter 8 shows, this shift in demand and decline in processing requirements have consequences for factor utilization and return on investment in exporting countries, which must forego the foreign exchange and substantial gains in employment and skill associated with downstream processing activities and face reduced incentives for capital investment.

Shifts in Global Production

Since the 1980s globalization has deepened, with an increasing number of developing-country firms participating in GVCs, typically by producing intermediate inputs or performing final assembly. GVCs expanded at different rates, with apparel and automobiles growing in the 1960s and 1970s in terms of the dispersion and complexity of the supply chain; the electronics industry leading the way in the 1990s and 2000s; and the services sector, and especially business process outsourcing, being the most recent example of dynamic GVCs. While it is difficult to generalize across all industries, the 2008–09 crisis accelerated consolidation trends, under way since the 1990s, in several industries.

Consolidation of GVCs

Milberg and Winkler (chapter 2) provide evidence of geographic consolidation with the onset of the crisis. They find that consolidation is most pronounced in textiles, iron and steel, machinery, and transportation. In some sectors, including handbags, apparel, and footwear, consolidation began in the 1990s. The level of consolidation varies from sector to sector, and within each sector, depending on the structure of production and trade. For example, in the context of the crisis, the authors suggest that buyer-driven value chains, where large retailers like Walmart act as order-placing lead firms, have experienced higher consolidation than have producer-driven chains, where branded manufacturers and technology companies like Ford and Hewlett Packard lead GVCs. This could be because technology, capital, and skill-intensive value chain activities are harder to relocate and scale up in specific country locations than is labor-intensive work.

Nevertheless, the consolidation phenomenon has been observed across the spectrum of the sectors covered by this volume. Sturgeon and Kawakami (chapter 7) suggest that the crisis sped up a process of consolidation in electronics that had been under way since the bursting of the technology bubble in 2001. Production locations in electronics value chains have been less dispersed than in other sectors, such as apparel, but since the 2001 dot.com crisis and accelerated by the 2008–09 crisis, a shift to emerging countries, especially China, has accelerated.

Gereffi and Frederick (chapter 5) document a consolidation process in the apparel industry spurred by the phaseout of the Multi-Fibre Arrangement's quotas at the end of 2004. They show that large, low-cost Asian producers (China, Bangladesh, Indonesia, and Vietnam) have increased their export market shares at the expense of regional sourcing countries such as Mexican, Central American, and Caribbean suppliers for the United States, as well North African and Eastern European suppliers for the EU. The shift to large countries in East and South Asia has come at the expense of less-developed countries in Sub-Saharan Africa and smaller economies in Southeast Asia.

In the automobile sector, Van Biesebroeck and Sturgeon (chapter 6) observe the beginning of a historic market shift within the automotive industry to large developing countries, most likely accelerated by the crisis. The authors predict that the current decline in more mature markets is likely to be permanent and that China will soon occupy the top spot and keep it for the foreseeable future. In the automotive industry, production has tended to follow markets.

Consolidation is taking place not only at the country level, but also at the firm level. There is a tendency by lead firms to prefer larger, more capable, globally operating, first-tier suppliers. This can be observed in the apparel, automobile, and electronics sectors. This trend predates the crisis; however, lead firms used the crisis to consolidate their supply bases further and focus on big, well-established companies with whom they have ongoing strategic relationships. Thus, the elimination and shutdown of marginal suppliers during the crisis could exacerbate asymmetric buying patterns when demand recovers. Because large orders give them an advantage in credit markets, global suppliers will be in a better position to expand when the market rebounds, further reinforcing the consolidation of GVCs at the firm level.

Challenges for development

Developing-country firms seeking entry and upgrading opportunities in GVCs find that changing roles in export hierarchies is not an easy task. The consolidation of GVCs has allowed those developing countries and firms that have specific capabilities to remain in the game; they may find upgrading opportunities as their relationships with lead firms become closer and more strategic, or they may find their paths blocked as they get too close to competing with their customers. Clearly, market size is central to lead firms' sourcing and production decisions as the potential for local industrial growth often gravitates toward the largest developing countries. Van Biesebroeck and Sturgeon (chapter 6) provide an example of a virtuous cycle of development in large emerging economies in the automobile sector: lead firms sold final products in very large markets only, such as Brazil, China, or India; this led them to establish local design, engineering, and regional headquarters facilities, which provide opportunities for local suppliers.

Consolidation of GVCs has serious implications for those countries and firms with limited capabilities seeking to move up the value chain, and it may work to exclude potential new entrants entirely. If some countries and firms have a solid grip at the level of global first-tier suppliers, this could be an obstacle to new entry or upgrading for lower-tier countries and firms. For example, in the electronics and automotive industries, the emergence of powerful first-tier suppliers and the importance of strategic relationships with a handful of key component suppliers (or platform leaders) limit the entry and upgrading opportunities for lower-tier suppliers in supply chains. Van Biesebroeck and Sturgeon (chapter 6) conclude that small developing countries far from large existing markets have generally been unable to develop their automotive industries and will continue to have extreme difficulty doing so in the future. According to Sturgeon and Kawakami (chapter 7), countries and firms not yet involved in electronics GVCs appear to be out of the game for the foreseeable future. Gereffi and Frederick (chapter 5) argue that requirements for full-package services in the apparel industry (from design to distribution) put countries providing only assembly services (cut, make, and trim) at a severe disadvantage moving forward.

Countries and firms that benefit from consolidation also face challenges. The constant competition for foreign investment and contracts with global brand owners and other lead firms leaves many developing-country suppliers with little leverage in the chain. The result is an unequal partition of the total value-added and rewards along value chains in favor of lead firms. This is the case, for example, in the apparel sector (chapter 5). In electronics, chapter 7 shows that even the world's major contract manufacturers have been trapped in low value-added segments of the value chain. In the personal computer industry, most of the profits have been captured by branded lead firms such as Dell and Hewlett Packard, and especially by platform leaders in software operating systems (Microsoft) and central processing unit chip sets (Intel).

A further question to be discussed is whether these shifts in production to the largest developing countries are permanent. As explained by Sturgeon and Kawakami (chapter 7), innovation remains a challenge for developing-country firms. On one hand, local firms may encounter problems as new technologies come along or local consumers begin to ask for more sophisticated products. On the other hand, it is likely that the learning curve for local firms will help develop deeper expertise (for example, design) and increase competitiveness vis-à-vis multinational companies over the long run. In the services sector, the sustainability question relates to the ability of developing countries to supply enough skilled personnel to continue to host offshore facilities (chapter 9).

Some observers suggest, however, that developed countries are losing their leadership in innovation. For example, Fortune 500 companies now have 98 R&D centers in China and 63 in India; IBM employs more people in the developing world than in America; and in 2008, the Chinese telecom giant Huawei applied for more international patents than any other firm in the world. Developing countries have taken the lead in products tailored to the need of their home markets and other markets in the South. So-called "frugal innovation" (for example, the $300 notebook computer or the $3,000 car) for low-income consumers has become a real factor in new market creation (*Economist* 2010). However, these successes may have a short life span; in any case, they involve only a limited number of developing countries, leaving others, particular the least-developed countries, out of contention.

Conclusions

The authors in this volume support the conclusion that the crisis of 2008–09 has not reversed globalization. GVCs have proven resilient and have emerged as a long-term structural feature of the world economy. However, important shifts in global production and demand have taken place and the crisis has accelerated preexisting trends toward geographic and organizational consolidation. The crisis has also underlined the growing importance of markets in the South. These changes create opportunities for development, along with challenges, but the benefits and barriers are unevenly distributed among developing countries. This volume suggests that world production and demand patterns have remained global and that the role of the South has grown, but inequalities among developing countries threaten to rise.

In addition to the importance of these general patterns, industry dynamics matter. It is essential to understand conditions in specific industry value chains in the postcrisis world, and the opportunities and challenges they create for developing countries seeking to enter and upgrade within these chains. Accordingly, this volume initially provides a global perspective on the crisis and its impacts on global production and demand in the first three chapters, and then turns in the next five chapters to the specifics of GVCs in key industries that are driving integration of the world economy.

Notes

1. For more background on the global value chain perspective and related publications, see the Global Value Chains Web site: http://www.globalvaluechains.org/.
2. The Group of Twenty members are finance ministers and central bank governors of 19 countries (Argentina, Australia, Brazil, Canada, China, France, Germany, India, Indonesia, Italy, Japan, Republic of Korea, Mexico, Russia, Saudi Arabia, South Africa, Turkey, United Kingdom, and United States of America) and the European Union.
3. Statement of the Leaders of the Group of Twenty, London, April 2, 2009, paragraph 22.
4. Statement of the Leaders of the Group of Twenty, Pittsburgh, September 25, 2009, paragraphs 5–6.
5. "This crisis is not just a global crisis. This crisis is not a crisis in globalization. This crisis is a crisis of globalization," Nicolas Sarkozy, President of the French Republic, World Economic Forum, Davos, Switzerland, January 27, 2010.
6. The authors also acknowledge a number of accounting and other problems that might exaggerate the effect of the crisis on trade.
7. However, two caveats are important in the Chinese mobile phone case. First, multinational company brands quickly gained back market share with the transition to more feature-rich 3G phones. Local brands could not make this shift without giving most of their profits up to buy MediaTek chip sets platforms. They did not have the internal expertise to move with the market. Second, local production in China is often not carried out by local firms.

References

Baldwin, Richard, ed. 2009. *The Great Trade Collapse: Causes, Consequences and Prospects.* Centre for Economic Policy Research for VoxEU.org.

Borchert, Ingo, and Aaditya Mattoo. 2009. "The Crisis-Resilience of Services Trade." World Bank Policy Research Working Paper 4917. World Bank, Washington, DC.

Clothesource. 2008. "The Great Apparel Sourcing Issues of 2008—And How To Deal with Them." March Management Briefing. Aroq Limited, Worcestershire, UK.

Economist. 2010. "The New Masters of Management." 15 April. London.

Evenett, Simon J., Bernard Hoekman, and Olivier Cattaneo, eds. 2009. *Effective Crisis Response and Openness: Implications for the Trading System*. London: Centre for Economic Policy Research (CEPR) and World Bank.

Ferrantino, Michael J., and Aimee Larsen. 2009. "Transmission of the Recession through U.S. Trade." VoxEU.org. August 29.

Freund, Caroline. 2009. "The Trade Response to Global Downturns: Historical Evidence." World Bank Policy Research Working Paper 5015. World Bank, Washington, DC.

Fukao, Kyoji, and Tangjun Yuan. 2009. "Why Is Japan So Heavily Affected by the Economic Crisis? An Analysis Based on the Asian International Input-Output Tables." VoxEU.org. June 8.

Gereffi, Gary. 1994. "The Organization of Buyer-Driven Global Commodity Chains: How U.S. Retailers Shape Overseas Production Networks." In *Commodity Chains and Global Capitalism*, ed. Gary Gereffi and Miguel Korzeniewicz, 95–122. Westport, CT: Greenwood Press.

———. 1999. "International Trade and Industrial Upgrading in the Apparel Commodity Chain." *Journal of International Economics* 48 (1): 37–70.

Gereffi, Gary, John Humphrey, and Timothy Sturgeon. 2005. "The Governance of Global Value Chains." *Review of International Political Economy* 12 (1): 78–104.

Holland, Dawn, Ray Barrell, Tatiana Fic, Ian Hurst, Iana Liadze, Ali Orazgani, and Rachel Whitworth. 2009. "Consumer Spending and the Financial Crisis." *National Institute Economic Review* 210 (October): 9–15.

ILO (International Labour Organization). 2010. *Global Employment Trends*. Geneva: ILO.

Jansen, Marion, and Erik von Uexkull. 2010. *Trade and Employment in the Global Crisis*. Geneva: International Labour Organization.

Les Echos. 2010. "Zara pousse les feux dans les pays émergents." March 18. Paris.

Ma, Alyson, and Ari Van Assche. 2009. "When China Sneezes, Asia Catches a Cold: Effects of China's Export Decline in the Realm of the Global Economic Crisis." *Bureau of European Policy Advisers Monthly Brief* 27 (June): 32–36.

Malouche, Mariem. 2009. "Trade and Trade Finance Developments in 14 Developing Countries Post-September 2008: A World Bank Survey." World Bank Policy Research Working Paper 5138. World Bank, Washington, DC.

Reinhart, Carmen, and Andrew Felton. 2008. *The First Global Crisis of the 21st Century*. Centre for Economic Policy Research for VoxEU.org.

World Bank. 2010. *Global Economic Prospects 2010*. Washington, DC: World Bank.

WTO (World Trade Organization). 2009. *2009 International Trade Statistics*. Geneva: WTO.

———. 2010. *2010 International Trade Statistics*. Geneva: WTO.

PART II

THE CRISIS AND TRENDS IN GLOBAL TRADE, DEMAND, AND PRODUCTION

2

TRADE, CRISIS, AND RECOVERY: RESTRUCTURING GLOBAL VALUE CHAINS

William Milberg and Deborah Winkler

Global value chains (GVCs), which only recently entered into the purview of economists, are now at the center of the debate over the causes and consequences of the 2008–09 economic crisis and collapse of global trade. Feenstra (1998) noted the prominence of a global "disintegration" of production, but not until the essay by Grossman and Rossi-Hansberg (2006) on the welfare effects of offshoring was there broad acknowledgment by economists of the extraordinary nature of trade within GVCs—what the authors call "trade in tasks" rather than traditional trade in final goods. Previously, trade in intermediates was generally modeled as a refinement of the international division of labor according to principles of comparative advantage (for example, see Arndt and Kierzkowski, 2001). Since the global downturn, GVCs are seen as central to the dramatic collapse of world trade (see the array of contributions in Baldwin 2009a). Well documented, this collapse has been more severe, rapid, and persistent than trade collapses experienced in the past, including during the Great Depression. This chapter explores the role of GVCs in the 2009 trade collapse and the prospects for world trade and its geographic distribution in light of the dynamics of GVCs.

A trade decline has potentially devastating effects on export-oriented developing countries. As shown in figure 2.1a, the decline in U.S. goods imports in the fourth quarter of 2008 and the first two quarters of 2009 was greater than the decline in U.S. GDP, and the drop in the ratio of imports to GDP over that period represented by far the greatest three quarter decline in imports, both absolutely

Figure 2.1 U.S. and EU 27 Goods and Services Imports
% GDP

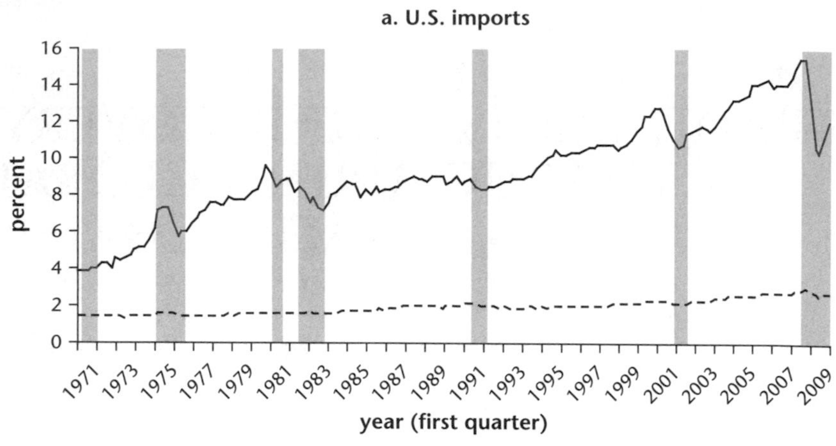

Sources: Authors' illustration using data for the United States from the U.S. Bureau of Economic Analysis, National Income and Product Accounts Table, Gross Domestic Product, seasonally adjusted at annual rates; data for the EU 27 are from Eurostat, National Accounts, seasonally adjusted and adjusted data by working days.
Note: In part a, the gray bars correspond to U.S. business cycle recessions according to the definition of the National Bureau of Economic Research. In part b, imports refer to extra-EU 27 countries.

and relative to GDP, since 1980 at least. The European Union (EU 27) has undergone a similar, if less dramatic, import decline (see figure 2.1b.). A similar pattern has been observed on a global scale as well. Ominously, the drop in trade in the 2008–09 crisis has been found to be even more rapid than the decline in world trade at the beginning of the Great Depression in 1929 (Eichengreen and O'Rourke 2009).

Leading up to the 2008–09 economic downturn, developed-country imports of goods and services were growing faster than output, as seen in the case of the United States and the European Union in figure 2.1. This was the result of a variety of factors, including the liberalization of trade and capital flows and the decline in the costs of international transportation and, especially, communications. Business strategies have also become increasingly international, and today a significant amount of world trade occurs within global value chains, that is, international systems of production typically governed by lead firms that coordinate sometimes elaborate networks of suppliers (see Gereffi 1994; Gereffi, Humphrey, and Sturgeon 2005. As a result of these factors, changes in the value and volume of trade over the business cycle are greater today than they were in the 1960s.

This chapter addresses three questions:

1. Will trade volumes rebound in a symmetric fashion as world economic growth rebounds?
2. Will the crisis result in a change in the structure of trade; in particular, will it lead to a reversal of the pattern of more diversified sourcing and thus to a consolidation of GVCs?
3. What policies can improve the prospects for developing-country growth in the event that trade volumes do not rebound symmetrically and there is a consolidation of some GVCs?

Previous research shows that, on average, over business cycles since 1975, the effect on international trade is (1) larger than the effect on GDP and (2) symmetric, like the movement of GDP. The 2010 International Trade Statistics released by the World Trade Organization (WTO) suggest a similar pattern for the 2008–09 crisis: after the sharpest decline in more than 70 years, world trade is set to rebound in 2010, growing at 9.5 percent, assuming a 2.9 percent global GDP growth (WTO 2010). However, the recent downturn has been deeper than and different from previous downturns, so there is a greater likelihood of a lag in the recovery of the volume of world trade. It has involved a credit crunch, and thus a collapse of trade credit. The crisis might also have brought a structural change in aggregate demand, as U.S. consumption, for example, may settle at a lower rate relative to income, and as the Chinese yuan is revalued relative to the dollar, further shifting the world pattern of trade. Therefore, it is likely that those factors will affect the pace and pattern of trade recovery.

Regarding the question of changing the structure of trade, this chapter presents an empirical analysis of the change in the concentration of trade flows, using a Herfindahl-Hirschman Index (HHI) that measures concentration in terms of trade flows by country, rather than in terms of market share by firms. This study finds that consolidation has been more likely in "buyer-led" GVCs and greater dispersion more likely in "producer-led" GVCs. The third question is discussed in terms of the prospects for developing-country fiscal stimulus and for South-South trade expansion. Preliminary analysis indicates promising growth potential for South-South trade based on the experience of the past 20 years, but suggests that this growth too may be limited if GVCs are consolidated, since the largest category of South-South trade is in intermediates.

The next section briefly assesses the degree of developing-country export success over the past 20 years in both goods and services. This success has created a greater reliance on export revenue in aggregate demand. The third section examines in more detail the role of GVCs in the decline in U.S. and EU import demand between 2008 and the third quarter of 2009, including estimates of the U.S. income elasticity of import demand during the crisis compared to long-run elasticities, as well as a discussion of the possibility of a shifting V-curve of import demand. This is followed by a closer look at the sectoral and developing-country impact of the import decline in the United States and European Union. We then propose a theory of vertical and horizontal GVC consolidation, and present data on changes in the geographic concentration of global exports in detailed product areas. Following that is a brief discussion of prospects for expanding South-South trade as a substitute for declines in North-South trade that may be long term because of both the changing structure of world demand and the consolidation of some GVCs.

The chapter ends with some policy conclusions, necessarily tentative, since the recovery is unfolding as the research is being conducted. These conclusions focus on the need for continued support of trade credit by the international financial corporations; the need for developing countries to find other, nonexport, sources of demand, or to diversify trade patterns to focus more on trade among developing countries; and the need for developed countries to resist trade protection measures, even in a time of high and persistent unemployment rates.

GVCs and the Export Reliance of Developing Countries

The expansion of GVCs began in the 1980s, as developing countries shifted from import substitution strategies to export-oriented development strategies. Their dramatic export success is evident in figure 2.2a., which shows that since the early

Figure 2.2 Exports from Low- and Middle-Income Countries

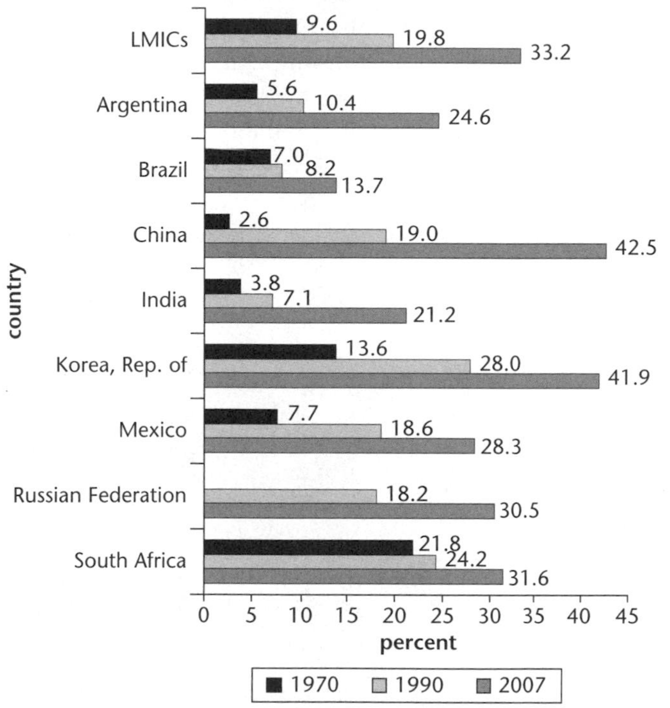

Source: Authors' illustration with data from World Development Indicators, World Bank 2009.
Note: LMICs = Low- and middle-income countries. This category covers most developing countries.

1980s, the share of low- and middle-income countries in world exports of goods and services rose almost steadily. The goods export share rose from 16 percent in 1986 to over 30 percent in 2008, while the services export share grew from 13 percent to 20 percent in 2007. This shift in world trade patterns also means that developing countries are much more reliant on export revenues for final demand. On average, low- and middle-income countries became steadily more export-oriented, with exports as a share of GDP growing to 33 percent in 2007, compared to just 15 percent in 1980. China's enormous success is well known; its export reliance went from around 3 percent of GDP in 1970 to almost 43 percent in 2007. But the increased export orientation was also dramatic in Argentina, the Republic of Korea, India, and Mexico, among others (figure 2.2b). (See annex 2A for export shares by region of origin.)

The increased export orientation of developing economies also involved a change in the structure of international trade resulting from the expansion of global production networks, also called GVCs. With the expansion of GVCs in the 1980s, trade in inputs grew dramatically as a share of total input use. Figure 2.3 shows that by 2008, low- and middle-income countries accounted for 35 percent of world exports of intermediate goods, with a rapid acceleration in this share in the 2000s. The growth of capital goods and consumption goods exports has remained relatively stable since the late 1980s. Milberg and Winkler (2010a) report that U.S. offshoring intensities, that is, the share of U.S. imported inputs of materials and

Figure 2.3 Goods Exports from Low- and Middle-Income Countries by Product Category, 1970–2008
% world exports in that product category

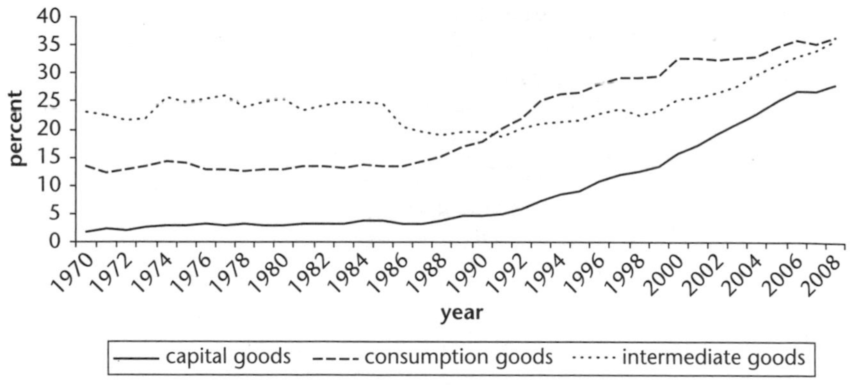

Source: Authors' calculations using data from UN Comtrade, 2009.
Note: See annex 2B for definitions of the product categories.

services in total non-energy input use, grew at an average annual rate of 2 percent and 1.7 percent, respectively, between 1998 and 2006, reaching more than 25 percent in some sectors, including apparel and motor vehicles, by 2006.

Standard offshoring measures capture only trade inputs, thus may understate the magnitude of trade within global supply chains. Global corporations in the major industrialized countries are not strictly involved in assembly. Much of the import activity in global supply chains is in fully finished goods. In fact, the purpose of corporate offshoring, whether at arm's length or through foreign subsidiaries, is precisely to allow the corporation to focus on its "core competence," while leaving other aspects of the process, often including production, to others. Many "manufacturing" firms now do not manufacture anything at all. They provide product and brand design, marketing, supply chain logistics, and financial management services.

Thus, an alternative proxy for offshoring may simply be imports from developing countries. Table 2.1 shows that Japan and the United States now rely heavily on

Table 2.1 Goods and Services Offshoring Intensities in Selected Countries, 1991 versus 2006
percent

Measure	Denmark	France	Germany	Japan	United Kingdom	United States
Goods offshoring intensity (narrow measure)						
1991	2.9	3.8	4.1	14.9	3.0	8.6
2006	6.5	6.3	8.2	29.1	8.2	23.1
CAGR	5.4	3.4	4.7	4.5	7.0	6.8
Goods offshoring intensity (broad measure)						
1991	9.0	15.2	14.6	49.3	14.1	40.1
2006	13.1	16.4	17.0	68.2	22.8	54.1
CAGR	2.5	0.5	1.0	2.2	3.3	2.0
Services offshoring intensity (narrow measure)						
1991	23.1	13.0	20.0	29.2	13.7	10.4
2006	20.0	28.0	26.1	24.3	22.6	18.6
CAGR	–1.0	5.2	1.8	–1.2	3.4	4.0
Services offshoring intensity (broad measure)						
1991	23.1	24.7	22.1	31.6	17.7	18.6
2006	22.3	33.4	31.6	27.0	32.9	22.6
CAGR	–0.2	2.0	2.4	–1.0	4.2	1.3

Source: Milberg and Winkler 2010b, with data from Organisation for Economic Co-operation and Development (OECD) National Accounts database, United Nations Conference on Trade and Development (UNCTAD) GlobStat Database.
Note: CAGR = compound annual growth rate.

goods imports from low-income developing countries (29 percent and 23 percent, respectively), here defined as the *narrow measure of goods offshoring*. While the European countries are at much lower levels, all countries have seen the narrow measure of goods offshoring more than doubling since 1991 (see annualized growth rates in table 2.1). However, offshore destinations also include developing countries with a higher income level, such as Brazil, Mexico, or South Africa. Thus, the *broad measure of goods offshoring*, including imports from all developing countries, shows that developing-country imports constitute over half of total imports by Japan (68 percent) and the United States (54 percent), while the European countries range from 23 percent in the United Kingdom to only 13 percent in Denmark.[1]

Since services import data by region of origin are not available for the relevant time period, this analysis defines a country's import share of "computer and information services" plus "other business services" in total services imports as *narrow measure of services offshoring*. The *broad measure of services offshoring* additionally takes "communication services" and "financial services" into account. Table 2.1 shows that Japan and Denmark saw a small decline in services offshoring between 1991 and 2006, while the other countries experienced compound annual growth rates of services offshoring of between 1.3 percent and 5.2 percent.

Economic development has become increasingly associated with "economic upgrading" or "industrial upgrading" within GVCs, requiring that firms move up through the chain of production of a particular commodity into higher value-added activities. This involves raising productivity and skills through training, mechanization, and the introduction of new technologies. It also requires fitting into existing corporate strategies by linking closely to lead firms. In manufacturing, such upgrading has also been associated with qualitative change, with firms moving from parts production or assembly, to design and more integrated production, to fully integrated production, to original brand design. Humphrey and Schmitz (2002) describe four types of upgrading in GVCs: product, process, functional, and chain. Product and process involve productivity gains, while the producer remains largely in the same place in the GVC. Functional upgrading involves moving into more technologically sophisticated and higher value-added aspects of an existing chain. And chain upgrading implies moving into a new, related value chain that also involves more skills, capital, and value added.

The economic theory of vertical integration focuses on transaction cost–minimizing behavior by lead firms and distinguishes hierarchical from market-based relations within GVCs (Williamson 2000; more recently, Grossman and Helpman 2005; for an extension, see Gereffi, Humphrey, and Sturgeon 2005). Gereffi (1994) shifts the focus of the analysis of GVCs, characterizing GVCs as "buyer-led" or "producer-led," depending on the nature of the lead firm. Large retailers (for example, Walmart, Sears, JCPenney, and Kmart) and firms with global brands (for example, Nike, Liz Claiborne) lead buyer-led GVCs and are more likely to work at arm's length with suppliers and to have supplier contracts of shorter duration. Manufacturers in more high-tech areas, such as automobile, aircraft, and aspects of electronics (for example, Ford, Boeing, Apple Computers) lead producer-led chains in which ownership of suppliers (through foreign direct investment) is more likely and in which supplier contracts are of longer duration.

The Role of GVCs in the Collapse of World Trade

Why did trade volumes collapse so dramatically relative to GDP in the 2008–09 downturn? To answer this question we examine the role of GVCs in the decline in U.S. and EU import demand between 2008 and the third quarter of 2009. In addition to discussing the various effects of the crisis on international trade, including estimates of the U.S. income elasticity of import demand during the crisis compared to long-run elasticities, the possibility of a shifting V-curve of import demand will be raised.

Cyclicality and the "Composition Effect"

In examining the trade collapse, Freund (2009) shows that historically trade flows are pro-cyclical and follow a more exaggerated cyclical pattern than GDP. She analyzes the effect on the value of international trade of global economic downturns in 1975, 1982, 1991, and 2001, and finds that global economic downturns in the recent past have been associated with declines in the volume of world trade proportionally greater than the change in GDP. On average over these downturns, GDP growth fell to 1.5 percent and the growth in trade value turned negative, to –1.0 percent. In the year leading to the trough of the cycle, she finds the percentage point fall in trade is five times that of world output. By this standard, if world GDP in the recent recession fell by 4.8 percentage points, then world trade would have fallen by more than 20 percentage points. Importantly, Freund (2009) also predicts that the GDP-trade relation is symmetric, that is, that the rebound in trade is greater than the rebound in GDP, and that the recovery of trade is as fast as was its decline. Most of the trade rebound occurs the same year as the GDP growth increase, but "it takes about 4 years for trade to pass pre-downturn levels" (Freund 2009, 8). According to the WTO, the 2010 trade rebound should help recover some, but not all, of the 2009 trade losses that occurred when the global crisis prompted a 12.2 percent contraction in the volume of global trade; the WTO forecasts that, should trade continue to expand at its current pace, it would take at least two years in developing countries, and three years in developed countries, for trade volume to surpass the peak level of 2008 (WTO 2010).

One reason trade reacts more strongly to changes in GDP during a recession than otherwise is the difference in the composition of trade and GDP. In a global downturn, the demand for goods falls more strongly than the demand for services, because goods represent the bulk of trade flows while services make up the bulk of GDP. In particular, the demand for "postponable" goods—consumer durables and investment goods-related intermediates, which make up a narrow slice of world GDP but a large percentage of world trade—dropped sharply during the crisis. Thus, the global crisis operated with full force on trade, but with less force on GDP as a whole (Baldwin 2009a).

Evidence of the composition effect is confirmed in figure 2.4, showing the sharp decline in "industrial supplies and materials" (–49 percent year-to-year [YTY] in August 2009). The decline in consumer goods imports (–17 percent YTY in August 2009) is much less, and the decline in the growth of services imports (–15 percent YTY in August 2009) is even less than for goods. Throughout the downturn, services trade, especially of business services, has been relatively unaffected (see Borchert and Mattoo 2009). Borchert and Mattoo list a number of reasons why the demand for services has contracted less than the demand for goods in the 2008–09 crisis, including the nonstorability of services and the fact that a larger part of services demand involves outsourced services (for example, bookkeeping) that are "necessities" for producers.

Figure 2.4 U.S. Goods and Services Import Growth, August 2008–December 2009
% growth year to year

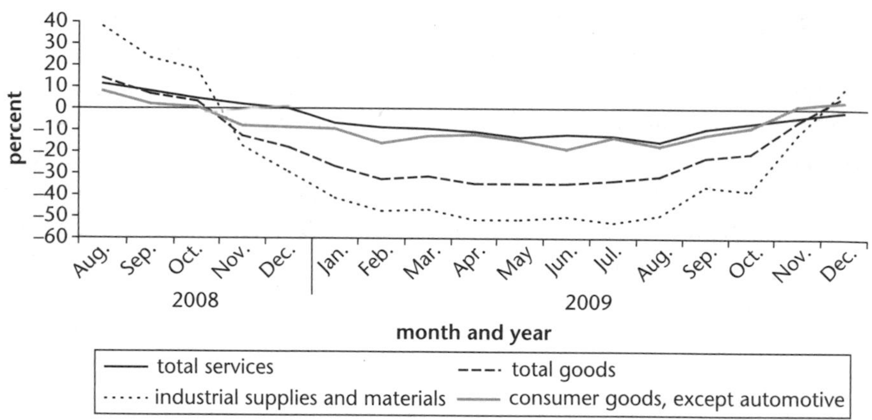

Source: Authors' illustration using data from the Bureau of Economic Analysis, International Accounts Products, quarterly imports of goods, balance of payments–based data, seasonally adjusted.

Globalization in the Long Run versus "Crisis Elasticities" of Trade

A second explanation of the collapse in world trade in the recent downturn is that economic globalization has resulted over decades in a steady increase in the income elasticity of world trade, so that the relatively large GDP decline in recent years has been matched by a historic decline in the volume of world trade. Freund (2009) reports estimates showing a monotonic increase in the income elasticity of world trade over successive decades, rising from 1.94 in the 1960s to 3.69 in the 2000s. As a result, an identical percentage drop in GDP now leads to a greater percentage decline in trade than previously. Thus, a 1 percent reduction in real income lowered real trade by around 2 percent in the 1960s, and that has increased gradually to 3.7 percent in recent years.

The income elasticity of import demand ε_M, for example, is given by:

$$\varepsilon_M = \frac{\partial M/M}{\partial Y/Y} = \frac{\partial M}{\partial Y}\cdot\frac{Y}{M}. \tag{2.1}$$

Using quarterly GDP and import data, the U.S. income elasticities of import demand are approximated as follows:

$$\varepsilon_{M,t} = \frac{\Delta M_t}{\Delta Y_t}\cdot\frac{Y_t}{M_t}, \tag{2.2}$$

where subscript t denotes the quarter, $\Delta M_t = M_t - M_{t-4}$, and $\Delta Y_t = Y_t - Y_{t-4}$. Figure 2.5a confirms the increase in the income elasticity of imports for the United States over the past four decades. The data for 2008:Q4 to 2009:Q4 are not shown, as the drop and subsequent increase were extremely high.

Note that greater economic openness per se—the result of trade liberalization, or technological change, or changing business strategies—does not imply a higher income elasticity of import demand. To the contrary, other things being equal, a higher import propensity, M/Y, lowers the income elasticity of import demand as evident in equation 2.1.[2] However, if the increase in the import propensity is matched by a larger increase in the incremental import–GDP ratio, $\partial M/\partial Y$, then the elasticity will indeed rise. Figure 2.5b shows that the U.S. incremental import–GDP ratio was higher (in absolute value terms) in the last two business cycles than previously and that during the recent downturn, the incremental import–GDP ratio was larger (again in absolute value) in the past two years than ever since 1970.

An important issue is whether the recent downturn resulted in a structural break in historical elasticity patterns. To judge whether that history is a useful

Figure 2.5 U.S. Income Elasticities and Incremental Import–GDP Ratios, First Quarter 1970 to Third Quarter 2008

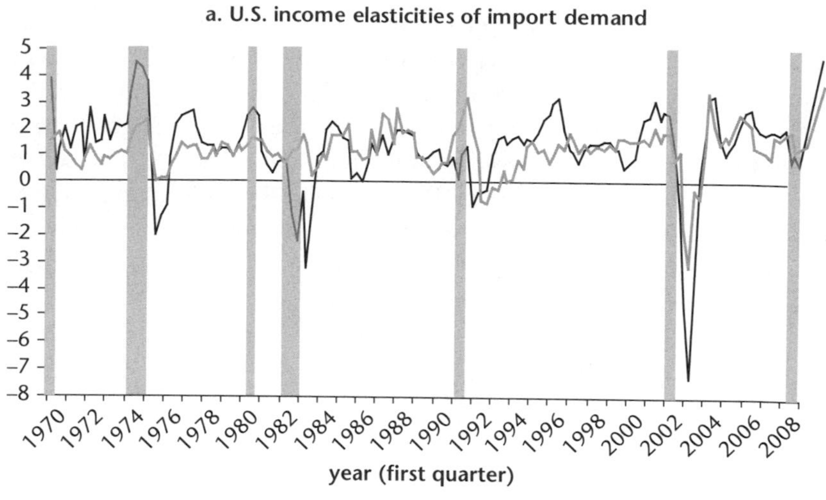

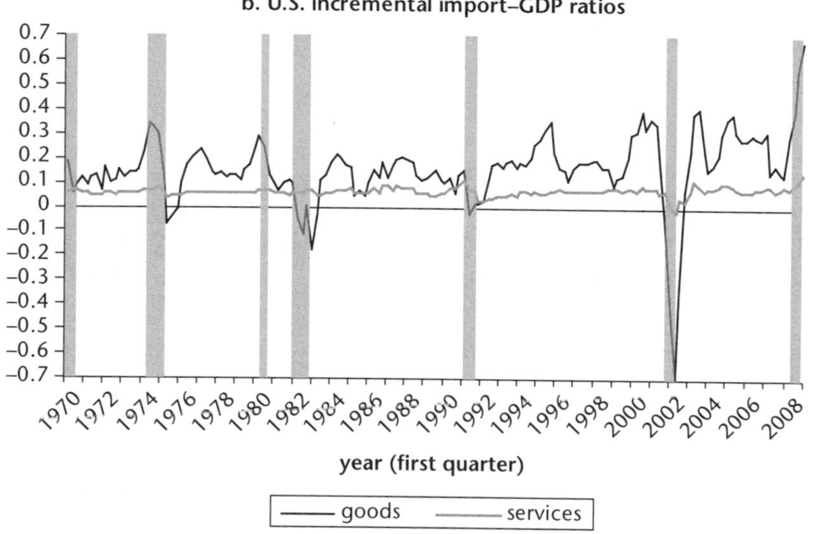

Source: Authors' calculations using U.S. data from the U.S. Bureau of Economic Analysis, National Income and Product Accounts Table, Gross Domestic Product, seasonally adjusted at annual rates.
Note: The gray bars correspond to U.S. business cycle recessions according to National Bureau of Economic Research definition.

guide in the current context, we estimated long-run income elasticities of import demand in the United States for 16 countries and compared these to the current experience. The latter are referred to as "crisis elasticities." The long-term elasticities for goods and services were estimated separately using bilateral, quarterly trade data for the period 1999–2008. An autoregressive distributed lag (ARDL) approach was applied to co-integration, which yields consistent estimates of the long-run coefficients, regardless of whether the regressors are I(1) or I(0), and thus does not require pretesting for unit root (Pesaran, Shin, and Smith 2001). The ARDL approach adds short-run dynamics to a long-run estimation equation as given in equation 2.3:

$$\Delta \ln M_t^j = \alpha + \sum_{i=1}^{n} \beta_i \Delta \ln Y_{t-i} + \sum_{i=1}^{n} \gamma_i \Delta \ln E_{t-1}^j + \sum_{i=1}^{n} \delta_i \Delta \ln M_{t-i}^j + \nu_1 \ln Y_{t-1} + \nu_2 \ln E_{t-1}^j + \nu_3 \ln M_{t-1}^j + \varepsilon_t, \tag{2.3}$$

where M designates real import demand for imports from country j; Y, real domestic income; and E, real bilateral exchange rate between the United States and country j at time t. E is defined as the number of units of foreign currency per U.S. dollar, and ε_t denotes the random error term. The lagged level variables constitute the so-called lagged error-correction term, which should be retained or excluded from the equation based on the F-statistics. Annexes 2E and 2F give full details of the estimation procedures, sample, and the estimation results. The long-run relations are given by the estimates of ν_3 in annex table 2E.1 (column 4). Only six countries show significant results, while others miss the 10 percent level narrowly. The highest elasticities are for China and India. They imply that a 1.0 percent U.S. income increase is expected to raise goods imports demand for China and India by 8.6 percent and 8.1 percent, respectively. Germany and Brazil show elasticities of 1.9 and 1.2, respectively. Interestingly, four Asian and two Latin American economies show negative elasticities, which is significant however only for Hong Kong, China.

Regarding services imports, the estimates become more significant. The F-tests show that only India, República Bolivariana de Venezuela, and the United Kingdom should not include the error-correction term when calculating short-run effects. The long-run elasticities are nearly all positive and significant in 13 economies. Canada; China; France; Germany; and Hong Kong, China, show the largest service import elasticities, which range between 7.6 and 4.7 percent. Given the high absolute value of services imports from India, an elasticity of 2.1 percent still seems very high.

Table 2.2 shows the long-run income elasticities of U.S. import demand for goods (column 1) and the "crisis elasticities," which are derived from data for the last half of 2008 for the major trading partners of the United States (column 3). In many cases, the long-run estimate is many times less than what was experienced in the crisis period. For Brazil, for example, the long-run elasticity of 1.24 jumps to 11.6 in the crisis period. For Taiwan, China, it jumps from 0.77 to 7.6 and for

Table 2.2 "Crisis" versus Long-Run Income Elasticities of U.S. Import Demand

	Income elasticities			
	Estimations		During crisis	
	1999:Q1–2008:Q4		2008:Q3–2008:Q4	
Country	Goods	Services	Goods	Services
Argentina	..	2.25	–0.9	–4.6
Brazil	1.24	–0.60	11.6	1.0
Canada	..	7.56	16.3	22.7
China	8.65	6.02	5.5	1.0
France	..	5.41	2.3	10.8
Germany	1.86	4.70	5.4	5.9
Hong Kong, China	2.75	5.50	13.3	–2.0
India	8.06	2.07	6.0	–3.2
Japan	..	1.74	5.0	0.8
Korea, Rep. of	..	0.68	6.7	13.1
Mexico	..	0.79	10.6	2.4
Singapore	..	1.92	7.6	7.0
South Africa	1.21	0.69	28.9	8.6
Taiwan, China	0.77	2.34	7.6	0.4
United Kingdom	..	..	13.1	7.4
Venezuela, R.B. de	..	..	61.3	0.1

Source: Authors' calculations using data from the Bureau of Economic Analysis.
Note: Income elasticities 2008:Q3 to 2008:Q4 are calculated based on equation 2.2, where $\Delta M_t = M_t - M_{t-1}$ and $Y_t = Y_t - Y_{t-1}$. Stastically insignificant estimates are indicated by··

South Africa from 1.21 to 28.9. For Mexico, the estimate is statistically insignificantly different from zero in the long-run estimate, jumping to 10.6 in the crisis. In the cases of China and India, the long-run elasticities are not so different from the crisis period, falling slightly in both cases but from already extremely high long-run values. Our findings support the results of Levchenko, Lewis, and Tesar (2009) who find an enormous gap ("wedge") between predicted U.S. imports based on historical data and the actual drop in U.S. import demand.

The evidence on services trade is quite different. While only one sector has a negative income elasticity in the long-run analysis, three economies have a negative relation in the crisis period, and three other economies have values lower than 1 (that is, very low). Argentina; Hong Kong, China; and India have negative elasticities in the crisis period, reflecting that U.S. services imports of some types have increased, even as national income has fallen. Business processing services are part of fixed rather than variable costs and thus are likely to rise, especially when profits are squeezed, while expenditures on variable inputs (imported and domestic) fall with the decline in final goods and services orders.

GVCs: Flexibility and Synchronicity

There is no doubt that the globalization of production has raised the ratio of global imports and exports per unit of output over time. Freund (2009, 6), for example, writes that "an increase in GDP may lead to more outsourcing and much more measured trade, as an increasing number of parts travel around the globe to be assembled, and again to their final consumer." Greater vertical specialization in production means that the import content of exports has also risen (Yi 2009).

With vertical specialization, a decline in final demand reduces trade in both final and intermediate goods and services. In a study of the United States, Ferrantino and Larsen (2009, 177) note the connection between imports and exports: "[T]he drop in U.S. imports for computers and cell phones leads indirectly to a drop in U.S. exports of semiconductors and components." In a study of the recent export decline in Japan, Fukao and Yuan (2009) find that adding to the decline in U.S. demand for Japanese final goods is the decline in demand for intermediate goods intended for assembly in East Asia for shipment to the United States.[3] The point is that such fragmentation contributes both to a rising trade propensity and to a rising incremental import–GDP ratio.

Lead firms with declining profits will seek drastic means to cut costs and thus may substitute cheaper foreign inputs for domestic inputs. This is the "substitution effect" having a positive effect on trade flows of intermediates. There are reports, for example, that with the burst of the dot-com bubble in 2001, IT firms faced a profit squeeze and turned increasingly to offshore sourcing for both hardware and software (reported in Friedman 2005). Scott (2009) notes that an important part of U.S. auto companies' adjustment to their current unprofitable position is likely to be a significant increase in offshoring, especially from Mexico. Van Biesebroeck and Sturgeon (2010, 42) identify the likelihood of such a substitution effect by lead firms in the automobile sector in the United States and Western Europe (sourcing in Mexico and Eastern and Central Europe, respectively) if market shares continue to decline.

This substitution effect is further influenced by the heightened uncertainty of future demand after the crisis, which may encourage firms to externalize further their sourcing in order to increase their flexibility in response to future demand stagnation or volatility. Nonetheless, the large declines in the volume of trade seen in the recent crisis indicate clearly that the demand effect has so far swamped the substitution effect.

The rise in trade elasticities, then, does not result from a rise in trade openness but from the rising sensitivity of trade to changes in GDP, that is, to the nature of GVCs, not to the globalization of production per se. There are at least two reasons why the expansion of GVCs has increased trade openness and raised incremental import–GDP ratios. The rise in the incremental import–GDP ratio is the result of the magnitude and speed with which adjustments take place when supply chains are well coordinated by lead firms. An important reason for lead firms to establish global production networks in the first place is the flexibility they provide. GVCs allow adjustment to changes in market demand to occur quickly and enable the risk of demand declines and inventory adjustment to be borne to a greater extent by supplier firms. Innovations in lean retailing, fast fashion, just-in-time inventory management control, and full-package outsourcing have all been built on GVC governance strategies. Suppliers too have developed in a way that seeks to manage the environment of flexibility-seeking lead firms. Modular production processes give supplier firms the capacity to serve different product lines and even different GVCs (Sturgeon 2002). Adding to the speed of adjustment in trade in a downturn is the fact that firms might make use of accumulated inventories first (Baldwin 2009b; Freund 2009).

In a world of disintegrated production and lean retailing, the 2008–09 GDP downturn resulted not only in larger declines in trade than had occurred previously but also declines that were more rapid. Recent research confirms that the trade collapse was "synchronized" across countries, which Baldwin (2009b) also attributes to the internationalization of the supply chain. GVCs are a channel for the rapid transmission of both real and financial shocks. Shifts in demand for final goods can immediately affect flows of intermediates, especially when supplier contracts are short term. And credit market problems can cascade throughout the chain; for example, a denial of credit to importers in one country can reduce access to credit for sellers in others, thus affecting their ability to import (Escaith and Gonguet 2009).

Trade Credit Crunch

There are strong indications of an additional factor at work today that has driven down international trade activity: the freezing up of lines of credit for undertaking international trade transactions, also known as trade finance. A survey of multinational buyers (that is, lead firms and higher-tier supplier firms in GVCs) indicates that the drop in orders may be more a function of "new credit bottlenecks" than declining final demand per se (Auboin 2009; see ICC 2009 for a survey measuring the decline in the volume of trade credit). Trade finance comprises a number of financial instruments, including letters of credit, pre-export financing, factoring and forfeiting, advance payment guarantees, export credit insurance, and export credit guarantees (drawn from Chauffour and Farole 2009, appendix 1). The slowdown in trade credit provision has come as a result of more stringent bank credit and capital allocation criteria, growing distrust between international banking counterparts who must cooperate in the provision of trade credit, more stringent requirements on borrowers' invoice and payment systems, and a drying up of the secondary market for trade financing instruments.

A trade credit crunch will put a more severe damper on the volume of international trade when such trade is organized in global value chains. There are two reasons for this. One, a bottleneck resulting from lack of credit in one part of the chain can reduce trade for the entire chain. As described by ICC (2009, 4): "Supply chains have produced undesirable side effects. Exporters in international supply chains are better shielded from financial turmoil because they have access to credit from buyers. However, with their own access to finance drying up, global buyers will become more restrictive in providing finance along their supply chains."

The second reason is that GVCs are potentially a channel for the rapid transmission of financial shocks, in particular through credit markets, which can have a negative international "cascade effect" as the denial of credit to importers in one country leads to credit problems for sellers in others, reducing their access to credit, affecting in turn their ability to import, and so on. This is a vicious cycle between the real and the financial sides of the economy (Amiti and Weinstein 2009; Escaith and Gonguet 2009; Mora and Powers 2009).

The implication is that the decline in world trade is greater when the credit crunch occurs within a production system organized through GVCs. This combination is a unique feature of the recent crisis and thus may account for the break from historical output-demand relations as seen in the elasticity estimates presented in the next section. For this reason, the Group of Twenty (G-20) provision of $250 billion to support trade finance over the next two years is an important step in easing the financial side of the trade collapse (Auboin 2009, 6).

The Shifting V-Curve of Trade

The recent WTO prediction of a rapid trade recovery includes an acknowledgment that its forecasts could be either overly optimistic (for example, if there are unexpected increases in oil prices, appreciation or depreciation of major currencies, or additional adverse developments in financial markets) or overly pessimistic (for instance, if unemployment rates in developed countries were to drop faster than anticipated) (WTO 2010). As seen in figure 2.1 and in more detail in the elasticity estimates, the decline in trade relative to GDP is greater than the historical pattern would predict, and thus elasticities estimated on data from past cycles are not a reliable guide to future trends.

Freund (2009) identifies a distinct V-shaped curve in the volume of world trade over the business cycle, and Baldwin and Taglioni (2009) use the past V-curve to predict a relatively rapid recovery of trade volumes to precrisis levels.

To date, this recovery of trade is not following the historical V-curve, as seen in figure 2.6, which compares the historical pattern of the past two U.S. recessions to the recent experience. The import decline is larger and more rapid, as noted earlier. Moreover, the recovery in imports is in the form of a smaller percentage of quarterly declines. Thus, two years from the previous business cycle peak, U.S. imports are still falling at a 10 percent rate. The V-curve appears to have shifted to the right.

There are a number of possible explanations for the shift in the V-curve. For one, the recent downturn may involve a macroeconomic restructuring in many industrial countries, as debt burdens are worked off, household consumption is reduced, and government spending partly offsets declines in consumption and business investment demand. Consumption expenditure in the United States in particular is recovering much more slowly than in previous recoveries (Kaplinsky and Farooki [2010] and Ferrantino and Larsen [2009] make a similar argument). A second, but related, factor is China's development trajectory and exchange rate policy, with the renminbi generally considered undervalued compared to the U.S. dollar. While the renminbi appreciated in relation to the dollar until 2006, it has remained constant since then. This has been associated with an expanding Chinese market share for many U.S. and EU import products. But pressures for a revaluation remain, and a U.S. recovery at a higher rate of private saving, a higher

Figure 2.6 Quarterly U.S. Goods Import Growth Rates during the Past Three Crises: 1990, 2001, and 2007
% growth year to year

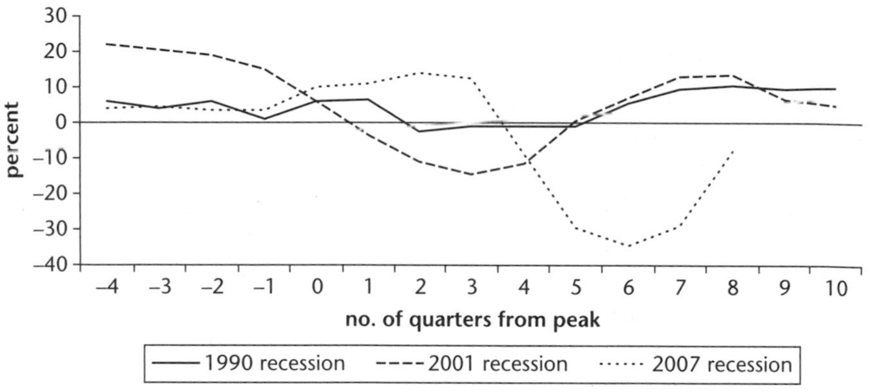

Source: Authors' illustration using data from the U.S. Bureau of Economic Analysis, National Income and Product Accounts Table, Gross Domestic Product, seasonally adjusted at annual rates.
Note: Zero on the y axis refers to the peak of the U.S. business cycles' recessions, as defined by the National Bureau of Economic Research.

rate of public dissaving, and a weakened dollar may bring a very different world trade picture, with lower levels of trade and consolidated GVCs (Kaplinsky and Farooki 2010).

Country and Product Profile of the Decline in U.S. and EU Import Demand

After reviewing how individual countries and sectors fared in the recent economic crisis, this section analyzes GVC consolidation.[4] It should be noted that the financial origins of this downturn resulted in a tightening of trade credit, which may contribute to the shift in the V-curve. The first part examines more closely the country and product profile of the decline in U.S. and EU import demand. It begins with a product-based analysis of U.S. and EU imports, then makes a regional analysis of developing-country exports.

Product-Based Analysis of U.S. and EU Imports

The country-level variation in import demand is a function of macroeconomic conditions (foreign demand growth and changes in the real effective exchange rate) and the commodity composition of trade. To get a closer look at the latter, it is necessary to explore the shifts in import demand in the United States and the European Union over the past 12–18 months in more detail. Figure 2.4, illustrating the U.S. import trends for broad commodity groupings, shows that industrial supplies and materials imports fell much more than consumer goods (except autos) and services. These data are aggregated up from the detailed goods import data presented in annex 2C. Total goods imports decreased by 31 percent in August 2009 on a year-to-year (YTY) basis. In the first analysis of the downturn described earlier (Milberg and Winkler 2009a), for February 2009, U.S. imports fell most in motor vehicles, oil, and construction on a YTY basis, and the smallest declines were seen in food and clothing, two consumer necessities.

The decline in motor vehicle demand in the United States has had significant international repercussions, because U.S. motor vehicle production relies more on imported inputs than any other sector of the economy, with over 25 percent of inputs imported (see figure 2.5; for a detailed analysis, see Van Biesebroeck and Sturgeon 2010). The first analysis in this chapter, using February 2009 YTY data, showed rapid declines in imports of various categories of auto and truck parts by dramatic amounts: imports of unfinished metals (largely used for motor vehicles) declined 55 percent; automotive vehicles, parts, and engines declined 54 percent, of which bodies and chassis for passenger cars constituted the largest drop at a 71 percent decline.

These declines are the result of a combination of a sudden collapse of consumer demand for new automobiles and the highly developed GVCs developed by the United States and U.S.-based firms. As discussed above, the fact that the demand drop was concentrated at first in consumer durables and investment goods—such as construction materials ("postponables" in Baldwin's [2009b] terminology)—meant that there was a much more drastic impact on trade than on GDP, since the latter is dominated by services. Borchert and Mattoo (2009) list a number of reasons why the demand for services has contracted less than the demand for goods in the recent crisis, which include the nonstorability of services and the fact that a larger part of services demand involves outsourced services (for example, bookkeeping) that are "necessities" for producers. (See annex 2D for the detailed services import data.)

The sectoral declines in U.S. imports give some indication of the composition of shifts in labor demand. Since it is medium-technology goods for which demand has fallen most, it would be expected that low-skill manufacturing workers in developing countries would have suffered most in terms of employment and wages. Services workers—of both low and high skill—have so far been affected less, because private services have continued to grow, and even the most affected services sector (other transportation) has declined considerably less than the average decline for goods.

The pattern of import decline for the European Union is similar to that in the United States, but less pronounced. EU goods import growth is shown in figure 2.7. Total goods imports fell by almost 29 percent in August 2009 on a YTY basis. Manufactured goods showed the biggest decline, reaching more than –40 percent since the second quarter of 2009. This, again, supports the finding that demand fell most strongly for "postponables," that is, consumer durables and investment goods. As in the United States, the demand for imported industrial supplies and materials (mineral fuels, lubricants, and related materials; animal and vegetable oils, fats, and waxes; crude materials, inedible, except fuels) showed a sharp decline, while more necessary consumer goods, such as food and miscellaneous manufactured articles (including clothing and footwear), dropped less.[5]

Regional Analysis of Developing-Country Exports

While China's exports to the United States declined during the downturn more than those in other countries (see figure 2.8a), it is only China among the top five exporters to the United States that has seen a significant rebound in trade volume. This means that China's share of U.S. imports has grown significantly, reaching 20 percent in September 2009, which represents the highest share since January 2007 (except for January 2009). China has gained market share despite the decline in U.S. imports. Canada's import share has fallen between 1 and 2 percentage

Figure 2.7 EU 27 Goods Imports by Product Category, Ranked by August 2009 Growth
% change year to year

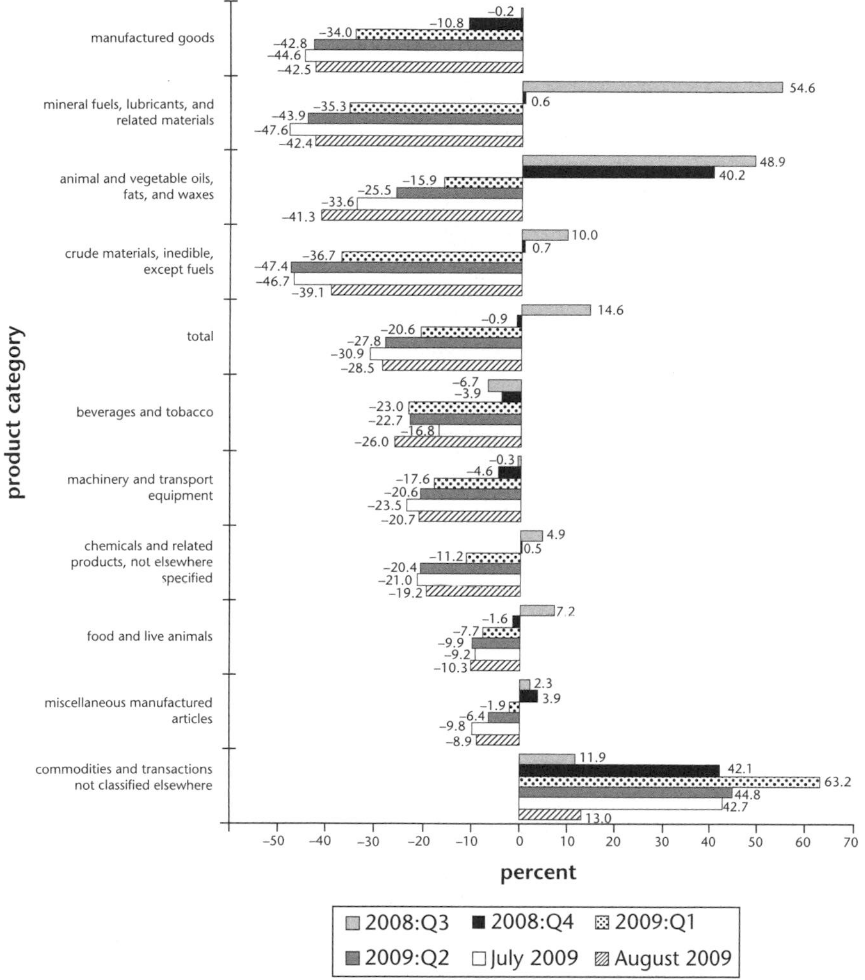

Source: Authors' illustration using data from Eurostat, External Trade by Standard International Trade Classification (SITC).

points since the outbreak of the crisis, but the top five importers combined have gained market share from 52.6 percent in August 2008 to 55.4 percent in September 2009.

A similar pattern holds for the EU import market. While imports from the United States have continued to fall through July 2009, Chinese imports were already rising for four consecutive months (figure 2.8b). Since March 2009,

Figure 2.8 U.S. and EU 27 Goods Imports of Top-Five Importers

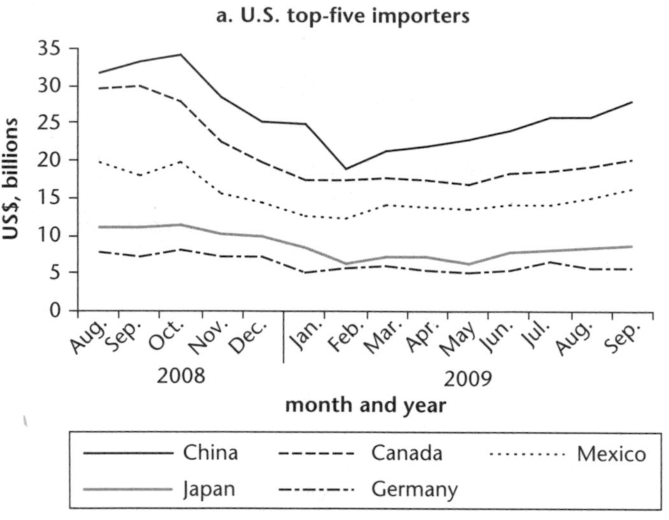

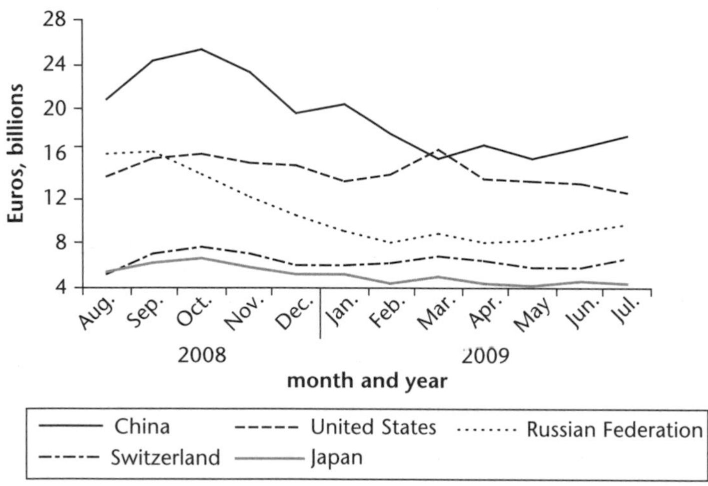

Source: Authors' illustration using data from U.S. International Trade Commission; Eurostat, External Trade.
Note: Top-five importers are as of August 2008.

Chinese imports have gained market share at the cost of the second biggest importer, the United States. China's import share reached 17.6 percent in July 2009, while the U.S. market share was only 12.4 percent. The total market share of the top-five importers was 50.9 percent in July 2009, compared to 48.1 percent in August 2008.

China's outstanding performance in U.S. and EU markets appears to have been matched by some other economies in late 2009, as seen in figure 2.9, where goods export growth on a YTY basis is compared across all economies for which data were available. While most economies saw smaller declines in exports in the third quarter 2009 compared to the second quarter, a small number of economies began to see export increases (on a YTY basis) in November, including Bosnia-Herzegovina; Chile; Indonesia; Taiwan, China; and Thailand. Still, many economies showed considerable export declines in the third quarter 2009, greater than 25 percent compared to a year earlier. This confirms that even a delayed recovery in world trade is likely to take place at very different rates across economies, again, depending on their specialization patterns and trends in GVC consolidation.

Consolidation of GVCs: Theory and Evidence

Through the 1980s and 1990s, more and more countries entered into global export markets, typically producing intermediate inputs or performing assembly in global value chains. Different GVCs expanded at different rates, with apparel and automobiles expanding in the 1960s and 1970s, in terms of the dispersion and complexity of the supply chain, and the services sector and business services of other sectors falling among the more recent parts of growing and expanding GVCs. But the onset of the 2008–09 crisis brought broader evidence of consolidation of some types of supply chains.

Historical Trends in GVC Structure

We measured GVC structure using a modified version of the Herfindahl-Hirschman Index (HHI) calculated for each product category by taking the total sum of the squared market shares of all countries exporting that product and multiplying the sum by 10,000, thus:

$$HHI_j = \sum_i (S_{ij})^2 \cdot 10{,}000,$$

where S_{ij} is the share of country *i* expressed as a percentage of total world exports of product *j*.[6] The HHI can range between $1/n$ * 10,000 (if each of the n countries has the same share), and 10,000, if one country exports all, where *n* designates the total number of countries exporting this product. A decline reflects a decrease in "concentration," or, more accurately, a greater degree of spatial dispersion of export sourcing in that sector. The U.S. Department of Justice Antitrust Division considers HHIs between 1,000 and 1,800 points to be moderately concentrated, and those

Figure 2.9 Goods Exports of Low- and Middle-Income Countries, 2009
% change year to year

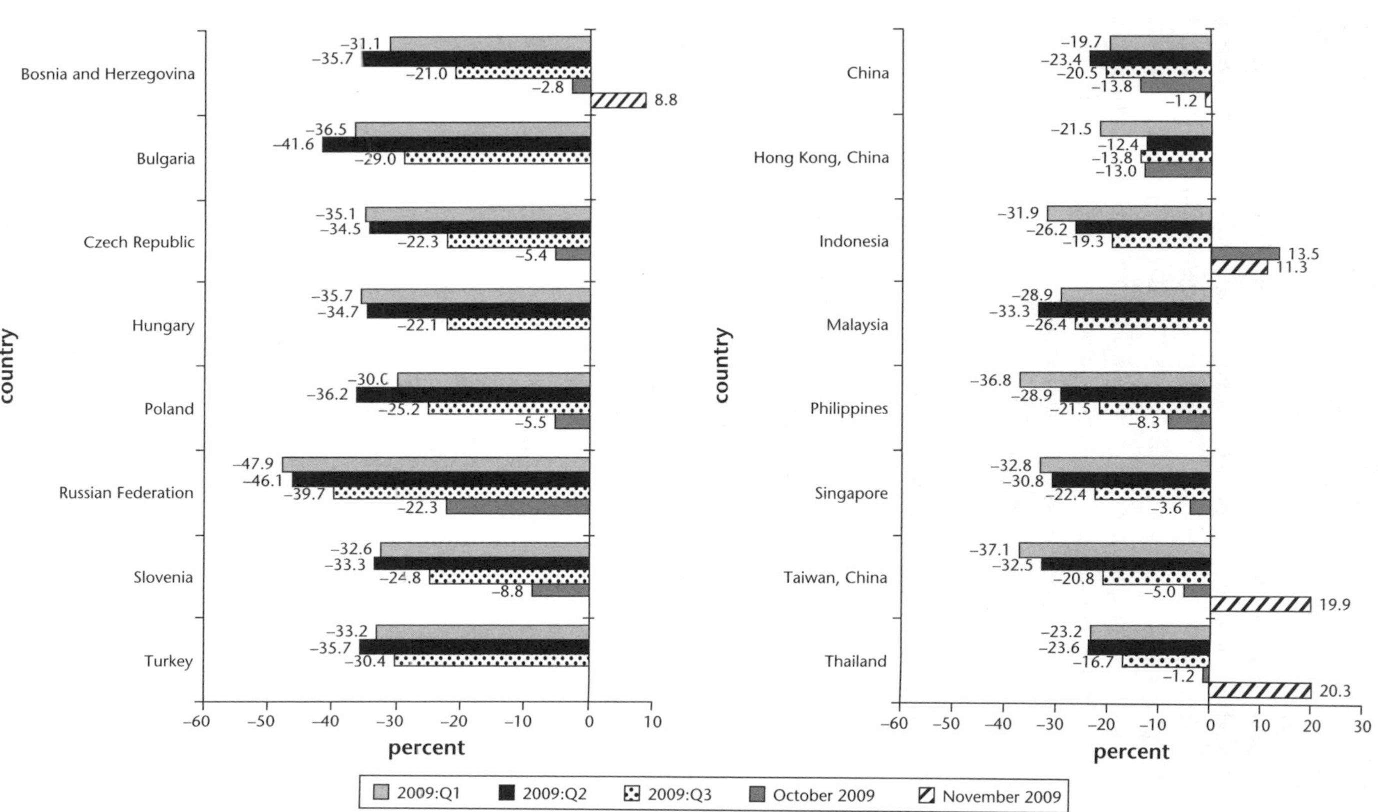

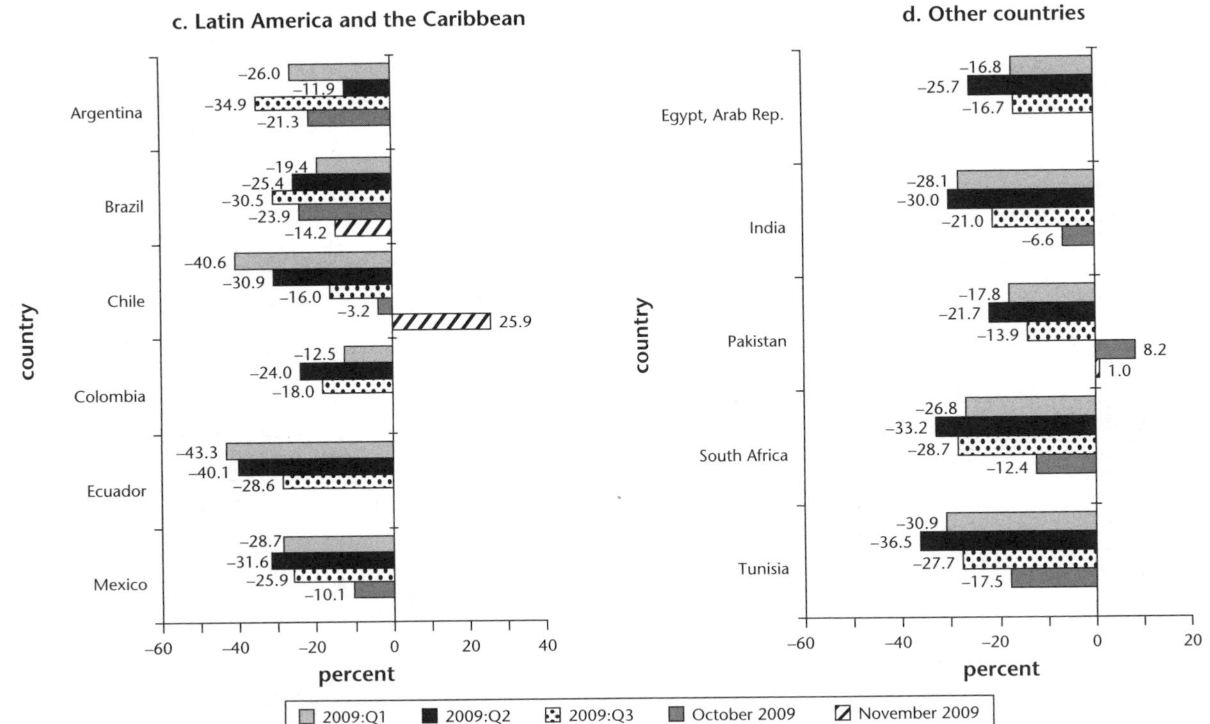

Source: Authors' illustration using data from Economist Intelligence Unit Country Data.

exceeding 1,800 points to be concentrated.[7] Although this rule of thumb refers to the original HHI, that is, to firms' market shares in a particular market rather than to the market shares of exporting countries, it provides a convenient benchmark for judging export market concentration.

Figure 2.10 shows the graph of the index of industrial concentration for a selection of three-digit sectors for selected years from 1970 to 2008. Note that recent data should be interpreted with caution because export data might not be published yet for all individual countries, which—at a given level of world trade—would overestimate the share of countries for which data are available and thus yield a higher HHI. Most of the product areas experience a dispersion of trade (a decline in the HHI), although there are a number of exceptions. This is most clearly the case in the subsectors of textiles, iron and steel, machinery, and transportation. In some sectors, however, consolidation already began in the 1990s, including handbags, clothing, and footwear. These are sectors in which China made enormous gains in world market share, pushing out competitors, especially those from Africa and Latin America, but also those from smaller East and South Asian countries (Gallagher, Moreno-Brid, and Porzecanski 2008; Kaplinky and Morris 2008; Wood and Mayer 2009).

Downturn, Recovery, and GVCs: A Simple Taxonomy of Consolidation

A theory of the relation between the number of suppliers in a GVC and the level of demand or stage of the business cycle has not been completely developed. The expansion of GVCs internationally and in terms of numbers of suppliers has been understood from the perspective of transaction cost considerations, following the insights of Coase (1937) and Williamson (1975). The approach is largely static and independent of underlying demand conditions, since the focus is on the ownership pattern in the vertical production structure. Moreover, the transaction cost model is not typically understood as symmetric, that is, as applying to both expansion and consolidation of GVCs; this is true because transaction costs are generally viewed as falling monotonically over time as transportation, communication, search, and policy (for example, tariffs) costs fall (for example, Langlois 2003; Williamson 1979).[8]

Two types of consolidation are distinguished in this chapter, vertical and horizontal. Vertical consolidation is a reduction in the number of tiers of suppliers. Horizontal consolidation is a reduction in the number of suppliers in a particular tier of a GVC. Vertical consolidation is driven by a shrinking of market size, reducing the rationale for the existing number of tiers of suppliers. This follows Adam Smith's notion that "the division of labor is limited by the extent of the market." Stigler (1951) developed the insight to apply precisely to the degree of vertical

Figure 2.10 Herfindahl-Hirschman Index by Standard International Trade Classification, 1970–71 to 2007–08

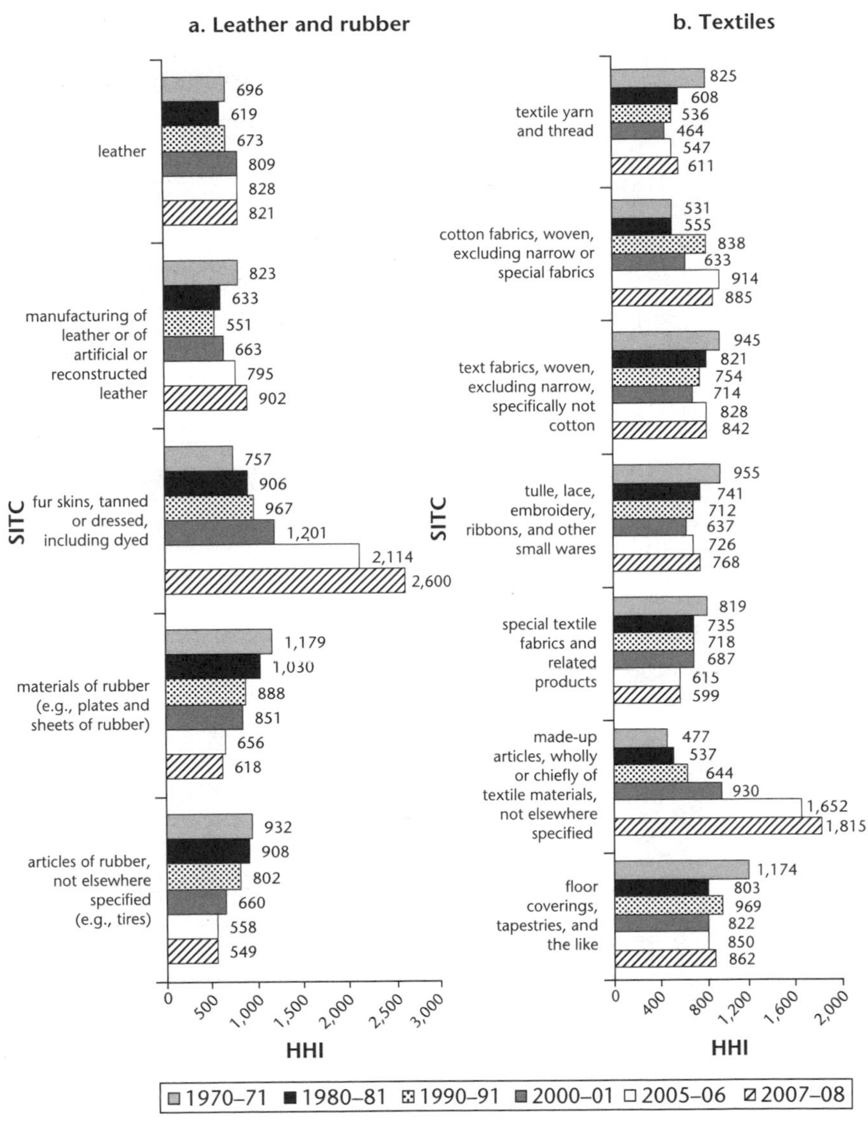

(*continued next page*)

Figure 2.10 *continued*

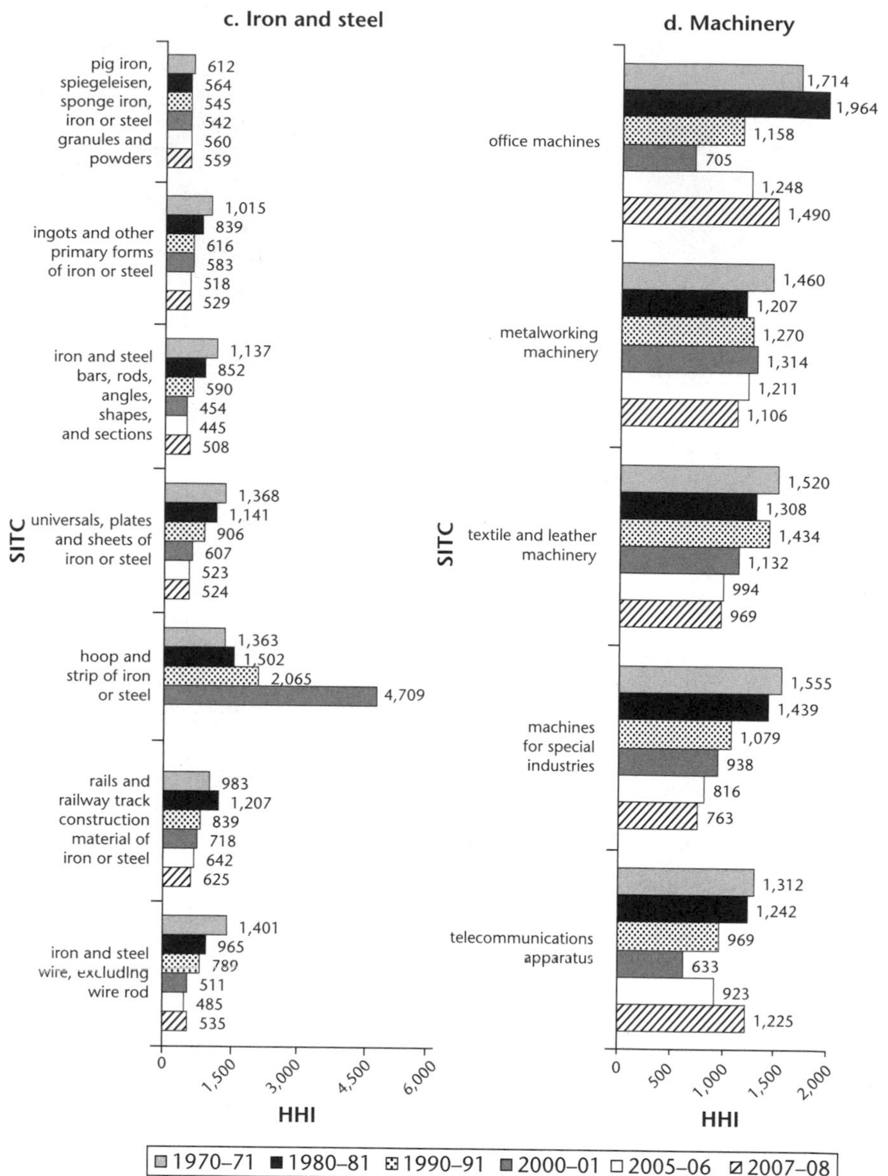

Figure 2.10 *continued*

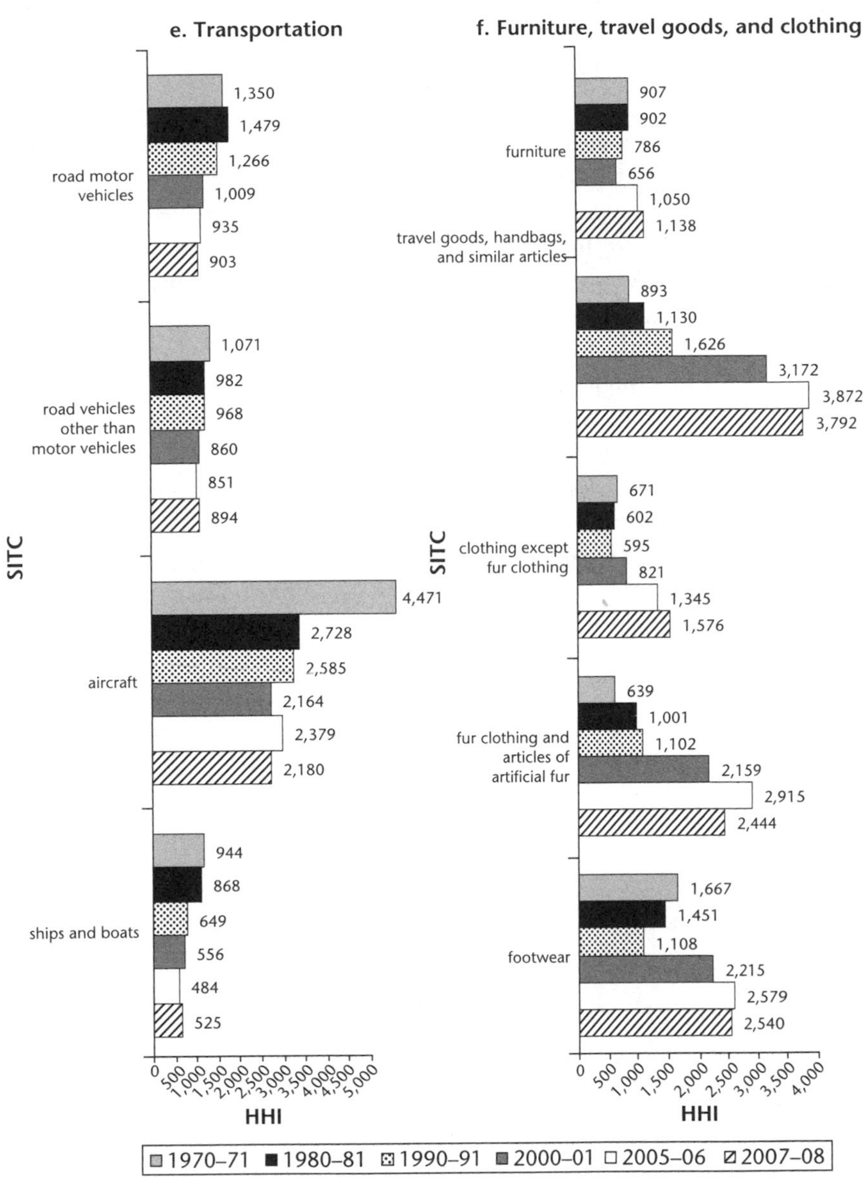

Source: Authors' calculations using data from UN Comtrade, retrieved from World Integrated Trade Solution.

Note: The Standard International Trade Classification (SITC) used was Revision 1. HHI = Herfindahl-Hirschman Index.

integration of the firm. Levy (1984) formalized the process and tested it empirically for the domestic operations of U.S. firms. The logic for this calculation is depicted in figure 2.11.

Assume there are economies of scale and that the lower curve represents the cost structure of a vertically integrated lead firm and the higher cost curve represents the costs of a specialized supplier firm. In a small market such as Q_1, the supplier firm is not cost-competitive compared to a vertically integrated lead firm. If the market expands and more firms enter the supplier industry while the lead firm maintains its production, then supplier firms' costs, C_3, are lower than lead firm costs C_1. As Levy (1984, 382) states, "Because the specialized [supplier] firm can produce at lower costs than the integrated [lead] firm, the integrated [lead] firm spins off the decreasing cost activity and buys from the specialized firm at a price lower than its average costs." The reverse of this logic predicts that a shrinking market would lead to a vertical consolidation of the GVC, whereby the lead firm can produce at lower cost by remaining integrated. Chung, Lu, and Beamish (2008), in a related study, find that majority-owned subsidiaries of parent firms perform relatively better compared to arm's-length suppliers in periods of economic downturn.

The notion of horizontal consolidation comes from Ricardo's theory of rent, according to which marginal suppliers are driven out of business as the market shrinks. Consolidation in the number of suppliers occurs in a downturn as marginal

Figure 2.11 Vertical Consolidation of Global Value Chains

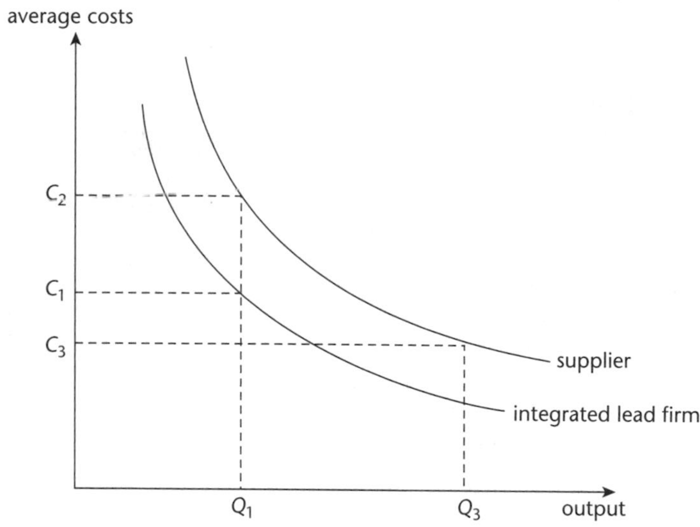

Source: Authors' illustration based on Levy (1984, 382).

suppliers are squeezed out with the decline in demand. Horizontal consolidation might be more likely in buyer-driven GVCs, where supplier contracts are shorter and where lead firm commitments to, and technology sharing with, supplier firms are less. This process is depicted in figure 2.12. Production costs are indicated in the figure by prices in foreign currency, where p_i is domestic price and e_i is the exchange rate for country *i*. Lead firms will be more likely to maintain suppliers with whom they have already invested in technology, capital, or cooperation.

Both types of consolidation are logical in a downturn. The central issue here is the reversibility of these processes. Will a rebound in demand generate a reversal of consolidation? The focus in the analysis here is primarily on horizontal consolidation. Is there a rationale for asymmetry or hysteresis in the relation between demand and GVC structure? The answer would seem to hinge on the possibility of surviving suppliers expanding capacity and capturing scale economies, creating new entry barriers for firms that did not survive the downturn. The duration of the economic downturn and speed of the recovery potentially allow surviving suppliers to expand productive capacity and to further capture scale economies. Such suppliers may also develop new production capabilities. At the same time, suppliers forced to shut down during the slump face considerable fixed costs in reopening operations, and thus may be at a further disadvantage even when demand returns to pre-downturn levels. Thus, in the case of GVC consolidation, the shutdown of marginal firms can lead to an asymmetric pattern when demand recovers. The high-productivity suppliers are in a better position to expand when the market rebounds, leading to a consolidation of the GVC.

GVC Restructuring in the Crisis

What has been the trend in the HHI over the recent downturn period? Those sectors or products that saw the greatest decline in trade might be expected to exhibit

Figure 2.12 Horizontal Consolidation of Global Value Chains

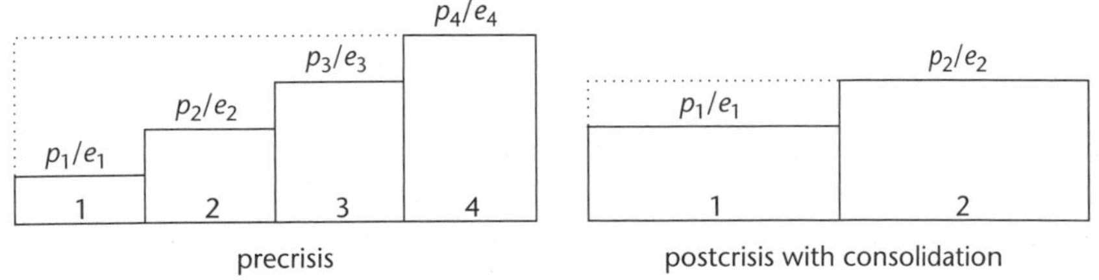

Source: Authors' illustration.

the greatest degree of consolidation, according to our HHI measure. But there appears to be no correlation between the percentage decline in trade and the change in GVC structure. This may be a result of the fact that the 2007–08 period does not capture enough of the downturn's effect, since its major impact began in 2008. However, if we recalculate the HHI index for a different grouping of sectors, we do find some regularities. That is, while the volume of trade does not seem correlated, as yet, with consolidation, the type of sector or GVC does seem to matter for the pattern of consolidation and diversification.

The hypothesis that emerges from this brief theoretical consideration of global value chain consolidation is that buyer-led chains will experience the most consolidation and producer-led chains, the least. This hypothesis gets some support when considering consolidation in sectors measured by "Broad Economic Category," which characterizes goods as consumption goods, capital goods, and intermediate goods (see annex 2B for definitions). The changes in HHI for these product categories between 2007 and 2008 are presented in figure 2.13. Note that an almost equal number of product areas experienced diversification as experienced consolidation. Consolidation occurs more often in consumption goods sectors (categories 1, 6, and 7, for example), where buyer-led chains are more pervasive, and diversification occurs in intermediates (categories 2 and 5), where producer-led chains are more often the governing norm. Finally, we find that there is a weak positive relationship between consolidation and export growth, as indicated by the upward sloping line in figure 2.14.

This result of consolidation in buyer-driven GVCs is consistent with the fact that in the downturn there were some significant shifts in product market shares, with China often gaining in U.S. import markets, while smaller East Asian nations were found to be losing U.S. market share in the United States. Table 2.3 provides some evidence of how particular countries have fared in particular markets as U.S. imports declined. These selected sectors reveal a pattern of China gaining market share despite the decline in U.S. imports. Other countries have also gained, depending on the product area. Countries that have lost market share include high-cost producers (for example, Italy in the handbag market) and low-cost, especially East Asian, producers (for example, Cambodia in apparel, Thailand in rubber products and plumbing and heating fixtures, and Malaysia in telecommunications products). Thus, this evidence would indicate that the import decline that occurred with the economic downturn created winners and losers in terms of market share. China's continued success in exporting to the United States, aided no doubt by the adjustable dollar peg, is taking a toll on exporters in both high-cost markets and low-cost markets, the latter especially among smaller East Asian countries. This finding is confirmed by surveys by Hurst, Buttle, and Sandars (2009) of small and medium enterprises in East

Figure 2.13 Herfindahl-Hirschman Index by Broad Economic Category, Ranked by 2007–08 Growth Rate
percent

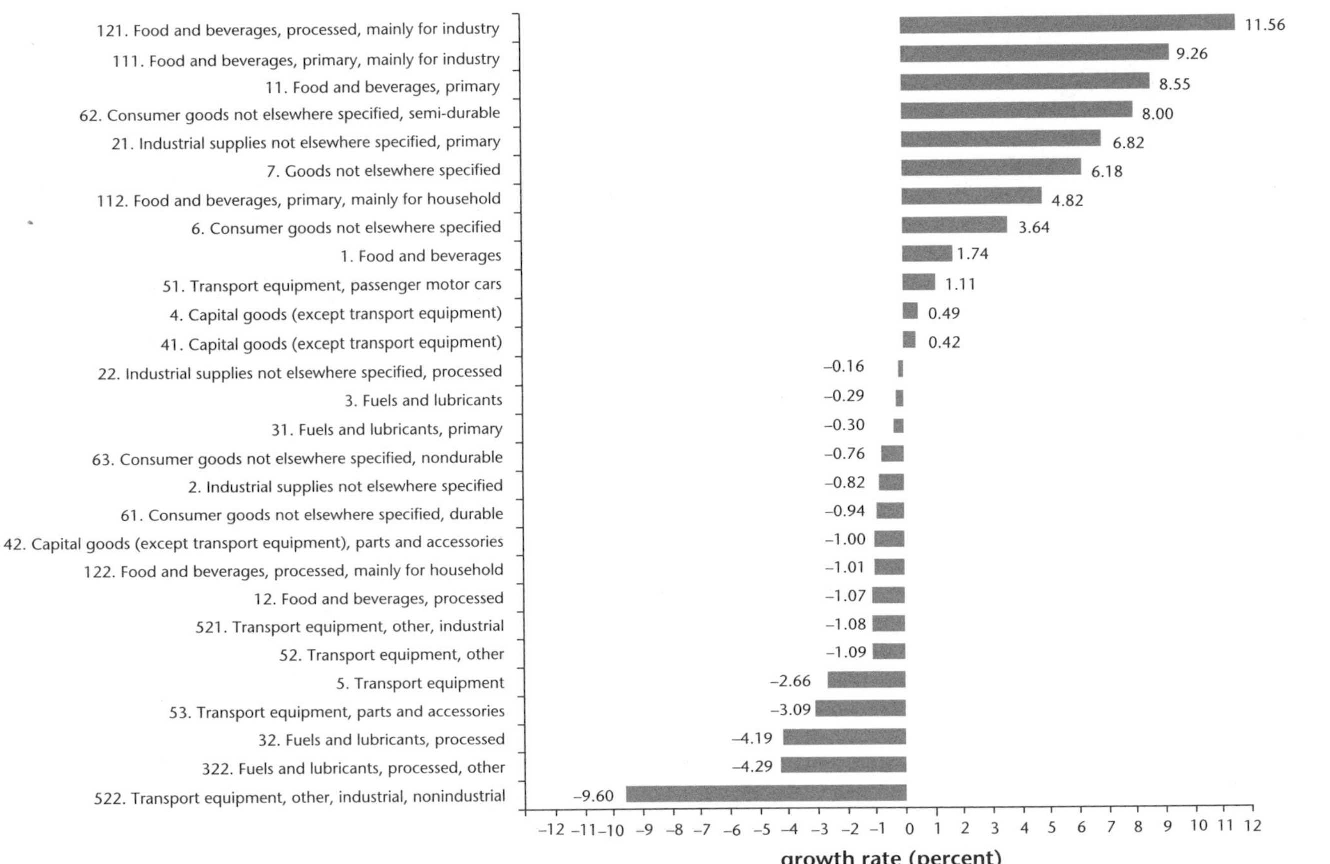

Source: Authors' calculations with data from UN Comtrade, retrieved from World Integrated Trade Solution.

Figure 2.14 Export Growth and Herfindahl-Hirschman Index Growth by Broad Economic Category, 2007–08
percent

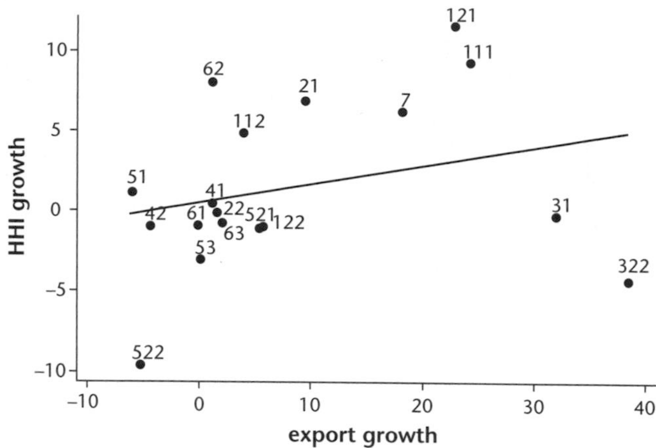

Source: Authors' illustration using data from UN Comtrade, retrieved from World Integrated Trade Solution.

Asia, which have reported massive declines in orders and cutbacks in employment across a variety of consumer goods.

Conclusions: Alternative Sources of Demand and Policy Responses

Joseph Stiglitz (2009)[9] has noted that the 2008–09 downturn was the first economic crisis in the era of globalization, in that the crisis was felt globally (rather than in just some regions) and spread in part as the result of the globalized nature of financial markets. But his characterization also holds true for the production and trade sides of the economy. This has been the first economic crisis since the globalization of production (the expanded use of global value chains) became extensive and sophisticated. It occurred since highly export-dependent developing countries have been participating in the world economy largely through these global value chains. Our analysis of the effects of the economic crisis on export-oriented developing countries confirms that the economic crisis that began in the United States in 2007, and quickly evolved into a large drop in demand for exports from developing countries, has had a magnified effect on trade because of the prominence of GVC-based trade. Trade volumes had risen much more rapidly than GDP for 25 years, and the reverse occurred in the recent recession.

Table 2.3 U.S. Sectoral Import Shares by Top-10 Importers, January–September 2008 versus January–September 2009
percent

Economy	January–September 2008	January–September 2009	Change
62. Rubber manufactures, n.e.s.			
China	21.3	24.4	3.2
Canada	17.8	18.4	0.6
Japan	13.5	13.6	0.1
Mexico	7.1	6.7	–0.4
Korea, Rep. of	6.6	6.2	–0.4
Germany	4.9	4.6	–0.3
Thailand	3.5	3.3	–0.2
Brazil	2.7	2.7	–0.1
Taiwan, China	3.4	2.8	–0.5
Indonesia	1.5	1.8	0.3
All other	17.8	15.6	–2.2
65. Textile yarn, fabrics, made-up articles, n.e.s., and related products			
China	33.7	35.1	1.4
India	10.2	10.6	0.5
Mexico	6.9	7.4	0.6
Canada	7.0	6.9	–0.2
Pakistan	6.7	7.6	0.8
Korea, Rep. of	3.4	3.4	–0.1
Turkey	2.4	2.1	–0.3
Taiwan, China	2.7	2.3	–0.3
Japan	2.5	2.1	–0.4
Israel	1.5	1.7	0.2
All other	22.9	20.9	–2.1
76. Telecommunications and sound recording and reproducing apparatus and equipment			
China	39.6	40.5	1.0
Mexico	23.7	24.1	0.4
Korea, Rep. of	7.9	9.6	1.6
Taiwan, China	4.6	4.8	0.2
Japan	5.6	4.2	–1.4
Malaysia	5.0	4.1	–0.9
Thailand	2.8	2.5	–0.3
Canada	2.8	2.9	0.0
Indonesia	0.7	0.9	0.2
Germany	0.9	0.7	–0.2
All other	6.3	5.7	–0.6

(continued next page)

Table 2.3 *continued*
percent

Economy	January–September 2008	January–September 2009	Change
81. Prefabricated buildings: sanitary, plumbing, heating and lighting fixtures and fittings, n.e.s.			
China	54.6	57.4	2.8
Mexico	18.6	19.0	0.3
Canada	8.9	8.5	–0.3
Germany	2.6	2.5	–0.1
France	1.0	1.2	0.2
Taiwan, China	1.4	1.0	–0.4
India	0.9	0.9	–0.1
Italy	1.8	1.3	–0.5
Japan	0.7	0.7	0.0
Thailand	1.1	0.9	–0.2
All other	8.4	6.6	–1.8
84. Articles of apparel and clothing accessories			
China	33.6	38.2	4.6
Vietnam	6.6	7.3	0.7
Indonesia	5.4	5.9	0.5
Mexico	5.4	5.1	–0.3
Bangladesh	4.4	5.1	0.8
India	4.2	4.5	0.3
Cambodia	3.1	2.7	–0.4
Honduras	3.3	3.0	–0.3
Thailand	2.7	2.5	–0.2
Pakistan	2.0	2.0	0.0
All other	29.3	23.7	–5.6
85. Footwear			
China	74.0	76.3	2.3
Vietnam	5.9	7.5	1.6
Italy	5.9	4.3	–1.6
Indonesia	2.0	2.5	0.5
Brazil	2.7	2.2	–0.5
Mexico	1.2	1.3	0.1
India	1.0	0.9	–0.1
Dominican Republic	0.6	0.7	0.0
Thailand	1.3	0.9	–0.3
Canada	n.a.	0.3	n.a.
All other	5.3	3.1	–2.3

Source: Authors' calculations using data from U.S. International Trade Commission.
Note: Top-10 importers as of September 2009 by SITC category. n.e.s = not elsewhere specified.

And this reverse effect has been more pronounced and the upturn more delayed in the recent downturn.

While this magnified effect has been observed across sectors, there appears to be considerable variation based on recent U.S. import data. Motor vehicles and parts imports and construction materials imports fell by over 50 percent at an annual rate, while apparel and food imports fell by 10 percent or less and professional services imports continued to expand. The effect to date on developing countries thus depends on their export profile, that is, on their role in global value chains, on the nature of the GVCs (buyer or producer-driven), and on the net effect of the forces of import demand and substitution.

We argue that because of structural changes that occurred in this recession, there are more reasons than previously to be concerned about the possibility of a longer recovery of trade. Moreover, the recession occurred at a time when GVCs are expansive and are subject to consolidation. We found evidence that some consolidation of GVCs occurred in 2008, especially in buyer-led chains. China's expanded market share across a spectrum of product categories, which seems to have come at the expense of other East Asian countries' exports, supports this finding. Producer-led chains appear to be continuing the longer-term trajectory of diversification.

If trade volumes do not rebound symmetrically with the economic recovery, then the consolidation of GVCs is more likely, because the consolidation that occurred with the downturn will lead to a longer period of time for surviving suppliers to expand capacity and raise productivity.

The analysis presented in this chapter leads to three policy conclusions:

1. Declines in export demand translate immediately into declines in foreign exchange reserves. In an environment where developing-country foreign exchange reserves are growing more slowly or declining, the provision of $250 billion in trade credit by the G-20 is a useful stopgap measure and should be allocated quickly. The expanded resources of the International Monetary Fund should also be tapped quickly and with reduced conditionality.
2. Countries need to find other, nonexport sources of demand, or to diversify trade patterns to focus more on trade among developing countries. One source is expansionary fiscal policy. China's large stimulus package is a prime example, and China's growth has picked up following a large increase in unemployment from the initial shock to world trade. But China's success in domestic stimulus in some ways points out the difficulty of drawing any general conclusions about the possibilities for stimulus across the developing world. Capacity for stimulus depends to a great extent on the prior accumulation of foreign exchange reserves. China is, of course, exceptional in that it has accumulated

substantial reserves over the past 15 years. Most developing countries have very small reserve stocks.

The other prospect is to expand other sources of export demand. South-South trade is often cited as a potential source of growth in developing countries. This deep embedding in GVCs also appears in the structure of developing-countries' imports. Figure 2.15 shows low- and middle-income country exports to other low- and middle-income countries (that is, South-South trade) by Broad Economic Category (BEC) as a percentage of total exports of BEC. During the past two decades, the export shares to other developing countries have been continuously growing for capital goods, consumption goods, and intermediates. This reflects the growing importance of South-South trade. By definition, high-income countries have absorbed a declining percentage of exports from developing countries. Preliminary data for 2009 point to a strong increase of South-South trade, indicating that this is a potentially promising source of demand growth in the future.

Regarding the composition of South-South trade, more than a third of developing-countries' exports of intermediates went to other developing countries in 2008. The preliminary 2009 data even indicate a jump to almost 50 percent. Capital and consumption goods, however, are increasingly exported to developing countries as well, reaching precrisis shares of 30 percent and 20 percent, respectively. But here, again, the structure of world trade according

Figure 2.15 South-South Trade by Broad Economic Product Category, 1970–2009
% total exports in that product category

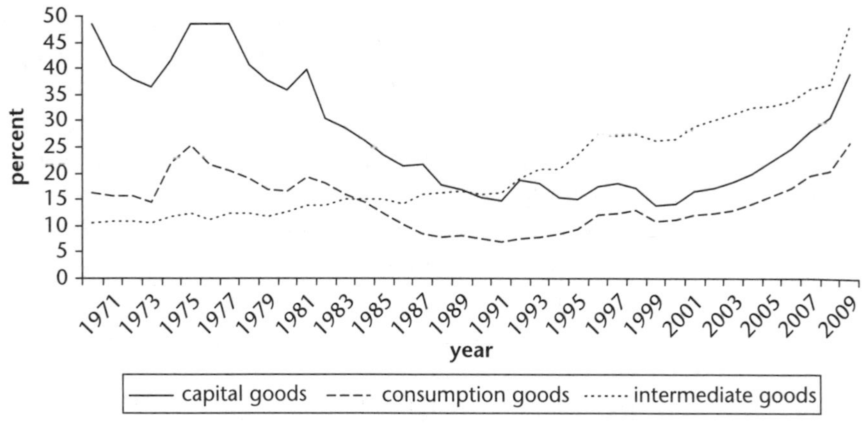

Source: Authors' calculations using data from UN Comtrade.
Note: Figures are exports from low- and middle-income countries to other low- and middle-income countries by Broad Economic Category.

to GVCs may create an obstacle in the short run to South-South trade growth. Figure 2.15 shows that the greatest growth potential of developing-countries' exports over the past decade has been in intermediates. This indicates that South-South trade is also molded to some extent by GVCs and the processing of intermediates to serve these chains. In this sense, the expansion of South-South trade still depends on the functioning of GVCs.

3. A final policy conclusion has to do with trade politics in industrialized countries during a severe economic downturn. Because of the extent of global value chains, firms in developed countries—generally the lead firms in the GVCs—depend on imports for their inputs and profitability (for some econometric-based evidence, see Milberg and Winkler 2009b); thus, these firms are less inclined to support trade protection than they were in earlier periods of steep economic decline (for example, when the Smoot-Hawley tariff adopted by the United States in 1930 raised U.S. import tariff rates to 60 percent). Nonetheless, popular sentiment remains in developed countries for protectionism. Resisting such a move will be very important for developing countries as the world economy recovers from the crisis.

Annex 2A: World Exports by Region from 1970 to 2007

Annex figures and tables begin on the next page.

Figure 2A.1 World Exports by Region, 1970–2007
% GDP

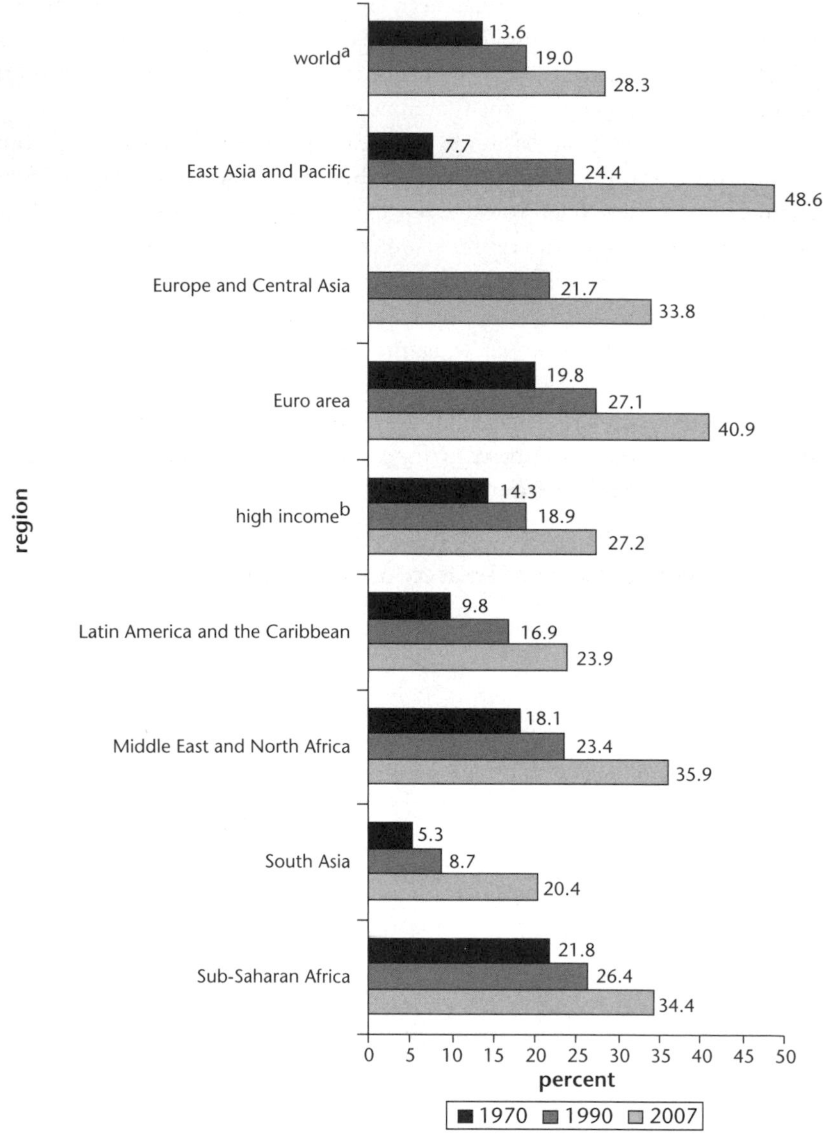

Source: Authors' illustration using data from World Bank, World Development Indicators.

a. Data are from 2006.

b. Data are from 2006, and this category includes members of the Organisation for Economic Co-operation and Development.

Annex 2B: Classification of Sectors by Broad Economic Category

The Broad Economic Category (BEC) classification, as defined by the United Nations, comprises 19 basic categories that are assigned to the final use of the good, namely, capital good, consumption good, and intermediate good (see table 2B.1). Two categories (motor spirit, passenger motor cars, and goods n.e.s. [not elsewhere specified]) are not assigned to these categories. We suggest classifying motor spirit as intermediate goods and passenger motor cars as consumption goods, while the assignment of goods that are not specified elsewhere cannot be done.

Table 2B.1 Classification of Sectors by Broad Economic Category

Broad Economic Category	Final use
1 Food and beverages	
11 Primary	
111 Mainly for industry	Intermediate goods
112 Mainly for household consumption	Consumption goods
12 Processed	
121 Mainly for industry	Intermediate goods
122 Mainly for household consumption	Consumption goods
2 Industrial supplies not elsewhere specified	
21 Primary	Intermediate goods
22 Processed	Intermediate goods
3 Fuels and lubricants	
31 Primary	Intermediate goods
32 Processed	
321 Motor spirit	Intermediate and consumption goods
322 Other	Intermediate goods
4 Capital goods (except transport equipment)	
41 Capital goods (except transport equipment)	Capital goods
42 Parts and accessories	Intermediate goods
5 Transport equipment	
51 Passenger motor cars	Intermediate and consumption goods
52 Other	
521 Industrial	Capital goods
522 Nonindustrial	Consumption goods
53 Parts and accessories	Intermediate goods
6 Consumer goods not elsewhere specified	
61 Durable	Consumption goods
62 Semi-durable	Consumption goods
63 Nondurable	Consumption goods
7 Goods not elsewhere specified	Intermediate, consumption, and capital goods

Source: UN "Classification by Broad Economic Categories" 2002.

Annex 2C: U.S. Goods Imports Ranked by Fourth-Quarter 2009 Growth

Figure 2C.1 U.S. Goods Imports by Product Category, Ranked by Fourth-Quarter 2009 Growth

% change year to year

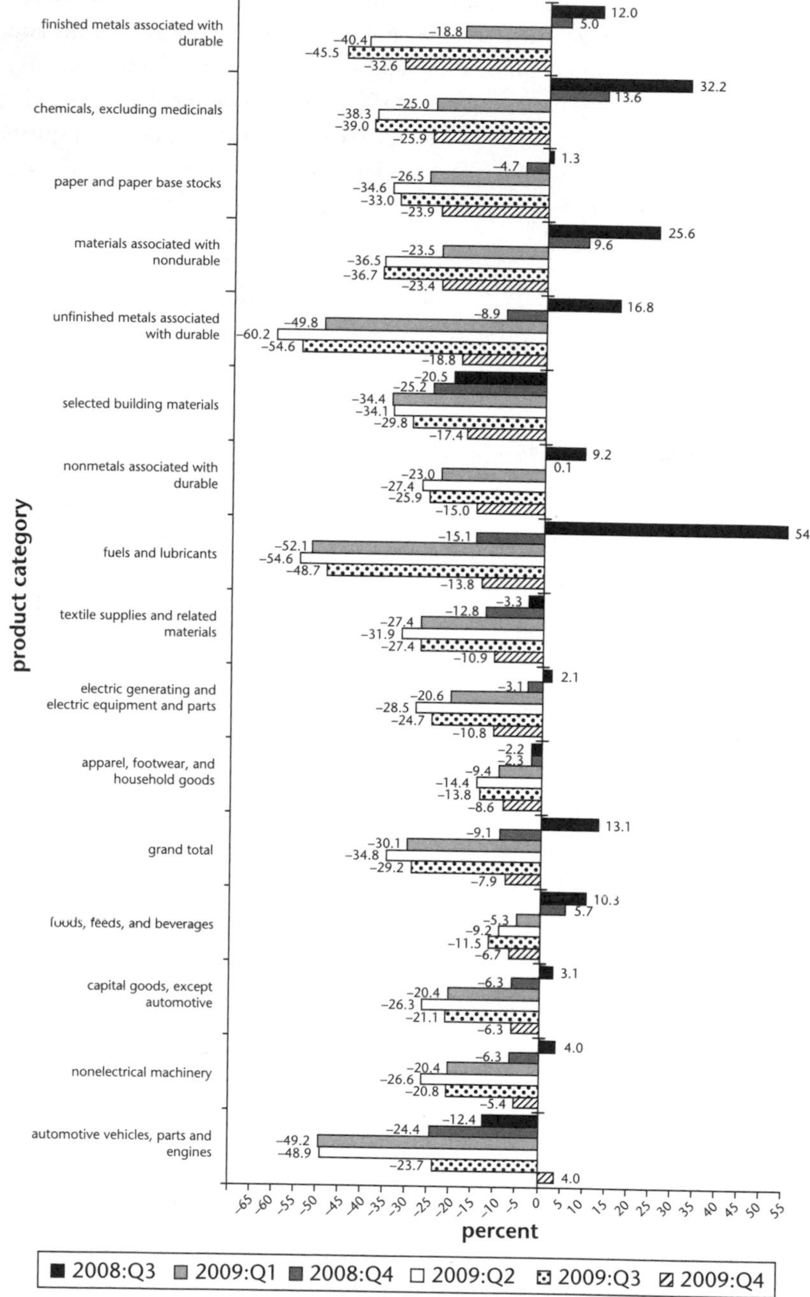

Source: Authors' illustration using data from Bureau of Economic Analysis, International Accounts.

Note: Product, monthly, and quarterly imports of goods, and balance of payments–based data are seasonally adjusted.

Annex 2D: U.S. Services Imports Ranked by Fourth-Quarter 2009 Growth

Figure 2D.1 U.S. Services Imports by Service Category, Ranked by Fourth-Quarter 2009 Growth
% change year to year

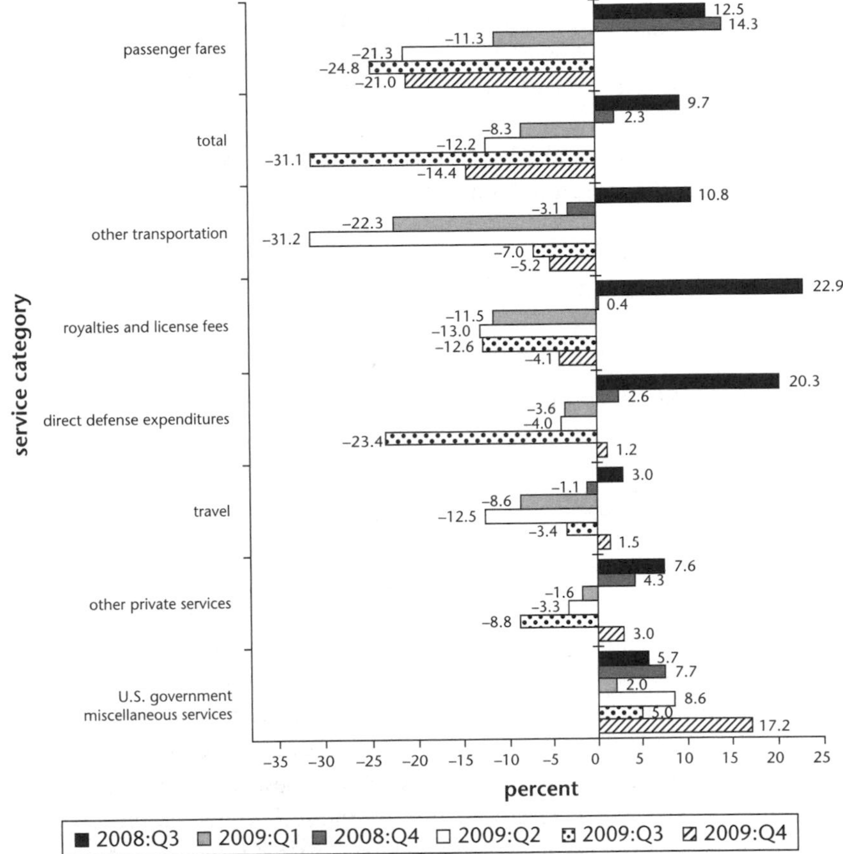

Source: Authors' illustration using data from Bureau of Economic Analysis, International Accounts.
Note: Product, monthly imports of services, and balance of payments–based data are seasonally adjusted.

Annex 2E: Income Elasticity Estimates

Following Bahmani-Oskooee, Goswami, and Talukdar (2005), U.S. import demand is assumed to be the following:

$$\ln M_t^j = \alpha + \beta \ln Y_t + \gamma \ln E_t^j + \varepsilon_t, \qquad \text{(E.1)}$$

where M designates real import demand for imports from country j; Y, real domestic income; and E, real bilateral exchange rate between the United States and country j at time t. E is defined as units of foreign currency per U.S. dollar, and ε_t denotes the random error term. Annex 2F describes the data used in the regressions. We hypothesize β to be positive, that is, higher income is related to higher import demand. γ is also expected to be positive, that is, an appreciation of the U.S. dollar is associated with a higher import demand.

An autoregressive distributed lag (ARDL) approach to co-integration is applied, which yields consistent estimates of the long-run coefficients, regardless of whether the regressors are I(1) or I(0) and thus does not require pretesting for unit root (Pesaran, Shin, and Smith 2001). The ARDL approach adds short-run dynamics to the long-run estimation as given in equation E.1:

$$\begin{aligned}\Delta \ln M_t^j &= \alpha + \sum_{i=1}^{n} \beta_i \Delta \ln Y_{t-i} + \sum_{i=1}^{n} \gamma_i \Delta \ln E_{t-1}^j + \sum_{i=1}^{n} \delta_i \Delta \ln M_{t-i}^j \\ &\quad + \nu_1 \ln Y_{t-1} + \nu_2 \ln E_{t-1}^j + \nu_3 \ln M_{t-1}^j + \varepsilon_t.\end{aligned} \tag{E.2}$$

The lagged level variables constitute the so-called lagged error-correction term, which should be retained or excluded from the equation based on the F-statistics. Pesaran, Shin, and Smith (2001) provide lower and upper critical value bounds and show that the null hypothesis of $\nu_1 = \nu_2 = \nu_3 = 0$ is rejected if the calculated F-statistics are greater than the upper critical value bound. In such a case, the lagged level variables are co-integrated.

Table 2E.1 reports the income and price elasticities, differentiating between goods imports (columns 1–4) and services imports (columns 5–8). Column 1 shows the F-statistics for goods imports based on the optimal number of lags (column 2), which were determined using Akaike's information criterion. Due to the limited number of quarters, we restricted the maximum lag to be six. We also tested for autocorrelation using Durbin's alternative test (column 3). In case the specification showed autocorrelation, we used the second best lag structure. We consider the error correction model with an unrestricted intercept and no trend. At the 10 percent significance level the critical value bounds for the F-statistics are 3.17 and 4.14 (Pesaran, Shin, and Smith 2001). Column 1 shows that only Argentina, China, India, Korea, and the United Kingdom exceed the critical level. The F-statistics for Germany and Hong Kong, China, fall within the band, which leads to inconclusive results. Following Bahmani-Oskooee and Brooks (1999), the error-correction term should be retained in such a case. The short-run effects of income on import demand are determined by the coefficient estimates of the first differenced income variables (with or without the error correction term). These results are mostly insignificant so are not reported here.

Table 2E.1 U.S. Import Elasticities, 1999–2008

	Long-run income and price elasticities of import demand									
	U.S. goods imports					*U.S. services imports*				
	(1)	(2)	(3)	(4)	(5)	(6)	(7)	(8)	(9)	(10)
Economy	F-statistics[a]	Lags[b]	Durbin's test[c]	Income elasticities	Price elasticities	F-statistics[a]	Lags[b]	Durbin's test[c]	Income elasticities	Price elasticities
Argentina	15.07	5	Prob> X^2 = 0.54	–0.5528 (0.109)	–0.1318* (0.071)	4.80	6	Prob> X^2 = 0.73	2.2540** (0.034)	–0.5155 (0.426)
Brazil	2.87	3	Prob> X^2 = 0.41	1.2441** (0.018)	–0.0898 (0.255)	5.70	2	Prob> X^2 = 0.45	0.2577 (0.515)	–0.5986*** (0.006)
Canada	0.13	5	Prob> X^2 = 0.74	0.0488 (0.956)	–0.0569 (0.932)	9.44	6	Prob> X^2 = 0.21	7.5568*** (0.000)	3.2146*** (0.006)
China	4.19	4	Prob> X^2 = 0.20	8.6450*** (0.006)	1.8407*** (0.007)	8.39	1	Prob> X^2 = 0.72	6.0187*** (0.000)	0.2330 (0.534)
France	1.61	1	Prob> X^2 = 0.24	0.4724 (0.294)	–0.0615 (0.663)	3.29	5	Prob> X^2 = 0.14	5.4116** (0.012)	1.0838 (0.132)
Germany	3.34	2	Prob> X^2 = 0.89	1.8615*** (0.007)	–0.0774 (0.617)	5.21	4	Prob> X^2 = 0.65	4.7037*** (0.003)	0.4846 (0.121)
Hong Kong, China	3.69	3	Prob> X^2 = 0.79	–2.7530** (0.011)	0.3589 (0.544)	4.02	2	Prob> X^2 = 0.46	5.4964** (0.012)	–1.9867* (0.052)
India	11.96	6	Prob> X^2 = 0.48	8.0550*** (0.000)	0.9567* (0.093)	1.94	2	Prob> X^2 = 0.53	2.0745** (0.039)	–0.0496 (0.930)
Japan	2.07	4	Prob> X^2 = 0.30	–0.1623 (0.582)	0.2765 (0.188)	3.65	3	Prob> X^2 = 0.78	1.7411** (0.011)	–0.0555 (0.658)

(continued next page)

Table 2E.1 *continued*

	Long-run income and price elasticities of import demand									
	U.S. goods imports					*U.S. services imports*				
	(1)	(2)	(3)	(4)	(5)	(6)	(7)	(8)	(9)	(10)
Economy	**F-statistics[a]**	**Lags[b]**	**Durbin's test[c]**	**Income elasticities**	**Price elasticities**	**F-statistics[a]**	**Lags[b]**	**Durbin's test[c]**	**Income elasticities**	**Price elasticities**
Korea, Rep. of	8.89	4	Prob> X^2 = 0.66	–0.1243 (0.759)	–0.2833 (0.247)	7.17	1	Prob> X^2 = 0.93	0.6843** (0.037)	–0.2796 (0.143)
Mexico	0.91	1	Prob> X^2 = 0.16	0.2330 (0.277)	0.1021 (0.627)	5.32	4	Prob> X^2 = 0.93	0.7879*** (0.004)	–0.1401 (0.784)
Singapore	1.91	1	Prob> X^2 = 0.85	–0.1663 (0.444)	0.1832 (0.516)	3.57	3	Prob> X^2 = 0.25	1.9245** (0.032)	0.0829 (0.838)
South Africa	2.16	1	Prob> X^2 = 0.94	1.2101 (0.104)	0.1832 (0.516)	3.26	1	Prob> X^2 = 0.53	0.6918* (0.094)	–0.1552 (0.446)
Taiwan, China	2.69	6	Prob> X^2 = 0.59	0.7715* (0.082)	–0.7135 (0.281)	4.14	1	Prob> X^2 = 0.51	2.3392*** (0.004)	0.2649 (0.356)
United Kingdom	4.53	2	Prob> X^2 = 0.73	–0.1623 (0.655)	0.5044** (0.026)	1.36	4	Prob> X^2 = 0.74	0.5222 (0.405)	0.3048 (0.477)
Venezuela, R.B. de	0.23	2	Prob> X^2 = 0.95	–0.1587 (0.766)	–0.0146 (0.948)	0.55	5	Prob> X^2 = 0.38	–1.1244 (0.514)	–0.0248 (0.960)

Source: Authors' calculations.
Note: The table represents quarterly data. The *p* values are in parentheses.
a. We consider the error correction model with an unrestricted intercept and no trend. At the 10 percent significance level, the critical value bounds for the F-statistics are 3.17 and 4.14. F-statistics are based on the optimal lag structure.
b. The optimal lag structure is determined by Akaike's Information Criterion for specifications with no autocorrelation.
c. We used Durbin's alternative test to test for serial correlation in the disturbance. This test does not require that all the regressors be strictly exogenous.
$*p < 0.1$ $**p < 0.05$ $***p < 0.001$.

Annex 2F: Data Description and Sources

For the regressions, quarterly data for 16 countries for the period 1999:Q1–2008:Q4 were used. U.S. imports by country of origin are available from the Bureau of Economic Analysis (BEA), U.S. International Transactions Accounts Data (release date: March 18, 2009). Real imports were calculated using the U.S. consumer price index (CPI) as deflator (2000 = 100). Real GDP data were retrieved from the BEA National Economic Accounts Data in order to match the income variable. As real exchange rates were not available, we corrected the bilateral nominal exchange rates for price differences using the foreign and U.S. CPI as price deflators, that is, $E_r = E_n \cdot (P^{us}/P^j)$. The CPI was used instead of the producer price index, as the latter was not available for all countries. Nominal exchange rates and CPIs were retrieved from the International Monetary Fund's International Financial Statistics database except for China and Taiwan, China (from Economist Intelligence Unit Country Data).

Notes

1. For relevant economic groupings of developing countries according to UNCTAD, see http://www.unctad.org/sections/stats/docs//gds_csirb_c&td-2-9_en.pdf.

2. In fact, there is some debate over Freund's elasticity estimates. Escaith, Lindenber, and Miroudout (2010) find that trade elasticities rose in the 1990s compared to the previous decade, but then were lower in the 2000s compared to the 1990s.

3. Note that this does not mean there is more value-added in international trade, but simply that there is more trade per unit of output and likelihood of a greater change in the volume of trade for a given change in real output. There is some double counting of value-added in GVC-based trade, as the value of imported inputs is included in the value of exports. The greater import content of exports (vertical specialization) accounts for a significant amount of the measured growth in world trade. Chen, Kondratowicz, and Yi (2005) find that double counting of value in trade figures occurs more in manufacturers than in services. For the United States in 2000, adjusted exports would be $198 billion, or 9 percentage points less than reported in 2000 trade figures. Koopman, Wang, and Wei (2008) calculate value-added in Chinese exports in 2002 to be about 51 percent of total export value. Linden, Kramer, and Dedrick (2007) show that Chinese value-added in its export of the $143 Apple 30GB video iPod (retail price of $299) was $5.

4. Freund (2009), in fact, predicts some worsening of the U.S. current account imbalance based on past experience.

5. Unfortunately, Eurostat does not report trade data for services.

6 This measure was used by Mayer, Butkevicius, and Kadri (2002) and Milberg (2004).

7. See http://www.justice.gov/atr/public/testimony/hhi.htm.

8. Williamson (1979, 260) thus addresses the issue: "As generic demand grows and the number of supply sources increases, exchange that was once transaction-specific loses this characteristic and greater reliance on market-mediated governance is feasible."

9. Blog posting by Joseph Stiglitz in 2009.

References

Amiti, M., and D. E. Weinstein. 2009. "Exports and Financial Shocks." mimeo, Federal Reserve Bank of New York and Columbia University, September.

Arndt, S., and H. Kierzkowski, eds. 2001. *Fragmentation: New Production Patterns in the World Economy.* Oxford, UK: Oxford University Press.

Auboin, M. 2009. "Boosting the Availability of Trade Finance in the Current Crisis: Background Analysis for a Substantial G20 Package." *CEPR Policy Insight* 35, June.

Bahmani-Oskooee, M., and T. Brooks. 1999. "Bilateral J-curve between U.S. and Her Trading Partners." *Review of World Economics* 135 (1): 156–65.

Bahmani-Oskooee, M., G. G. Goswamil, and B. K. Talukdar. 2005. "Exchange Rate Sensitivity of the Canadian Bilateral Inpayments and Outpayments." *Economic Modeling* 22 (4): 745–57.

Baldwin, R., ed. 2009a. *The Great Trade Collapse: Causes, Consequences and Prospects.* Centre for Economic Policy Research (CEPR) for VoxEU.org. CEPR, The Graduate Institute, Geneva.

Baldwin, R. 2009b. "The Great Trade Collapse: What Caused It and What Does It Mean?" In *The Great Trade Collapse: Causes, Consequences and Prospects,* ed. R. Baldwin. Centre for Economic Policy Research (CEPR) for VoxEU.org, 1–14. CEPR, The Graduate Institute, Geneva.

Baldwin, R., and D. Taglioni. 2009. "The Great Trade Collapse and Trade Imbalances." In *The Great Trade Collapse: Causes, Consequences and Prospects,* ed. R. Baldwin. CEPR for VoxEU.org, 47–55. CEPR, The Graduate Institute, Geneva.

Borchert, I., and A. Mattoo. 2009. "The Crisis-Resilience of Services Trade." Policy Research Working Paper 4917, World Bank, Washington, DC.

Chauffour, J., and T. Farole. 2009. "Trade Finance in Crisis: Market Adjustment or Market Failure?" mimeo, World Bank, Washington, DC.

Chen, H., M. Kondratowicz, and K. Yi. 2005. "Vertical Specialization and Three Facts about U.S. International Trade." *North American Journal of Economics and Finance* 16 (1): 35–59.

Chung, C., J. Lu, and P. Beamish. 2008. "Multinational Networks during Times of Economic Crisis versus Stability." *Management International Review* 48 (3): 279–95.

Coase, Ronald H. 1937. "The Nature of the Firm." *Economica* 4 (16): 386–405.

Eichengreen, B., and K. H. O'Rourke. 2009. "A Tale of Two Depressions." April 6, VoxEU.org. http://www.voxeu.org/index.php?q=node/3421, accessed April 15, 2009.

Escaith, H., and F. Gonguet. 2009. "Supply Chains and Financial Shocks: Real Transmission Channels in Globalised Production Networks." June 16, VoxEU.org. http://www.voxeu.org/index.php?q=node/3662, accessed June 16, 2009.

Escaith, H., N. Lindenber, and S. Miroudout. 2010. "International Supply Chains and Trade Elasticities in Times of Crisis." mimeo, World Trade Organization, Geneva.

Feenstra, R. 1998. "Integration of Trade and Disintegration of Production in the Global Economy." *Journal of Economic Perspectives* 12 (4): 31–50.

Ferrantino, M., and A. Larsen. 2009. "Transmission of the Global Recession through U.S. Trade." In *The Great Trade Collapse: Causes, Consequences and Prospects,* ed. R. Baldwin. CEPR for VoxEU.org, 173–82. CEPR, The Graduate Institute, Geneva.

Freund, C. 2009. "The Trade Response to Global Downturns: Historical Evidence." Policy Research Working Paper 5015. World Bank, Washington, DC.

Friedman, T. 2005. *The World Is Flat: A Brief History of the Twenty-first Century.* New York: Farrar, Straus and Giroux.

Fukao, K., and T. Yuan. 2009. "Why Is Japan So Heavily Affected by the Global Economics Crisis? An Analysis Based on the Asian Input-Output Tables." posted June 8 on VoxEU.org. http://www.voxeu.org/index.php?q=node/3637, accessed June 16, 2009.

Gallagher, Kevin P., Juan Carlos Moreno-Brid, and Roberto Porzecanski. 2008. "The Dynamism of Mexican Exports: Lost in (Chinese) Translation?" *World Development* 36 (8): 1365–80.

Gereffi, G. 1994. "The Organization of Buyer-Driven Global Commodity Chains: How U.S. Retailers Shape Overseas Production Networks." In *Commodity Chains and Global Capitalism,* ed. G. Gereffi and M. Korzeniewicz, 95–122. Westport, CT: Greenwood Press.

Gereffi, G., J. Humphrey, and T. Sturgeon. 2005. "The Governance of Global Value Chains." *Review of International Political Economy* 12 (1): 78–104.

Grossman, G. M., and E. Helpman. 2005. "Outsourcing in a Global Economy." *Review of Economic Studies* 72 (1): 135–59.

Grossman, G. M., and E. Rossi-Hansberg. 2006. "The Rise of Offshoring: It's Not Wine for Cloth Anymore." In *The New Economic Geography: Effects and Policy Implications*, 5–102. Jackson Hole: Federal Reserve Bank of Kansas City.

Humphrey, J., and H. Schmitz. 2002. "How Does Insertion in Global Value Chains Affect Upgrading in Industrial Clusters?" *Regional Studies* 36 (9): 1017–27.

Hurst, R., M. Buttle, and J. Sandars. 2009. "The Impact of the Global Economic Slowdown on Value Chain Labour Markets in Asia." Background paper for conference, Impact of the Global Economic Slowdown on Poverty and Sustainable Development in Asia and the Pacific. September 28–30, Hanoi, Vietnam.

ICC. 2009. "Rethinking Trade Finance in 2009: An ICC Global Survey." Document 470-1120, March. International Chamber of Commerce, Paris, France.

Kaplinsky, R., and M. Farooki. 2010. "What Are the Implications for Global Value Chains When the Market Shifts from the North to the South?" Policy Research Working Paper 5205, World Bank, International Trade Department, Washington, DC.

Kaplinsky, R., and M. Morris. 2008. "Do the Asian Drivers Undermine the Export-Oriented Industrialisation in SSA [Sub-Saharan Africa]?" *World Development* 36 (2): 254–73.

Koopman, R., Z. Wang, and S. Wei. 2008. "How Much of Chinese Exports Is Really Made in China? Assessing Domestic Value Added When Processing Trade Is Pervasive." NBER Working Paper 14109. National Bureau of Economic Research, Cambridge, MA.

Langlois, R. N. 2003. "The Vanishing Hand: The Changing Dynamics of Industrial Capitalism." *Industrial and Corporate Change* 12 (2): 351–85.

Levchenko, A., L. Lewis, and L. Tesar. 2009. "The Collapse of U.S. Trade: In Search of the Smoking Gun." In *The Great Trade Collapse: Causes, Consequences and Prospects*, ed. R. Baldwin, CEPR for VoxEU.org, 71–77. CEPR, The Graduate Institute, Geneva.

Levy, D. 1984. "Testing Stigler's Interpretation of 'The Division of Labor Is Limited by the Extent of the Market.'" *The Journal of Industrial Economics* 32 (3): 377–89.

Linden, G., K. Kramer, and J. Dedrick. 2007. "Who Captures Value in a Global Innovation System? The Case of Apple's iPod." Personal Computing Industry Center, University of California, Irvine. http://www.escholarship.org/uc/item/1770046n.

Mayer, J., A. Butkevicius, and A. Kadri. 2002. "Dynamic Products in World Exports." UNCTAD Discussion Paper No. 159. United Nations Conference on Trade and Development, Geneva.

Milberg, W. 2004. "The Changing Structure of International Trade Linked to Global Production Systems: What Are the Policy Implications?" *International Labour Review* 143 (1–2): 45–90.

Milberg. W., and D. Winkler. 2009a. "Economic Crisis, Global Value Chains and the Collapse of Developing Country Exports." Concept Note for Department for International Development/Social Research Council project, "Capturing the Gains: Economic and Social Upgrading in Global Production Networks." University of Manchester, United Kingdom.

———. 2009b. "Outsourcing Economics: Power, Profits and the Globalization of Production." Mimeo. Department of Economics, New School for Social Research, New York, NY.

———. 2010a. "Financialisation and the Dynamics of Offshoring in the U.S.A." *Cambridge Journal of Economics* 34 (2): 275–93.

———. 2010b. "Economic Insecurity in the New Wave of Globalization: Offshoring and the Labor Share under Varieties of Capitalism." *International Review of Applied Economics* 24 (3): 285–308.

Mora, J., and W. Powers. 2009. "Did Trade Credit Problems Deepen the Great Trade Collapse?" In *The Great Trade Collapse: Causes, Consequences and Prospects*, ed. R. Baldwin, 115–25. CEPR for VoxEU.org. CEPR, The Graduate Institute, Geneva.

Pesaran, M. H., Y. Shin, and R. J. Smith. 2001. "Bounds Testing Approaches to the Analysis of Level Relationships." *Journal of Applied Econometrics* 16 (3): 289–326.

Santos-Paulino, A. U., and A. P. Thirlwall. 2004. "The Impact of Trade Liberalization on Exports, Imports and the Balance of Payments of Developing Countries." *Economic Journal* 114: F50–F72.

Scott, R. 2009. "Invest in America: Essential Policies Needed to Secure U.S. Jobs and Broadly Shared Prosperity in the Auto Industry." EPI Briefing Paper 233, Economic Policy Institute, Washington, DC.

Stigler, J. 1951. "The Division of Labor Is Limited by the Extent of the Market." *The Journal of Political Economy* 59 (3): 185–93.

Sturgeon, T. 2002. "Modular Production Networks: A New American Model of Industrial Organization." *Industrial and Corporate Change* 11 (3): 451–96.

Van Biesebroeck, J., and T. Sturgeon. 2010. "Effects of the Crisis on the Automotive Industry in Developing Countries: A Global Value Chain Perspective." Chapter 6 in this volume.

Williamson, O. 1979. "Transactions-Cost Economics: The Governance of Contractual Relations." *Journal of Law and Economics* 22 (2): 233–62.

Williamson, O. E. 1975. *Markets and Hierarchies: Analysis and Antitrust Implications: A Study in the Economics of Internal Organization*. New York: Free Press.

———. 2000. "The New Institutional Economics: Taking Stock, Looking Ahead." *Journal of Economic Literature* 38 (3): 595–613.

Wood, A., and J. Mayer. 2009. "Has China De-industrialised Other Developing Countries?" QEH Working Paper series 175, Department of International Development, University of Oxford, United Kingdom.

WTO (World Trade Organization). 2010. "International Trade Statistics: Trade to Expand by 9.5% in 2010 after a Dismal 2009, WTO Reports." Press Release 598, March 26, Geneva.

Yi, K. 2009. "The Collapse of Global Trade: The Role of Vertical Specialisation." In *The Collapse of Global Trade, Murky Protectionism, and the Crisis: Recommendations for the Crisis*, eds. R. Baldwin and S. Evenett, 45–48. CEPR for VoxEU.org. CEPR, The Graduate Institute, Geneva.

3

GLOBAL VALUE CHAINS AND THE CRISIS: RESHAPING INTERNATIONAL TRADE ELASTICITY?

Hubert Escaith, Nannette Lindenberg, and Sébastien Miroudot

The recent phase of globalization—beginning with the emblematic year 1989 when many political and regulatory barriers fell[1]—saw the emergence of new business models that built on new opportunities to develop comparative advantages (Krugman 1995; Baldwin 2006). With the opening of new markets, the technical revolution in information technology (IT) and communications, and the closer harmonization of economic models worldwide, trade became much more than just a simple exchange of merchandise across borders: it developed into a constant flow of investment, of technologies and technicians, of goods for processing and business services, in what has been called "global manufacturing."

While providing renewed opportunities for increasing productivity and promoting industrialization in developing countries, the greater industrial interconnection of the global economy has created newer and faster channels for the propagation of adverse external shocks.[2] Referring to the economic crisis in global manufacturing of 2008–09, some authors have pointed out that the breakdown of international supply chains and consequent breakdown in global manufacturing may explain the abrupt decrease in trade or the synchronization of the trade collapse. This crisis has been dubbed the "Great Trade Collapse" for its impact on international commerce. This trade collapse is unprecedented, even compared to the Great Depression of the 1930s (Eichengreen and O'Rourke 2009). The shock, emanating from the United States, the largest world financial center, spread very quickly and almost simultaneously to most industrial and emerging countries. International trade, which dropped five times more rapidly than global GDP, was both a casualty of the 2008–09 crisis and one of its main channels of transmission. The Great Trade Collapse was not only sudden and severe, but also synchronized, and this was another distinguishing feature of this crisis.

While a decrease in trade is expected when world output falls following a severe financial crisis, the magnitude of this collapse surprised observers, because it was reflected in high trade elasticities. One reason for blaming global value chains (GVCs) and trade in tasks for the depth of the crisis is the inherent magnification effect of global production networks: intermediate inputs cross the border several times before the final product is shipped to the final customer. All the different production stages of the GVC rely on each other—as suppliers and as customers. Thus, if a shock occurs in one of the participating sectors or countries, the shock is transmitted quickly to the other stages of the supply chain through both backward and forward linkages.

But has the impressive collapse in world trade really been caused by global value chains? Did the GVCs reshape international trade elasticities fundamentally? The question is important for its economic and financial implications, but also for its social impact, as the reorganization of GVCs implies the destruction and creation of jobs at different locations. If the answer is yes, we should expect a deeper decrease of trade in those countries and sectors that participate in global production networks and a smoother reaction in those that produce mainly for the domestic market. Moreover, GVCs are likely to play a role in the synchronization of the trade collapse as well as its size. These transmission channels apply both to financial shocks, for example, a credit crunch in one country, and to trade policy shocks, for example, rising tariffs and nontariff barriers or implementing "buy local" campaigns.

Another explanation for trade being affected harder than GDP during the 2008–09 downturn is the composition effect. Trade flows are composed mainly of durable goods (about two-thirds or more), while GDP consists mainly of services. Trade in goods was strongly affected by the crisis, while services showed some resilience (Borchert and Mattoo 2009). Finally, an accounting bias exists, as GDP is measured as value-added and trade in gross values; that is, for *GDP*, only the value that has been added is considered, rather than the total value of all domestic commercial transactions (correcting for any double counting when transactions involve intermediate goods), whereas *trade* is measured as the sum of the commercial values imported or exported. The increase in trade in intermediate goods resulting from GVCs led to significant double counting as goods for processing were criss-crossing borders when moving up in the supply chain. A measure of trade in value-added, as promoted by the World Trade Organization (WTO), would correct this accounting bias.

The remainder of the chapter is organized as follows. The next section explores some of the stylized facts that sustain the hypothesis of a structural change in world trade. It is followed by a brief overview of the related literature on outsourcing, offshoring, and vertical integration. The fourth section analyzes vertical integration and trade multipliers compiled from international input-output (I-O) statistics. Section five extends the exploration of trade data patterns by estimating import multipliers for a larger selection of countries, regions, and sectors. The sixth section develops a formal dynamic model incorporating short-run and long-term components. The last section offers conclusions and policy implications of the analysis.

Stylized Facts: Global Value Chains and Trade Elasticity

As mentioned, trade reacted very strongly to the first signals of recession in 2008 (figure 3.1), with a decrease of much higher magnitude than the fall in GDP. These differing reactions imply a high trade elasticity (see box 3.1 for a definition). Concretely, the income elasticity of trade measures the percentage increase in trade

Figure 3.1 World Merchandise Exports and GDP, 1960–2009
real annual % change

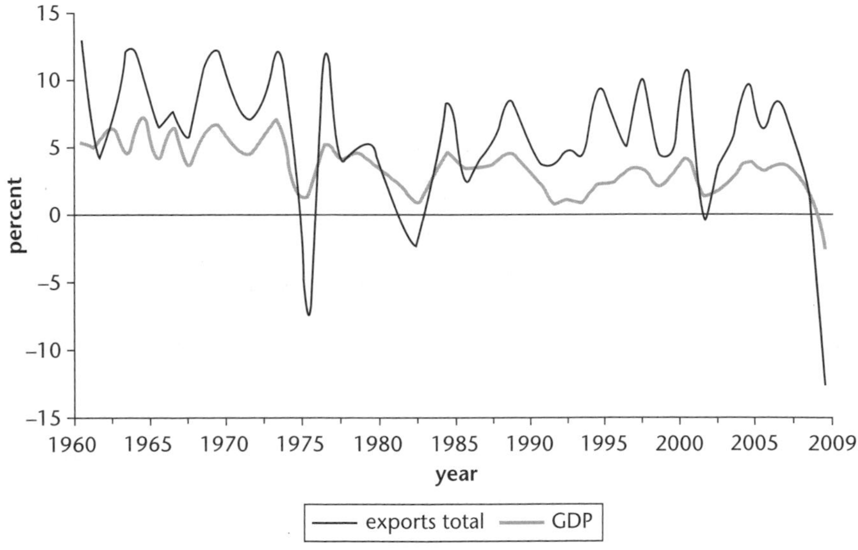

Source: WTO 2009.

Box 3.1 Trade Elasticities

Elasticities measure the responsiveness of demand or supply to changes in income, prices, or other variables. Two prominent representatives of elasticities are the income elasticity and the price elasticity of demand. While the former measures the percentage change in the quantity demanded resulting from a 1 percent increase in income, the latter measures the percentage change in the quantity demanded resulting from a change of 1 percent in its price. Thus,

$$E_P = \frac{\Delta Q/Q}{\Delta P/P} = \frac{P}{Q}\frac{\Delta Q}{\Delta P} \quad \text{and} \quad E_I = \frac{\Delta Q/Q}{\Delta I/I} = \frac{I}{Q}\frac{\Delta Q}{\Delta I},$$

with E = elasticity, Q = quantity demanded, P = price, and I = income.

In consumer theory, price elasticity is complemented by elasticity of substitution between competing goods and services, leading to the concept of indifference curves. This chapter focuses on the macroeconomic income elasticities of trade—in short, trade elasticities.

It is important to remember that in most of the literature reviewed in this chapter, neither price effects nor substitutions effects are explicitly taken into consideration in this context. Thus, the trade elasticities reflect the pure effect of a change in domestic income (measured by GDP) to the quantity of imports. This convention is used throughout the chapter.

The variation in the relative price of exports and imports is, nonetheless, implicitly taken into consideration in the calculation of the domestic product. Because GDP, on the demand side, is equal to the sum of consumption, investment, and the net balance between exports minus imports (*X–M*), any changes in the terms of trade that affect (*X–M*) will be reflected, ceteris paribus, into the domestic product. The terms of trade effect is immediate when GDP is computed at current prices; it is formally imputed by national accounts when elaborated at constant prices.

when there is a 1 percent increase in GDP (or, conversely, its drop when GDP decreases).

The income elasticity of trade at the aggregated world level can be econometrically estimated by ordinary least squares (OLS)[3]:

$$m_t = \alpha + \beta y_t + \varepsilon_t, \tag{3.1}$$

with m_t = logarithmized imports, y_t = logarithmized GDP, and ε_t = residuals. The trade elasticity has been on average, that is, over the complete sample from 1980 to 2009, 2.28 ($R^2 = 0.99$ for 30 observations with the above-mentioned OLS estimation).

As a robustness check and to provide a benchmark for subsequent calculations, a state space object containing GDP and imports was estimated, to which a Kalman filter was applied, with maximum likelihood

$$\text{Signal: } m_t = \alpha_t + \beta_t y_t + \varepsilon_t, \tag{3.2}$$

$$\text{State: } \beta_t = \beta_{t-1} + \nu_t. \tag{3.3}$$

The estimated elasticity is also 2.28. However, this elasticity is not at all constant but changes significantly over the years. To visualize the changing characteristics over time, the estimations are recalculated both with OLS and with Kalman filter for rolling time windows of each 10 years, that is, the estimation sample subsequently changes by one year, the first sample comprising 1980–89, the second 1981–90, and so forth. Results are displayed graphically in figure 3.2.

Each data point of the graph in figure 3.2 reflects the estimated coefficient for the previous 10 years, for example, the displayed value in the year 2000 reflects the GDP elasticity of imports computed for the 10-year window between 1991 and 2000. From 1989 to 1998, a steady increase in the elasticity can be seen, from about 1.6 to 3.0, which in the following six years decreases again to an elasticity of about 2.3 between 2004 and 2008. This pattern gives ground to the assumption that GVCs have led to an increase of the GDP elasticity of imports and that a transition from one steady state (without GVCs) to another one (with GVCs) has taken place. The graphs indicate quite closely the trend that should be expected if this hypothesis of the impact of GVCs on trade elasticities were correct: it seems that trade elasticity has increased in the years of rising globalization in the 1990s and turned back to a new steady state that

Figure 3.2 Worldwide GDP Elasticity of Imports, 10-Year Rolling Window, 1980–2009
constant prices

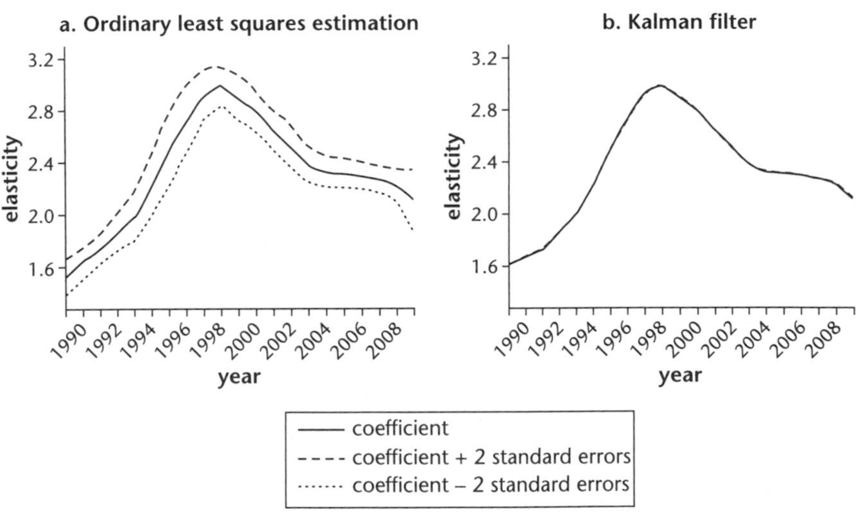

Source: Authors' calculations; see text for data description.
Note: Both parts are calculated for rolling time windows of 10 years, that is, the estimation sample subsequently changes by 1 year.

was reached around 2004. Moreover, the new steady state has adjusted to a higher level than the old one, that is, trade volumes today react more to changes in GDP than they did 30 years ago.

Hence, there might have been a mutation in the way the economic pandemic spread across the world. In previous instances of global turmoil, the transmission of shocks was mainly of a macroeconomic nature: a recession in a foreign economy reduced demand for exports, which in turn depressed the activity in the home country. This traditional vision is compatible with the Ricardian model of the international economy.[4] When countries exchange finished products (consumer or investment goods), they are therefore vulnerable to fluctuations in the level of their trading partner's final demand.

GVCs have introduced new microeconomic dimensions that run parallel to the traditional macroeconomic mechanism of shock transmission, explaining in large part the magnifying effect of the crisis on international trade. Some of the mechanisms are purely of an accounting nature: while GDP is computed on a net basis, exports and imports are registered on their gross value. In addition, because value chains cover various countries, a lot of double counting takes place while goods for processing cross the borders at each step of the production process.

But the core of the explanation is to be found in the economic implications of the structural changes that have affected world production since the late 1980s. In the contemporaneous context, adverse external shocks affect firms not only through their sales of finished goods (the final demand of national accounts), but also through fluctuations in the supply and demand of intermediate inputs. Therefore, it has been tempting to attribute the large trade-GDP elasticity, close to 5 in 2009, to the leverage effect induced by this geographical fragmentation of production.

Looking at the impacts of the recent crisis again, table 3.1 shows that the most affected sectors were fuels and minerals, resulting from a strong price effect, and machinery and transport equipment, because of a strong demand effect. Indeed, consumer durable and capital goods were on the front line, as demand for these products relies on credit, which dried up as banks closed their loan windows and flocked to liquidity. In turn, the lower industrial activity brutally reversed the trend in the prices of key primary commodities, which had been rising substantively since 2003.

But even if these stylized facts seem to support the hypothesis of a structural change in world trade—compatible with the role of GVCs in explaining the increased elasticity of imports to GDP—it should be pointed out that, so far, there is no information on the causes of the observed change. Another important, but unanswered, question is whether this reshaping of the trade elasticity also holds at the disaggregated level and can be observed for individual countries. Consequently,

Table 3.1 Quarterly Growth of World Manufactures Exports by Product, First Quarter 2008 to Fourth Quarter 2009

% change over previous quarter, current US$

	2008				2009			
Sector	Q1	Q2	Q3	Q4	Q1	Q2	Q3	Q4
Manufactures	–1	9	–2	–15	–21	7	9	9
Office and telecommunications equipment	–12	5	5	–10	–27	13	14	16
Automotive products	1	6	–14	–18	–33	14	13	21
Iron and steel	11	23	7	–34	–31	–8	10	10
Ores and other minerals	10	20	4	–33	–35	13	24	7

Source: WTO Short Term Statistics in International trade and tariff data Web site.

the remainder of the chapter attempts to identify the causative factors by examining the literature review, then conducting an empirical analysis to probe some of the hypotheses discovered.

Global Value Chains and Trade in Recent Literature

Trade in tasks and the fragmentation of production along global value chains have challenged the validity of the traditional Ricardian models, based on the exchange of final goods, each country specializing in certain types of products. Contrary to the Ricardian model, countries that are similar in factor endowment and technology have developed a significant part of their trade in the same products, and trade intermediate goods between their industries (box 3.2). The new trade theory, by introducing imperfect competition, consumer preference for variety, and economies of scale, looks to explain divergence from this traditional model.

An early appraisal of the extent of outsourcing can be found in Feenstra (1998), who compares several measures of outsourcing and argues that all have risen since the 1970s. On the descriptive side, Agnese and Ricart (2009) provide details on the extent of offshoring during 1995–2000 for several countries worldwide, showing that offshoring is not only a phenomenon among large developed economies but also a widespread phenomenon among smaller economies. In addition, the authors provide evidence that offshoring is much more prominent in the manufacturing sector.[5]

An illustrative example of a globalized value chain can be found in Linden, Kramer, and Dedrick (2007), who study the case of Apple's iPod. Hanson, Mataloni, and Slaughter (2005) conduct a firm-level analysis with U.S. multinationals and analyze

Box 3.2 Offshoring, Outsourcing, and the Measure of Vertical Integration

The recent world economic crisis has important implications because its consequences are not only of an economic and financial nature. There is also a social impact caused by the reorganization of GVCs, which involves the destruction and creation of jobs at different locations. During the 1990s, firms offshored and outsourced—two phenomena that define globalization and are often poorly understood—part of their production and built "global value chains."[a] The relevant process in GVCs is "offshoring," which comprises both offshore-outsourcing and foreign direct investments (FDI). Outsourcing to another domestic firm is not considered. Figure B3.2 gives an overview of the distinction between outsourcing and offshoring.

Figure B3.2 Differences between Outsourcing and Offshoring

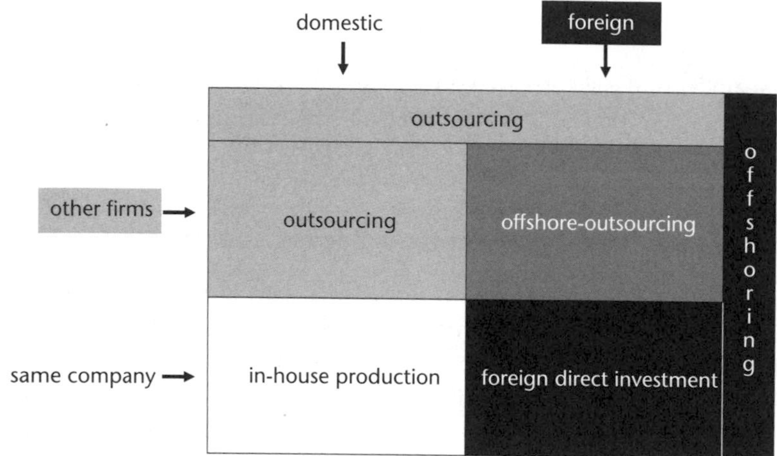

Several factors favor the tendency to locate production stages in other countries. First, overall trade costs have decreased in the past two decades; that is, not only have tariffs fallen, but transport and communications costs, as well as the time cost of transport, have also decreased (Jacks, Meisner, and Novy 2008). A second important factor is that through better infrastructure and logistic services, the reliability and timeliness of delivery have improved significantly (Hummels, Ishii, and Yi 2001; Nordås, Pinali, and Grosso 2006). Finally, technological improvements, that is, advances in IT, have made it possible to geographically separate an increasing number of services tasks (Jones and Kierzkowski 1990).

This fragmentation of the value chain can be measured using three different methods. Some authors use firm surveys to account for the fragmentation of the value chain. Others use foreign trade statistics and consider, for example, the share of parts and components in trade flows as an indicator for increases

Box 3.2 *continued*

in international production-sharing. A third possibility is offered by international input-output tables, which relate the output of one industry to the inputs of other industries. These input-output tables account for different countries, giving information on how each industry depends on other domestic or foreign industries, both as customer and as supplier of intermediate inputs. For example, Hummels, Ishii, and Yi (2001) calculate the extent of vertical specialization, that is, the share of imported inputs needed to produce total exports. This measure is widely used to account for the above-mentioned fragmentation.

Two shortcomings, however, of international input-output tables are that often the data quality needs to be improved and they are not available yearly. Nonetheless, they are a powerful tool for measuring the size of production linkages and tracking the international transmission of demand and supply shocks.

a. Practitioners (engineers and business managers) refer usually to "supply chains" (for example, the "just-in-time" model), while "value chains" is more commonly used by economists to refer to the addition of value-added from commodities to increasingly complex manufacture goods. These two terms are broadly comparable, albeit the latter refers more to the outcome, and the former to the process and its management.

the driving forces of interfirm trade in intermediate inputs. Paul and Wooster (forthcoming) study the financial characteristics of outsourcing firms in the United States; they find that compared to non-outsourcing firms, the former have higher costs and lower profitability and must perform in more competitive industries. Coucke and Sleuwaegen (2008) analyze a firm data set of the Belgian manufacturing sector, arguing that firms that engage in offshoring activities improve their chances of survival in a globalizing industry. Nordås (2005) reviews vertical specialization and presents six country case studies—Brazil, China, Germany, Japan, South Africa, and the United States—analyzing production-sharing in the automotive and electronics industries. Sturgeon and Gereffi (2009) contribute to the understanding of the phenomenon from a business perspective, providing an overview of the microeconomic evidence and the role of outsourcing in industrial upgrading and competitiveness, while pointing out some crucial data issues.[6]

Still working from a descriptive perspective, but approaching the issue from a global angle, Daudin, Rifflart, and Schweisguth (2009) propose a new measure for "value-added trade," and shed some light on the question of "who produces for whom," using the Global Trade Analysis Project (GTAP) database for 1997, 2001, and 2004. Johnson and Noguera (2009) also calculate bilateral trade in value-added for 87 countries and regions in 2001, using a modified version of the vertical integration index, to incorporate two-way trade. Lanz, Miroudot, and Ragoussis (2009) estimate trade flows of intermediate goods and services over the period 1995–2005, with a disaggregation by industry of origin and using industry. Koopman, Wang, and Wei (2008) develop a formula for computing the domestic and foreign content of exports, including a mathematical program to estimate relevant input-output coefficients that may be missing in most of the available input-output tables. The authors apply their methodology to China, a country that participates to an important extent in tariff- and tax-favored processing exports.

On the conceptual side, the critique of the traditional Ricardian hypotheses and the development of new concepts have led to a vast literature (see Helpman 2006 and WTO 2008a for reviews). This chapter focuses on a few of the articles that have a direct relation to the authors' analysis.

Hummels, Ishii, and Yi (2001) compute vertical specialization using input-output tables for 10 Organisation for Economic Co-operation and Development (OECD) countries and 4 emerging market economies and find that it increased by 30 percent between 1970 and 1990.[7] Yi (2003) builds on these findings and proposes a dynamic Ricardian trade model of vertical specialization that can explain the bulk of the growth of trade.

A stock-taking of offshore outsourcing and how it is perceived by economists and noneconomists is made in Mankiw and Swagel (2006). A straightforward introduction to the economics of offshoring and its underlying motivations and effects is given in Smith (2006). Grossman and Rossi-Hansberg (2008) present a model of offshoring where the production process is represented as a continuum of tasks. Thus, the authors focus on tradable tasks rather than on trade of finished goods, that is, during the production process, different countries participate in GVCs by adding value. Yet another model of offshoring is proposed by Harms, Lorz, and Urban (2009) who allow for variations of the cost-saving potential along the production chain and consider transportation costs for unfinished goods. Within this framework they can explain large changes in offshoring activities with small variations of the parameters of their model. The link between the offshoring literature and the research on firm heterogeneity is established in Mitra and Ranjan (2008). They construct an offshoring model with firm heterogeneity and externalities and study the effects of temporary shocks on offshoring activities.

Grossman and Helpman (2005) develop a model to study outsourcing decisions focusing on equilibria where some firms outsource in the home country and others abroad. In an earlier paper (Grossman and Helpman 2002), the authors propose a general equilibrium model of the "make-or-buy-decision," that is, the decision between insourcing and outsourcing. A model that allows firms to choose between vertical integration and outsourcing, as well as between locating the production at home or in the low-wage South, is proposed by Antràs and Helpman (2004). They point out that the more productive firms source inputs in low-cost countries, whereas less productive firms do so in the high-cost countries of the North. Besides, if both types of firms acquire inputs in the same country, the former insource and the latter outsource.

An explanation for the steady increase in outsourcing activities is offered by Şener and Zhao (2009), who analyze the globalization process by setting up a dynamic model of trade with endogenous innovation, in which a local-sourcing-targeted and an outsourcing-targeted R&D race take place at the same time. The latter represents the so called "iPod cycle" where firms combine innovation activity with simultaneous outsourcing, a form of R&D strategy that is becoming more and more important. Ornelas and Turner (2008) propose another model that explains the current trend toward foreign outsourcing and intrafirm trade. That the motivation for outsourcing can also be strategic rather than cost-motivated is shown by Chen, Ishikawa, and Yu (2004). They model strategic outsourcing as a response to trade liberalization in the intermediate-product market.

Of particular relevance for the present analysis, papers by several authors help to understand the volatility linked to globalized activities. Du, Lu, and Tao (2009) elaborate a model on bi-sourcing, that is, simultaneous outsourcing and insourcing for the same set of inputs, a strategy that is being more and more often adopted by multinational enterprises. The use of this strategy, with the inherent options of preferring either the external or the internal source of intermediate inputs, may explain part of the reduction of trade flows in times of economic crisis.

A model of in-house competition, that is, between the different facilities of a multiplant firm, is introduced by Kerschbamer and Tournas (2003). Their model shows that in downturns, firms may decide to produce in the establishment that has higher costs, even when it would also be possible to locate production to the lower-cost facility. The stability of value chain networks is studied in Ostrovsky (2008), who proposes a model of matching in supply chains. The author deduces the sufficient conditions for the existence of stable networks; however, these networks rely on the assumptions of the model of same-side substitutability and cross-side complementarity. Bergin, Feenstra, and Hanson (2009) analyze empirically the volatility of the Mexican export-processing industry compared to their U.S. counterparts with a difference-in-difference approach; they find that, on average, the fluctuations in value-added in the Mexican outsourcing industries are twice as high as in the United States. In addition, the authors propose a theoretical model of outsourcing that can explain this stylized fact.

Finally, Tanaka (2009) and Yi (2009), among others, explain the collapse of trade during the recent worldwide crisis as a systematic overshooting due to the globalization of value chains. However, Bénassy-Quéré et al. (2009), using a multiregion/multisector computable general equilibrium (CGE) model, reject this hypothesis. Freund (2009) analyzes the effects of a global downturn on trade with a historical perspective. She finds that the elasticity of trade to GDP (see box 3.1) has increased significantly in the last 50 years, and that in times of crisis, trade is even more responsive to GDP. McKibbin and Stoeckel (2009) point out that the distinction between durable and nondurable goods is fundamental to explain the overreaction of trade to the contraction of GDP in the recent crisis. Borchert and Mattoo (2009) emphasize that services trade is much less affected in the crisis than goods trade. They argue that this can probably be explained by lower demand cyclicality and less dependence on external finance. Escaith and Gonguet (2009) study the international transmission of financial shocks through the supply chains and propose an indicator of supply-driven shocks. A series of studies in Inomata and Uchida (2009) examines the various dimensions (trade, employment, finance) of the global crisis in the Asian Pacific region.

Vertical Integration and Trade Multipliers from an Input-Output Perspective

The investigation in this section focuses on the United States and Asia, a subset of countries that epitomize the vertical integration phenomenon from both micro and macro perspectives. The investigation, based on observed data, relies on national accounts and statistics on intersectoral trade in inputs produced by IDE-Jetro for various benchmark years.[8] The information is presented as a set of interlinked input-output tables to form an estimate of the composition of intermediate and final flows of goods and services between home and foreign countries. The calculation of a "Leontief inverse matrix" derived from these input-output matrices is used to estimate the resulting effect of the series of direct and indirect effects on all domestic sectors of activity. This procedure allows the imported content of exports to be estimated and the vertical integration of productive sectors to be measured.

Imported Content of Exports and Trade in Intermediate Goods

As table 3.2 shows, the observations of the United States and Asia, one of the most dynamic trade compacts in the recent history of international trade, tend to support the "magnifying hypothesis," that is, trade in intermediate inputs induced by the fragmentation of value chains increases faster than trade in final

Table 3.2 Asia and the United States: Annual Growth of Intermediate Inputs and Exports, 1990–2008
percent

Sector	Total imported intermediates	Exports		
		Intermediate inputs	Final goods and services	Total
Agriculture	9.5	3.5	13.0	5.9
Mining quarrying	15.6	7.6	—	7.9
Manufacturing	9.0	10.7	6.6	9.1
Total sectors	9.1	10.2	7.1	9.1

Source: Authors' calculation, based on IDE-Jetro Asian Input-Output matrices.
Note: The sum of China; Indonesia; Japan; Republic of Korea; Malaysia; the Philippines; Singapore; Taiwan, China; Thailand; and the United States is in nominal values in U.S. dollars. Total sectors includes services and other sectors; 2008 estimates. Imports and exports include exchanges with the rest of the world.

products. While exports of final products (consumer and investment goods) increased 7 percent in annual average over the 1990–2008 period, exports of inputs (intermediate consumption, in the national account terminology) rose by more than 10 percent per year. In the same period, imports of such intermediate goods increased by 9 percent.[9]

Because intermediate goods include commodities, particularly fuels, and are valuated at nominal prices, imports of intermediate goods show the highest growth rate for mining and quarrying. But manufacturing is the sector where exports of intermediate products increased most since 1990, supporting the hypothesis that vertical integration and trade in intermediate goods drove international trade in the recent past and explained the trade collapse after September 2008.

Retrospectively, the literature provides a clear signal that export-led growth among developing economies has been associated with higher reliance on imported inputs. To mention a recent study on production-sharing and the value-added content of trade, Johnson and Noguera (2009) show that countries systematically shift toward manufacturing exports, which have lower value-added content on average, as they grow richer; this depresses the per-unit value of the aggregate value-added to export ratio.[10] These authors show that the largest exporters among developed countries (Germany and the United States) see their value-added content scaled down as a result of a more integrated production structure with their respective regional partners (the North American Free Trade Agreement for the United States and the European Union for Germany).

These findings support the claim that supply chains and the fragmentation of manufacture production explain the "overshooting" of trade elasticity during the crisis (Tanaka 2009; Yi 2009), that is, the unusual high value observed in

2008–09. Other experts, nevertheless, contest the hypothesis that higher demand elasticity behind the Great Trade Collapse could have been caused by vertical integration (Bénassy-Quéré et al. 2009) because it affects only the relative volume of trade in relation to GDP levels, while elasticity should remain constant in a general equilibrium context.

The data compiled from national accounts data on Asian and U.S. economies since 1990 (table 3.3) confirm the positive relationship between export orientation (share of export over total output) and reliance on imported inputs. Figure 3.3 shows that the relationship is rather stable over time between 1990 and 2000, at least on manufactured products, where it is stronger than for other product groups.[11] Table 3.3 also indicates that all Asian economies increased their exposure to exports during the 1990–2008 period, while the United States registered a slight reduction, especially before 2000.

The ratio of imported inputs in relation to total exports (all sectors together) is stable for most economies (aggregated results for column 3—growth rate of imported inputs to growth rate of exports—are close to 1). The exceptions are the United States and Japan, where elasticity is about 1.7 percent (that is, an increase of 1 percentage point in exports necessitates a 1.7 percent increase in imported inputs). Considering the size of these economies, this would indicate that the increase in the weight of intermediate goods in world trade is the result of the change in business models in developed economies, rather than the result of the emergence of developing countries. Moreover, the latter may both be a result of and explain the former, as the recent industrialization phase of developing countries is closely linked to the outsourcing strategy of transnational corporations (Sturgeon and Gereffi 2009).

Vertical Integration and Trade Elasticity

The previous results relate to the imported content of exports, a level variable, and do not have direct implications for the debate on the stability of the trade-GDP elasticity. Table 3.4 goes further, examining the weight of imported inputs in sectoral value-added (and in GDP). Contrary to some preconceived ideas about export-led growth, emerging countries are not only reprocessing goods for export, but also incorporating a sizable domestic content in their exports. While the share of domestic value-added in total inputs (including factorial costs) for manufacture is still lower for developing economies compared with developed economies, the gap is closing for China.

More important for the purpose of the present study on trade and GDP elasticity, the weight of imported inputs in sectoral value-added (and in GDP) has been increasing from 1990 to 2008 in all countries. The rate of increase is above

Table 3.3 Asia and the United States: Changes in Exports and Imported Inputs Elasticity, 1990–2008

percent

Country/sector	1990–2008[a]			1990–95			1995–2000			2000–08[a]		
	1. Exports (YoY)	2. d(export/output) (PoP)	3. Elasticity (imported inputs/exports) (YoY)	1. Exports (YoY)	2. d(export/output) (PoP)	3. Elasticity (imported inputs/exports) (YoY)	1. Exports (YoY)	2. d(export/output) (PoP)	3. Elasticity (imported inputs/exports) (YoY)	1. Exports (YoY)	2. d(export/output) (PoP)	3. Elasticity (imported inputs/exports) (YoY)
China												
Agriculture	7.5	–0.6	1.4	3.6	–0.4	3.5	9.1	0.2	—	8.9	–0.4	2.3
Mining quarrying	6.0	–6.8	4.1	2.2	–4.4	14.9	0.9	–1.8	36.8	11.9	–0.6	1.2
Manufacturing	20.7	6.5	0.9	26.1	1.8	0.9	15.8	1.7	0.7	20.5	2.9	0.9
Total sectors	20.1	3.7	0.9	27.3	1.5	0.9	14.3	0.7	0.9	19.5	1.6	0.9
Indonesia												
Agriculture	15.3	3.3	1.0	15.8	0.4	0.3	9.1	2.3	2.9	19.1	0.6	0.8
Mining quarrying	7.4	–17.6	3.1	1.4	–8.7	4.5	4.5	1.6	4.9	13.3	–10.5	2.7
Manufacturing	9.7	–2.3	0.9	18.2	–0.7	0.9	6.4	7.9	—	6.7	–9.4	1.6
Total sectors	8.8	–1.9	1.1	10.5	–2.4	1.4	5.3	5.7	0.2	10.1	–5.1	1.2
Japan												
Agriculture	7.2	0.4	0.8	5.9	0.0	0.7	2.3	0.1	1.2	11.3	0.4	0.8
Mining quarrying	5.7	1.6	1.0	6.8	0.1	—	–1.5	0.3	—	9.7	1.2	2.2
Manufacturing	5.1	6.1	0.9	10.9	1.0	0.5	0.5	1.5	3.8	4.5	3.6	1.4
Total sectors	5.4	2.0	1.0	11.6	0.1	0.5	0.8	0.5	1.5	4.6	1.4	1.7
Malaysia												
Agriculture	0.1	–16.3	—	–12.0	–13.9	—	–1.3	–1.9	3.6	9.4	–0.6	1.5
Mining quarrying	9.3	–5.7	1.7	–2.6	–5.0	0.9	6.3	–11.7	5.9	19.6	11.1	0.9

(continued next page)

Table 3.3 *continued*
percent

Country/sector	1990–2008[a]			1990–95			1995–2000			2000–08[a]		
	1. Exports (YoY)	2. d(export/ output) (PoP)	3. Elasticity (imported inputs/ exports) (YoY)	1. Exports (YoY)	2. d(export/ output) (PoP)	3. Elasticity (imported inputs/ exports) (YoY)	1. Exports (YoY)	2. d(export/ output) (PoP)	3. Elasticity (imported inputs/ exports) (YoY)	1. Exports (YoY)	2. d(export/ output) (PoP)	3. Elasticity (imported inputs/ exports) (YoY)
Manufacturing	13.6	13.5	0.9	29.1	9.3	1.0	7.0	7.5	1.1	8.9	–3.4	0.7
Total sectors	11.7	5.4	1.1	20.1	2.8	1.4	7.4	5.1	1.1	9.5	–2.5	0.6
Thailand												
Agriculture	16.0	15.8	0.6	1.2	–1.4	11.3	–4.2	–0.1	1.7	42.4	17.2	0.5
Mining quarrying	8.0	2.7	1.2	–15.5	–14.1	—	8.0	1.4	—	25.9	15.5	1.4
Manufacturing	11.8	10.8	0.7	22.7	4.5	0.7	5.1	7.4	0.3	9.7	–1.0	0.8
Total sectors	12.1	8.7	0.7	20.9	2.0	0.8	5.3	4.7	—	11.2	1.9	0.8
United States												
Agriculture	4.6	1.7	2.1	5.0	0.7	2.0	–6.1	–1.5	—	11.8	2.6	1.2
Mining quarrying	2.1	–0.4	7.2	–3.1	–0.2	—	–4.5	–0.4	—	10.0	0.3	1.7
Manufacturing	5.1	0.2	1.5	12.0	0.9	0.7	1.0	–0.5	9.3	3.6	–0.3	1.8
Total sectors	5.0	–0.1	1.7	10.8	0.2	0.9	0.6	–0.3	—	4.3	0.0	1.7

Source: Authors' calculations based on IDE-Jetro Asian Input-Output matrices.

Note: Nominal values in national currencies are converted into U.S. dollars using average International Monetary Fund exchange rates. d = change; PoP = point to point; accumulated variation from initial to final year, in percentage points; YoY = year over year; average annual changes; — = not available. Exports includes final goods and intermediate consumption. Intermediate inputs includes oil and other commodities. Total sectors includes other industries and services.

a. Data are 2008 preliminary estimates. Results should be interpreted with caution, as variations in exchange rates can greatly affect the comparison between benchmark years.

Figure 3.3 Asia and the United States—Export Orientation and Imports of Intermediate Goods: 1990, 1995, 2000, and 2008
percent

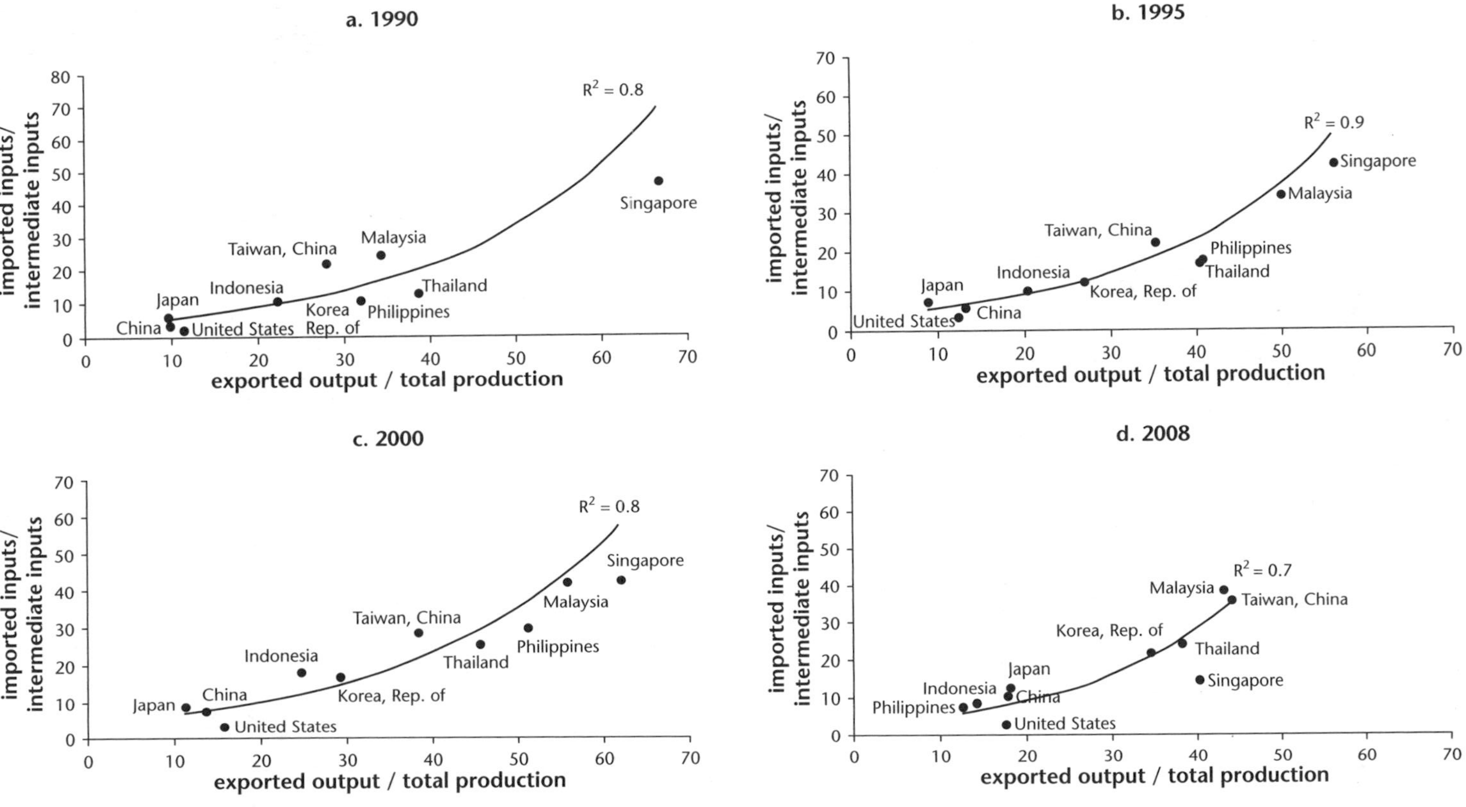

Source: Authors' calculations based on IDE-Jetro database.
Note: The figure is based on national input-output tables, converted to U.S. dollars using commercial exchange rates: 2008, preliminary estimates.

Table 3.4 Share of Value-Added and Imported Inputs, 1990–2008
percent

		VA/total production costs		Imported inputs/VA	
Country	**Sector**	**1990**	**2008**	**1990**	**2008**
China	Agriculture	64.3	77.6	2.9	2.3
	Mining quarrying	46.2	77.1	1.6	4.6
	Manufacturing	28.2	32.2	24.9	37.3
	Total sectors	40.1	46.4	11.2	18.1
Indonesia	Agriculture	80.8	64.7	1.4	4.6
	Mining quarrying	80.3	67.0	1.3	11.4
	Manufacturing	33.2	30.5	44.3	32.3
	Total sectors	55.1	44.6	13.9	16.0
Japan	Agriculture	57.0	60.0	2.6	6.6
	Mining quarrying	48.6	45.0	3.3	10.5
	Manufacturing	34.0	35.5	18.5	32.8
	Total sectors	50.2	55.2	7.5	12.1
Malaysia	Agriculture	69.3	66.8	10.9	15.4
	Mining quarrying	80.8	50.8	5.2	22.4
	Manufacturing	30.2	24.7	78.7	131.2
	Total sectors	47.3	41.4	31.6	51.4
Thailand	Agriculture	66.2	53.3	8.4	18.4
	Mining quarrying	72.3	82.5	4.0	5.0
	Manufacturing	32.1	27.9	81.4	98.3
	Total sectors	47.5	45.0	32.0	39.6
United States	Agriculture	34.4	34.2	4.7	16.0
	Mining quarrying	75.1	55.3	3.5	28.2
	Manufacturing	39.9	36.2	17.1	30.9
	Total sectors	54.3	54.0	5.6	9.2

Source: Authors' calculation based on IDE-Jetro data.
Note: Total sectors includes other sectors, in particular, services. Total production costs includes factorial inputs (labor and capital) and taxes, as measured by total value-added (VA).

60 percent, except in Indonesia (16 percent) and Thailand (24 percent). The change is particularly significant when considering the manufacturing sectors of the two developed economies, Japan and the United States, where the participation of imported inputs in total production costs has increased by an average of 80 percent between 1990 and 2008. With imported inputs contributing to more than 30 percent of their production costs in manufactures, these two industrialized countries are not far from the two largest developing countries in the table: China (37 percent) and Indonesia (32 percent).

Finally, the intensity of the interindustry linkages varies greatly from sector to sector. The reliance on imported inputs is consistently larger in manufacture than in other productive sectors, and also larger in smaller countries. At the extreme, the value of imported inputs may be more than industry's value-added, as is the case of manufacture in Malaysia.

The four building blocks identified above—the fragmentation of global manufacturing, its magnifying effect on trade, the interindustry linkages as transmission effect, and the external vulnerability of export-oriented countries—are, in particular, central for explaining the specificities of the 2008–09 great trade collapse, in which trade in some industries fell by more than 30 percent in two consecutive quarters (see table 3.1). When industrial production is spread across various countries, and all segments of the chain are critical to the other ones (supplied constrained networks), a shock affecting one segment of the chain will reverberate through the entire network. In contrast to the traditional macroeconomic transmission of shocks, impacts are moving forward from supplier to clients, and not backward as in the traditional demand-driven Leontief model (from client to suppliers). The intensity of the supply shock will vary according to the affected industry; if the origin of the shock is a systemic credit crunch, it will disproportionately affect the international segments of the global supply chains, through increased risk aversion and shrinking trade finance (Escaith and Gonguet 2009).

The following subsections analyze in more detail the implications of GVCs on world trade elasticity, first by looking at the long-term perspective through the possible changes in structural relationships and, second, by investigating their contribution to the increased short-term volatility observed during the recent economic crisis.

Long-term perspective

The following equations formalize the empirical observations obtained from the U.S.-Asian compact from a demand-oriented input-output perspective.[12] In the absence of structural changes affecting production function (that is, when technical coefficients, as described by an input-output matrix, are constant), the relationship linking demand for intermediate inputs with an external shock can be described by the following linear relationship:

$$\Delta m^{IC} = u' \cdot M^{\circ} \cdot (I - A)^{-1} \cdot \Delta D\,, \tag{3.4}$$

where, in the case of a single country with s sectors,[13] Δm^{IC} is the variation in total imported inputs (scalar); u' is the summation vector ($1 \times s$); M° is the diagonal matrix of intermediate import coefficients ($s \times s$); $(I - A)^{-1}$ is the Leontief inverse, where A is the matrix of fixed technical coefficients ($s \times s$); and ΔD is the initial shock on final demand ($s \times 1$).[14]

Similarly, changes in total production caused by the demand shock (including the intermediate inputs required to produce the final goods) are obtained from

$$\Delta Q = A \cdot \Delta Q + \Delta D \,. \tag{3.5}$$

Solving for ΔQ yields the traditional result:

$$\Delta Q = (I - A)^{-1} \cdot \Delta D \,. \tag{3.6}$$

Aggregating impacts across all sectors s, the total additional output derived from this demand shock is equal to

$$\Delta q = u' \cdot \Delta Q \,. \tag{3.7}$$

The comparison between equations 3.4 and 3.7 is illustrative. Since $[M^o \cdot (I - A)^{-1}]$ is a linear combination of fixed coefficients, the ratio $(\Delta m^{IC} / \Delta q)$ is a constant, and trade elasticity is 1. This result is consistent with the critique advanced by Bénassy-Quéré et al. (2009) against the hypothesis of the large trade multiplier observed during the crisis being attributed to supply chains and vertical integration.[15]

Short-term aspects

The "steady-state approach" embedded in structural input-output relationships described in the preceding subsection tells only part of the story.[16] In the short term (and we see later that the "short term" can last up to four years), trade elasticity can deviate significantly from its long-term value as a result of two effects, "composition" and "inventory."

The first cause for deviation, called "composition effect," is related to the fact that sectors of activity (agriculture, manufacture, services) react differently in the face of a macroeconomic shock. We should remember that the initial shock ΔD analyzed in the preceding section is not a scalar, but a vector $(1 \times s)$. The individual shocks affecting each particular sector do not need to be always in the same proportion from one year to the next. We already saw in the analysis of the Asian–United States epitome that the reliance on imported inputs is sector-specific. As the sectoral import requirements M^o_s differ from sector to sector, then the apparent import elasticity for the national economy will change according to the sectoral distribution of the shock.[17]

This was the case in particular after the financial crisis of September 2008, during which the demand for consumer durable and investment goods (consumer electronics, automobile and transport equipment, office equipment and computers, and so forth) was particularly affected by the sudden stop in bank credits. Because these sectors are also vertically integrated, the impact on international trade in intermediate and final goods was high. Table 3.5 shows that the coefficient of imported inputs, derived from equation 3.4, is much larger than in other sectors, for example, agriculture or services.

Table 3.5 Asia and the United States: Imported Inputs Coefficients, 2008

Sector	China	Indonesia	Japan	Malaysia	Thailand	United States
Agriculture	0.04	0.07	0.09	0.17	0.20	0.12
Mining quarrying	0.06	0.10	0.12	0.17	0.07	0.20
Manufacturing	0.21	0.17	0.21	0.48	0.40	0.18
Services	0.10	0.09	0.04	0.12	0.15	0.04
Total sectors	0.20	0.13	0.17	0.41	0.35	0.15

Source: Authors' calculations based on IDE-Jetro Asian Input-Output matrices.
Note: Normalized imported inputs requirements ($\Delta m^{IC} / \Delta d$). Total sectors includes other sectors.

Services sectors—the main contributors to GDP in developed countries and also less dependent on imported inputs—were more resilient to the 2008–09 financial crisis than was the manufacturing sector. But services and other nontradable sectors will eventually be affected by the external shock (see figure 3.4).

Because the initial shock was concentrated on manufactured and other tradable goods, the most vertically integrated sectors, the apparent trade-GDP elasticity soared to approximately 5. In a second phase, the initial shock reverberates through the rest of the economy, transforming the global financial crisis into a great recession. GDP continues to slow down, but the decrease in trade tends to decelerate as the import content of services sectors (its sectoral imported input-VA ratio, as shown in table 3.4) is much lower than for manufacturing sectors.

After the initial overshooting of trade, therefore, a regression to normality of the trade elasticity can be expected in 2010. Or, in econometrics terms, the data generation process should follow an error correction model (ECM). This hypothesis is tested in the penultimate section of this chapter. Nevertheless, as is shown in the next section, this does not mean that observed trade multipliers should be constant in the long run, as in the steady-state situation.

Indeed, the structural changes that were deep enough to flatten the planet, as proclaimed by Thomas Friedman in his book, *The World Is Flat: A Brief History of the Globalized World in the Twenty-First Century*, were probably also strong enough to shift the parameters governing CGE models. Thus, shifting trade multipliers may indeed exist in the long run, and they may reflect the move from one "steady state" to another one (Hicks [1973] would have used the word "traverse" for this transition path toward a new growth regime). According to the stylized facts that were identified using the Asian–United States compact in the previous section, the long-run transition should also vary from country to country, depending on its stage of industrial development and its export specialization. This heterogeneity is more systematically explored in the next section.

Figure 3.4 Change in World Production and GDP Response, 1980–2009

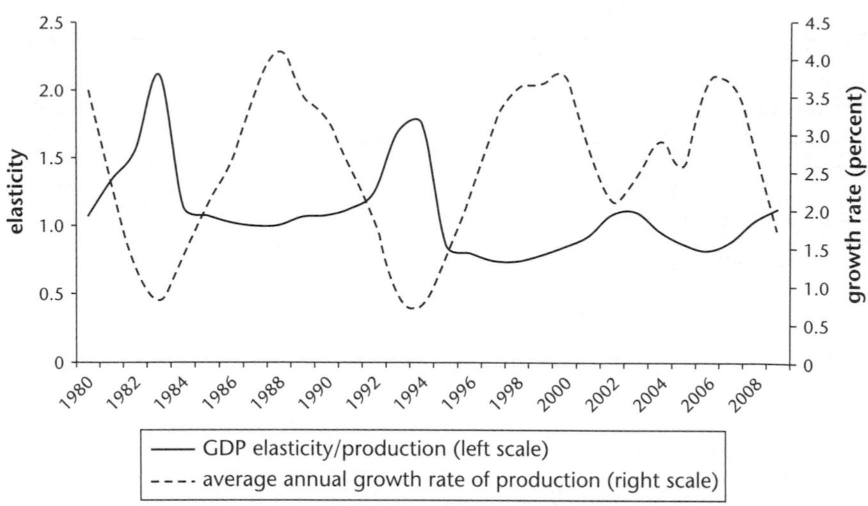

Source: Based on WTO International Trade Statistics database.
Note: Five-year rolling periods, constant prices. Average annual growth rate of production includes agriculture, mining, and manufactures.

The second short-term determinant, called the "inventory effect," is closely linked to the functioning of GVCs. Recent changes in the apparent trade elasticity are also probably linked to changes in inventories, as mentioned by various analysts (for example, Baldwin 2009; Bénassy-Quéré et al. 2009), as retailers run down their stocks in reaction to a large drop in final demand. Here, again, this traditional macroeconomic effect on inventories is amplified on the microeconomic side by the new business model that surged in the late 1980s and opened the way to international vertical integration. Even under "just-in-time" management (production-to-order) favored by GVC managers, geographically fragmented networks need to maintain a minimum level of inventories (buffer stocks) in order to face the usual risks attached to international transportation. While large players try to keep their inventories at the lowest possible level, considering their sales plans and the acceptable level of risk, they tend at the same time to force their suppliers to maintain large stocks (production-to-stock) so that they are able to supply them quickly upon request. In addition, some upstream suppliers, engaged in highly capitalistic processes such as foundries, need to process large batches in order to benefit from economies of scale and lower their unit costs.

As a result, there is always a significant level of inventories in a global supply chain, translating into a higher demand for banking loans (Escaith and Gonguet

2009). When a drop in final demand reduces the activity of downstream firms, or when these firms face a credit crunch, their first reaction is to run down their inventories. Thus, a slowdown in activity transforms itself into a complete standstill for the supplying firms that are located upstream.

These amplified fluctuations in ordering and inventory levels result in what is known as a "bullwhip effect" in the management of production-distribution systems (Stadtler 2008). This effect is more sensitive in an international setting. Alessandria, Kaboski, and Midrigan (forthcoming) provide direct evidence that participants in international trade face more severe inventory management problems. Importing firms have inventory ratios that are roughly twice those of firms that only purchase materials domestically, and the typical international order tends to be about 50 percent larger and half as frequent as the typical domestic one. The related international trade flows, at the microeconomic level, are therefore lumpy and infrequent. As long as the downstream inventories of imported goods have not been reduced to their new optimum level, foreign suppliers are facing a sudden stop in their activity and must reduce their labor force or keep them idle.

The timing and intensity of the international transmission of supply shocks may differ from traditional demand shocks that apply to final goods. For example, the supply-side transmission index proposed by Escaith and Gonguet (2009) implicitly assumes that all secondary effects captured by the I-O matrix occur simultaneously, while these effects may actually propagate more or less quickly depending on the length of the production chain. Also, there might be contractual precommitments for the order of parts and materials that manufacturers must place well in advance in order to secure just-in-time delivery in accordance with their production plans (Uchida and Inomata 2009).

Nevertheless, in closely integrated networks, these mitigating effects are probably reduced, especially when the initial shock is large. A sudden stop in final demand is expected to reverberate quickly through the value chain, as firms run down their inventories in order to adjust to persistent changes in their market. This inventory effect magnifies demand shocks and is principally to blame for the initial collapse of trade in manufacture that characterized the world economy from September 2008 to June 2009. A study of the electronic equipment sector during that crisis (Dvorak 2009) indicates that a fall in consumer purchase of 8 percent reverberated into a 10 percent drop in shipments of the final good and a 20 percent reduction in shipments of the related intermediate inputs (for example, computer chips and other parts). The velocity of the cuts was much faster than in previous slumps—as reordering is now done on a weekly basis, instead of the monthly or quarterly schedules that prevailed up to the early 2000s.

Global, Sectoral, and Regional Trade Elasticity Patterns

The preceding sections presented some stylized facts at the global trade level and provided information on the diversity of the country and sectoral situation in an epitome of GVCs (the United States–Asian compact), using accounting relationships. This section extends the data analysis to the rest of the world in order to identify patterns illustrative of the GDP elasticity of imports and the putative role of GVCs.

The following analysis examines how the parameters of interest vary according to specific groupings of observations or how they change with time. It should be noted that the results presented in this section are exploratory and do not pretend to provide a strong statistical basis for confirmatory inferences or predictions. For this purpose, more formal dynamic specifications are presented in the next section of this chapter.

This explorative data analysis is conducted by looking at subgroups of countries. If the GVCs were the cause of the observed change in elasticities, the results should be similar for countries participating heavily in GVCs and a different trend should be observed in the rest of the countries.

Exploring Country Patterns

The objective of the section is to explore in detail the data generation process and identify possible clusters of countries in order to abstract from the country level and to derive some more generalized stylized facts. The following analysis is conducted with the group of the 50 most important exporters[18] as listed by the WTO (2008b, p. 12 table I.8). Data for the analysis are taken from the International Monetary Fund's *World Economic Outlook* (*WEO*) 2009,[19] namely, imports of goods (volume) and gross domestic product (in constant prices) in a sample from 1980 to 2009. In order to address the tradeoff between number of observations and disaggregation, we take advantage of the panel dimension of our data and cluster the countries in an appropriate way.[20]

As a first approach to defining groups among countries, the countries were clustered according to observed data patterns. For this purpose, we estimate the elasticity of imports to GDP using a state space object for each individual country and apply a Kalman filter (see, for example, Harvey 1987) for three different samples: 1980–90, 1990–2000, and 2000–08. The results provide a first idea of how the elasticity of imports is evolving for each country in the sample. Then, we construct up to nine different clusters (3 × 3) with the following logic:

- Does the elasticity from sample one to sample three increase, remain stable, or decrease (three options)?

- If so, does the elasticity of the second sample lay above, in between, or beneath the two other elasticities (another three possible cases)?

After elimination of clusters 4, 5, 6, and 9,[21] the following country groups were selected (see annex table 3A.2): Cluster 1 comprises countries with an increasing elasticity over the full sample, which overshoots in the middle of the sample; cluster 2, countries with an increasing elasticity over the full sample; cluster 3, countries with an increasing elasticity over the full sample, but with a drop in the middle of the sample; cluster 7, countries with a decreasing elasticity over the full sample, but with an increase in the middle of the sample; and cluster 8, countries with a decreasing elasticity over the full sample. The results of the panel OLS estimation with fixed cross-section effects and rolling windows of five years are displayed in figure 3.5.

As the data show, only the first cluster of countries features a trend compatible with our hypothesis of global value chains being the cause of the change in elasticities. If this cluster contained all the countries that participate in GVCs, this hypothesis would be enormously strengthened. Annex table 3A.2 shows that many of the participants in GVCs are actually in the first cluster. However, many others that are known for their participation in GVCs, such as China, Germany, and Mexico, are missing, which suggests that it might be just coincidence that some of the countries show the data structure that confirms our hypothesis.

Overall, given these findings, the hypothesis that GVCs explain all by themselves the changes in trade-income elasticity seems highly unlikely. However, this does not imply that the emergence of global production networks since the late 1980s did not play a role, only that other factors may also be at work to explain the results observed when estimating equations 3.1 to 3.3.

Clustering by Export Specialization

As clustering by pure elasticity patterns (an empirical concept) cannot confirm the hypothesis that GVCs are the driving force behind the change in the GDP elasticity of imports, the countries are now clustered in an alternative way, based on an economic approach. (An overview of all clusters ordered by country can be found in annex table 3A.1.) All countries that have the same export specialization are grouped together.[22] Thus, the following five clusters were obtained (see annex table 3A.2 for details): fuel exporters; ores, metals, precious stones, and nonmonetary gold exporters; manufactured goods exporters; machinery and transport equipment exporters; and other manufactured goods exporters.[23] Results of panel OLS estimations with fixed cross-section effects and rolling windows of five years are shown in figure 3.6.

Figure 3.5 GDP Elasticity of Imports: Clusters Based on Elasticity Patterns, 1989–2009

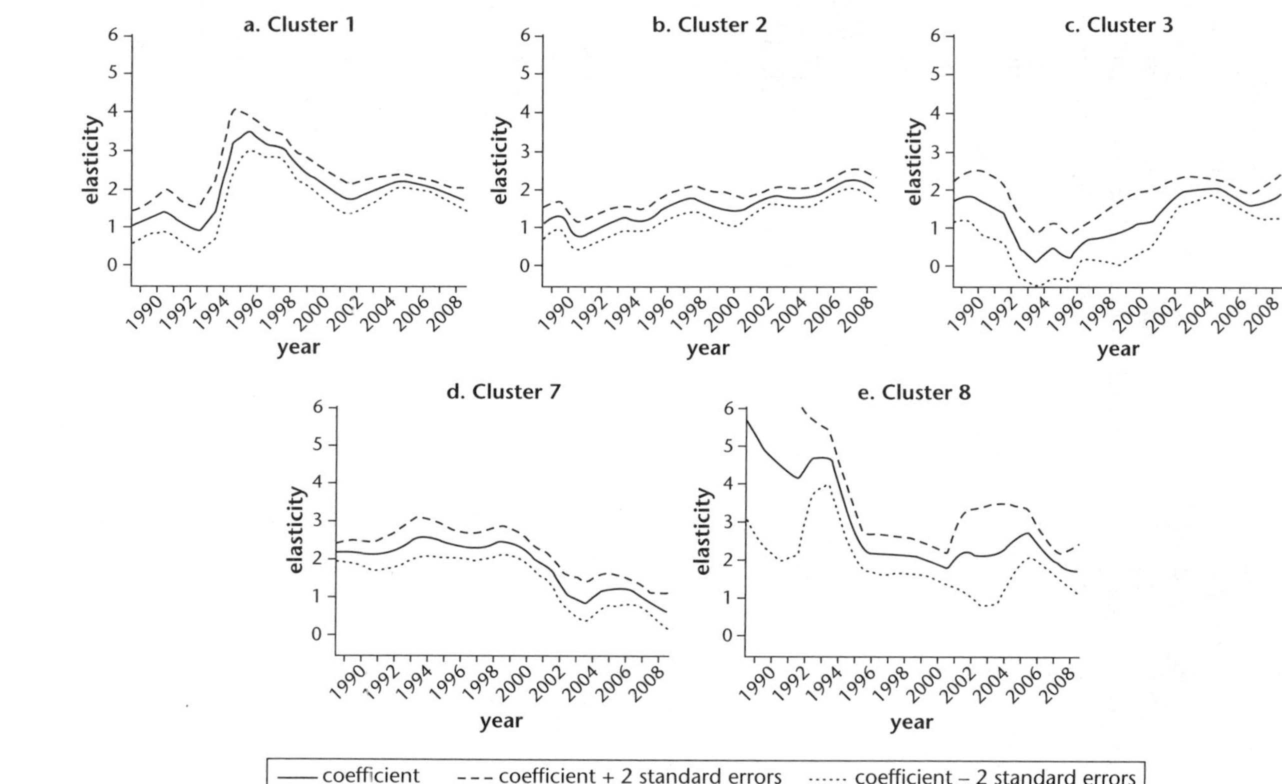

Source: Authors' calculations.

Note: The graphs display the results of the panel ordinary least squares estimation with fixed cross-section effects and rolling windows of five years. Prices are constant. Country groupings are based on the combined changes in trade elasticity in the three periods: 1980–90, 1990–2000, and 2000–08 (see text and annex table 3A.2).

Figure 3.6 GDP Elasticity of Imports, 10-Year Rolling Window: Hypothesis of Clusters Based on Export Specialization, 1980–2009

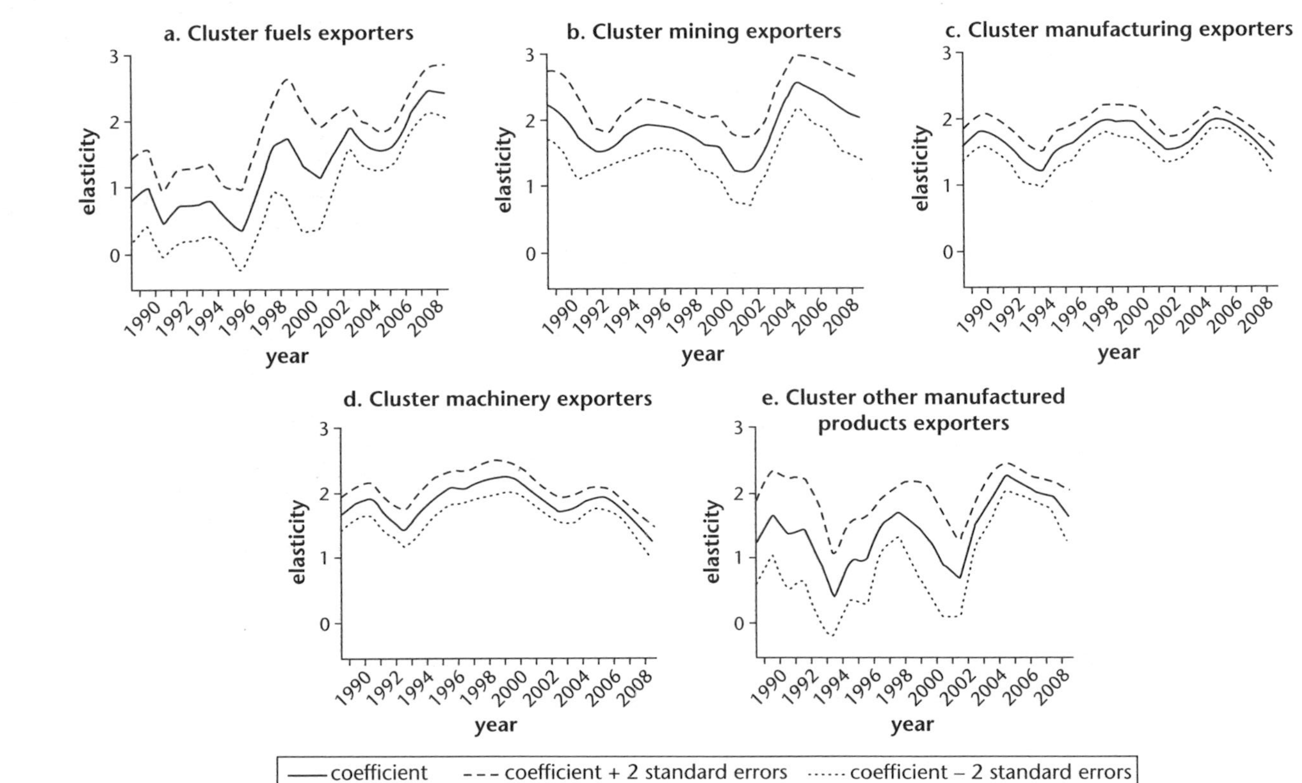

Source: Authors' calculations.
Note: The graphs display the results of the panel ordinary least squares estimation with fixed cross-section effects and rolling windows of five years. Prices are constant. See text and annex tables 3A.1 and 3A.2 for methodology and groupings.

Again, the patterns of the calculated elasticities change significantly among the different country clusters. The elasticity of the group of fuel exporters increases steadily; however, this is certainly a terms-of-trade effect and has nothing to do with the globalization of value chains. For the manufacturing sector, both for the aggregate (manufacturing exporters) and for the two subgroups (machinery exporters and other manufactured goods exporters), there were three peaks in trade elasticity, the first one in 1990, the second in 1998, and the third in 2005. Each time, elasticity has decreased between the peaks. However, this does not support the hypothesis of an impact of GVCs on the elasticity either. Thus, there is still no supporting evidence that implicates GVCs in the changes of trade elasticities.[24]

Clustering by Regions

To complete the exploration of trade elasticity patterns, the countries were clustered by (geographical) regions. Within one regional cluster, the countries often dispose of a similar endowment (for example, natural resources) or have similar comparative advantages and, accordingly, may have assumed a similar role in the world trade economy. For example, the literature often refers to "Central and Eastern European Countries" or "Emerging Asia" as single entities when discussing offshoring. Therefore, we construct the following set of clusters: Latin America, emerging Asia, new EU member states, Middle East, G-7 countries, and western European countries (see annex table 3A.2). Results of the panel OLS estimation with fixed cross-section effects for rolling windows of five years of the GDP elasticity of imports are displayed in figure 3.7.

As figure 3.7 shows, elasticities vary substantially among the regions, but overall there is no evidence for a strengthening of the supply-chain hypothesis. The evolution of the elasticity of the new EU member countries could be an illustration of a transition that has taken place, but at the same time, the graph for the Middle East countries clearly alludes to the limitations of the trade elasticity approach: exploration of the data patterns does not say anything about the causes of the change in elasticity. In the case of the latter group of countries, the increase in elasticity most probably is due to changes in relative prices and is not at all related to the globalization of value chains.

To sum up, even ignoring the known limitations of the model, we cannot find strong evidence for the role of global value chains for the changes in the GDP elasticity of imports. Although on the aggregated world level, trade elasticity is changing in a way that one could be tempted to interpret as confirming evidence (trade elasticity increased in the years of rising globalization in the 1990s, then fell back to a lower level in the mid-2000s), the disaggregated analysis does not support this

Figure 3.7 GDP Elasticity of Imports: Hypothesis of Clusters Based on Regions, 1989–2009

% trade decrease

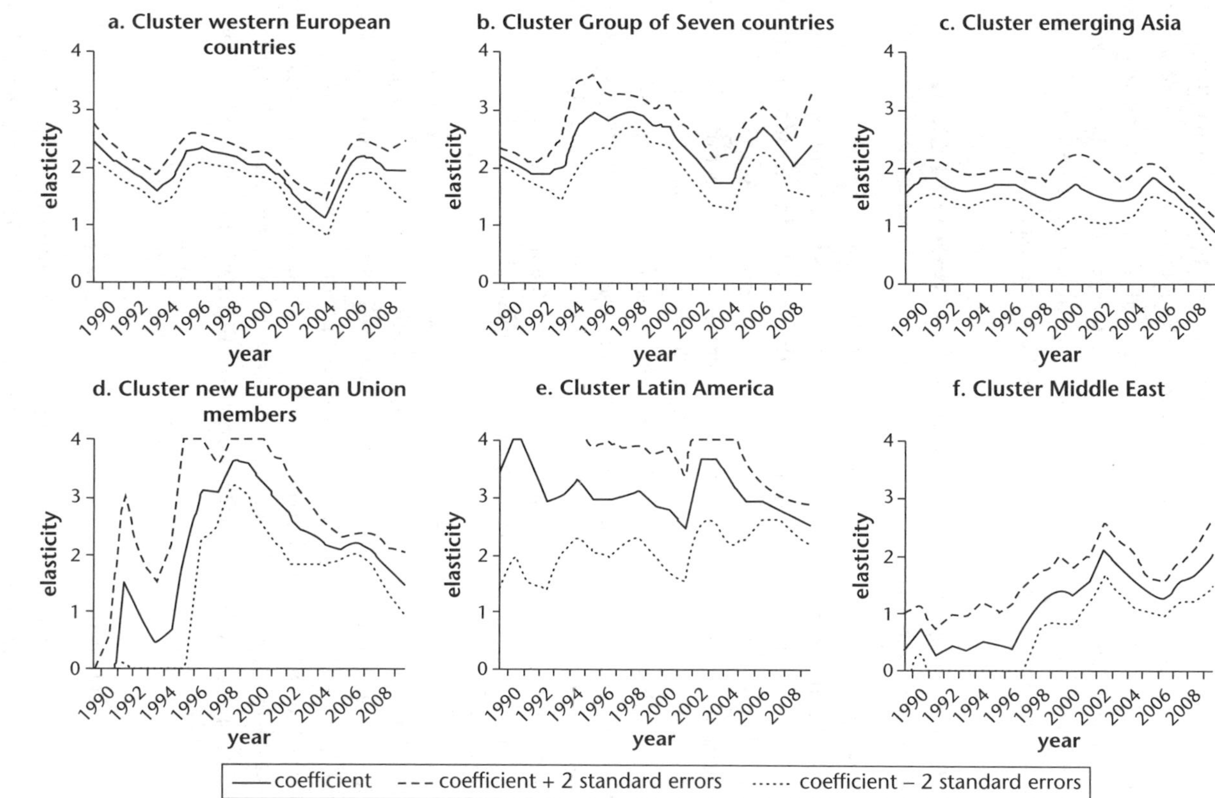

Source: Authors' calculations.

Note: The graphs display the results of the panel ordinary least squares estimation with fixed cross-section effects and rolling windows of five years. Prices are constant. See text and annex tables 3A.1 and 3A.2 for methodology and groupings.

hypothesis. Some countries that are part of GVCs do not show significant differences in the evolution of their elasticities, while countries less integrated in global production networks tend to do so. Although trade elasticities in general are quite volatile, the exploration of elasticity patterns does not support the hypothesis that deeper vertical integration is *the* driving force behind this development. There are probably more causal factors at work. We mentioned the changes in relative prices that inflated the value of primary commodities. Other factors might be the lowering of trade barriers after the conclusion of the Uruguay Round in 1995 and increasing consumer preferences for diversity as their incomes increase.

New Dynamics of Trade and GDP in the Context of Global Value Chains: An Estimation with the Error Correction Model

The previous sections were exploratory, and no formal assumption was made on the relationship between imports and GDP. The analysis now assumes that there is a long-run equilibrium relationship between the growth of trade and the growth of GDP, that is, that the elasticity is stable in the long run. As described at the beginning of the chapter and evidenced in figure 3.2, we expect the elasticity of trade to GDP to have increased during the 1990s because of outsourcing and offshoring, but then to have *decreased* afterwards, once a new steady state had been reached. The elasticity that we measure through trade and GDP data is a short-run elasticity that reflects both the long-run equilibrium and the stochastic fluctuations that lead to volatility, such as those illustrated in the previous section on vertical integration from an I-O standpoint (sequential nature of sectoral shocks, inventory effects, and so on).

We use an error correction model (ECM) to account for both the long-run equilibrium and the stochastic fluctuations, and to estimate the steady-state elasticity. Quarterly data were used from the OECD National Accounts database over the period 1961–2009[25] in order to have a consistent data set with time-series for the OECD area (based on 24 OECD economies) and individual data for 30 OECD countries. The data, in constant prices, allow controlling for the changes in relative price, one of the sources of fluctuations identified in the previous sections.

Steady-State Elasticity

The analysis starts with a very simple proportional relationship between trade and GDP: $M_t = QY_t$, where M_t are imports (in volume), Y_t is real GDP, and Q is the share of imports in GDP. In log form, the equation can be written: $m_t = q + y_t$ with m, q, and y the natural logs of the previous variables. Adding the lagged values of both trade (m_{t-1}) and GDP (y_{t-1}), as well as stochastic fluctuations (u_t), the model can be written as follows:

$$m_t = \alpha_0 + \alpha_1 m_{t-1} + \beta_1 y_t + \beta_2 y_{t-1} + u_t. \quad (3.8)$$

Assuming that there is a long-run equilibrium relationship between M and Y, and that $m*$ and $y*$ are the equilibrium values of m and y, we have

$$m* = \alpha_0 + \alpha_1 m* + \beta_1 y* + \beta_2 y* . \quad (3.9)$$

At the equilibrium, we set u_t equal to zero and the above equation implies that

$$m* = \frac{\alpha_0}{1-\alpha_1} + \frac{\beta_1 + \beta_2}{1-\alpha_1} y * . \quad (3.10)$$

This equation is consistent with $m_t = q + y_t$ if we have $q = \frac{\alpha_0}{1-\alpha_1}$ and $\frac{\beta_1+\beta_2}{1-\alpha_1} = 1$. This is the long-run equilibrium relationship between trade and GDP. We can interpret $\gamma = \frac{\beta_1+\beta_2}{1-\alpha_1} = 1$ as the long-run equilibrium trade elasticity.

We can then model a divergence from equilibrium in the presence of stochastic shocks. Taking the first difference of m_t, adding and subtracting both $\beta_1 y_{t-1}$ and $(\alpha_1 - 1)y_{t-1}$ from the right-hand side, the model can be rewritten as

$$\Delta m_t = \alpha_0 + (\alpha_1 - 1)(m_{t-1} - y_{t-1}) + \beta_1 \Delta y_t + (\beta_1 + \beta_2 + \alpha_1 - 1)y_{t-1} + u_t. \quad (3.11)$$

The coefficients β_1 and β_2 indicate the short-run impact of a change in GDP on imports. Then $(\alpha_1 - 1)$ is the speed at which trade adjusts to the discrepancy between trade and GDP in the previous period. This is the error correction rate.

The above equation is the classic specification in an ECM. Before proceeding to its estimation, we check for the degree of integration. Running Phillips-Perron unit root tests shows that m and y have unit roots, but we reject the assumption that Δm and Δy contain unit roots. A Johansen test further shows that the rank of co-integration of m and y is one. This justifies the use of the above specification.

We can estimate the model in the following way:

$$\Delta m_t = \alpha_0 + \delta_1 m_{t-1} + \delta_2 \Delta y_t + \delta_3 y_{t-1} + \varepsilon_t. \quad (3.12)$$

The latter equation is similar to the former with $\delta_1 = \alpha_1 - 1$, $\delta_2 = \beta_1$, and $\delta_3 = \beta_1 + \beta_2$. The advantage of the specification is that we can derive directly the long-run equilibrium trade elasticity from the estimated coefficients: $\gamma = \frac{\beta_1+\beta_2}{\alpha_1 - 1} = \frac{\delta_3}{\delta_1}$. Furthermore, δ_1 is the speed at which imports adjust to trade, and δ_2 is the short-term impact of GDP on trade (short-term elasticity).

First, the regression is run on aggregate data for 24 OECD economies (1971–2009). The results are presented in table 3.6 below. Over the period 1971–2009, all the variables of the model are significant, and the model explains 63 percent of the variance in the data. We find strong coefficients (both in terms of statistical and economic significance) for the short-term adjustment of trade to GDP changes (Δy_t) in all periods. The speed at which imports converge to their equilibrium value is generally less significant and the coefficient is relatively small.

Of special relevance to the present concern, the last row of table 3.6 reports the implied long-run trade elasticity (γ). Its overall value of 2.43 over the 1971–2009 period is slightly higher than the elasticity measured in the previous section (that is, 2.28), but it remains close despite a different statistical model and different data. As hypothesized, the trade elasticity has increased up to the 1990s and appears to have decreased afterwards. However, in the last regression for the 2000s, the computed value for lags of imports and GDP are not significant; therefore, some caution should be exercised when interpreting these results, despite the relatively good fit to the data.

It is nonetheless very interesting to see that the long-term elasticity, according to this model, is almost the same in the 1980s and 2000s. This result would confirm that vertical specialization, as suggested by theory, has no reason to increase the equilibrium elasticity of trade to GDP and that the 1990s, with their higher trade elasticity, can be interpreted as a transition period to a new "steady state."[26]

Table 3.6 Estimation of the Error Correction Model and Long-Run Trade Elasticity for 24 OECD Countries

	Time period				
Variables	**1971–2009**	**1970s**	**1980s**	**1990s**	**2000s**
Dependent variable: Δm_t					
m_{t-1}	–0.021*	–0.122	–0.162*	–0.212***	0.006
	(0.012)	(0.108)	(0.088)	(0.076)	(0.139)
Δy_t	2.533***	2.046***	1.436***	1.819***	3.228***
	(0.263)	(0.613)	(0.299)	(0.508)	(0.289)
y_{t-1}	0.052**	0.184	0.320**	0.592***	–0.012
	(0.024)	(0.142)	(0.158)	(0.202)	(0.318)
Number of observations	153	35	40	40	38
R-squared	0.63	0.53	0.60	0.55	0.83
Long-run trade elasticity (δ_3/δ_1)	2.43	1.51	1.98	2.79	1.90

Source: Authors' calculations.

Note: Ordinary least squares estimation with robust standard errors. OECD = Organisation for Economic Co-operation and Development.

***$p < 0.01$, **$p < 0.05$, * $p < 0.1$.

Variation across Countries

To examine discrepancies across countries and relate those possible differences to vertical integration, table 3.7 reports the results of similar regressions at the country level. Generally, the model works quite well in explaining the variations across the growth rate of trade and GDP. However, for some countries, coefficients are not significant and the trade elasticity is not calculated. All countries demonstrate an increase in their trade elasticity until 1990. Afterwards, countries differ in the evolution of the elasticity between the 1990s and 2000s. In Australia, Denmark, Finland, Republic of Korea, Norway, and Portugal, the trade elasticity continues to increase after 2000. In the case of Mexico, the Netherlands, New Zealand, Spain, and Turkey, there is a decrease in the elasticity, as seen in the aggregate data in table 3.6. For other countries, the results are not significant enough to assess the trend.

Trade Response to External Shocks

Figure 3.8 shows the "impulse response function" (IRF) of imports when there is an exogenous shock on GDP (calculated on the basis of the estimation of the OECD time-series for 1999–2009). When there is a 1 percent decrease in GDP, it is observed that during the first year following the shock, trade decreases more than proportionally and, in fact, "overreacts" (there is a 3 percent decrease in imports). Then, there is a convergence toward a new equilibrium value. Trade recovers during the second and third years; four years after the shock, the decrease in trade is about 2 percent, in line with the multiplier observed in table 3.6 (1.9).

Role of Vertical Specialization

In order to check more precisely for the influence of GVCs on the change in trade elasticity, a vertical specialization variable is introduced to alter the model.[27]

The estimated equation becomes

$$\Delta m_t = \alpha_0 + \delta_1 m_{t-1} + \delta_2 \Delta y_t + \delta_3 y_{t-1} + \delta_4 VS.y_{t-1} + \delta_5\, VS + \varepsilon_t, \qquad (3.13)$$

where *VS* is the country vertical specialization share, calculated as in Hummels, Ishii, and Yi (2001).[28] *VS* is closely related to the imported content of intermediate goods derived previously from equation 3.4 in an input-output context.

The vertical specialization variables slightly increase the goodness-of-fit of the model for most countries, but they are not always significant. To see to what

Table 3.7 Estimation of the Error Correction Model at the Country Level

Country	Period	Estimation-dependent variable: Δm_t			Long-run trade elasticity		
		m_{t-1}	Δy_t	y_{t-1}	All years	1990s	2000s
Australia	1961:Q2–2009:Q2	–0.049*	0.757**	0.087*	1.77	2.15	2.85
Austria	1961:Q2–2009:Q3	–0.139***	1.888***	0.266***	1.91	—	—
Belgium	1961:Q2–2009:Q3	–0.066**	1.597***	0.120**	1.82	2.40	1.84
Canada	1961:Q2–2009:Q3	–0.046**	1.809***	0.081**	1.75	—	2.12
Czech Republic	1995:Q2–2009:Q3	–0.038	1.190**	0.067	—	—	2.06
Denmark	1961:Q2–2009:Q2	–0.025	1.273***	0.045	—	2.23	3.82
Finland	1961:Q2–2009:Q3	–0.164***	1.990***	0.271***	1.65	1.73	2.06
France	1961:Q2–2009:Q3	–0.038**	2.124***	0.081**	2.13	2.98	—
Germany	1961:Q2–2009:Q3	–0.029	0.802***	0.06	—	—	—
Greece	1961:Q2–2009:Q3	–0.050**	3.136***	0.110**	2.22	3.25	—
Hungary	1995:Q2–2009:Q2	–0.094*	2.868***	0.252	—	—	—
Ireland	1961:Q2–2009:Q2	–0.019	0.485**	0.028	—	—	0.89
Italy	1961:Q2–2009:Q2	–0.052**	1.406***	0.092**	1.78	3.17	2.67
Japan	1961:Q2–2009:Q3	–0.037**	1.165***	0.055**	1.50	—	2.47

Korea, Rep. of	1970:Q2–2009:Q3	–0.132**	2.029***	0.205**	1.56	1.83	2.06
Luxembourg	1961:Q2–2009:Q2	–0.079***	0.208	0.108***	1.37	—	1.64
Mexico	1961:Q2–2009:Q2	–0.021	2.653***	0.060**	—	3.65	2.34
Netherlands	1961:Q2–2009:Q3	–0.033	0.383***	0.054	—	2.42	2.16
New Zealand	1961:Q2–2009:Q2	–0.116***	0.753***	0.200***	1.73	1.97	1.91
Norway	1961:Q2–2009:Q3	–0.076***	0.435	0.071**	0.93	1.33	2.62
Poland	1995:Q2–2009:Q3	–0.256**	3.474***	0.510**	1.99	—	1.75
Portugal	1961:Q2–2009:Q3	–0.02	0.960***	0.038	—	2.62	3.66
Slovak Rep.	1993:Q2–2009:Q3	–0.061	0.793*	0.076	—	—	—
Spain	1961:Q2–2009:Q3	0.004	–0.273	–0.036	—	3.73	2.21
Sweden	1961:Q2–2009:Q3	–0.148***	0.868***	0.266***	1.79	—	1.86
Switzerland	1961:Q2–2009:Q3	–0.02	1.081***	0.045	—	—	1.84
Turkey	1961:Q2–2009:Q2	–0.054*	2.199***	0.109*	2.03	2.68	1.74
United Kingdom	1961:Q2–2009:Q3	–0.188***	1.343***	0.385***	2.05	2.56	—
United States	1961:Q2–2009:Q3	–0.077***	1.695***	0.154***	1.99	2.72	—

Source: Authors' calculations.

Note: Ordinary least squares estimation with robust standard errors. — = not available.

***$p < 0.01$, **$p < 0.05$, * $p < 0.1$. The multiplier is not reported when the coefficients used to calculate it are not significant.

Figure 3.8 Impulse Response Function: Impact of an Exogenous Decrease in GDP on Trade in 24 OECD Countries

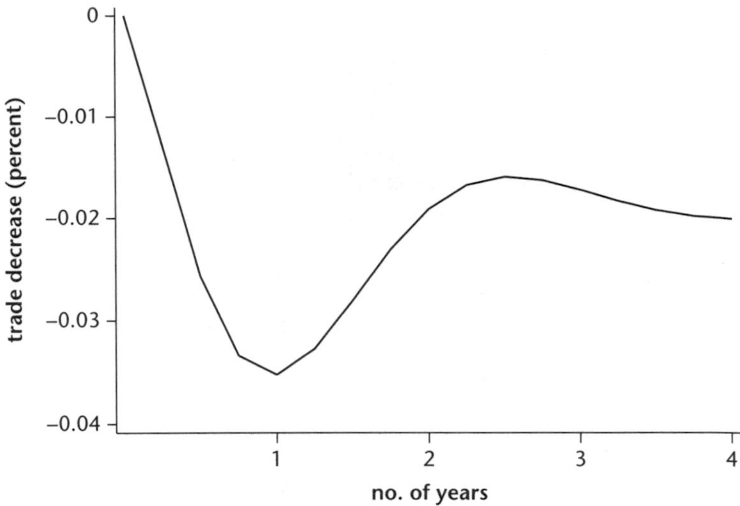

Source: Authors' calculations.
Note: Orthogonalized impulse response function is based on the estimation of the OECD model for the period 1999–2009. OECD = Organisation for Economic Co-operation and Development.

extent vertical specialization can help explain the trade collapse during the crisis, we do a forecasting exercise, predicting for each quarter the value of imports based on the estimated model. We then compare the results between the first model (without vertical specialization) and the second model (with vertical specialization). As can be seen in annex table 3A.3, the discrepancy between the predicted change in trade and the observed trade collapse is only marginally reduced when using the specification with vertical specialization. The difference in percentage points tends to be lower for most countries, but not in a way that significantly increases the ability of the model to predict the trade collapse, even if vertical specialization has shaped the dynamics of transmission.

The results of formal modeling thus confirm the evidence presented in exploratory analysis and input-output relationships. The long-term elasticity of trade to GDP increased in the 1990s before lowering at the end of the 2000s. This pattern suggests that the 1990–2000 period marked a transition to a new steady state, where the share of trade in GDP is higher. Global value chains played a significant role in explaining the short- and medium-term dynamics of trade and GDP elasticity observed during this transition period, but the longer-term trade elasticities remain of a magnitude comparable to those observed before the 1990s.

Conclusions

The 2008–09 financial crisis has highlighted new interdependencies in world trade and GDP and pointed out the role that global value chains played in the transmission of macroeconomic shocks. Looking at the evolution of trade elasticities over the past two decades shows that there were clear signals that an important structural change occurred in the middle of the 1990s and that the world economy has undertaken a "traverse," that is, a shift between two underlying economic models. Using exploratory analysis, input-output analysis, and formal modeling and working with different data sets, the authors obtained the results presented in this chapter, which converge to support the hypothesis that long-term trade elasticity rose during the 1990s before lowering in the late 2000s.

This pattern observed from the data is compatible with a structural change from a "Ricardian" economy, where countries trade final goods, to a "trade in tasks" economy. Trade in tasks is a consequence of the new "global manufacturing" model, where countries trade intermediate goods for further processing, in the context of global value chains resulting from the fragmentation of the production process. Accordingly, from the late 1980s onward, the internationalization of production has caused a shift from one steady state to a new one. Trade elasticities rose only during the transition phase, coming back then to their long-run equilibrium level, now at a new steady state where trade represents a higher share of GDP. The concept of steady-state equilibrium implies that vertical integration should only affect the level of trade relative to GDP but not the elasticity.

While we expect the trade elasticity to be stable in the long run, we also recognize that the results obtained highlight that import elasticities in general have been very volatile and that, at a more disaggregated level, countries have experienced changes in their elasticities that should be explained beyond the internationalization of production and that imply that other variables have been at work. Indeed, a more detailed analysis showed significant differences among trade elasticities for different countries and sectors. The direct observation of intrasectoral trade, using input-output models, as well as standard time-series econometrics, tends to identify the aggregate pattern in many countries, including Japan and the United States. However, other countries that are also known for their participation in global value chains, like China, Germany, and Mexico, are not showing the expected long-term increase in trade elasticity, suggesting that it might just be coincidence that some of the countries show the data structure that confirms the above hypothesis.

These results also indicate that the "trade collapse" of 2008–09 cannot be explained by the long-term structural change observed in the data and that the high trade elasticities measured in the course of the crisis are of a short-term nature. In the short run, a shock that has very different effects on different sectors of the economy will have a transitory impact on the trade elasticity of the whole economy, which explains some of the volatility observed in the data. Moreover, two factors related to value chains are at work to explain the overshooting of trade elasticity that occurred during the 2008–09 trade collapse. The first one is the composition effect, as the initial demand shocks linked to the credit crunch concentrated disproportionably on consumer durables and investment goods, the most vertically integrated industrial sectors. The second factor is the "bullwhip effect," where inventory adjustments are amplified as one moves upstream in the supply chain. But the disturbance is expected to dissipate in the medium term and the elasticity to return to its long-run value. The regression to normality can take up to four years, albeit most of the overshooting dissipates in the first two years.

These findings have several policy implications. Overall, they seem to disprove the hypothesis that global value chains explain all by themselves the change in trade-income elasticity and that participating in global production networks is a source of increased macroeconomic volatility or a risk for small, open economies. The 2008–09 crisis has highlighted new short-term and long-term dynamics in trade and GDP, but, in the end, the financial crisis hit all economies. The severity of the downturn is not explained by the nastiness of the transmission channels created by the fragmentation of the production chain, but by the sheer size of the initial financial shock. Thus, it is not because of global value chains that industries, like automotive, were severely impacted, but rather because of underlying trends, in particular shifts in demand and consumer preferences (see Van Biesebroeck and Sturgeon, chapter 6 in this volume). Global value chains can be important sources of productivity gains for both developed and developing economies, and the conclusions drawn from the 2008–09 crisis should *not* be that global value chains are at the origin of increased macroeconomic risks.

Furthermore, global value chains highlight that trade and investment are more and more intertwined and that in the context of vertical specialization, imports of intermediate inputs are associated with more exports to third countries. This trend should help developing countries to further reassess the detrimental impact of policies aimed at discouraging trade or foreign direct investment (or both), as well as local content requirements. Moreover, the current reorganization of Asian production networks (Inomata and Uchida 2009) shows that countries that were originally part of North-South global value chains and specialized in final assembly are now shifting to the production of upstream inputs and are part of regional production networks that produce for domestic consumers who have benefited from increased income in the context of global production (see Kaplinsky and Farooki, chapter 4).

Finally, this chapter dealt principally with trade in goods. With services representing two-thirds of GDP and less than 20 percent of world trade, the high trade elasticities observed during the crisis are also explained by the discrepancy between the share of services in domestic value-added and in international trade. While services are by nature less tradable, this discrepancy has nonetheless its roots in restrictive trade policies and the lack of any substantive multilateral services trade liberalization since the entry into force of GATS (General Agreement on Trade in Services) 15 years ago. Albeit the outsourcing of services is still incipient, it offers very promising potential for further development (see Gereffi and Fernandez-Stark, chapter 9). In addition, the crisis resilience of services trade should encourage further services trade liberalization, as a mean for reducing both trade volatility and exposure to external shocks.

Annex

Annex tables and figures begin on the next page.

Table 3A.1 Overview of Clusters Ordered, by Country

Economy	1	2	3	7	8	LA	EA	New EU	ME	G-7	Europe	Fuels	Mining	Manufac-turing	Machines and transport equipment
Algeria			x									x			
Argentina					x	x									
Australia		x											x		
Austria	x													x	x
Belgium				x										x	
Brazil	x					x								x	x
Canada				x						x				x	x
Chile		x				x							x		
China		x					x							x	x
Czech Republic	x							x						x	x
Denmark		x									x			x	x
Finland	x										x			x	x
France	x									x	x			x	x
Germany		x								x	x			x	x
Great Britain				x						x	x			x	x
Hong Kong, China				x			x							x	x
Hungary	x							x						x	x
India	x						x							x	
Indonesia							x					x		x	
Iran, Islamic Rep. of			x						x			x			
Ireland					x						x			x	
Israel				x					x				x	x	x
Italy				x						x	x			x	
Japan	x									x				x	x
Korea, Rep. of		x					x							x	x
Kuwait		x							x			x			
Malaysia		x					x							x	x
Mexico					x	x								x	x
Netherlands		x									x			x	x
Nigeria		x										x			
Norway		x									x	x			
Philippines				x			x							x	x
Poland	x							x						x	x
Portugal		x									x			x	
Russian Federation		x										x			
Saudi Arabia		x							x			x			
Singapore			x				x							x	x
Slovak Republic	x							x						x	x
South Africa	x												x	x	x
Spain					x						x			x	x
Sweden	x										x			x	x
Switzerland				x										x	
Thailand			x				x							x	x
Turkey	x													x	
Ukraine			x											x	
United Arab Emirates		x							x			x			
United States				x						x				x	x
Venezuela, R.B. de		x				x						x			
Vietnam		x												x	

Source: Authors' calculations. See text for data description.

Note: The table provides information on the clustering of countries according to a series of characteristics, for example, linked to their export specialization or the specific behavior of their trade elasticity. The clusters are described as follows: for clusters 1, 2 ,3, 7, and 8, the countries were grouped together according to the consecutive patterns observed for the estimated elasticities of total imports to GDP through three subperiods: 1980–90, 1990–2000, and 2000–08. Elasticity characteristics of the groups are the following: cluster 1 = countries with an increasing elasticity over the full sample, which overshoots in the middle of the sample; cluster 2 = countries with an increasing elasticity over the full sample; cluster 3 = countries with an increasing elasticity over the full sample, but with a drop in the middle of the sample; cluster 7 = countries with a decreasing elasticity over the full sample, but with an increase in the middle of the sample; and cluster 8 = countries with a decreasing elasticity over the full sample (although the total number of possible clusters is

Other manufactures	Metals	Coal	Petroleum	Gas	Medicine	pc	Communications	- Electronics	Vehicles	Other transport equipment
			x	x						
			x							
	x	x								
									x	
					x				x	
	x									
			x	x					x	
	x									
						x	x			
					x	x			x	
			x		x					
							x			
									x	x
									x	
			x		x		x		x	
						x	x	x		
						x	x			
x			x							
x		x	x	x						
			x							
					x	x				
					x		x			
x									x	
								x	x	
			x				x	x	x	x
			x							
			x			x	x	x		
			x				x		x	
			x			x				
			x							
			x	x						
						x		x		
									x	
x									x	
			x	x						
			x							
			x			x	x	x		
			x				x		x	
		x							x	
									x	
					x		x		x	
x										
						x		x		
x										
x			x							
			x							
								x		x
			x							
x			x							

nine, some of them were empty). LA = Latin America; EA = emerging Asia; New EU = new member countries of the European Union; ME = Middle East; G-7 = Group of Seven countries; Europe = European countries. Fuels = fuels; mining = ores, metals, precious stones, and nonmonetary gold; manufacturing = manufactured goods; machines and transport equip. = machinery and transport equipment; other manufactures = other manufactured goods; metals = metaliferous ores and metal scrap; coal = coal, coke, and briquettes; petroleum = petroleum, petroleum products, and related materials; gas = natural and manufactured gas; medicine = medicinal and pharmaceutical products; pc = office machines and automatic data-processing machines; communications = telecommunications and sound-recording and reproducing apparatus and equipment; electronics = electrical machinery, apparatus, and appliances, n.e.s., and electrical parts thereof; vehicles = road vehicles (including air-cushion vehicles); other transport equipment = other transport equipment.

Table 3A.2 Overview of Countries in Each Cluster

Clusters by observed elasticity patterns	
Cluster 1	Austria, Brazil, Czech Republic, Finland, France, Hungary, India, Japan, Poland, Slovak Republic, South Africa, Sweden, Turkey
Cluster 2	Australia, Chile, China, Denmark, Germany, Republic of Korea, Kuwait, Malaysia, Netherlands, Nigeria, Norway, Portugal, Russian Federation, Saudi Arabia, United Arab Emirates, República Bolivariana de Venezuela, Vietnam
Cluster 3	Algeria, Islamic Republic of Iran, Singapore, Thailand, Ukraine
Custer 7	Belgium; Canada; Great Britain; Hong Kong, China; Israel; Italy; Philippines; Switzerland; United States
Cluster 8	Argentina, Ireland, Mexico, Spain
Clusters by export specialization	
Fuel exporters	Algeria, Indonesia, Islamic Republic of Iran, Kuwait, Nigeria, Norway, Russia, Saudi Arabia, United Arab Emirates, República Bolivariana de Venezuela
Ores, metals, precious stones, and nonmonetary gold exporters	Australia, Chile, Israel, South Africa
Manufactured goods exporters	Austria; Belgium; Brazil; Canada; China; Czech Republic; Denmark; Finland; France; Germany; Great Britain; Hong Kong, China; Hungary; India; Indonesia; Ireland; Israel; Italy; Japan; Korea; Malaysia; Mexico; Netherlands; Philippines; Poland; Portugal; Singapore; Slovak Republic; South Africa; Spain; Sweden; Switzerland; Thailand; Turkey; Ukraine; United States; Vietnam
Machinery and transport equipment exporters	Austria; Brazil; Canada; China; Czech Republic; Denmark; Finland; France; Germany; Great Britain; Hong Kong, China; Hungary; Israel; Japan; Korea; Malaysia; Mexico; Netherlands; Philippines; Poland; Singapore; Slovak Republic; South Africa; Spain; Sweden; Thailand; United States
Other manufactured goods exporters	India, Indonesia, Italy, Portugal, Switzerland, Turkey, Ukraine, Vietnam

Clusters by export specialization (export product)	
Metalliferous ores and metal scrap exporters	Australia, Brazil, Chile
Coal, coke, and briquettes exporters	Australia, Indonesia, South Africa
Petroleum, petroleum products, and related materials exporters	Algeria, Argentina, Canada, Denmark, Great Britain, India, Indonesia, Islamic Republic of Iran, Korea, Kuwait, Malaysia, Mexico, Netherlands, Nigeria, Norway, Russia, Saudi Arabia, Singapore, Slovak Republic, Ukraine, United Arab Emirates, República Bolivariana de Venezuela, Vietnam
Gas, natural and manufactured, exporters	Algeria, Canada, Indonesia, Norway, Russia
Medicinal and pharmaceutical products exporters	Belgium, Czech Republic, Denmark, Great Britain, Ireland, Israel, Sweden
Office machines and automatic data-processing machines exporters	China; Czech Republic; Hong Kong, China; Hungary; Ireland; Malaysia; Netherlands; Philippines; Singapore; Thailand
Telecommunications and sound-recording and reproducing apparatus and equipment exporters	China; Finland; Great Britain; Hong Kong, China; Hungary; Israel; Korea; Malaysia; Mexico; Singapore; Slovak Republic; Sweden
Electrical machinery, apparatus and appliances, n.e.s., and electrical parts thereof exporters	Hong Kong, China; Japan; Korea; Malaysia; Philippines; Singapore; Thailand; United States
Road vehicles (including air-cushion vehicles) exporters	Austria, Belgium, Canada, Czech Republic, France, Germany, Great Britain, Italy, Japan, Korea, Mexico, Poland, Portugal, Slovak Republic, South Africa, Spain, Sweden
Other transport equipment exporters	France, Korea, United States
Clusters by region	
Latin America	Argentina, Brazil, Chile, Mexico, República Bolivariana de Venezuela
Emerging Asia	China; Hong-Kong, China; India; Indonesia; Korea; Malaysia; Philippines; Singapore; Thailand
New EU member states	Czech Republic, Hungary, Poland, Slovak Republic
Middle East	Islamic Republic of Iran, Israel, Kuwait, Saudi Arabia, United Arab Emirates
G-7 countries	Canada, France, Germany, Great Britain, Italy, Japan, United States
Western European countries	Denmark, Finland, France, Germany, Great Britain, Ireland, Italy, Netherlands, Norway, Portugal, Spain, Sweden

Source: Classification based on authors' calculations and UNCTAD (2008).
Note: The table provides information on the countries included in each cluster.

Figure 3A.1 GDP Elasticity of Imports: Export Specialization (Main Product)

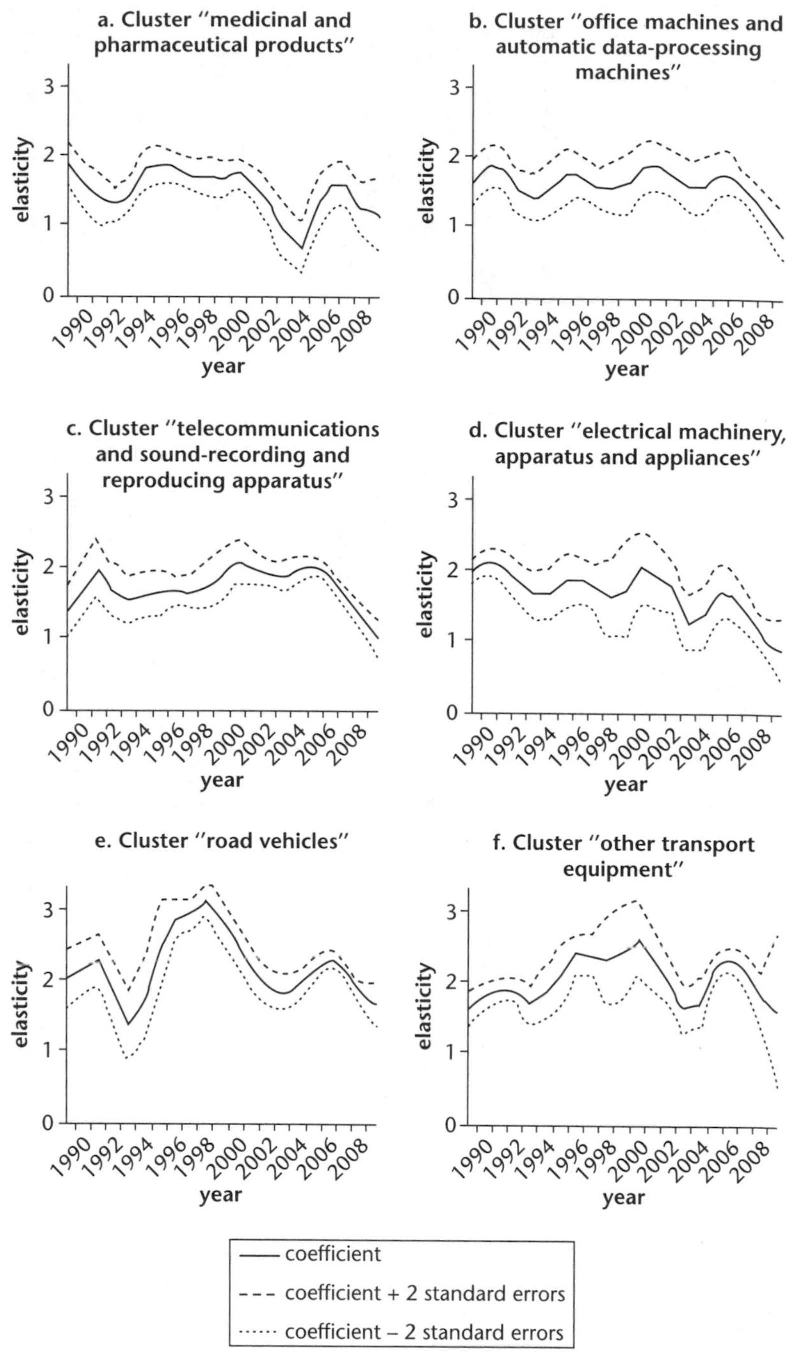

Figure 3A.1 *continued*

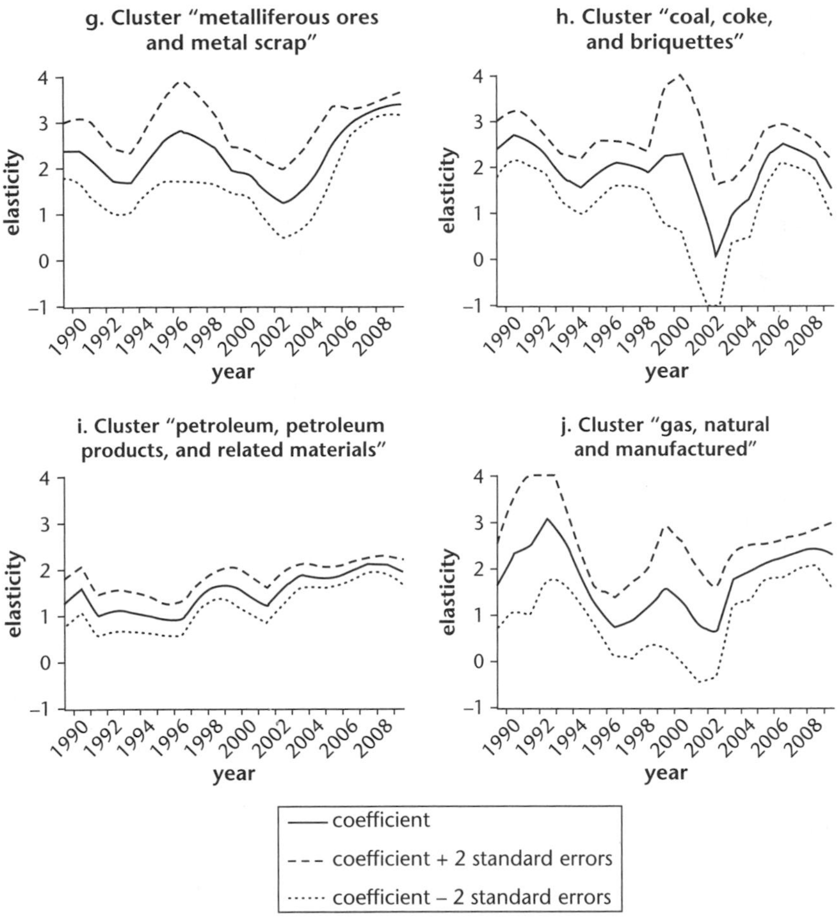

Source: Authors' calculations. See text for data description.
Note: Country clusters were constructed using the "export structure by product" as compiled by UNCTAD (2008, table 3.2D [2005–06]. For each of the 49 countries, all export products with a share among the country's exports of 5 percent or higher were extracted (if no product exceeds 5 percent, the most important product is used). These export groups are classified on a SITC Rev.3 3-digit basis. Then, clusters of countries were constructed with the same export products on a 2-digit basis (in order to have clusters with a significant number of countries); the analysis was conducted with those clusters that make up at least three countries. The analysis was conducted with the following export-product-country groups: Metalliferous ores and metal scrap exporters; coal, coke, and briquettes exporters; petroleum, petroleum products, and related materials exporters; natural and manufactured gas exporters; medicinal and pharmaceutical products exporters; office machines and automatic data-processing machines exporters; telecommunications and sound-recording and reproducing apparatus and equipment exporters; electrical machinery, apparatus, and appliances, n.e.s., and electrical parts thereof exporters; road vehicles (including air-cushion vehicles) exporters; and other transport equipment exporters.

Table 3A.3 Predicted Change in Imports and Observed Values

	Observed change in imports (percent)			Model 1 (no *VS* variable)						Model 2 (with vertical specialization)					
				Predicted change (percent)			Difference in percentage points			Predicted change (percent)			Difference in percentage points		
Country	2008:Q4	2009:Q1	2009:Q2	2008:Q4	2009:Q1	2009:Q2	2008:Q4	2009:Q1	2009:Q2	2008:Q4	2009:Q1	2009:Q2	2008:Q4	2009:Q1	2009:Q2
Australia	–8.2	–7.9	2.1	–2.1	0.5	2.0	–6.1	–8.5	0.1	–2.3	–0.5	0.4	–5.9	–7.5	1.7
Austria	–4.2	–5.8	–2.4	–2.7	–5.4	–1.6	–1.5	–0.4	–0.8	–3.0	–5.6	–2.2	–1.3	–0.2	–0.2
Belgium	–8.6	–5.8	–1.2	–6.1	–3.9	1.0	–2.6	–1.9	–2.2	–6.2	–3.9	0.9	–2.4	–1.9	–2.0
Canada	–6.7	–12.5	–1.8	–5.0	–6.1	–1.4	–1.6	–6.3	–0.4	–4.7	–5.6	–0.1	–2.0	–6.8	–1.7
Czech Republic	–6.0	–8.3	–1.4	–0.2	–4.6	1.0	–5.8	–3.7	–2.3	–0.4	–4.0	4.3	–5.6	–4.3	–5.7
Denmark	–3.2	–8.2	–4.0	–3.9	–3.6	–4.7	0.6	–4.7	0.7	–4.0	–3.7	–3.7	0.8	–4.5	–0.3
Finland	–7.4	–18.7	–4.6	–11.3	–13.8	1.0	4.0	–4.9	–5.6	–10.5	–14.8	–2.2	3.1	–3.9	–2.4
France	–3.3	–6.2	–2.7	–4.7	–4.4	0.7	1.4	–1.8	–3.4	–4.9	–5.1	–0.2	1.5	–1.1	–2.4
Germany	–4.3	–5.8	–5.6	–2.9	–5.1	–0.3	–1.4	–0.7	–5.2	–3.1	–5.0	–0.2	–1.1	–0.8	–5.4
Greece	2.3	–14.4	–2.9	–2.8	–2.6	–1.3	5.1	–11.8	–1.6	–3.9	–5.4	–2.3	6.3	–9.0	–0.6
Hungary	–9.1	–9.5	–2.2	–6.2	–7.9	–5.9	–2.9	–1.6	3.6	–6.2	–8.4	–6.3	–2.9	–1.1	4.1
Ireland	–4.5	–3.1	1.0	–1.6	–0.4	0.6	–2.9	–2.7	0.4	–3.0	–3.4	–3.1	–1.5	0.3	4.1
Italy	–5.9	–9.4	–3.1	–5.4	–7.2	–0.7	–0.5	–2.2	–2.3	–5.9	–7.9	–2.1	0.0	–1.6	–1.0
Japan	–1.6	–16.2	–3.5	–5.7	–8.6	1.5	4.1	–7.6	–4.9	–6.1	–9.6	–0.2	4.5	–6.7	–3.3
Korea, Rep. of	–15.3	–8.7	8.4	–16.7	–0.8	7.8	1.4	–7.9	0.7	—	—	—	—	—	—
Luxembourg	–8.9	–9.0	–0.8	–2.6	–0.5	2.5	–6.3	–8.5	–3.3	–3.3	–0.7	2.7	–5.6	–8.2	–3.5
Mexico	–12.7	–13.2	–6.2	–6.2	–15.7	–0.5	–6.5	2.5	–5.7	—	—	—	—	—	—
Netherlands	–3.8	–5.6	–2.3	–1.9	–4.2	–1.1	–1.9	–1.4	–1.1	–2.0	–4.3	–1.2	–1.9	–1.3	–1.0
New Zealand	–7.0	–8.6	–3.8	–2.0	–0.3	3.0	–5.0	–8.4	–6.9	–5.4	–4.3	–1.8	–1.6	–4.3	–2.0
Norway	–6.0	–8.1	1.5	–1.1	–0.6	0.4	–4.9	–7.5	1.0	–1.0	–0.3	0.8	–5.0	–7.8	0.6
Poland	–7.9	–7.0	–6.1	–3.2	–0.4	2.7	–4.7	–6.6	–8.9	–3.6	–0.7	2.5	–4.3	–6.3	–8.6
Portugal	–6.7	–8.1	–2.2	–4.8	–4.9	1.1	–1.8	–3.2	–3.3	–4.7	–4.6	1.1	–2.0	–3.5	–3.3
Slovak Republic	–4.6	–15.5	–1.1	0.1	–8.0	0.7	–4.7	–7.5	–1.8	–0.2	–7.8	1.9	–4.3	–7.7	–3.1
Spain	–6.5	–11.8	–2.4	–7.3	–9.3	–3.0	0.8	–2.5	0.6	–7.5	–9.2	–2.3	1.0	–2.5	–0.1
Sweden	–3.1	–12.8	–0.9	–5.8	–2.3	0.9	2.7	–10.5	–1.9	–5.8	–2.3	1.0	2.7	–10.5	–1.9
Switzerland	–4.6	–1.6	–4.2	–1.8	–2.0	–0.2	–2.8	0.4	–3.9	—	—	—	—	—	—
Turkey	–18.7	–7.6	3.1	–11.8	–7.4	8.5	–6.8	–0.1	–5.4	–11.7	–7.3	8.6	–6.9	–0.3	–5.6
United Kingdom	–5.6	–7.3	–2.2	–5.3	–7.2	–0.7	–0.3	–0.1	–1.5	–5.1	–7.0	–1.7	–0.6	–0.2	–0.5
United States	–4.6	–11.3	–4.0	–4.2	–4.8	–0.7	–0.4	–6.6	–3.3	–4.5	–6.0	–1.9	–0.1	–5.3	–2.1

Source: Authors' calculations.

Note: Estimates are from the error correction model. — = not available.

Notes

1. In 1989 the fall of the Berlin Wall brought down the barriers that had split the post–World War II world; the year is remembered for the Brady Bonds, that is, US-dollar-denominated bonds issued by emerging markets that were used as an instrument of debt reduction, which put an end to the decade-long debt crisis that plagued many developing countries. In a continuation, the 1990s saw the conclusion of the Uruguay Round, that is, the eighth round of multilateral trade negotiations of the General Agreement on Tariffs and Trade (GATT) (1986–94), and the birth of the World Trade Organization, which brought down many trade barriers and led to further liberalization in areas like telecommunications, financial services, and information technologies.

2. Incidentally, by helping U.S. firms improve their productivity, global manufacturing contributed significantly to the low-interest-rate policy that paved the ground for the financial bubble that burst in 2008. Thanks to higher domestic productivity, the potential output in manufacturing increased in line with actual production. The gains in total factor productivity sustained a long period of higher activity without creating the inflationary pressures that would have forced a change in the lenient monetary policy.

3. The data supporting the regression are obtained from the International Monetary Fund (IMF) *World Economic Outlook* (*WEO*) 2009. World GDP weighted at market exchange rates is constructed by combining World GDP at 2000 prices from the World Development Indicators (WDI) database (World Bank) with GDP growth rates (market exchange rate) from the *WEO* 2009. World GDP is usually weighted with purchasing power parity (PPP), which, however, is inadequate when investigating demand on international markets (that is, GDP–trade elasticity). The sample comprises annual data between 1980 and 2009.

4. According to Ricardo's theory, the pattern of trade between countries is explained by their comparative advantages in producing the traded goods. A country has a comparative advantage in producing a particular good if the opportunity cost of producing that good is lower in that country than in other countries. The Ricardian theory did not consider that the production of the final good itself could be fragmented among different countries (see WTO 2008a for a discussion of the model and its extensions).

5. Although service offshoring has been rising significantly in recent years, it still accounts for only a small fraction of total offshoring; see OECD (2008) for an overview.

6. Information about some aspects of the production process is missing, and there are generally only few product details provided. More generally, it is empirically difficult to disentangle the role of outsourcing on productivity from other concomitant enhancing factors such as investment in IT or changes in business practices.

7. An update in 2005 for 40 countries is provided in Miroudot and Ragoussis (2009). An alternative methodology based on international input-output tables can be found in Inomata (2008).

8. This study used a seven sectors aggregation for 1990, 1995, 2000, and 2008 matrices. The data for 2008 are estimates; other years are derived from national accounts and countries' official statistics. For a presentation and evaluation, see IDE-Jetro (2006); Oosterhaven, Stelder, and Inomata (2007); and Inomata and Uchida (2009).

9. Differences between imports and exports are due to the rest of the world (ROW). Within an international I-O, trade among the 10 countries covered by the input-output matrix is symmetric (bilateral exports within the matrix should equal bilateral imports); however, this symmetry is not necessarily respected when considering trade with the ROW (all other countries) as exports from the 10 countries to ROW can differ from their imports from ROW.

10. Obviously, this strategy of diversifying into manufacture allows the developing countries to increase labor productivity and generate more income per capita. Thus, richer countries are not defined by the intensity of the creation of value-added, but by its extension.

11. The data for 2008 tend to indicate a reduction in the reliance on imported inputs. Yet, because the 2008 data are based on estimates rather than official national account statistics, this result should be understood with caution.

12. Analyzing the supply shocks from the quantity space would pose a series of methodological issues (Escaith and Gonguet 2009). Notation uses macroeconomic practices and differs from usual I-O conventions.

13. The model can be extended easily to the case of *n* countries by modifying matrix A, extending the I-O relationship to include intersectoral international transactions of intermediate goods, and adapting the summation vector *u*.

14. In this traditional I-O framework considering one country and the rest of the world, exports of intermediate goods are considered part of the final demand. The situation differs when extending the I-O relationship to include international transactions of intermediate consumptions, as in equation 3.4.

15. Using a slightly different approach, the authors conclude that "the growth rate of imports of domestic goods is the same as that of domestic GDP. . . . When the trend of globalization is correctly accounted for, the income elasticity of imports is generally close to unity" (Bénassy-Quéré et al. 2009, 15). Exploring the potential impact of the 2008–09 downturn using a CGE model, using appropriate benchmarks for trade and GDP, the authors do not find any multiplier effect on trade.

16. "Steady state" is used here in a loose sense of structurally stable dynamics; we are aware that the coexistence of such a Walrasian concept with the Keyenesian model of Leontief is particularly unnatural. Despite the conceptual contradiction, it is better suited to the CGE approach used by most contemporary trade analysts.

17. The more complex the production process, the more are potential gains in outsourcing a part of it; thus, it is usual to expect much more vertical integration in the manufacturing sector. Miroudot and Ragoussis (2009) show that manufacturing sectors in OECD countries generally use more imported inputs than other industrial and services sectors. It is especially the case for final consumer goods, such as motor vehicles; radio, TV, and communication equipment; or computers. As expected, services are less vertically integrated into the world economy. But even these activities show an upward trend in the use of imported services inputs (for example, business services).

18. Taiwan, China, is excluded due to lack of available data. Thus, we analyze the remaining 49 economies of the group of the 50 leading exporters in world merchandise trade in 2007, namely, Algeria; Argentina; Australia; Austria; Belgium; Brazil; Canada; Chile; China; Czech Republic; Denmark; Finland; France; Germany; Hong Kong, China; Hungary; India; Indonesia; Islamic Republic of Iran; Ireland; Israel; Italy; Japan; Republic of Korea; Kuwait; Malaysia; Mexico; Netherlands; Nigeria; Norway; Philippines; Poland; Portugal; Russian Federation; Saudi Arabia; Singapore; Slovak Republic; South Africa; Spain; Sweden; Switzerland; Thailand; Turkey; Ukraine; United Arab Emirates; United Kingdom; United States; República Bolivariana de Venezuela; and Vietnam.

19. The 1980–91 data for GDP and imports for Russia and the Ukraine are missing in WEO2009. These missing values are replaced with the corresponding values from *WEO* 2008. As all GDP values of Russia in *WEO* 2009 were multiplied with 1.1362 (in comparison to the *WEO* 2008), the added values were also multiplied with the same factor.

20. It is important to note that contrary to the world aggregate, where countries are weighted by their GDP, all countries have the same weight in the following clusters. Thus, comparison with the results of Figure 3.2 is somehow biased.

21. The actual number of clusters (see annex tables 3A.1 and 3A.2) is smaller, as no country pertains to clusters 4, 5, or 6, which have in common that the elasticity from sample 1 to sample 3 remains stable. Cluster 9 (decrease, with the second elasticity beneath the first and the third elasticity) is omitted, as only one country falls in this category.

22. The main export activities are from table 3.1, titled "Country Trade Structure by Product Group," in UNCTAD (2008).

23. The following three product groups were not considered in the analysis, because they each comprise fewer than three countries: all food items, agricultural raw materials, and chemical products.

24. Yet another way of clustering the countries—by export specialization, using the main export products of each country—does not change the result qualitatively either: the hypothesis of an impact

of the global supply chains on the changes in GDP elasticity of imports still cannot be confirmed by our explorative data analysis. The results of this robustness check can be found in annex figure 3A.1.

25. Year-to-year change, volumes in US dollars (fixed PPPs, OECD reference year), seasonally adjusted. Market exchange rates are used for the OECD aggregation.

26. As mentioned, we use "steady state" in the very limited sense of "long-term outcome"; the trade patterns that emerged in the 2000s witnessed the accumulation of large macroeconomic imbalances, and these patterns were not sustainable.

27. Cheung and Guichard (2009) suggest that the way vertical specialization affects trade is by raising its elasticity with respect to income.

28. Data are from Miroudot and Ragoussis (2009). Time-series have been created over the period 1995–2009 with three data points (1995, 2000, and 2005 for most countries). Because data are interpolated and extrapolated, there is no guarantee that the variable accurately reflects the variation over time of the vertical specialization share. The assumption is that this share is relatively stable over years and that the trend suggested by the three data points is enough to account for its evolution.

References

Agnese, P., and J. E. Ricart. 2009. "Offshoring: Facts and Numbers at the Country Level." Working paper, IESE Business School, Universidad de Navarra, Barcelona, Spain.

Alessandria, G., J. Kaboski, and V. Midrigan. Forthcoming. "Inventories, Lumpy Trade, and Large Devaluations." *American Economic Review.*

Antràs, P., and E. Helpman. 2004. "Global Sourcing." *Journal of Political Economy* 112 (3): 552–80.

Baldwin, R., ed. 2009. *The Great Trade Collapse: Causes, Consequences and Prospects.* Centre for Economic Policy Research (CEPR) for VoxEU.org. CEPR, The Graduate Institute, Geneva.

Baldwin, R. 2006. "Globalisation: The Great Unbundling(s)." Study for Economic Council of Finland, 20 September. Graduate Institute of International Studies, Geneva.

Bénassy-Quéré, A., Y. Decreux, L. Fontagné, and D. Khoudour-Casteras. 2009. "Economic Crisis and Global Supply Chains." Document de Travail 2009-15, Centre d'Etudes Prospectives et d'Informations Internationales (CEPII). Paris.

Bergin, P. R., R. C. Feenstra, and G. H. Hanson. 2009. "Offshoring and Volatility: Evidence from Mexico's Maquiladora Industry." *American Economic Review* 99 (4): 1664–71.

Borchert, I., and A. Mattoo. 2009. "The Crisis-Resilience of Services Trade." Policy Research Working Paper Series 4917, World Bank, Washington, DC.

Chen, Y., J. Ishikawa, and Z. Yu. 2004. "Trade Liberalization and Strategic Outsourcing." *Journal of International Economics* 63 (2): 419–36.

Cheung, C., and S. Guichard. 2009. "Understanding the World Trade Collapse." OECD Economics Department Working Papers 729, Organisation for Economic Co-operation and Development, Paris.

Coucke, K., and L. Sleuwaegen. 2008. "Offshoring as a Survival Strategy: Evidence from Manufacturing Firms in Belgium." *Journal of International Business Studies* 39 (8): 1261–77.

Daudin, G., C. Rifflart, and D. Schweisguth. 2009. "Who Produces for Whom in the World Economy?" Documents de Travail de l'OFCE 2009-18, Observatoire Francais des Conjonctures Economiques (OFCE), Paris.

Du, J., Y. Lu, and Z. Tao. 2009. "Bi-sourcing in the Global Economy." *Journal of International Economics* 77 (2): 215–22.

Dvorak, P. 2009. "Clarity Is Missing in Supply Chain" *Wall Street Journal*, May 18.

Eichengreen, B., and K. H. O'Rourke. 2009. "A Tale of Two Depressions." VoxEU.org, updated March 18, 2010. http://www.voxeu.org/index.php?q=node/3421.

Escaith, H., and F. Gonguet. 2009. "International Trade and Real Transmission Channels of Financial Shocks in Globalized Production Networks." WTO Working Paper ERSD-2009-06, May. World Trade Organziation, Geneva.

Feenstra, R. C. 1998. "Integration of Trade and Disintegration of Production in the Global Economy." *Journal of Economic Perspectives* 12 (4): 31–50.

Freund, C. 2009. "The Trade Response to Global Downturns: Historical Evidence." Policy Research Working Paper Series 5015, World Bank, Washington, DC.

Grossman, G. M., and E. Helpman. 2002. "Integration Versus Outsourcing in Industry Equilibrium." *The Quarterly Journal of Economics* 117 (1): 85–120.

———. 2005. "Outsourcing in a Global Economy." *Review of Economic Studies* 72 (1): 135–59.

Grossman, G. M., and E. Rossi-Hansberg. 2008. "Trading Tasks: A Simple Theory of Offshoring." *American Economic Review* 98 (5): 1978–97.

Hanson, G. H., R. J. Mataloni, and M. J. Slaughter. 2005. "Vertical Production Networks in Multinational Firms." *The Review of Economics and Statistics* 87 (4): 664–78.

Harms, P., O. Lorz, and D. M. Urban. 2009. "Offshoring along the Production Chain." CESifo Working Paper Series 2564, CESifo Group, Munich.

Harvey, A. C. 1987. "Applications of the Kalman Filter in Econometrics." In *Advances in Econometrics: Fifth World Congress*, Vol. 1, ed. T. F. Bewley, 285–313. Cambridge, UK: Cambridge University Press.

Helpman, E. 2006. "Trade, FDI, and the Organization of Firms." *Journal of Economic Literature* 44 (3): 589–630.

Hicks, J. R. 1973. *Capital and Time: A Neo-Austrian Theory*. New York: Oxford University Press.

Hummels, D., J. Ishii, and K.-M. Yi. 2001. "The Nature and Growth of Vertical Specialization in World Trade." *Journal of International Economics* 54 (1): 75–96.

IDE-JETRO 2006. "How to Make Asian Input-Output Tables." Institute of Developing Economies, Japan External Trade Organization (IDE-JETRO), Tokyo.

Inomata, S. 2008. "A New Measurement for International Fragmentation of the Production Process: An International Input-Output Approach." IDE Discussion Papers 175, Institute of Developing Economies, Japan External Trade Organization (IDE-JETRO), Tokyo.

Inomata, S., and Y. Uchida, eds. 2009. *Asia beyond the Crisis: Visions from International Input-Output Analyses.* IDE Spot Survey 31, Institute of Developing Economies, Japan External Trade Organization (IDE-JETRO), Tokyo.

International Monetary Fund (IMF). 2008. *World Economic Outlook.* Washington, DC: IMF.

———. 2009. *World Economic Outlook.* Washington, DC: IMF.

Jacks, D. S., C. M. Meissner, and D. Novy. 2008. "Trade Costs, 1870–2000." *American Economic Review* 98 (2): 529–34.

Johnson, R. C., and G. Noguera. 2009. "Accounting for Intermediates: Production Sharing and Trade in Value Added." Manuscript, Dartmouth College, Hanover, NH; available at http://sites.google.com/site/robjohnson41/research.

Jones, R. W., and H. Kierzkowski. 1990. "The Role of Services in Production and International Trade: A Theoretical Framework." Oxford and Cambridge, Mass. RCER Working Papers, University of Rochester, Center for Economic Research (RCER), Rochester, NY.

Kerschbamer, R., and Y. Tournas. 2003. "In-house Competition, Organizational Slack, and the Business Cycle." *European Economic Review* 47 (3): 505–20.

Koopman, R., Z. Wang, and S.-J. Wei. 2008. "How Much of Chinese Exports Is Really Made in China? Assessing Domestic Value-Added When Processing Trade Is Pervasive." NBER Working Paper 14109, National Bureau of Economic Research, Cambridge, MA.

Krugman, P. 1995. "Growing World Trade: Causes and Consequences." *Brookings Papers on Economic Activity* 26 (1): 327–77.

Lanz, R., S. Miroudot, and A. Ragoussis. 2009. "Trade in Intermediate Goods and Services." OECD Trade Policy Working Paper 93, Trade and Agriculture Directorate, Organisation for Economic Co-operation and Development, Paris.

Linden, G., K. Kramer, and J. Dedrick. 2007. "Who Captures Value in a Global Innovation System? The Case of Apple's iPod." Personal Computing Industry Center, University of California, Irvine. http://www.escholarship.org/uc/item/1770046n.

Mankiw, N. G., and P. Swagel. 2006. "The Politics and Economics of Offshore Outsourcing." *Journal of Monetary Economics* 53 (5): 1027–56.

McKibbin, W. J., and A. Stoeckel. 2009. "The Potential Impact of the Global Financial Crisis on World Trade." Policy Research Working Paper Series 5134, World Bank, Washington, DC.

Miroudot, S., and A. Ragoussis. 2009. "Vertical Trade, Trade Costs and FDI." OECD Trade Policy Working Papers 89, Trade and Agriculture Directorate, Organisation for Economic Co-operation and Development, Paris.

Mitra, D., and P. Ranjan. 2008. "Temporary Shocks and Offshoring: The Role of External Economies and Firm Heterogeneity." *Journal of Development Economics* 87 (1): 76–84.

Nordås, H. K. 2005. "International Production Sharing: A Case for a Coherent Policy Framework." WTO Discussion Papers 11, World Trade Organization, Geneva.

Nordås, H. K., E. Pinali, and M. G. Grosso. 2006. "Logistics and Time as a Trade Barrier." OECD Trade Policy Working Papers 35, Trade and Agriculture Directorate, Organisation for Economic Co-operation and Development, Paris.

OECD. 2008. "Staying Competitive in the Global Economy—Compendium of Studies on Global Value Chains." OECD Publishing, Organisation for Economic Co-operation and Development, Paris.

Oosterhaven, J., D. Stelder, and S. Inomata. 2007. "Evaluation of Non-Survey International IO Construction Methods with the Asian-Pacific Input-Output Table." IDE Discussion Paper 114. July. Institute of Developing Economies, Japan External Trade Organization (IDE-JETRO), Tokyo.

Ornelas, E., and J. L.Turner. 2008. "Trade Liberalization, Outsourcing, and the Hold-Up Problem." *Journal of International Economics* 74 (1): 225–41.

Ostrovsky, M. 2008. "Stability in Supply Chain Networks." *American Economic Review* 98 (3): 897–923.

Paul, D. L., and R. B. Wooster. Forthcoming. "An Empirical Analysis of Motives for Offshore Outsourcing by U.S. Firms." *International Trade Journal.*

Ricardo, David. 1821. *On the Principles of Political Economy and Taxation.* London: John Murray.

Şener, F., and L. Zhao. 2009. "Globalization, R&D and the iPod Cycle." *Journal of International Economics* 77 (1): 101–08.

Smith, D. 2006. "Offshoring: Political Myths and Economic Reality." *World Economy* 29 (3): 249–56.

Stadtler, H. 2008. "Supply Chain Management—An Overview." In *Supply Chain Management and Advanced Planning*, 4th ed., ed. Hartmut Stadtler and Christoph Kigler. Berlin: Springer-Verlag.

Sturgeon, T., and G. Gereffi. 2009. "Measuring Success in the Global Economy: International Trade, Industrial Upgrading, and Business Function Outsourcing in Global Value Chains." *Transnational Corporations* 18 (2): 1–36.

Tanaka, K. 2009. "Trade Collapse and International Supply Chains: Evidence from Japan." May 7. VoxEU.org.

Uchida, Y., and S. Inomata. 2009. "Vertical Specialization in the Time of the Economic Crisis." In *Asia beyond the Crisis,* ed. S. Inomata and Y. Uchida, 70–83. Tokyo: Institute of Developing Economies, Japan External Trade Organization (IDE-JETRO).

UNCTAD (United Nations Conference on Trade and Development). 2008. *UNCTAD Handbook of Statistics 2008.* Geneva: United Nations Commission on Trade and Development, Geneva.

WTO (World Trade Organization). 2008a. *World Trade Report 2008.* Geneva: World Trade Organization.

———. 2008b. *International Trade Statistics 2008.* Geneva: World Trade Organization.

———. 2009. *International Trade Statistics 2009.* Geneva: World Trade Organization.

Yi, K.-M. 2003. "Can Vertical Specialization Explain the Growth of World Trade?" *Journal of Political Economy* 111 (1): 52–102.

———. 2009. "The Collapse of Global Trade: The Role of Vertical Specialisation." In *The Collapse of Global Trade, Murky Protectionism, and the Crisis: Recommendations for the G20R,* ed. R. Baldwin and S. Evenett, 45–48. VoxEU publication.

4

GLOBAL VALUE CHAINS, THE CRISIS, AND THE SHIFT OF MARKETS FROM NORTH TO SOUTH

Raphael Kaplinsky and Masuma Farooki

The first decade of the 21st century arguably marks a significant structural shift in the global economy. Since the early 19th century, the historic dominance of China and India as contributors to global output was increasingly undermined by the rapid deepening of industrialization, initially in England, then spreading to western and northern Europe, North America, Japan, and the newly industrializing economies in Southeast Asia. The latter phase of this dominance of the global economy by predominantly "northern" economies was marked by deepening globalization with an increasing number of producers in low-income economies participating in global value chains (GVCs) involving the increasing fragmentation of production and specialization of tasks. This latter period was also characterized by the accelerated growth of the financial sector.

Since the mid-1980s, this historical trajectory of northern dominance began to wane, driven by two sets of interrelated developments. The first was the very rapid growth of productive capabilities in the two large Asian Driver economies, China and India (http://asiandrivers.open.ac.uk/). The second was the growth of structural weaknesses in many of the key previously dominant northern economies, which resulted in a major financial meltdown in 2008 in most of the major northern economies, with an accompanying fall in global output (especially from those economies). If sustained, these two trends will have a major impact on the location of production and consumption in the global economy in the 21st century.

But what impact will this potential change in global growth trajectories have on low-income producers participating in global value chains?

To address this question, this chapter focuses on two sets of issues. The first concerns the nature of the structural imbalances in the global economy, which leads to the assumption that there will be a decisive shift in the dominance of production and consumption from Europe, North America, and Japan to China and India in the coming decades. Working on this presumption, the second issue relates to the patterns of demand in southern drivers of growth. The analysis examines the distinctive nature of consumption in the Asian Driver economies and considers the likely impact this will have for southern producers who participate in the GVCs that feed into southern, as opposed to northern, final markets. Before undertaking these two sets of analyses, the importance of focusing on demand in the evolution of GVCs is explained. The final section reviews the main implications of these potential shifts for the participation of low-income countries in GVCs.

Buyers, Markets, and Global Value Chains

Until the late 1950s, economic growth was largely explained by the quantum of available labor, investment, and land, and growth was assumed to occur at the extensive margin, that is, through the application of more resources to production. High savings-investment rates were at the center of the Harrod-Domar family of growth models that informed development policy in the immediate post-war period. However, the "discovery" by Solow in the 1950s that an increase in the volume of productive inputs accounted for only around 87.5 percent of economic growth in the United States increasingly shifted the focus of attention in growth models from the extensive to the intensive margin (Solow 1957). The improvement in the quality of productive inputs has thus risen to center stage.

The emphasis on both the extensive and intensive margins reflects a preoccupation in growth theory and development policy with factors determining the augmentation of supply. However, in recent years, there has been an increasing awareness of the role that demand plays in economic growth and its derived impact on the growth of supply capabilities.

A key demand-related factor affecting economic growth is the size and rate of market growth. Rapidly expanding and large markets both spur productivity growth by allowing for scale economies in production and send a signal to producers that they can have confidence in investing for the future. This trend leads to a virtuous circle of growth and innovation and is particularly influential in the context of very large domestic markets or when producers sell into global markets.

However, it is not just the *volume* and rate of demand growth that affects productivity and capabilities. The *nature* of demand also has a significant impact on capabilities as well as on the returns to alternative patterns of production. Around the late 1960s, there was an important transition in final markets in the northern economies (Piore and Sabel 1984). Once post–World War II reconstruction had been achieved and basic needs of most consumers had been met, consumers became increasingly discerning about the products they consumed. They demanded higher levels of quality, much greater product differentiation, and faster rates of product innovation. In the context of this change in the pattern of demand, the ideal archetype in production organization moved from mass production to mass customization (Pine 1993), in which producers developed the capabilities to meet different critical success factors (CSFs) in proliferating and dynamic market segments. Variety and flexibility—with little tradeoff in costs—became the name of the game in competitive production.

A direct consequence of this search for low-cost flexibility was a transition in production organization, from "just-in-case" mass production to "just-in-time" lean production (Kaplinsky 1994; Womack and Jones 1996). A series of related changes in quality assurance procedures (with "zero-defects" becoming an essential building block of just-in-time production) and reduced batch size, coupled with the drive by firms to concentrate on their core competencies, meant that lead firms were required to take responsibility for the systemic efficiency of their increasingly global value chains (Gereffi 1994). One important component of the toolbox this entailed was the development of standards in production, often usefully summarized as "QCD." The Q stood for standards over quality (increasingly measured in parts per million), the C for cost (annual reductions in price paid to suppliers), and D for delivery (more frequent deliveries in smaller batches).

Most of these standards were firm specific. But in some cases, industry-specific standards were also developed as the outcome of collaboration between private sector firms searching for competitive advantage. Increasingly, too, standards were introduced to foster the capabilities of suppliers to meet the new requirements of lean production, notably the cross-sector ISO9000 quality procedures, and subsequently ISO14000 environmental standards. The development and extension of these process standards began in the Japanese auto industry in the 1960s, then gradually spread to the global electronics sector, and then more widely and rapidly to many sectors in subsequent decades. By the end of the 20th century, these private sector standards had become an integral component in most GVCs that fed production into global markets, particularly for intermediate and final consumption goods characterized by variety.

A further development of standards reflected a different process, one in which the key drivers were final consumers and the state concerned with consumer welfare, rather than private sector firms searching for competitive advantage. In some cases, standards were set by governments to promote product safety, particularly in the food sector. However, increasingly, consumers' organizations became concerned with the processes involved in producing products to meet their needs, requiring fair returns to producers (Fair Trade) and organic certification. Table 4.1 summarizes the growing complexity of these standards, covering both product and process and involving various types of codification, including both private and public sectors.

How have the producers that find themselves inserted into GVCs been informed about the growing prevalence and nature of these evolving standards? Where the supply function has been internalized within a diversified firm, it has been the firm that has driven the standards through its subsidiaries. And to the extent that the large firm has focused on the systemic efficiency of its value chain (as, for example, in the Japanese auto industry during the 1980s; see Cusumano 1985), it has driven standards to its suppliers through supply chain management procedures, usually informing suppliers of the standards they are required to achieve, and in some cases also assisting them to achieve those standards (Bessant, Kaplinsky, and Lamming 2003). But in a growing number of GVCs, suppliers have often been left to make their own way in identifying the core relevant standards, as well as in establishing the procedures required to meet those standards. It is in these sectors that global buyers have come to play an important role. By defining the role played by individual parties in the chain, the buyers can also block the upgrading paths of producers.

If we relate these functions performed by global buyers to the challenge of capability building, the story becomes a little more complicated. Understanding these complexities requires that the term "upgrading," implicit in the concept of "capabilities," is explained. Arising out of the GVC approach is an augmentation of the understanding in the innovation literature that has historically been predominantly focused on process upgrading, with an ancillary focus on

Table 4.1 Drivers of Standards over Process and Product, by Firms, Governments, and Civil Society

Standard	Firms	Governments	Civil society
Product	Quality standards such as permitted parts per million defects	Food hygiene standards Lead content in toys	Organic products
Process	Quality control procedures, such as ISO9000	Hygiene standards, such as Hazard Analysis and Critical Control Point conformance (HACCP)	Sustainability standards, such as FSC (Forest Stewardship Council) (timber)
	Frequency of on-time delivery	Traceability of pesticide content	Child labor standards

Source: Authors.

product upgrading. The GVC framework recognizes the centrality of dynamic rents to the global fragmentation and relocation of economic activity (Kaplinsky 2005). It distinguishes four types of upgrading activity (Humphrey and Schmitz 2001). The first two are familiar to the innovation literature: the upgrading of process and product. The third is central to the GVC approach, referring to the upgrading of function. That is, firms may change their positioning in the chain, perhaps moving from physical transformation to design or marketing. Often, as in table 4.2, there is a hierarchy in the process of upgrading as firms move from assembly and manufacturing transformation to design and branding (or often a combination of these functions). In mature chains, when firms have developed capabilities, they may also upgrade by moving to a new chain.

The reason these categories of upgrading are important is that the buyers, who play a key role in informing suppliers of market requirements, have their own interests to protect, thus will generally limit the upgrading path of their suppliers. Buyers naturally are focused on protecting their own rents in the chain and will therefore "guide," and often limit through contractual conditions, the upgrading path of suppliers. The nature of these constraints on upgrading will depend on the particular competencies of the buyers. For example, in the furniture global value chain, large global buyers such as Ikea will allow, and indeed foster, process upgrading by their suppliers that reduces costs. But, at the same time, they will zealously guard the design and branding functions and keep those functions off limits to suppliers (Kaplinsky, Morris, and Readman 2002). The more variety and

Table 4.2 Hierarchy of Upgrading Firm Capabilities

Item	Process upgrading	Product upgrading	Functional upgrading	Chain upgrading
Trajectory	↓ ———————————————→			
Examples	Original equipment assembly (OEA) ↓ Original equipment manufacture (OEM) →	Original design manufacture →	Original brand manufacture →	Moving chains, e.g., from black-and-white TV tubes to computer monitors
Degree of disembodied activities	Disembodied content of value-added increases progressively ———————→			

Source: Kaplinsky and Morris 2001.

brand conscious the markets are, the more likely that lead chain buyers will strive to maintain their control over design and branding.

Of course, the understanding of capability growth must reflect both supply and demand factors. But it also will reflect the interaction between these two sets of factors. For example, responding to a series of analyses on the growth of supply capabilities in the newly industrializing economies (NIE), Feenstra and Hamilton (2005) point to the role played by the U.S. retail sector in the evolving East Asian "export miracle." They show how the growing concentration of buying power in the United States during the 1960s led to intense competition to find low-cost, high-volume sources of supply. This led Walmart and other large retail chains to actively foster the growth of supply capabilities in Hong Kong, China; Republic of Korea; Singapore; and Taiwan, China during the 1970s and 1980s—a process extended to Chinese and other global suppliers in the 1980s and 1990s. This dovetailed with the simultaneous investment in the supply of capabilities by governments and producers in these NIEs (Amsden 1989; Wade 1990).

In summary, therefore, although economic growth is ultimately a story of augmented supply capabilities, there has been growing recognition of the key role that final markets play in inducing this growth in supply capabilities. Market size and market growth are one part of this story. But another part involves the nature of final markets, and the role that this plays in guiding the direction of capability growth among suppliers. Intermediation into final markets, and therefore the nature of buying power in global markets, is a further factor affecting economic growth, particularly in economies in which external trade plays a key role.

Economic Crisis and the Southern Drivers of Demand Growth

The 2008–09 recession following the financial crisis of autumn 2008 sparked the largest fall in output in the North since World War II, with an associated decline in output and exports in many low-income economies, including the stellar-growth economies in East and South Asia. Between the onset of the crisis and the first quarter of 2009, global output fell by 2.4 percent, and that of countries in the Organisation for Economic Co-operation and Development[1] (OECD) fell by 4 percent (Holland et al. 2009). The unknown issue (as of December 2009), is how this crisis will unfold and whether and how it will be resolved. While output revived in most of the major northern economies in late 2009, much of Europe began to experience growing concerns with the fear of a sovereign debt crisis in 2010, leading to concerted fiscal tightening. This is likely to constrain demand and throw the European, and potentially the northern, economies back into a double-dip recession.

Essentially two major schools of analysis and policy response dominate the public debate on the evolution and resolution of the crisis. (Krugman amusingly refers to these schools in the United States context as comprising "saltwater" economists on the east and west coasts, and the "freshwater" economists in Chicago, located on one of the Great Lakes, and other inland universities [Krugman 2009]). On one hand, the "saltwater" Keynesians, who have dominated policy responses, argue that a necessary transitory mechanism is government financing to sustain demand growth and prevent a downward spiral of confidence and economic activity. On the other hand, the "freshwater" mainstream economists are suspicious of big government and fearful that deficit-financing will induce inflation; they argue for a very rapid rebalancing of government budgets.

What is missing from this polarized debate is a structural analysis of the crisis, which is what must be understood in order to assess the likely role China and other large southern economies will play in the coming decade and beyond. Before presenting this structural analysis, it is helpful to think through a number of possible final outcomes to the recent financial and economic crisis. The first possible outcome is the "V scenario"—a rapid downturn followed by a fairly rapid upturn. In late 2009, growth was beginning to revive in the United States and parts of Europe, as well as in China and elsewhere in Asia, which is the positive (or rather, the "least negative") hoped-for outcome. The "U scenario"—sometimes described as the "bath scenario" when the upturn is delayed—suggests a similar outcome, but with a more protracted dip. Less comfortable is the "W scenario"—a double-dip growth path, but with a subsequent retreat to past growth trajectories. This is an outcome considered more realistic by some (such as the CEO of the Hong Kong and Shanghai Bank, who said, "Is this a V recovery or a W? I think it's the latter" [*Financial Times*, October 5, 2009]).

The most pessimistic possible outcome of the financial crisis is that it will follow the same path as that experienced by Japan after its financial bubble burst in the early 1990s, that is, a sharp downturn followed by a protracted period of stagnation. This is the "L scenario." Somewhere between the L and the W scenarios is the "square root scenario" ($\sqrt{\ }$), that is, a sharp downturn, followed by a small rise (consistent with the revival of activity in late 2009), followed by a period of protracted stagnation. A recent study supports the likelihood of this outcome: Holland et al. (2009) expected growth to resume by the end of 2009 in most countries, except for OECD countries, whose level of output they expect will remain permanently lower (Holland et al. 2009, 9).

It is important, however, to avoid treating the global economy as a homogeneous entity and recognize the possibility—the likelihood, in fact—of diverse regional outcomes. The structural analysis that follows contrasts the likely outcome in the northern economies with that in two key southern economies, the Asian Driver economies of China and India.

Structural Crisis in the North

High rates of global economic growth during the 1990s and the first decade of the new century were essentially fueled by high rates of consumption in key northern economies, particularly in the large economies of the United States, the United Kingdom, and Spain, as well as in some smaller economies, such as Ireland, Greece, and Iceland. In each case, this consumption boom was made possible through a series of financial bubbles, particularly in housing, which allowed consumers to drawn on the "wealth" arising from inflating house prices. This resulted in two sets of related phenomena—falling rates of household and personal savings (in some cases, falling into dissavings) and a rise in balance of payments deficits. These deficits in external payments were filled by large payment surpluses in key exporting economies, particularly China, Japan, and Germany, made possible by restrained personal consumption arising from high rates of personal—and in recent years, corporate—savings, or low rates of consumption, or both.

Table 4.3 shows the extent of external payments deficits and surpluses in key large trading economies. The two most notable cases are the largest deficit economy, the United States (its payments deficit hovered around 5 percent of GDP) and China (whose payments surplus in 2008 was 11 percent of GDP). Also notable is the case of Spain (deficit of almost 10 percent of GDP in 2008) and the United Kingdom (a deficit of almost 3 percent of GDP). Some of the other smaller OECD economies showed even greater trade deficits, notably Greece (15 percent of GDP) and Iceland (40 percent of GDP in 2008). A significant feature of this performance was the growth in these structural imbalances during the 2000s.

Table 4.3 Country Current Account Balance
percentage of country GDP

Year	Brazil	India	China	Germany	Japan	Spain	United Kingdom	United States
1985	–0.1	–1.8	–3.7	2.5	3.8	1.6	0.7	–3.0
1990	–0.8	–2.2	3.4	2.8	1.5	–3.5	–3.9	–1.4
2000	–3.8	–1.0	1.7	–1.7	2.6	–4.0	–2.7	–4.3
2005	1.6	–1.0	7.2	5.1	3.6	–7.4	–2.6	–5.9
2008	–1.7	–1.0	11.0	6.7	3.2	–9.6	–2.8	–4.7

Source: Organisation for Economic Co-operation and Development database, November 2009.

Table 4.4 shows the disparities in savings and consumption rates that underpinned these structural trade imbalances. The striking characteristics of these data are, first, the relatively low rates of final household consumption expenditure in China and, second, the high rate of private consumption (especially compared to the low rate of savings) in three key bubble economies, Spain, the United Kingdom,

Table 4.4 Savings and Household Consumption Expenditure
percentage of country GDP

Country/year	Gross domestic savings	Household final consumption expenditure	Savings-to-consumption ratio
Brazil			
1990	21	59	0.36
2000	16	64	0.26
2008	19	61	0.31
China			
1990	40	46	0.86
2000	38	47	0.80
2008	49	37	1.34
India			
1990	23	66	0.35
2000	23	64	0.36
2008	33	56	0.59
Germany			
1990	23	58	0.40
2000	22	59	0.38
2007	25	57	0.45
Japan			
1990	34	53	0.65
2000	27	56	0.48
2006	25	57	0.44
Spain			
1990	23	60	0.38
2000	23	60	0.39
2007	25	57	0.44
United Kingdom			
1990	18	62	0.29
2000	16	65	0.25
2007	15	63	0.24
United States			
1990	16	67	0.24
2000	17	69	0.24
2006	14	70	0.20

Source: World Development Indicators, November 2009.

and the United States. Concomitant with these imbalances has been the growth of foreign exchange reserves in the two leading surplus economies, China and Japan, which together accounted for nearly half of total global foreign exchange reserves (table 4.5).

The imbalances in trade—feeding off the financial bubble—represent a core structural feature that is unsustainable in the medium and long terms, particularly for very large global economies such as the United States and China. To be resolved, they require either a reduction in consumption in the surplus economies or a rise in consumption in the deficit economies, or a combination of the two, which would result in a fall in net exports in surplus economies and a rise in net exports in the deficit countries. These changes may work their way through the system through changes in exchange rates, personal consumption expenditure, and government expenditure, and they may or may not involve price deflation or inflation. The precise mechanisms involved in the resolution of the imbalances are less important for this discussion than the level of output and output growth in which the structural rebalancing will be achieved.

Some changes are already occurring. For example, household savings rates are beginning to rise, with consumption falling and trade deficits narrowing in key deficit economies. At the same time, payments surpluses have been falling in some economies, including China (table 4.6).

Table 4.5 Foreign Exchange Reserves, 2009

Year	Country	US$, millions	Percentage of world total
	World (sum of all countries)	**7,520,566**	
2009	China (including Hong Kong)	2,292,300	30
2009	Japan	1,044,327	14
2008	Euro Area[a] (European Union member states that have adopted the euro, including the European Central Bank)	569,213	8
2008	India	313,354	4
2009	Brazil	223,713	3
2008	Germany	150,377	2
2008	United Kingdom	99,956	1
2008	United States	67,000	1

Source: Sovereign Wealth Fund (SWF) Institute, November 2009.

a. Euro Area members include Austria, Belgium, Cyprus, Finland, France, Germany, Greece, Ireland, Italy, Luxembourg, Malta, Netherlands, Portugal, Slovenia, and Spain.

Table 4.6 Changes in Trade and Savings for Major Economies, 2008–09

	Current account balance (percentage of GDP)		Gross national savings (percentage of GDP)		Trade (percentage change in $ value June 2008/09 year to year)	
Country	2008	2009[a]	2008	2009[a]	Imports	Exports
Germany	6.4	2.9	26	20	33	34
Japan	3.2	1.9	27	23	26	24
United Kingdom	–1.7	–2.0	15	12	31	31
United States	–4.9	–2.6	13	11	24	–0.29

Source: International Monetary Fund (IMF) World Economic Outlook (WEO) and Direction of Trade Statistics (DOTS) database, November 2009.
a. Estimated by IMF WEO.

However, the outcome of falling consumption in most northern economies has been a sharp rise in unemployment almost everywhere, with aggregate employment in the OECD falling by 2.2 million between the second quarters of 2008 and 2009 (Holland et al. 2009), and unemployment growing to exceed 10 percent of the labor force in the United States in late 2009. It has also led to a sharp fall in exports in major surplus economies (table 4.6). In June 2009, Germany's exports had declined by 34 percent and Japan's by 24 percent compared to the same period in the previous year. China, too, saw a fall in employment after global trade fell significantly in the first year after the financial meltdown (13 percent fall in exports between June 2008 and June 2009).

This decrease in output in the North, and increase in unemployment—both arising out of falling personal consumption—have been met by a massive "saltwater Keynesian" injection of funds through bank bailouts and quantitative easing in most of the deficit economies, fueling a "freshwater" response warning of the dangers of inflation. Although not historically unprecedented, government debt as a share of GDP has risen sharply in almost all economies as actual (and projected) fiscal deficits have grown (table 4.7). Without this growth in government expenditure, there is little doubt that the almost unprecedented large fall in output and rise in unemployment would have been substantially greater. As a result, there has been some revival in economic activity, with both the United States and the European Union (EU) (but not the United Kingdom) moving out of recession (in the sense that output stopped falling) in the final quarter of 2009 and China's exports being revived. Virtually no observer doubts the reflationary

Table 4.7 General Government Fiscal Balance
percentage of GDP

Year	Germany	Japan	Spain	United Kingdom	United States
1980	–3	–5	–2	–3	–3
1990	–2	2	–4	–2	–4
2000	1	–8	–1	1	2
2005	–3	–5	1	–3	–3
2008	0	–6	–4	–5	–6
2009	–4	–10	–12	–12	–12
2010	–5	–10	–12	–13	–10
2011	–4	–8	—	–11	–8
2012	–2	–8	—	–9	–6
2013	–1	–8	—	–8	–7
2014	0	–8	—	–7	–7

Source: International Monetary Fund World Economic Outlook database, November 2009.
Note: Shaded areas are estimates. — = not available.

consequences of government deficit financing—the debate is on the sustainability and long-term consequence of this deficit-spending program and the extent of the economic revival.

Thus, there are two clear medium- to long-term trends that emerge from these developments in major northern economies. First, personal consumption has fallen back and is unlikely to rise in the near term to midterm, as households rebuild their savings and cut personal debt. Second, continued government dissaving has limited the fall in aggregate consumption and output, but it is unsustainable in the medium and long terms, both for fiscal reasons and because of sustained trade deficits. So, the issue is in what other ways can the structural deficits in key northern economies be resolved if the past growth trajectory is to be sustained—that is, if any of the V, U, or W scenarios are to be achieved. One possibility is for there to be a rapid growth in consumption and imports in China, Japan, Germany, and other economies in trade surplus. Here, the portents are not positive. Scarred by its history of inflation during the 1920s, Germany has made it clear that it wishes to minimize deficit financing. It has also explicitly committed itself to remaining an economy with a substantial trade surplus. Japan, despite efforts to reflate consumption in the past, also does not suggest itself as an economy capable of pulling in significant imports from the deficit economies and allowing them to benefit from rapid, export-led growth. As a recent International Monetary Fund report concluded, "The scope for advanced economies such as Germany and Japan to contribute to rebalancing is limited, given their need to build savings to prepare for population aging" (IMF 2009, 33). So China and, to a lesser extent, India hold the hopes of sustaining the V, U, or W scenarios.

The problem is that there is little realistic sign that China-led reflation will draw in the imports to allow the major deficit economies to resume past levels of consumption growth while at the same time rebalancing their external payments accounts. It is true that the Chinese government has embarked on a major spending program. However, much of this has focused on infrastructure and on public services where, as of March 2009, government spending had expanded rapidly at an annual rate in health (38 percent), education (24 percent), and social safety (22 percent) (World Bank 2009a). These infrastructural expenditures do have derived import requirements but, as shown below, these are unlikely to have a direct first-round impact on the exports of the United States and the EU.

Of course, there are indirect trade multipliers operating in both these forms of domestic expenditure in China, but they are likely to be small, at least insofar as they affect the demand for goods and services exported by high-income northern economies.[2] Moreover, employment growth in China has been key in sustaining political stability in the face of rising inequality, and, insofar as China's labor-intensive exports decline, the emphasis will necessarily be placed on promoting domestic production to meet rising consumer demand. In addition, despite China's rapid economic growth and large size, it remains a relatively small player in international trade. In 2008, total Chinese demand was equivalent to less than one-quarter of total consumption in the United States and the EU. All of these factors also apply to India, but since its global footprint is smaller than China's, its capacity to stimulate exports from the northern economies is even more limited.

This leads to the conclusion that, beyond the short-term unsustainable deficit financing by governments in the large deficit economies, in reality, rebalancing these economies will occur through a reduction in consumption, and hence in imports. This should not be viewed as a historical aberration. Rather, it was the post-1990s boom in consumption in the large deficit economies that was aberrant, arising from a series of financial bubbles and leading to growing consumption in the (high-income) deficit economies being subsidized by high savings in some (low-income) surplus economies (notably China and India). This fall in northern consumption can also be anticipated to persist for some time, perhaps even as long as the 18-year post-bubble recession that the Japanese economy has experienced since 1991. Thus, the real issue is whether these northern economies will experience an L or a $\sqrt{\ }$ scenario, that is, whether output grows, but below precrisis levels, before it stabilizes and stagnates.

Sustained Consumption in the South

China's recent growth, at least since the beginning of the 1980s, has been stellar, averaging more than 9 percent annually over the period. India, too, has experienced very rapid and sustained growth, albeit only since the early 1990s. It is tempting to see these growth trajectories as exceptional—an "economic miracle." Yet neither of these two countries' growth experiences is unique. By charting the evolution of their growth paths—both in relation to output and exports—since the onset of their growth inflection, and comparing these with the similar experiences of Japan (after 1960) and Republic of Korea (after 1963), it is evident that other economies have experienced similar economic "miracles" in the past (Kaplinsky and Messner 2008). What is significant about the China-India experience is the size of these economies. Together, Japan and Korea never exceeded 5 percent of the global population. In 2008, China alone accounted for 20 percent of the global population, and together with India, for almost 37 percent of the global total (part of the reason they are increasingly referred to as the "Asian Drivers"; see http://asiandrivers.open.ac.uk/).

Three key features stand out with regard to the recent growth experience of these two Asian Driver economies. The first is that their growth rates have been significantly greater than those of key northern economies. If these past trajectories are sustained, then it is estimated that China will be the second-largest economy by 2010 and India, the third largest by 2027 (Goldman Sachs 2009). Of course, if past growth relativities are not sustained in the future (for example, if as suggested above, the northern economies experience a protracted period of stagnation), then China's and India's relative share of global output and trade will grow in a shorter time span than these projections of past performance suggest. Second, both China and India are in substantial trade surplus. They do not need to reduce or hold back consumption in the same way the large northern economies do. And, third, by virtue of their large size, they have the capacity to grow and realize scale economies by expanding their very large domestic markets. An illustration of the size of these Asian Driver markets is provided by a recent analysis of the locus of consumption by the global consuming class ("the middle class"), defined as those consumers with annual incomes of between $10 and $100 per day in 2009 (in 2005 purchasing power parity, PPP$) (Kharas 2009). Projecting forward to 2030 on the basis of growth rates in the past two decades, the center of gravity of the global middle-class consumption shifts decisively (table 4.8). The share of Europe and the United States falls from 64 percent in 2009 to 30 percent in 2030, while that of the South in general and Asia in particular rises. The share of Asia and the Pacific in the global consuming class is projected to increase from 23 percent in 2009 to 59 percent in 2030. Bear in mind, though, that these projections are based on past growth relativities. If northern economies do stagnate and the Asian Drivers and the surrounding regional economy continue to grow (albeit at a reduced rate), the shift of global consumption power to Asia, and to low-income economies in Asia, will be accentuated.

Table 4.8 Regional Share of Global Middle-Class Spending, 2009–30
percentage share

Region	2009	2030
North America	26	10
Europe	38	20
Central and South America	7	6
Asia-Pacific	23	59
Sub-Saharan Africa	1	1
Middle East and North Africa	4	4

Source: Information from Kharas (2009, table 3).
Note: The percentage of global GDP is in 2005 purchasing power parity dollars.

Nothing guarantees sustained growth in the Asian Driver economies. The fall in consumption in the northern deficit economies may be so large that it undermines export-oriented growth in China and India, with a potential combination of negative multiplier effects on economic activity and political disruption as unemployment grows. It may also be that environmental externalities grow so substantially, exacerbated by changing and unpredictable climate, that output growth is not sustainable. And it may be that global political instability spills over into the Asia-Pacific region, with a harmful impact on economic growth. So, as in the case of the analysis of likely growth paths in the northern economies, there are clear uncertainties in projecting forward, particularly in the context of a disruptive global financial crisis. Nevertheless, it is the authors' judgment that just as growth is likely to be reduced or to stagnate in the northern economies in the future, so growth in Asia in general and in China and India in particular, is likely to be sustained. If nothing else, the relativities in growth paths between these two worlds in the past two decades are likely to be sustained, and even to increase. If this is the case, then it is important to understand the nature of demand in these two large southern drivers of growth, which is considered in the next section.

Patterns of Demand in Southern Drivers of Growth

Despite differences in country size and endowments, there are well-established paths of development through which most economies pass (Kuznets 1966; Chenery and Syrquin 1975). Low-income economies tend to be agrarian, with the primary sector dominating GDP. As incomes rise and manufacturing expands, the industrial sector takes over as the major driver of GDP growth. Continued income growth leads to higher demand for services, and at higher income levels it becomes the dominant contributor to GDP. These structural shifts represent a well-established pattern, observed in a large number of countries over time. The interesting question in this analysis is that, in the context of China (and India) becoming the major drivers of global demand in the coming decades, what implications do the structural shifts in these Asian Driver economies have for low-income country exporters in general, and for low-income country exporters of commodities in particular? Thus, there are two major issues—the structure and the nature of import demand—and both cases are considered here in relation to the evolution of the Chinese economy.

The Structure of Import Demand

Three major consequences of changing economic structures affect the product composition of imports. First, at low per capita incomes, the income elasticity of demand for agricultural products in general, and food in particular, is relatively high. As incomes rise, the relative income elasticity of demand for manufactures grows, and as incomes increase further, the demand for services becomes increasingly important in final demand. Second, with the changing sector distribution of GDP, there is a shift in labor and employment across sectors. As the industrial sector expands, labor and employment migrate from agriculture in the rural areas to the manufacturing sector in the cities. Third, as economic output becomes more diversified, specialization and interchange grow. Together with the growth of urbanization, this requires heavy investments in infrastructure.

These three trends result in a growing demand for commodities. "Soft commodities" feed agricultural inputs into food and provide intermediate inputs (such as cotton and timber) into manufacturing. The demand for "hard commodities" (such as minerals and metals) and energy grows as a consequence of investments in infrastructure and the expansion of the manufacturing sector.

China's (and India's) growth paths reflect each of these trends. Significantly, they reflect the experience of an economy at an early stage in the evolution of this growth path. This is illustrated by focusing on some of the key parameters of China's recent growth trajectory (see Farooki 2009). China's economy has shown a rapid transition from agriculture to industry. The share of agriculture in GDP fell from 27 percent in 1990 to 11.3 percent in 2008. In the same period, the share of industry increased from 42 percent to 49 percent of GDP. This was accompanied by a large-scale rural-urban migration. In 2007, 45 percent of the population (594 million) lived in urban centers. By 2015, the urban population is projected to rise to 684 million, and to 890 million in 2030.

This process of urbanization is reflected in the growth in demand for infrastructure in general, and new infrastructure and housing in particular. It is one of the reasons leading observers to conclude that infrastructure intensity is highest at the early stages of industrialization and at relatively low levels of per capita income (Canning 1999; Auty 2008). New projects tend to be much more commodity intensive compared with expansion and reconstruction investments (World Bank 2009b). As table 4.9 shows, the share of new projects in urban fixed investments in China increased from less than a third to almost a half between 1995 and 2007.

Second, the growth of China's manufacturing sector has also made extensive use of commodities, particularly hard commodities and energy. To a considerable extent, this is reflected in the metals and minerals intensity of China's rapidly growing manufactured exports that constituted the bulk of exports between 1990 and 2006 (figure 4.1).

Table 4.9 Percentage Share of Total Investment in Fixed Assets in Urban Areas, by Type of Construction in China, 1995–2007

Year	New construction	Expansion	Reconstruction	Maintenance and equipment
1995	30	29	12	29
2000	32	24	15	29
2007	44	17	12	27

Source: Government of China 2008.

Figure 4.1 China's Intensity of Metals and Minerals Exports in Total Manufactures Exports, 1990–2006

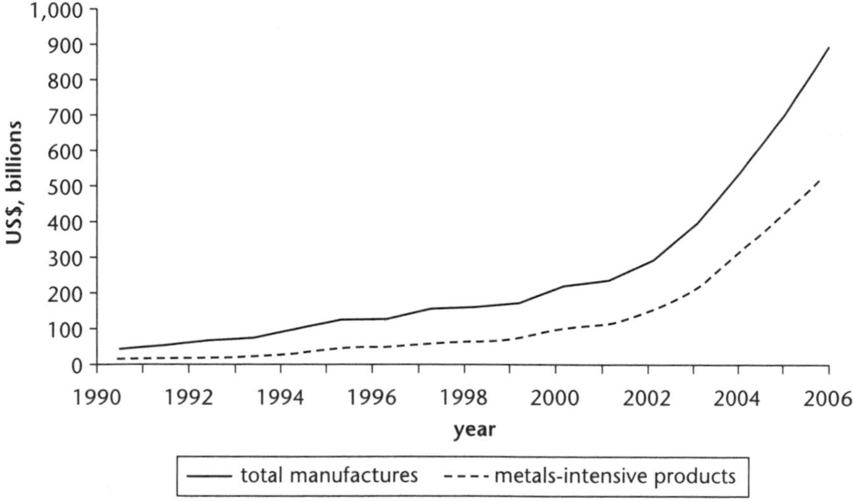

Source: Farooki (2009), calculated from Comtrade, data accessed via WITS in November 2008.
Note: The listing of metals-intensive sectors is available in Farooki (2009, annex 1).

As a result of these combined factors, the elasticity of demand for energy and metals grew rapidly between the 1990s and the 2000s, and for key resource inputs—such as coal, pig iron, crude steel, and rolled steel—it comfortably exceeded a value of 1 (table 4.10). Thus, for example, every 1 percent increase in GDP saw a more than 2 percent increase in the demand for rolled steel.

With regard to agricultural inputs, a key component of demand at low per capita incomes is for food products. Studies of urban consumers in China show that the income elasticity of demand for food falls from almost unity (0.96) at household incomes around yuan 2,500 (US$375) per year to 0.4 for household incomes of Y7,500 ($1,125) and to 0.33 for household incomes of Y10,000 ($1,500) (adapted from Gale and Huang 2007). Thus, even though incomes are growing, and the income elasticity of demand for food is falling, there is considerable scope for sustained demand for food, particularly because in 2007, around 75 percent of Chinese households had an annual income of less than Y38,000 ($5,500) (figure 4.2). Moreover, as incomes grow, the demand for meat expands, and this makes intensive use of grain (approximately four kilos of grain are required to produce one kilo of meat [Conceição and Mendoza 2009]). Thus, food availability is likely to be of considerable importance in China's future, not the least reason being that while it has 20 percent of global population, China possesses only 7 percent of global arable land.

These data show that China's growth path is particularly commodity intensive. There is nothing exceptional in this resource-intensive growth path; in fact, it closely reflects China's per capita income, which in 2008 was $5,510 compared to $43,000 for the United States (PPP$). However, two factors are worth mentioning. First, as figure 4.3 shows, there is a considerable way to go in per capita income levels before the resource intensity of growth declines. On the basis of the historic intensity of demand for aluminum, copper, and steel in Korea, Japan, the EU 12, and the United States, it seems unlikely that China's (and India's) demand for minerals and metals will decline in the foreseeable future, despite rapid economic growth and rising per capita incomes.

Second, both China and India, as already seen, are very large economies. Thus, in analyzing their impact on global trade, it is necessary to suspend the small

Table 4.10 Elasticity of Energy Consumption and Metal Production in China, 1991–2005

Period	Coal	Crude oil	Pig iron	Crude steel	Rolled steel
1991–95	0.441	0.569	0.900	0.614	0.958
2001–05	1.105	0.832	2.222	2.340	2.545

Source: Zhang and Zheng (2008).

Figure 4.2 Disposable Income Brackets of Households in China, India, Russian Federation, and Brazil, 2002–07

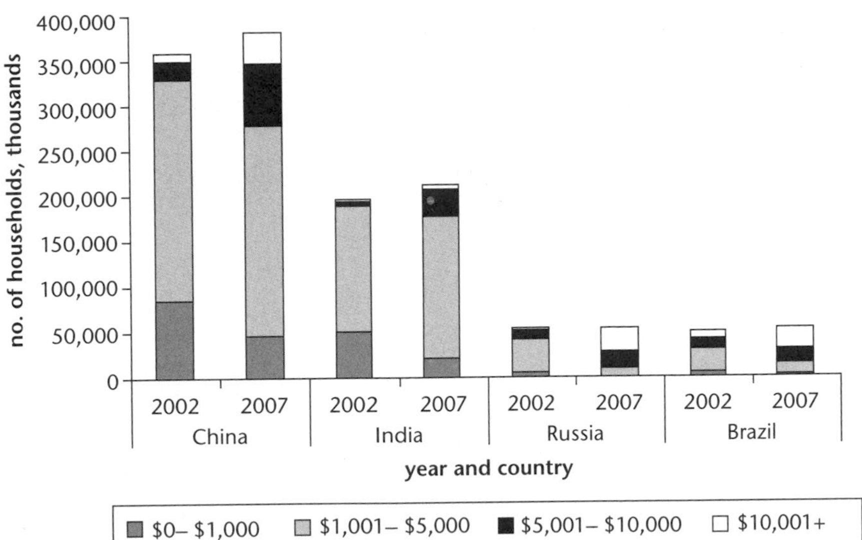

Source: Euromonitor International from national statistics (Eghbal 2008).
Note: The currency is U.S. dollars.

country assumption that no single economy's trade pattern will shift the structure of global trade or the prices at which products are traded. Table 4.11 shows that China accounts for a rapidly growing share of global consumption of key base metals and meat, which has led some commentators (including the present authors [Kaplinsky 2006, 2009; Farooki 2009]) to conclude that, at the least, this helped explain the boom in commodity prices between 2001 and 2008 and, perhaps, may also play a historically significant role in promoting a structural shift in the global commodities-manufactures terms of trade in favor of commodities.

The Nature of Import Demand

Thus, it can be seen that Chinese growth has led to a sharp rise in its share of global demand for commodities and perhaps also for a structural upward shift in the relative global price of commodities. But there is more to be observed about China's demand for commodities, which is of relevance to global commodity value chains feeding into the Chinese economy. The key relevant factors are the demand preferences of low-income consumers, the consequent relative insignificance of standards in value chains, and the preference for the importation of relatively unprocessed products.

Demand preferences of low-income consumers

The median income of individual consumers in the United States in 2007 according to the U.S. Census Bureau was $26,625. The figure representing the poverty

Figure 4.3 Per Capita Consumption of Base Metals, 1960–2005

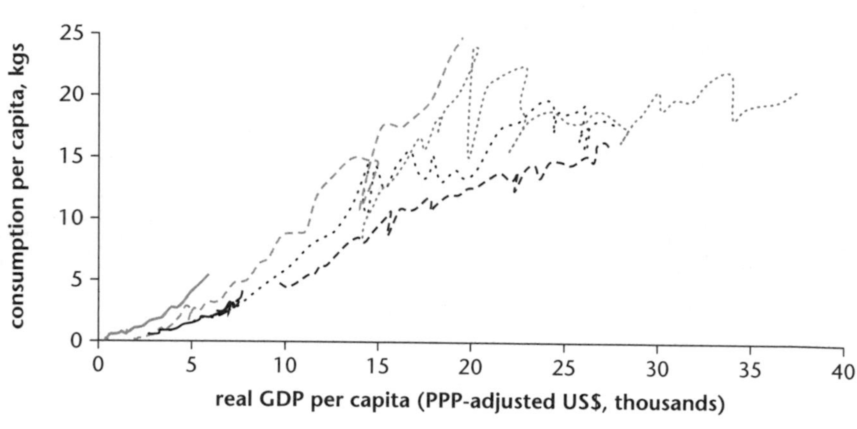

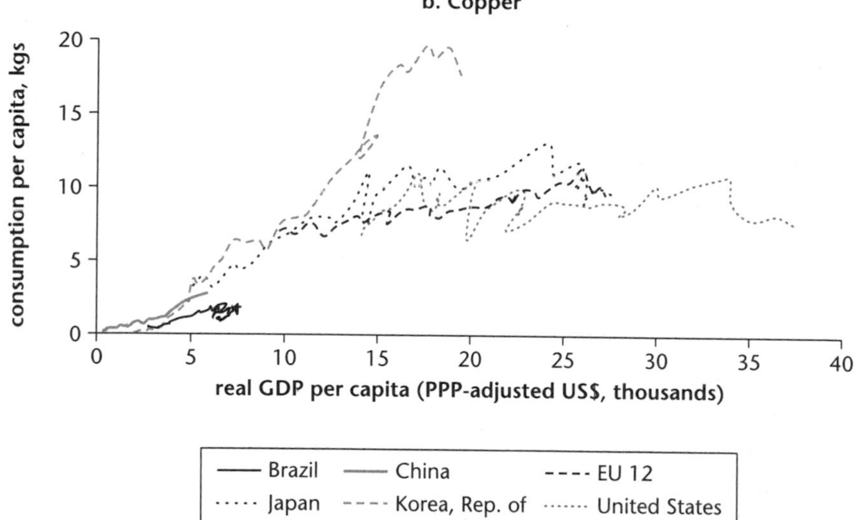

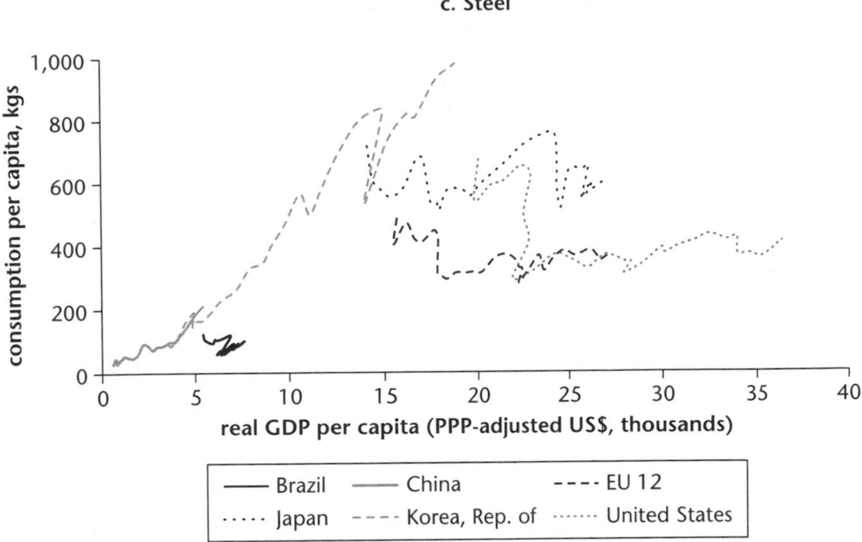

Source: International Monetary Fund World Economic Outlook, September 2006.
Note: EU 12 = Austria, Belgium, Denmark, Finland, France, Germany, Italy, the Netherlands, Norway, Sweden, Switzerland, and the United Kingdom (industrial production for the group was aggregated using 2005 purchasing-power-parity adjusted real GDP values as weights); kgs = kilograms; PPP = purchasing power parity.

Table 4.11 China's Share of Global Consumption of Base Metals and Meat
percentage of demand/consumption

Commodity	1990	2000	2007
Base metals (percentage share of world demand)			
Aluminum	5	13	33
Zinc	8	15	31
Lead	7	10	31
Iron ore	4	16	48
Copper	7	12	26
Food products (percentage share of world consumption)			
Poultry	9	18	17
Pork	35	47	46
Beef	2	10	12
Soybeans	—	—	40

Sources: Base metals, Macquarie Commodities Research 2008; food products, Conceição and Mendoza 2008.
Note: — = not available.

threshold in the United Kingdom (defined as 60 percent of average [median] annual incomes in 2007) was $35,432.[3] There is no gainsaying the existence of poverty in all of the high-income economies, particularly when poverty is defined as relative income.[4] Undoubtedly, cases of significant absolute poverty can be found in the North, for example, fuel poverty among the aged. However, whatever the degrees of inequality and deprivation in the North, the incomes involved are, in almost all cases, far greater than those earned in low-income economies such as China. Figure 4.2 shows the dispersion of incomes in the BRIC economies (Brazil, Russia, India, and China) in 2007. It is evident that more than 270 million *households* in China and more than 170 million *households* in India had total annual incomes of less than $5,000. By contrast, the 2007 median household income was $50,233 in the United States and $49,800 in the United Kingdom.

In many cases, these households in low-income countries lived above the minimum $1 per day MDG (Millennium Development Goal) threshold, particularly in China. However, it is significant that most of these households in all the BRIC economies were cash consumers, that is, they bought in a range of products, consumer, intermediate, and capital goods. For these consumers, price is an overwhelming consideration in consumption. That is not to say that they do not care about quality and variety (the two key drivers of consumer demand in northern economies in recent decades—see previous section), but that these preferences play a minor role in their consumption choices. Product differentiation (variety and quality) gives way to product "commodification" (standardization in order to achieve low prices). To the best of our knowledge, there is not statistical evidence to prove this assertion, although the idea that low-income markets provide scope for profitable production through the sale of low-value items is now widely acknowledged under the banner of the "fortune at the bottom of the pyramid" (Prahalad 2005).

Imported inputs are not standards intensive

Following on from the preferences of low-income consumers, implications for the role that standards play in value chains can be derived. The earlier discussion of buyers, markets, and GVCs (see table 4.1) distinguished between "process" and "product." A tendency was observed for the standards intensity in GVCs to grow, reflecting a combination of factors—firm–specific concerns with standards (such as QCD) to meet consumer needs for product diversity and product quality, government standards to protect consumers, and civil society–induced standards reflecting growing concerns with the ethics of productions systems and their environmental impact. In the context of the dominance of very low consumer incomes in countries such as China and India, each of these drivers of standards is likely to be of very diminished significance (table 4.12). In general, firms are less

Table 4.12 The Importance of Standards Driven by Firms, Governments, and Civil Society in Value Chains Feeding into China and India

Standard	Countries	Firms	Governments	Civil society
Product	High income	Quality standards such as permitted parts per million defects	Food hygiene standards; lead content in toys	Organic products
	China, India	Low emphasis and weak enforcement	Low emphasis and weak enforcement	None, or very weak
Process	high income	Quality control procedures—such as ISO9000	Hygiene standards—such as Hazard Analysis and Critical Control Point conformance (HACCP)	Sustainability standards—such as FSC (Forest Stewardship Council) (timber)
		Frequency of on-time delivery	Traceability of pesticide content	Child labor standards
	China, India	Low emphasis and weak enforcement	None, or very weak	Low emphasis and weak enforcement

Source: Authors.
Note: This table is an elaboration of table 4.1.

concerned with product variety than with cost, so that the imperatives to achieve flexibility through just-in-time production (and hence QCD standards) are weak. Governments may either have poorly developed safety standards or fail to implement existing standards effectively. Recent cases in both China (baby milk) and India (pesticide in soft drinks) provide striking evidence of this.[5] Finally, the nongovernmental organizations (NGOs) that have driven public opinion on issues such as FairTrade, labor standards, and the environment are muted in low-income countries and are likely to have little effect with regard to the incorporation of ethical and environmental standards in global value chains. Indeed, particularly in China, NGOs often have a tenuous identity.

Growth in imports of relatively unprocessed products

A key objective of economic and industrial policy in most low-income countries is to add value to natural resources: in South Africa, for example, the call is for the "beneficiation" (that is, downstream processing) of the country's extensive mineral and agricultural products. Although there are dangers to this policy agenda (beneficiation, particularly of hard commodities, is often very capital and technology intensive) there is a natural logic to this in many cases. Many commodities degrade rapidly or involve significant weight loss in processing. There are also cases in evidence of economies that have used their natural resources to drive forward their industrialization (Wright and Czelusta 2004). And, particularly in the processing of soft commodities, this is often a labor-intensive process, and wage costs in low-income exporting economies are generally a fraction of those in high-income economies. Moreover, commodity processing is often very polluting.

This logic of processing at source (rather than in the importing economy) applies easily—or relatively easily—when low-income economies export commodities to high-income economies. The high-income economies are happy to see the pollution-generating and energy-intensive production processes located in low-income countries; the high-technology, skill-intensive, high-wage, and safe working environments in their producing sectors are generally more appropriate to the provision of capital and intermediate goods for resource-processing industries rather than for the direct processing of commodities. However, when low-income resource economies trade with low-income importing economies, many of these factors that promote a win-win division of labor do not apply (table 4.13). Low-income economies care little about the polluting nature and energy intensity of processing. Their industrial structures are well pitched in terms of technological and skill intensity to specialize in processing, and their low labor costs enable them to do so at similar cost profiles to those operating in low-income exporting economies.

In the case of China importing food products, there is an additional factor affecting the degree of processing involved in these imports. As noted above, the ratio of China's population to its arable land suggests that, however effective its agricultural sector might become, it seems likely that it will have to draw on agricultural imports as its economy continues to grow, and as its population's food tastes shift increasingly toward meat products. After a brief flirtation with the

Table 4.13 High- and Low-Income Commodity Importing Economies: Complementarity and Competition with Low-Income Commodity-Exporting Economies

	Importing economy	
Difference in perspectives	**High income**	**Low income**
Pollution and energy intensity	High preference to outsource to exporting economy	Indifferent to location
Complementary or competitive industrial structures	Complementary—focus on technologies with high barriers to entry	Competitive—importers also have low technology industrial structures
Labor costs	High wages militate against labor-intensive processing	Low wages facilitate labor-intensive processing
Labor standards	Working conditions are effectively protected by enforcement legislation	Weak protective environment of working conditions

Source: Authors.

importation of food products, the experience of global shortages of key food crops in 2007, and the associated rise in political tension in countries as diverse as Cameroon and Indonesia, the minds of Chinese policy makers have become increasingly focused on ensuring food security through the domestic production of cereals. In fact, China has pursued a strong self-sufficiency policy in grains since 1995, with the objective of domestic production meeting 95 percent of its domestic demand (Anderson and Peng 1998). As a consequence, agricultural production shifted toward grains and away from other crops like cotton, sugar beets, and soybeans (Fang and Beghin 1999). Given the shortage of arable land, this has meant that China's agricultural imports have increasingly been concentrated in animal feeds (such as soy and palm oil) and products that compete with grains for land use (such as inputs).

Another policy-related factor also affects China's growing importation of agricultural products. With a growing global perception of an unfolding energy crisis, China has—like the United States and the EU—begun to promote the production of biofuels. These products need agricultural inputs, and China has increasingly sought to source these inputs from abroad: given its political commitment to food self-sufficiency and food security, China can ill afford to use land for biofuel crops that could be planted in food crops.[6]

Conclusions: Shifting Markets and Participation of Low-Income Countries in Global Value Chains

The rapid growth of the East Asian newly industrializing economies in the 1970s and 1980s and of China, India, Indonesia, Vietnam, Central America, and other emerging economies in the 1990s and 2000s, was to a significant extent based on the expansion of their exports. Incorporated in global value chains, their exports were either directed to northern economies or fed as intermediate products into other countries' exports to northern economies.

The earlier section on southern drivers of demand growth reflected on the likely trajectory of the global economy after the 2008–09 economic crisis. Even without stagnation and falling growth rates in the North, the growth rates of the past two decades in China and India are likely to lead to an outcome in which, by virtue of their size, these countries increasingly come to dominate the global economy in this century. However, there are persuasive reasons to believe that key large northern economies (notably the United States, the United Kingdom, and Spain) will reduce imports as they rebalance their global orientation, given their large structural trade and fiscal deficits. This will further accentuate the dominance of China, India, and other low-income economies in the growth of global demand in the coming decades.

We believe that this change in the drivers of global demand—from northern to southern economies—will, by hypothesis, have four major sets of implications for global value chains in the South that arise as a direct consequence of the particular characteristics of demand in China and India. First, low levels of per capita income, coupled with rapid urbanization and the growth of exchange as their economies become more diversified, will lead to a sustained growth in their demand for hard and soft commodities, both as a source of food and as inputs into infrastructure. Second, low levels of per capita income mean that the nature of demand will be for cheap, undifferentiated goods with low acquisition cost, which runs against the major trends in demand in northern economies after 1970 that increasingly favored differentiated, high-quality positional products. Third, the standards intensity of GVCs feeding into northern economies has grown significantly and has become much more complex and demanding in recent decades. By contrast, GVCs feeding southern markets are likely to have much lower levels of standards, in relation to both products and processes. And, fourth, northern and southern economies are often complementary in terms of economic structures. Northern economies have much higher wages costs and are much more sensitive to the harmful externalities of polluting economic activities than are southern economies; thus, the North has increasingly outsourced processing to developing economies. By contrast, low-income producing countries have similar economic structures and industrial trajectories to low-income consuming economies, with the prospect of greater competition in the division of labor in GVCs.

Evidence from two southern value chains—cassava in Thailand and timber in Gabon—provides corroboration for this broad argument (Kaplinsky, Terheggen, and Tijaja, chapter 8 in this volume). In both cases, the market has shifted from the EU to China, which resulted in a reduction in the degree of value-added and in the importance of process and product standards. But cassava and timber are relatively undifferentiated products, with low degrees of coordination and governance in their value chains. It remains to be seen, therefore, whether our hypotheses will also be evidenced in value chains historically producing more differentiated products for northern markets. We believe—but this belief necessarily requires testing—that the nature of the developments sketched out in earlier sections will be even more relevant in the case of less commodified products.

What might this mean for meeting development objectives in low-income economies? Naturally, this is a complex picture, reflecting different sectors and different types of low-income economies. However, some general observations can be made. First, on the positive side, enhanced demand from the rapidly growing and very large Asian Driver economies provides the potential for a significant income-enhancing effect, with either an increase in export earnings or some level of compensation for falling exports to the North. A second possible positive outcome is that there is often a link between process and product technologies such that products for low-income consumers often involve labor-intensive process technologies (Kaplinsky 2010). Third, meeting the standards in GVCs serving northern markets generally is not just a costly exercise, but requires a literate and numerate labor force and forms of management that may be beyond the reach of many small-scale enterprises. Accessing the Asian Driver markets may therefore promote the role played by small and medium enterprises in GVCs.

On the "dark side," achieving standards can often contribute to the development of upgrading capabilities by the firm, so that exclusion from demanding standards-intensive markets may undermine the drive to capability building in the firm. Further, from the perspective of both the firm and the economy as a whole, the blocking of attempts to deepen value-added by advancing along the value chain means that producers are likely to be stuck in pockets of static comparative advantage. Moreover, being confined to niches of low productivity (for example, value-added per worker) is likely to undermine the move into the higher value-added activities that underwrite high incomes.

It is clear from this examination that there is much ambiguity in possible outcomes. To some extent, this ambiguity reflects sector and technological constraints. But it also reflects the way in which individual producers and economies respond to these challenges posed by the transition in final markets. Will the advance of China and India as the major poles of consumption lead to a restructuring of value chains that will be "bad" or "good" for development in other low-income economies? The answer is yet to be seen.

Notes

1. OECD member countries are Australia, Austria, Belgium, Canada, Czech Republic, Denmark, Finland, France, Germany, Greece, Hungary, Iceland, Ireland, Italy, Japan, Republic of Korea, Luxembourg, Mexico, Netherlands, New Zealand, Norway, Poland, Portugal, Slovak Republic, Spain, Sweden, and Switzerland.
2. There undoubtedly will be a positive second-round general equilibrium impact on high-income country exports to those countries to meet China's expanding infrastructure investments. But these indirect impacts are likely to be delayed; moreover, increasingly, low-income countries' imports are being sourced from China and India rather than the EU and the United States.
3. Source: The median income before tax in 2007 was £17,700 (HM Revenue and Customs).
4. As Wilkinson and Pickett (2009) show, most indicators of welfare are more affected by relative than by absolute poverty levels. However, this discussion is not focusing on the welfare implications of income levels, but on their translation into the demand characteristics of consumption, so it is absolute income levels that draw our attention.
5. http://www.businessweek.com/globalbiz/content/aug2006/gb20060810_826414.htm.
6. In addition, Von Braun (2007) estimates that if current biofuel and investment plans were to be extended, by 2020 the world price of major food crops could rise by 11 percent for cassava, 26 percent for maize, 18 percent for oilseeds, about 12 percent for sugar, and 8 percent for wheat.

References

Amsden A. 1989. *Asia's Next Giant: South Korea and Late Industrialization.* New York: Oxford University Press.

Anderson, K., and C. Y. Peng. 1998. "Feeding and Fueling China in the 21st Century." *World Development* 26 (8): 1413–29.

Auty, R. 2008. "Natural Resources and Development." In *International Handbook of Development Economics,* vol. 1, ed. Amitava Krishna Dutt and Jamie Ros. Cheltenham, UK: Edward Elgar.

Bessant, J., R. Kaplinsky, and R. Lamming. 2003. "Putting Supply Chain Learning into Practice." *International Journal of Production Management* 23 (2): 167–84.

Canning, D. 1999. "Infrastructure's Contribution to Aggregate Output." Policy Research Working Paper 2246. World Bank, Washington, DC.

Chenery, H., and M. Syrquin. 1975. *Patterns of Development 1950–1970.* London: Oxford University Press.

Conceição, P., and R. U. Mendoza. 2008. "A Preliminary Anatomy of the Unfolding Global Food Crisis (draft)." Accessed October 2009. United Nations Development Programme.

———. 2009. "Anatomy of the Global Food Crisis." *Third World Quarterly* 30 (6): 1159–82.

Cusumano, M. A. 1985. *The Japanese Automobile Industry: Technology and Management at Nissan and Toyota.* Cambridge, MA: Harvard University Press.

Eghbal, M. 2008. "BRICS Economies Withstand Global Financial Crisis." *Euro-monitor International,* November 7.

Fang, C., and J. C. Beghin. 1999. "Food Self-Sufficiency, Comparative Advantage, and Agricultural Trade: A Policy Analysis Matrix for Chinese Agriculture." Staff General Research Papers 1627, Iowa State University, Department of Economics.

Farooki, M. Z. 2009. "The Southern Engine of Growth and Hard Commodity Prices: Does China Lead to Disruptive Development?" Ph.D. dissertation, Development Policy and Practice, Milton Keynes Open University.

Feenstra, R. C., and G. G. Hamilton. 2005. *Emergent Economies, Divergent Paths: Economic Organization and International Trade in South Korea and Taiwan.* New York: Cambridge University Press.

Gale, F., and K. Huang. 2007. "Demand for Food Quantity and Quality in China." Economic Research Services, United States Department of Agriculture, Washington, DC.

Gereffi, G. 1994. "The Organization of Buyer-Driven Global Commodity Chains: How U. S. Retailers Shape Overseas Production Networks." In *Commodity Chains and Global Capitalism,* ed. G. Gereffi and M. Korzeniewicz, 95–122. London: Praeger.

Goldman Sachs Global Economics Group. 2009. "The Long-Term Outlook for the BRICs and N-11 Post Crisis." Global Economics Paper 192. The Goldman Sachs Group, Inc., New York.

Government of China. 2008. *China Statistical Yearbook 2008.* National Bureau of Statistics of China, Beijing.

Holland, D., R. Barrell, T. Fic, I. Hurst, I. Liadze, A. Orazgani, and R. Whitworth. 2009. "Consumer Spending and the Financial Crisis." *National Institute Economic Review* 210 (1): 9–15.

Humphrey, J., and H. Schmitz. 2001. "Governance in Global Value Chains." In ed. G. Gereffi and R. Kaplinsky, *IDS Bulletin Special Issue on The Value of Value Chains* 32 (3): 19–29.

IMF (International Monetary Fund). 2009. "Beyond 2010: How Will the Global Economy Rebalance?" *World Economic Outlook.* International Monetary Fund, Washington, DC.

Kaplinsky, R. 1994. *Easternisation: The Spread of Japanese Management Techniques to Developing Countries.* London: Frank Cass.

———. 2005. *Globalisation, Poverty and Inequality: Between a Rock and a Hard Place.* Cambridge, UK: Polity Press.

———. 2006. "Revisiting the Terms of Trade Revisited: Will China Make a Difference?" *World Development* 34 (6): 981–95.

———. 2009. "China and the Terms of Trade: The Challenge to Development Strategy in Sub-Saharan Africa." In *Global Giant: Is China Changing the Rules of the Game?* ed. E. Paus, P. Prime, and J. Western, 115–34. New York: Palgrave Macmillan.

———. 2010. "Schumacher Meets Schumpeter: Appropriate Technology below the Radar." IKD Working Paper, Development Policy and Practice, Open University, Centre for Innovation, Knowledge and Development, Milton Keynes, UK.

Kaplinsky, R., and D. Messner. 2008. "Introduction: The Impact of the Asian Drivers on the Developing World." *World Development* (Special Issue on Asian Drivers and Their Impact on Developing Countries) 36 (2): 197–209.

Kaplinsky, R., and M. Morris. 2001. *A Handbook for Value Chain Research*. http://asianDrivers.open.ac.uk/documents/Value_chain_Handbook_RKMM_Nov_2001.pdf.

Kaplinsky, R., M. Morris, and J. Readman. 2002. "The Globalisation of Product Markets and Immiserising Growth: Lessons from the South African Furniture Industry." *World Development* 30 (7): 1159–77.

Kaplinsky, R., A. Terheggen, and J. P. Tijaja. 2010. "What Happens When the Market Shifts to China? The Gabon Timber and Thai Cassava Value Chains." Chapter 8 in this volume.

Kharas, H. 2009. "The Emerging Middle Class in Developing Countries." Working Paper, Organisation for Economic Co-operation and Development, Paris.

Krugman, P. 2009. "How Did Economists Get It So Wrong?" *New York Times*, September 2. http://www.nytimes.com/2009/09/06/magazine/06Economic-t.html.

Kuznets, S. 1966. *Modern Economic Growth*. New Haven, CT: Yale University Press.

Macquarie Commodities Research. 2008. "Overview of Commodities Outlook with Focus on Copper, Zinc and Coking Coal." Macquarie Capital Securities, London. September.

Pine, J. B. 1993. *Mass Customization: The New Frontier in Business Competition*. Cambridge, MA: Harvard Business School Press.

Piore, M. J., and C. Sabel, 1984. *The Second Industrial Divide: Possibilities for Prosperity*. New York: Basic Books.

Prahalad, C. K. 2005. *The Fortune at the Bottom of the Pyramid: Eradicating Poverty through Profits*. Upper Saddle River, NJ: Pearson Education/Wharton School Publishing.

Solow, R. 1957. "Technical Change and the Aggregate Production Function." *Review of Economics and Statistics* 39 (August): 312–20.

Von Braun, J. 2007. "The World Food Situation: New Driving Forces and Required Actions." *Food Policy Reports* 18, International Food Policy Research Institute (IFPRI), Washington, DC.

Wade, R. H. 1990. *Governing the Market: Economic Theory and the Role of Government in East Asian Industrialization*. Princeton, NJ: Princeton University Press.

Wilkinson, R., and K. Pickett. 2009. *The Spirit Level: Why More Equal Societies Almost Always Do Better*. London: Penguin.

Womack, J. P., and D. T. Jones. 1996. *Lean Thinking: Banish Waste and Create Wealth in Your Corporation*. New York: Simon & Schuster.

World Bank. 2009a. *China Quarterly Update*. March. Beijing: World Bank.

———. 2009b. *Global Economic Prospects 2009: Commodities at the Crossroads*. Washington, DC: World Bank.

Wright, G., and J. Czelusta. 2004. "The Myth of the Resource Curse." *Challenge* 47 (2): 6–38.

Zhang, Y., and C. Zheng. 2008. "The Implications of China's Rapid Growth on Demand for Energy and Mining Products Imported from Australia." *Economic Papers* 27 (1): 95–106.

PART III

GLOBAL VALUE CHAINS AND DEVELOPING COUNTRIES POSTCRISIS: SECTORAL PERSPECTIVES

5

THE GLOBAL APPAREL VALUE CHAIN, TRADE, AND THE CRISIS: CHALLENGES AND OPPORTUNITIES FOR DEVELOPING COUNTRIES

Gary Gereffi and Stacey Frederick

Apparel is one of the oldest and largest export industries, as well as the most globally prevalent: most countries make some type of product for the international textile and apparel market. It is a springboard for national development and often a starter industry for countries engaged in export-oriented industrialization because of its low fixed costs and emphasis on labor-intensive manufacturing (Adhikari and Weeratunge 2006; Gereffi 1999).

Although the global apparel industry has been expanding at a rapid rate since the early 1970s, during which it has been providing employment to tens of millions of workers in some of the least-developed countries in the world, the industry has experienced two major crises in the past five years. The first crisis is regulatory. The Multi-Fibre Arrangement (MFA)—which established quotas and preferential tariffs on apparel and textile items imported by the United States, Canada, and many European nations since the early 1970s—was phased out by the World Trade Organization (WTO) and replaced with the WTO Agreement on Textiles and Clothing (in effect 1995–2005).The concern of many poor and small developing economies that had relied on apparel exports was that they would be pushed out of the global trading system by much larger, low-cost rivals, such as China, India, and Bangladesh.

The second crisis is economic. The recent global recession, which was sparked by the banking meltdown in the United States in 2008 and quickly spread to most of the major industrialized and developing economies, brought the world to the brink of the most severe economic crisis since the Great Depression of the 1930s. Plant closures and worker layoffs in the industrialized nations led to slumping consumer demand, which resulted in fewer orders and shrinking markets for export-oriented economies in the developing world. The recession hit the apparel industry especially hard, leading to factory shutdowns, sharp increases in unemployment, and growing concerns over social unrest as displaced workers sought new jobs.

This chapter examines the impact of the MFA phaseout and the 2008–09 economic crisis on the changing patterns of supply and demand in the apparel global value chain (GVC) from 1995 to 2010, and also looks at how these crises have affected global sourcing and production networks among firms. Has there been greatly increased consolidation by the most successful exporting countries and among the leading firms in the apparel value chain? Who are the winners and losers in this industry, and what are the most viable upgrading strategies in today's global economy? Finally, recommendations and strategic options are discussed for how developing countries can deal with these challenges.

Effects of Dual Economic Crises on the Apparel Global Value Chain

Historically, global expansion of the apparel industry has been driven by trade policy. Apparel is one of the most trade protected of all industries, ranging from agricultural subsidies on input materials (cotton, wool, rayon) to a long history of quotas under the General Agreement on Tariff and Trade within the MFA and its successor pact under the WTO, the Agreement on Textiles and Clothing (ATC) (Adhikari and Yamamoto 2007). The MFA/ATC restricted exports to the major consuming markets by imposing country limits (quotas) on the volume of certain imported products. The system was designed to protect the domestic industries of the United States and the European Union (EU) by limiting imports from highly competitive suppliers such as China (Thoburn 2009).

Trade restrictions have contributed to the international fragmentation of the apparel supply chain, whereby low-wage countries typically sew together imported textile components and re-export the finished product. This reconfiguration began when exports from Hong Kong, China; the Republic of Korea; Taiwan, China; and later China reached their maximum levels under the quota system. Clothing assembly processes were then subcontracted to low-wage developing countries throughout the Asian Pacific region and other countries that had unused export quotas, such as Bangladesh, Sri Lanka, and Vietnam (Gereffi 1999; Audet 2004).

The removal of quotas on January 1, 2005 marked the end of more than 30 years of restricted access to the markets of the EU and North America. Retailers and other buyers became free to source textiles and apparel in unlimited amounts from any country, subject only to a system of tariffs and a narrow set of transitional safeguards that expired at the end of 2008. This caused a tremendous flux in the global geography of apparel production and trade, and a restructuring of firm strategies seeking to realign their production and sourcing networks to accommodate new economic and political realities (Gereffi 2004; Rasmussen 2008; Tewari 2006).

Apparel protectionism has declined in the past several years, with more garment-importing countries removing barriers to clothing trade than ever before (Frederick and Gereffi 2009a, 2009b; just-style.com 2009a). The economic recession and subsequent import slowdown in the United States, Europe, and Japan have sparked a reinvigoration of government policies to support the textile and clothing sector in leading apparel-exporting countries (see annex table 5A.1); however, overall, international restrictions on apparel trade are still relatively limited.

Changes in Global Supply and Demand

Consumption in the global apparel industry is concentrated in three main regions: the United States, the European Union, and Japan. In 2008, the European Union (EU 27, including intra-EU-27 trade) accounted for nearly half (47.3 percent) of total world apparel imports of US$376 billion, while the United States accounted for 22 percent, Japan for 6.9 percent, and the Russian Federation for 5.7 percent (see table 5.1). Together, the United States, the EU 27, and Japan represented over three-quarters of world apparel imports in 2008, which is down from 82.4 percent in 1995. Particularly notable is the steady decline in the U.S. share of global apparel imports, which fell from a peak of 32.1 percent in 2000 to 22 percent in 2008, and Japan's drop from 11.5 percent in 1995 to 6.9 percent in 2008.

At the onset of the recent 2008–09 crisis, global apparel imports increased by nearly 7 percent ($22.3 billion) between 2007 and 2008. U.S. imports declined during this period, but those of the EU 27, Japan, and Russia grew. Thus, the negative impact of the economic recession was not yet apparent in the annual import statistics for 2008 (see table 5.1).

A closer look at the shifting apparel imports of the United States, the EU 15, and Japan provides more detailed evidence of the impact of the economic recession on global apparel supply and demand.

Table 5.1 Changes in World's Top-15 Apparel Importers: 1995, 2000, 2005, and 2007–08

	1995		2000		2005		2007	2008	
Country/region	**Value (US$, billions)**	**Percent**	**Value (US$, billions)**	**Percent**	**Value (US$, billions)**	**Percent**	**Value (US$, billions)**	**Value (US$, billions)**	**Percent**
World	162.9		208.9		291.2		358.1	375.6	
European Union 27[a]	74.2	45.5	83.2	39.8	131.5	45.2	165.0	177.7	47.3
United States	41.4	25.4	67.1	32.1	80.1	27.5	84.9	82.5	22.0
Japan	18.8	11.5	19.7	9.4	22.5	7.7	24.0	25.9	6.9
Russian Federation[b]	n.a.	n.a.	2.7	1.3	7.9	2.7	14.5	21.4	5.7
Canada[c]	2.7	1.7	3.7	1.8	6.0	2.1	7.8	8.5	2.3
Switzerland	3.8	2.3	3.2	1.5	4.5	1.5	5.2	5.8	1.5
United Arab Emirates[d]	1.3	0.8	n.a.	n.a.	1.8	0.6	5.0	5.5	1.5
Australia[c]	1.3	0.8	1.9	0.9	3.1	1.1	3.7	4.3	1.1
Korea, Rep. of	1.1	0.7	1.3	0.6	2.9	1.0	4.3	4.2	1.1
Norway	1.4	0.9	1.3	0.6	1.8	0.6	2.3	2.7	0.7
Mexico[c,e]	1.9	1.2	3.6	1.7	2.5	0.9	2.5	2.5	0.7
China[f]	1.0	0.6	1.2	0.6	1.6	0.6	2.0	2.3	0.6

Singapore	1.6	1.0	1.9	0.9	2.1	0.7	2.4	2.2	0.6
Turkey	n.a.	n.a.	n.a.	n.a.	n.a.	n.a.	n.a.	2.2	0.6
Saudi Arabia	n.a.	n.a.	n.a.	n.a.	1.5	0.5	1.9	n.a.	n.a.
Honduras[f]	n.a.	n.a.	1.3	0.6	n.a.	n.a.	n.a.	n.a.	n.a.
Taiwan, China	0.9	0.5	1.0	0.5	n.a.	n.a.	n.a.	n.a.	n.a.
Top-15 share and percentage of world total imports	**151.3**	**92.9**	**193.0**	**92.4**	**269.9**	**92.7**	**325.5**	**347.8**	**92.6**
Hong Kong, China[g]	12.7	n.a.	16.0	n.a.	18.4	n.a.	19.1	18.5	n.a.

Source: WTO 2010; apparel is represented by SITC Code 84.

Note: Values are in billions of U.S. dollars at current prices, and percent is the country's or region's percentage of the year's world value. n.a. = not applicable, as the country was not in at current prices, top-15 apparel suppliers that year.

a. European Union (EU) values include intra-EU trade; values represent only the EU 15 in 1995.

b. Estimated value: coverage includes intratrade.

c. Method of valuation: imports are valued free-on-board (FOB).

d. Estimated value.

e. Coverage includes processing zones.

f. First-year processing zone trade is included; there is a break in data continuity with data from earlier years.

g. The value of Hong Kong, China, is not included in world totals because a large portion was re-exported and not retained.

United States

In 2008, U.S. consumers spent $200 billion on apparel, down 3.6 percent from 2007, and apparel spending in the first quarter of 2009 was also down 10 percent from the same period in the previous year (Driscoll and Wang 2009). Apparel sold and consumed in the United States has a very high import ratio, which has been increasing for decades. In 2006, the estimated overall apparel import penetration was 94 percent (Clothesource 2008). In 2008, the percentage of imports that were part of the apparent U.S. consumption of men's, women's, and children's apparel ranged from a low of 77.2 percent for finished socks to a high of 100 percent for men's dress and sports coats (in volume terms) (U.S. Census Bureau 2009a; 2009b).

Table 5.2 charts trends over time in the top-15 countries that supply U.S. apparel imports. Most striking is the dramatic increase in China's import share, which climbed from 13.3 percent of all U.S. apparel imports in 2000 to 26.4 percent in 2005 and 34.7 percent in 2008. The big losers during this period were Mexico, whose apparel import share fell from 13.1 percent in 2000 to just 5.2 percent in 2008, and the DR-CAFTA (Dominican Republic and the five countries in the Central American Free Trade Agreement[1]), whose import share dropped from 13.9 percent in 2000 to 9.6 percent in 2008. A more graphic illustration of the shifts in the regional structure of U.S. apparel imports is found in annex figure 5A.1.

European Union 15

In 2008, Europe accounted for 41 percent of the global apparel retail sales of $1,026 billion (Datamonitor 2009). In the EU 15, the apparel import penetration varies significantly among countries. In 2006, the estimated import shares for the main consuming countries were United Kingdom and Germany, 95 percent; France, 85 percent; Italy, 65 percent; and Spain, 55 percent (Clothesource 2008).

Table 5.3 highlights trends in the EU 15's source of apparel imports over time. China is the market leader, with 24 percent of total EU 15 apparel imports in 2009, up from 9.6 percent in 2000. The next three top importers in 2009 were Turkey (6.3 percent), Bangladesh (4.7 percent), and India (3.9 percent). The shifting regional structure of EU 15 apparel imports between 1996 and 2008 can also be seen in annex figure 5A. 2.

For the EU 15, it is important to note that all leading apparel suppliers, with the exception of China and Hong Kong, China, receive either duty-free or preferential tariff treatment. Morocco and Tunisia are part of the Euro-Mediterranean Partnership; Bulgaria, Hungary, Poland, and Romania are part of the EU 27; and Turkey has a Customs Union with the EU. To varying degrees, Bangladesh, India, Indonesia, Pakistan, Sri Lanka, Thailand, and Vietnam receive benefits from the U.S. Generalized System of Preferences (GSP) program. Whereas the United States

Table 5.2 Changes in U.S. Top-15 Apparel Importers: 1995, 2000, 2005, and 2007–09

Country/region	1995		2000		2005		2007	2008	2009	
	Value (US$, millions)	Percent	Value (US$, millions)	Percent	Value (US$, millions)	Percent	Value (US$, millions)	Value (US$, millions)	Value (US$, millions)	Percent
World	**41,367**		**67,115**		**80,071**		**84,853**	**82,466**	**72,064**	
China	6,170	14.9	8,924	13.3	21,138	26.4	28,530	28,575	28,201	39.1
DR-CAFTA	4,920	11.9	9,341	13.9	9,413	11.8	8,199	7,903	6,405	8.9
Vietnam	n.a.		n.a.		2,911	3.6	4,619	5,527	5,332	7.4
Indonesia	1,376	3.3	2,333	3.5	3,163	4.0	4,306	4,358	4,154	5.8
Mexico	2,904	7.0	8,809	13.1	6,374	8.0	4,743	4,250	3,580	5.0
Bangladesh	1,142	2.8	2,279	3.4	2,537	3.2	3,286	3,657	3,580	5.0
India	1,379	3.3	2,157	3.2	3,376	4.2	3,505	3,412	3,126	4.3
Cambodia	n.a.		n.a.		1,818	2.3	2,559	2,508	1,950	2.7
Thailand	1,209	2.9	2,276	3.4	2,351	2.9	2,311	2,238	1,765	2.4
European Union 15	2,003	4.8	2,644	3.9	2,535	3.2	2,602	2,412	1,646	2.3
Pakistan	n.a.		n.a.		1,447	1.8	1,696	1,691	1,467	2.0
Sri Lanka	1,029	2.5	1,609	2.4	1,796	2.2	1,711	1,620	1,319	1.8
Malaysia	1,253	3.0	1,380	2.1	n.a.		1,422	1,505	1,300	1.8
Philippines	1,685	4.1	2,037	3.0	1,949	2.4	1,821	1,443	1,071	1.5
Jordan	n.a.		n.a.		n.a.		n.a.	n.a.	791	1.1
Hong Kong, China	4,566	11.0	4,808	7.2	3,738	4.7	2,162	1,645	n.a.	
Korea, Rep. of	1,923	4.6	2,591	3.9	1,319	1.6	n.a.	n.a.	n.a.	
Taiwan, China	2,261	5.5	2,285	3.4	n.a.		n.a.	n.a.	n.a.	
Canada	896	2.2	1,933	2.9	n.a.		n.a.	n.a.	n.a.	
Top-15 totals and percentage of world total	**34,715**	**83.9**	**55,407**	**82.6**	**65,866**	**82.3**	**73,470**	**72,744**	**65,687**	**91.2**

Source: UN Comtrade; apparel represented by SITC 84. Values for 2009 are from United States International Trade Commission (USITC); apparel is represented by SITC 84; General CIF (cost, insurance, freight) Imports Value and General CIF Imports.

Note: Percent is the country's or region's percentage of the year's world value. DR-CAFTA = Dominican Republic–Central American Free Trade Agreement; n.a. = not applicable, as country was not in the top-15 apparel suppliers that year.

Table 5.3 Changes in EU 15 Top-15 Apparel Importers, 2000 and 2005–09

	2000		2005		2006	2007	2008	2009	
Country/region	**Value (€, millions)**	**Percent**	**Value (€, millions)**	**Percent**	**Value (€, millions)**	**Value (€, millions)**	**Value (€, millions)**	**Value (€, millions)**	**Percent**
World totals	64,517		73,909		80,392	84,172	86,935	81,300	
European Union 15 (intra)	26,180	40.6	29,544	40.0	30,993	33,710	34,601	31,507	38.8
China	6,190	9.6	13,061	17.7	14,789	16,865	19,139	19,491	24.0
Turkey	4,437	6.9	5,648	7.6	5,730	6,109	5,739	5,137	6.3
Bangladesh	1,907	3.0	2,596	3.5	3,381	3,208	3,536	3,800	4.7
India	1,805	2.8	2,455	3.3	2,922	2,838	2,998	3,138	3.9
Tunisia	2,496	3.9	2,359	3.2	2,386	2,500	2,526	2,196	2.7
Morocco	1,822	2.8	1,858	2.5	2,007	2,165	2,089	1,809	2.2
Romania	2,196	3.4	2,881	3.9	2,791	2,060	1,982	1,521	1.9
Poland	1,539	2.4	854	1.2	812	890	1,185	1,335	1.6
Vietnam	650	1.0	522	0.7	768	843	947	935	1.1
Indonesia	1,281	2.0	891	1.2	1,052	899	899	865	1.1
Bulgaria	722	1.1	977	1.3	1,088	1,054	1,035	823	1.0
Pakistan	645	1.0	697	0.9	787	802	813	779	1.0
Thailand	730	1.1	663	0.9	761	703	717	690	0.8
Switzerland	377	n.a.	519	n.a.	528	636	642	548	0.7
Sri Lanka	338	n.a.	331	n.a.	426	488	529	555	0.7
Hungary	1,001	1.6	687	0.9	706	677	582	445	n.a.
Hong Kong, China	1,885	2.9	1,006	1.4	1,557	1,005	510	258	n.a.

Source: Eurostat: Apparel Imports to Euro Area EU 15; apparel represented by SITC 84.
Note: Percent represents the country's or region's percentage of the year's world value. n.a. = not applicable, as country was not in top-15 apparel suppliers that year.

excludes textiles and apparel items from its GSP agreements, the EU 15 includes textiles and apparel, thereby favoring many of the least-developed exporters in the global economy.

Japan

As in the United States and the EU 15, Japan relies heavily on apparel imports. In 2006, the estimated apparel import penetration ratio was 93 percent (Clothesource 2008). Furthermore, Japan is highly dependent on one country, China, which represented 83 percent of total apparel imports in 2008 (WTO 2009). The top-five countries/regions (EU 27, Vietnam, Thailand, and Korea, plus China) accounted for 93.9 percent of total imports in 2008 (see table 5.4).

Characteristics of Top Apparel-Exporting Countries

By the end of 2009, the economic recession that hit the apparel retail markets of all the advanced industrial countries had rippled throughout the supply chain in developing economies as well. A striking trend is that the largest low-cost apparel producers in the developing world—China, India, Bangladesh, and Vietnam—actually managed to increase their export shares in major global markets (see table 5.5). This may reflect a substitution effect of the economic recession, in which the lowest cost suppliers gain market share vis-à-vis more expensive rivals.

China is the clear winner in the global apparel export race of the past 15 years. Between 1995 and 2008, China more than doubled its share of global apparel exports, from 15.2 percent to 33.2 percent, and it had a fivefold increase in the value of its apparel exports, from $24 billion to $120 billion. Other than the EU 27, which includes intra-European Union trade, the next six apparel exporters combined (Turkey, Bangladesh, India, Vietnam, Indonesia, and Mexico) account for less than half (15.4 percent) of China's export total in 2008 (see table 5.5).

Capabilities of leading global apparel exporters

Annex table 5A.3 lists the production capabilities of several main apparel-exporting countries. As countries like China, Turkey, and India develop capabilities that permit vertical integration in apparel, their reliance on apparel exports tends to diminish because their upgrading processes facilitate broader industrial diversification. Annex table 5A.4, which provides export-dependence ratios for major apparel suppliers, lends support to this argument. Those countries with the greatest apparel export dependence—Cambodia (85 percent), Bangladesh (71 percent), and Sri Lanka (41 percent)—emphasize CMT (cut, make, and trim) assembly with limited capabilities beyond manufacturing. Vietnam also emphasizes CMT

Table 5.4 Changes in Japan's Top-Five Apparel Importers: 1995, 2000, 2005, and 2007–08

	1995		2000		2005		2007	2008	
Country/region	**Value (US$, millions)**	**Percent**	**Value (US$, millions)**	**Percent**	**Value (US$, millions)**	**Percent**	**Value (US$, millions)**	**Value (US$, millions)**	**Percent**
World	**18,758**		**19,709**		**22,541**		**23,999**	**25,866**	
China	10,626	56.6	14,713	74.7	18,243	80.9	19,795	21,350	82.8
European Union 15	2,398	12.8	1,476	7.5	1,556	6.9	1,515	1,457	5.6
Vietnam	n.a.		591	3.0	610	2.7	717	865	3.4
Thailand	503	2.7	n.a.		n.a.		271	313	1.2
Korea, Rep. of	1,847	9.8	951	4.8	436	1.9	258	227	0.9
United States	1,096	5.8	468	2.4	296	1.3	n.a.	n.a.	
Top-five total and percentage of world imports	**16,469**	**87.8**	**18,200**	**92.3**	**21,141**	**93.8**	**22,555**	**24,213**	**93.9**

Source: UN Comtrade, SITC 84, rev. 3., Imports to Japan.
Note: Percent represents the country's or region's percentage of the year's world value. n.a. = not applicable as country was not in top-five apparel suppliers for the year.

Table 5.5 Changes in World's Top-15 Apparel Exporters: 1995, 2000, 2005, and 2007–08

Country/region	1995		2000		2005		2007	2008	
	Value (US$, billions)	Percent	Value (US$, billions)	Percent	Value (US$, billions)	Percent	Value (US$, billions)	Value (US$, billions)	Percent
World	**158.4**		**197.7**		**277.1**		**345.8**	**361.9**	
China	24.0	15.2	36.1	18.2	74.2	26.8	115.2	120.0	33.2
European Union 27[a]	48.5	30.6	56.2	28.4	85.5	30.8	105.1	112.4	31.1
Turkey	6.1	3.9	6.5	3.3	11.8	4.3	13.9	13.6	3.8
Bangladesh[b]	n.a.		5.1	2.6	6.9	2.5	8.9	10.9	3.0
India	4.1	2.6	6.0	3.0	8.6	3.1	9.8	10.9	3.0
Vietnam[b]	n.a.		n.a.		4.7	1.7	7.4	9.0	2.5
Indonesia	3.4	2.1	4.7	2.4	5.0	1.8	5.9	6.3	1.7
Mexico[c]	2.7	1.7	8.6	4.4	7.3	2.6	5.1	4.9	1.4
United States	6.7	4.2	8.6	4.4	5.0	1.8	4.3	4.4	1.2
Thailand	5.0	3.2	3.8	1.9	4.1	1.5	4.1	4.2	1.2
Pakistan	n.a.		n.a.		3.6	1.3	3.8	3.9	1.1
Tunisia	2.3	1.5	n.a.		3.1	1.1	3.6	3.8	1.0
Cambodia[b]	n.a.		n.a.		n.a.		3.5	3.6	1.0
Malaysia	2.3	1.4	n.a.		n.a.		n.a.	3.6	1.0

(continued next page)

Table 5.5 *continued*

Country/region	1995 Value (US$, billions)	1995 Percent	2000 Value (US$, billions)	2000 Percent	2005 Value (US$, billions)	2005 Percent	2007 Value (US$, billions)	2008 Value (US$, billions)	2008 Percent
Sri Lanka[b]	n.a.		2.8	1.4	2.9	1.0	n.a.	3.5	1.0
Hong Kong, China[d]	9.5	6.0	9.9	5.0	7.2	2.6	5.0	n.a.	n.a.
Morocco	n.a.		n.a.		2.8	1.0	3.5	n.a.	n.a.
Korea, Rep. of	5.0	3.1	5.0	2.5	n.a.		n.a.	n.a.	n.a.
Taiwan, China	3.2	2.0	3.0	1.5	n.a.		n.a.	n.a.	n.a.
Dominican Republic	n.a.		2.6	1.3	n.a.		n.a.	n.a.	n.a.
Philippines	2.4	1.5	2.5	1.3	n.a.		n.a.	n.a.	n.a.
Poland	2.3	1.5	n.a.		n.a.		n.a.	n.a.	n.a.
Top-15 total and percentage share of world exports	**127.5**	**80.5**	**161.5**	**81.7**	**232.6**	**83.9**	**299.1**	**315.0**	**87.0**

Source: WTO 2010; apparel exports represented by SITC 84.

Note: Values are in billions of U.S. dollars at current prices. Percent represents the country's or region's percentage of the year's world value. n.a. = not applicable as country was not in top-15 apparel suppliers for the year.

a. European Union (EU) values include intra-EU trade; values represent only EU 15 in 1995.

b. Some years include estimates.

c. Includes significant shipments through processing zones.

d. Domestic exports only.

assembly, but its apparel export dependence ratio is relatively low (14 percent) because of the importance of its agricultural exports.

The main apparel-exporting countries can be categorized as follows:

- *Steady-growth suppliers* (overall increasing market share since the early 1990s): China, Bangladesh, India, Vietnam, and Cambodia; Pakistan and Egypt as well, but with smaller market shares.
- *Split-market suppliers:* Indonesia is increasing its market share in the United States and Japan and decreasing it in the EU 15; conversely, Sri Lanka is increasing market share in the EU 15 and decreasing it in the United States.
- *Pre-MFA suppliers* (sharp declines after MFA quota phaseout that have accelerated during the crisis): Canada, Mexico, CAFTA, EU-12, Tunisia, Morocco, and Thailand.
- *Past-prime suppliers:* (decreasing market share since early 1990s): Hong Kong, China; Korea; Taiwan, China; Malaysia—also countries with smaller market shares: Philippines; Singapore; and Macao SAR, China.

The last two years have reinforced many of the trends occurring after the phaseout of quotas. China, Bangladesh, Vietnam, and Indonesia are increasing their market shares in North America and the European Union, primarily at the expense of near-sourcing options such as Mexico and the Central American and Caribbean suppliers to the United States, as well as apparel exporters from North Africa and Eastern Europe to the EU 15 (see annex figures 5A.1 and 5A.2).

Leading apparel suppliers like China, India, and Turkey, concerned about a slowdown in global exports, have also begun to focus more on sales to their domestic markets. This trend not only taps into the added purchasing power of those emerging economies, but it also allows them to accelerate the upgrading process associated with moving beyond assembly and full-package supply to original design manufacturing (ODM) and original brand manufacturing (OBM).

Regional Trends in Capturing Export Share

From a regional perspective, how have different apparel exporters managed to cope with the MFA phaseout and the economic recession? Since the export data for 2008 capture only the initial year of the economic recession, the following findings are provisional, yet they reveal some interesting trends.

The growth of regional suppliers for finished apparel to the European Union and the United States has decreased markedly since 2005, largely resulting from the expansion of China's exports to these markets (see tables 5.2 and 5.3). Regional and bilateral trade agreements in Asia are also increasing, for example, as are those in the South Asian region (SAFTA, South Asian Free Trade Area) and those involving the Association of Southeast Asian Nations (ASEAN), including the new China link that went into full effect on January 1, 2010 (see annex table 5A.1).

East Asia: China wins with functional upgrading

In East Asia, China has not only increased its share of overall exports, but it has also significantly diversified its export partners. In 1996, Japan and Hong Kong, China, represented nearly 60 percent of China's apparel exports of $25 billion, with the United States and the EU 15 accounting for another 22.6 percent. By 2008, China's apparel exports had nearly quintupled to $120 billion, and the EU 15 and the United States were the top-two export partners; but they accounted for only 39.3 percent of China's apparel exports, while Japan and Hong Kong, China, held 21.1 percent (see table 5.6). Thus, China's top-four export markets in 2008 had about the same share of China's total exports as did combined Japan and Hong Kong, China, in 1996. In this respect, China is decreasing its dependence on its traditional export partners while adding important new markets, such as Russia and former Soviet bloc countries. This pattern can help China to withstand the current demand slump in advanced industrial markets.

It is also important to recognize the size of China's apparel production for its domestic market. In 2007, the estimated value of sales to the Chinese apparel market totaled $93 billion, indicating that 56 percent of the overall apparel production activities in China were for local consumers (Clothesource 2008).

South Asia: Steady winners

In the long term, the South Asian countries have all increased market share to both the EU 15 and the United States. Post-MFA and during the recent crisis, Bangladesh performed well in both markets, but India, Sri Lanka, and Pakistan have not performed as well in the two markets. The U.S. market share and export value of India, Sri Lanka, and Pakistan has been decreasing, whereas it has increased since 2007 to the EU 15. South Asian countries receive preferential access to the EU under the GSP scheme, yet they do not receive U.S. benefits from GSP.

Southeast Asia: Split effects

Both Vietnam and Cambodia have been gaining EU 15 and U.S. market share since the early 1990s. During the crisis, however, Vietnam managed to maintain its value, volume, and market share far better than did Cambodia. Indonesia and Malaysia are more important suppliers to the U.S. market than to the EU market, and their post-2007 export values and market shares have affected exports to the

Table 5.6 China's Top-10 Apparel Export Markets: 1996, 2002, and 2008

1996			2002			2008		
Partner	Value (US$, millions)	Percent	Partner	Value (US$, millions)	Percent	Partner	Value (US$, millions)	Percent
Japan	8,170	32.6	Japan	11,197	27.1	European Union 15	28,760	23.9
Hong Kong, China	6,600	26.4	Hong Kong, China	7,084	17.2	United States	18,566	15.4
United States	3,187	12.7	United States	5,325	12.9	Japan	17,686	14.7
European Union 15	2,467	9.9	European Union 15	4,672	11.3	Hong Kong, China	7,757	6.4
Korea, Rep. of	649		Korea, Rep. of	2,250	5.4	Russian Federation	5,640	4.7
Russian Federation	635	2.5	Russian Federation	1,300	3.1	Kyrgyz Republic	5,091	4.2
Australia	453	1.8	Australia	1,027	2.5	Korea, Rep. of	3,340	2.8
Poland	275	1.1	Canada	731	1.8	Kazakhstan	3,022	2.5
Canada	267	1.1	Mexico	618	1.5	Canada	2,956	2.5
Saudi Arabia	192	0.8	Singapore	617	1.5	Australia	2,473	2.1
World	25,034		World	41,302		World	120,405	
Value of year's top-10 and percentage share of China's annual apparel exports	22,896	91.5		34,821	84.3		95,290	79.1
World apparel exports and China's share	166,077	15.1		203,664	20.3		361,888	33.3

Source: UN Comtrade: SITC code 84 rev. 3: Exports from China. World Textile Export Values from WTO Statistics Database.
Note: Percent represents the country's or region's partner's share of China's annual apparel exports to the world.

two markets differently, with increases in their share of the U.S. market and decreases in the EU 15. Furthermore, Indonesia and Malaysia have started to focus on growth in textile exports as well. Thailand has been negatively affected by the MFA phaseout, and the Philippines' market share in the United States and EU 15 has fallen since the early 1990s.

Regional suppliers: Declines in market share

The EU's outward processing trade (OPT) arrangement is analogous to the U.S. production sharing system (807) trade arrangement (Gereffi 1997). The United States and its periphery include the following: NAFTA members (United States, Mexico, Canada); the DR-CAFTA signatories (Central America and the Dominican Republic); and other economies in the Caribbean Basin Initiative. The EU and its periphery include EU 27, Turkey, non-EU Central and Eastern Europe countries, and North Africa.

Nearly all of the U.S. regional suppliers have been negatively impacted by the MFA phaseout. EU 15 regional suppliers are also experiencing declines in market share to the EU 15, but the EU as a whole is increasing its share of global apparel exports. Apparel exports from the EU 27 are increasing to emerging markets such as Russia.

Apparel GVCs: Changing Roles, Capabilities, and Networks

The global industry has undergone several production migrations, and production network configurations have been transformed over the last 30 years. As production and sourcing networks evolved and expanded to different global regions, new governance structures and upgrading opportunities arose in the apparel GVC.

Upgrading in the Buyer-Driven GVC

The apparel industry is the quintessential example of a buyer-driven production chain, marked by power asymmetries between the producers and global buyers of final apparel products. The most valuable activities in the apparel GVC are not related to manufacturing per se, but are found in the design, branding, and marketing of the products. These activities are performed by lead firms—large global retailers and brand owners in the apparel industry, which in most cases, outsource the manufacturing process to a global network of suppliers. Apparel manufacturing is highly competitive and becoming more consolidated, with increasing barriers to entry and upgrading. Developing countries are in constant competition for foreign investments and contracts with global brand owners, leaving many suppliers with little leverage in the chain. The result is an unequal partition of the total value-added along the apparel commodity chain in favor of lead firms.

Beginning in the 1970s, East Asian suppliers extended their upgrading opportunities in the apparel GVC from simple assembly to a series of new roles that included original equipment manufacturing (OEM) for full-package production, ODM for design, and OBM for brand development stages (Gereffi 1999). As intangible aspects of the value chain—marketing, brand development, and design, for example—have become more important for the profitability and power of lead firms, "tangibles" (production and manufacturing) have increasingly become "commodities." This has led to new divisions of labor and hurdles if suppliers wish to enter these chains (Bair 2005; Gereffi et al. 2001).

The main stages of functional capabilities and upgrading in the apparel GVC are described below (Gereffi and Memedovic 2003). Table 5.7 summarizes the current functional capabilities of the main apparel export countries. Annex table 5A.5 highlights the change in roles, associated governance structures, and

Table 5.7 Summary of Country Capabilities with Examples

Functional capabilities	Supplier tier	Recommendations, key facilitators	Country examples
Cut, make, trim (CMT) (assembly)	Marginal supplier	• Promote upstream foreign direct investment (FDI) • Government and regional organizations • Lead firm to commit to long-term supply	Cambodia, Vietnam, Sub-Saharan Africa, the Caribbean
Package contractor (OEM) sourcing	Preferred supplier	• Invest in machinery and logistics technology • Private investment	Bangladesh and Indonesia
	Niche supplier		Sri Lanka and Mexico
Full-package provider (ODM)	Strategic supplier	Next step: enter new emerging markets as a lead firm	European Union, Turkey, India, China
Service providers	Coordinators and foreign investors		Hong Kong, China; Taiwan, China; Singapore; Malaysia; Republic of Korea

Source: Authors.
Note: ODM = original design manufacturing; OEM = original equipment manufacturing.

required skills for contemporary upgrading in the global apparel GVC. The stages are as follows:

- *Assembly/CMT:* This is a form of subcontracting in which garment sewing plants are provided with imported inputs for assembly, most commonly in export processing zones (EPZs). CMT, that is, "cut, make, and trim," or CM (cut and make), is a system whereby a manufacturer produces garments by cutting fabric provided by the customer and sewing the cut fabric into garments for delivery to the customer in accordance with his or her specifications. In general, companies operating on a CMT basis do not become involved in the design of the garment, just the manufacture.
- *Original equipment manufacturing (OEM)/FOB/package contractor:* OEM is a business model that focuses on the manufacturing process. The contractor is capable of sourcing and financing piece goods (fabric) and trim, and providing all production services, finishing, and packaging for delivery to the retail outlet. In the clothing industry, OEMs typically manufacture according to customer specifications and design, in many cases using raw materials specified by the customer. Free-on-board (FOB) is a common term used in industry to describe this type of contract manufacturer. However, it is technically an international trade term in which, for the quoted price, goods are delivered onboard a ship or to another carrier at no cost to the buyer.
- *Original design manufacturing (ODM)/full package:* This is a business model that focuses on design rather than on branding or manufacturing. A full-package garment supplier carries out all steps involved in the production of a finished garment, including design, fabric purchasing, cutting, sewing, trimming, packaging, and distribution. Typically, a full-package supplier will organize and coordinate the design of the product; the approval of samples; the selection, purchasing, and production of materials; the completion of production; and, in some cases, the delivery of the finished product to the final customer.
- *Original brand manufacturing (OBM):* OBM is a business model that focuses on branding rather than design or manufacturing; this is a form of upgrading to move into the sale of the customer's "own brand" products. For many firms in developing countries, this marks the beginning of brand development for products sold in the home country or its neighbors.

The desire of buyers to reduce the complexity of their own operations, keep costs down, and increase flexibility to enable responsiveness to consumer demand has spurred the shift from CMT to OEM package contractors. Establishing and maintaining captive, buyer-supplier-dependent relationships is costly for the lead firm and leads to inflexibility as far as changing suppliers because of transaction-specific investments developed between parties. Modular production networks provide the lowest costs to lead firms. Thus, logistics coordination and sourcing are frequently the first functional activities lead firms are willing to give up, and they want to shift the responsibility for this to their first-tier suppliers. The CMT model is unnecessarily complex and the recession has accelerated awareness of the flaws in this model. This model is finally becoming obsolete; countries without capabilities beyond CMT need to prioritize investments in this area to stay in business and maintain market share.

Upgrading of Regional Capabilities in the Apparel GVC

In the past, the global apparel industry has been characterized by a large number of exporting countries as a result of the MFA quota system; however, these numbers have been sharply reduced and the exports have become more concentrated. The apparel supply chain is also marked by substantial country specialization. Higher-income nations generally predominate in more capital-intensive segments, while lower-income countries dominate labor-intensive segments (Kilduff and Ting 2006). The most labor-intensive activity is apparel production, followed by textile (yarn and fabric) production. The most capital-intensive segments, such as manmade fiber production and machinery manufacturing, are located upstream, where entry barriers become progressively higher (Gereffi and Memedovic 2003). As countries grow richer and wages rise, the comparative advantage in labor-intensive manufacturing is eroded, and the focus shifts to high value-added products or to other manufactured products with lower labor intensity (Adhikari and Weeratunge 2006).

Annex figure 5A.3 illustrates how this division between capital- and labor-intensive activities varies between countries at different levels of development and shapes the pattern of industrial upgrading in the Asian apparel GVC. The main segments of the apparel chain—garments, textiles, fibers, and machinery—are arranged along the horizontal axis, and they reflect low to high levels of relative value-added as capital intensity increases. Countries are grouped on the vertical axis by their relative level of development, with Japan at the top, China and India in the middle tier, and the least-developed exporters like Bangladesh, Cambodia, and Vietnam at the bottom.

This figure further reveals several important dynamics about the apparel GVC in Asia, and the GVC approach more generally (see Gereffi 2005, 172). First, individual countries tend to progress from low to high value-added segments of the chain sequentially over time. This shows the importance of looking at the entire constellation of value-added steps in the production process (raw materials, components, finished goods, related services, and machinery), rather than just the end product. Second, there is a regional division of labor in the apparel GVC, whereby countries at very different levels of development form a multitiered production hierarchy with a variety of export roles; for example, the United States generates the product designs and large orders, Japan provides the sewing machines, the East Asian newly industrializing economies (NIEs) supply fabric, and low-wage Asian economies (like China, Indonesia, or Vietnam) sew the apparel. Industrial upgrading occurs when countries change their roles in these export hierarchies. Finally, advanced economies like Japan and the East Asian NIEs do not exit the industry when the finished products in the chain become mature, as the "product cycle" model (Vernon 1966) implies, but rather they capitalize on their knowledge of production and distribution networks and thus move to higher value-added stages in the apparel chain.

Lead Firms in the Contemporary Apparel GVC

In the apparel GVC, there are three main types of lead firms: retailers, brand marketers, and brand manufacturers (highlighted in figure 5.1). These lead firms not only have significant market power because of their size, which is reflected in sales, but they also have moved beyond production to different combinations of high-value activities, including design, marketing, consumer services, and logistics.

Table 5.8 provides regional examples of each type of lead firm. The retailer category distinguishes between mass merchants that sell a diverse array of products and specialty retailers that sell only apparel items. Brand manufacturers traditionally formed production networks in which the brand owner was involved in the production process, either through ownership or through supplying inputs to production. In contrast to brand manufacturers, brand marketers and retailers opt for sourcing strategies that involve constructing networks with OEM or full-package producers. In this model, the buyer provides detailed garment specifications and the supplier is responsible for acquiring the inputs and coordinating all parts of the production process: purchase of textiles, cutting, garment assembly, laundry, as well as finishing, packaging, and distribution (Bair and Gereffi 2001; Bair 2006). As capabilities in the global apparel supply base improved, brand manufacturers, marketers, and retailers expanded their sourcing networks.

Changes in Apparel-Sourcing Strategies

Two major changes occurred during the MFA phaseout that caused a change in the sourcing strategies of lead firms in the apparel GVC. On the demand side,

Figure 5.1 Types of Lead Firms in the Global Apparel Value Chain

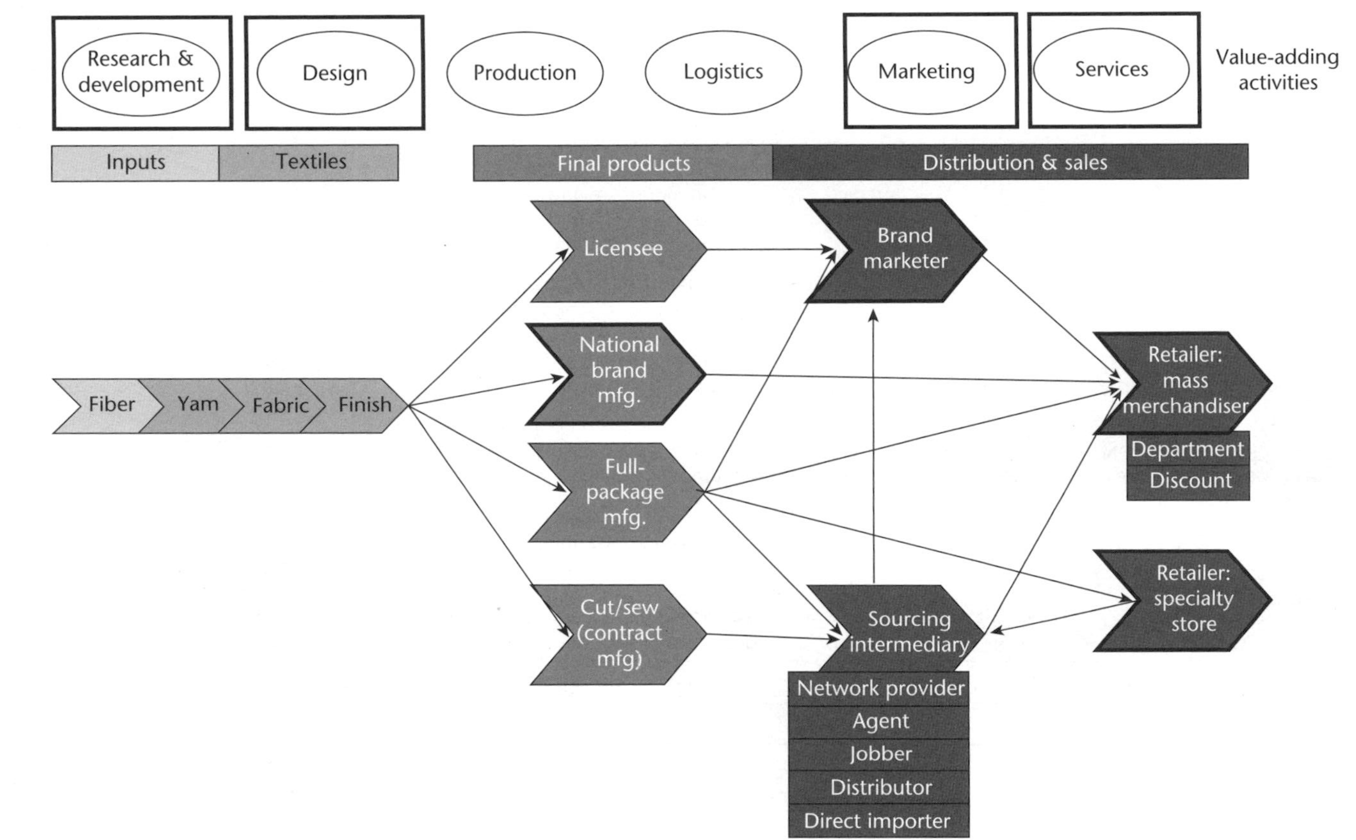

Source: Adapted from Frederick 2010, 80.

Table 5.8 Lead Firm Types and Brand Types with Regional Examples

			Examples	
Lead firm type	**Type of brand**	**Description**	**United States**	**European Union 27**
Retailers: mass merchants	Private label: the retailer owns or licenses the final product brand, but in almost all cases, the retailer does not own manufacturing.	Department/discount stores that carry private label, exclusive, or licensed brands that are only available in the retailers' stores in addition to other brands.	Walmart, Target, Sears, Macy's, JCPenney, Kohl's, Dillard's	Asda (Walmart), Tesco, C&A, Marks & Spencer
Retailers: specialty apparel		Retailer develops proprietary label brands that commonly include the store's name.	Gap, Limited Brands, American Eagle, Abercrombie & Fitch	HandM, Benetton, Mango, New Look, NEXT
Brand marketer	National brand: the manufacturer is also the brand owner and goods are distributed through multiple retail outlets.	Firm owns the brand name, but not manufacturing, that is, "manufacturers without factories." Products are sold at a variety of retail outlets.	Nike, Levi's, Polo, Liz Claiborne	Ben Sherman, Hugo Boss, Diesel, Gucci
Brand manufacturer		Firm owns brand name and manufacturing; it typically coordinates supply of intermediate inputs (CMT) to its production networks, often in countries with reciprocal trade agreements.	VF, Hanesbrands, Fruit of the Loom, Gildan	Inditex (Zara)

Source: Authors.

brand manufacturers were replaced by the suppliers of private-label merchandise (store brands) sourced by retailers. Retailers' strengths are in marketing and branding, but they tend to have limited knowledge of how to actually make the products they are procuring. Thus, retailers needed suppliers or agents capable of bundling and selling the entire range of manufacturing and logistics activities (OEM or ODM), creating a need for suppliers with increased capabilities. On the supply side, network relationships in the apparel supply chain became increasingly complex because of the breadth and specialization of apparel products and the growth of countries with production capabilities. The MFA had facilitated the entry of developing countries with limited technical or business skills into global apparel networks.

These two changes led to the need for new forms of coordination and management in the apparel supply chain. Two groups emerged to provide the key links between producers and retailers: East Asian transnational manufacturers with established buyer relationships who set up and managed global production networks, and traders (import-export companies) and agents who emerged as intermediaries between established buyers and sellers in the apparel GVC.

The traditional agent-sourcing model is most popular with buyers that require smaller volumes or larger buyers that need small quantities of certain items. Benefits of using a third-party sourcing agent include scale of operations, buying power, flexibility, and ability to spread risk among suppliers. Li and Fung Limited—based in Hong Kong, China, engaged in the trade of consumer goods since 1906, and pioneered the agent-sourcing model—is continuing to expand its roles into areas such as product development, marketing, and branding. Recently, Li and Fung adopted a more prominent role as the primary purchasing agent for giant retailers including Walmart and well-known apparel brands like Liz Claiborne.

Alternatively, as buyers developed expertise in assessing local capabilities, they started to establish direct sourcing relationships. To reduce cost and mitigate risk, many buyers established overseas sourcing offices in their main producing countries. Over the years, retailers shifted more responsibilities to these overseas sourcing offices, driven by cost and the skills of the staff based there. Many are also moving product development and design offices closer to the manufacturing process. Direct sourcing requires manufacturers to provide faster reaction times and better factory understanding of a retailer's particular needs. Sourcing agents charge clients 4 to 8 percent of the wholesale price as commission, representing an area to realize savings if this step is eliminated.

Annex tables 5A.6–5A.8 describe the sourcing channels and destinations used by several categories of lead firms in the global apparel GVC. Most retailers use a range of different channels depending on their levels of expertise and sales volumes (just-style.com 2009c).

New Roles and Relationships in the Apparel GVC

The roles and relationships among national and global lead firms, apparel manufacturers, and intermediaries have increasingly blended and overlapped in recent years. The following trends are closely tied to buyers' strategies and long-term objectives. These trends began before the economic crisis and will likely persist afterwards.

- *Brand owners becoming specialty retailers:* Brand manufacturers and marketers are increasingly opening their own stores. In addition, brands with existing retail operations are likely to focus more on their own stores rather than meeting the needs of their external customers (Euromonitor 2009).
- *Full-package "manufacturers" becoming intermediaries:* Rather than manufacture, they establish a network of global suppliers. Essentially, these suppliers are doing what brand marketers and manufacturers did 10 to 20 years ago. There are a host of firms in countries around the world that make products for multiple brands, based on the buyers' requirements. They provide full-package services along with production capabilities.
- *Intermediaries/agents expanding services:* These middlemen are expanding their roles to include an array of services to buyers, including design, product development, and quality control, in addition to providing a network of suppliers and logistics.
- *Private-label brands growing:* There is a sharp increase in the volume and diversity of retailer private labels. Retailers that develop proprietary brands use in-house design teams and outsourced manufacturing capacity, often by direct foreign product sourcing. By eliminating the middleman associated with national brands, retailers can shave costs and widen profit margins. Today, retailers are expanding the range of private-label products offered and developing higher-margin private-label goods (Euromonitor 2009).
- *Brand marketers creating exclusive product lines with mass merchant retailers:* Exclusive product lines are a new way for mass merchants to offer unique merchandise. Retailers are striking agreements with brand marketers to develop and distribute brands that are sold exclusively through the one retailer's stores instead of the traditional brand marketer model in which goods are sold via multiple retail outlets (Asaeda 2008; Euromonitor International 2009).
- *Social and environmental standards becoming more important:* This trend began with corporate social responsibility (CSR) campaigns and social advocacy groups. Now environmental compliance requirements and green initiatives are moving to the forefront (Asaeda 2008; Barrie and Ayling 2009; Driscoll and Wang 2009; International News Services 2009; Tucker 2009).

Consumers are demanding that lead firms become more responsible and transparent about their practices. The success of ethical clothing brands (for example, Patagonia) is a testament to the power of consumer demand and green credentials.

- *Dual sourcing strategies of "quick response" and "fast fashion" being adopted to keep competitive:* This is a system to design "hot" products with minimal production lead times and close matching of supply and demand.

Quick response is associated with replenishment purchases for basic products (Jassin-O'Rourke 2008). Fast fashion is actually quick response in new merchandise (with little or no replenishment), involving shipping fewer pieces, in a great variety of styles, and more often.[2] Fast fashion emerged from quick response, but the two are different. Buyers tend to source fashion-sensitive products from suppliers that can deliver in a flexible and speedy manner, while basic products are sourced from the lowest-cost countries (Technopak 2007), leading to the distinction between the two concepts.

The industry made predictions that fast fashion would lead to local sourcing, but this has not been the case. Asian suppliers have quickly adapted the capabilities to serve fast-fashion buyers, including reducing minimum-run requirements. These suppliers have also lowered the cost of goods, thus putting intense pressure on regional manufacturers (The Clothing Industry 2009).

Trends in Lead Firm Sourcing Strategies Accelerated by the Crisis

Activities and strategies of lead firms have a profound effect on suppliers' relationships and required capabilities throughout the value chain. Key trends in lead firms' sourcing strategies in the apparel GVC that have been accentuated by the MFA phaseout and economic recession include the following:

- *Avoid risk and increase diversity of suppliers:* Maintaining a diversified portfolio of vendors and countries is a necessity for successful sourcing organizations (Sauls 2008). The recession has increased buyers' interest in having backup suppliers in place in case factories go under and to cope with general uncertainty about the future (Barrie and Ayling 2009). Some predicted the recession would lead to more local sourcing, but this has not yet happened (The Clothing Industry 2009).
- *Reduce reliance on China:* Lead firms continue to source the majority of products from China, but they also seek to diversify into other countries to avoid putting all their eggs in one basket. The Japanese government has openly declared its interest in reducing reliance on China. This could have major

effects, since Japan is the world's second largest clothing importer and Southeast Asia and Bangladesh currently account for only 7 percent of imports. Japan's plan could double or triple the total current exports from these countries, putting price pressure on European and U.S. Asian importers (Talking Strategy 2008; *Jakarta Globe* 2009; just-style.com 2009b).

- *Decrease suppliers' dependence on few buyers:* Lead firms no longer want to be the main buyer for any one supplier because of the risks associated with controlling the majority of a factory's output. Buyers tend to follow the "30/70" rule in which it is desirable to have 30 percent of a factory's business, but not more than 70 percent (Fung, Fung, and Wind 2008). Now suppliers must be able to meet the requirements of several buyers, and buyers have less obligation (or benefit) to invest in upgrading their suppliers' factories.
- *Increase long-term relationships with suppliers:* During the era of quotas, trade was dominated by short-term, market relationships. Now that quotas are gone, buyers are streamlining the number of suppliers they work with and focusing on developing long-term strategic partnerships with their most important suppliers. These strategic suppliers are increasingly multinational manufacturers or network coordinators that do the logistics legwork for the lead firms.
- *Rationalize supply chain:* Most lead firms in the apparel industry are committed to significant reductions in the size and scope of their supply chains. They want to deal with fewer, larger, and more capable suppliers that are strategically located near major markets around the globe. Retailers seek to consolidate the number of wholesalers they purchase from and they want to buy a more comprehensive line of clothing, accessories, and footwear from these wholesalers (Barrie and Ayling 2009; Euromonitor 2009). The recession has caused lead firms to "cut the fat," and they are confining their relationships to their most capable and reliable suppliers.

Impact of the Crisis on Apparel Suppliers in Developing Economies

The economic crisis has had a similar impact on apparel suppliers in developing countries, but those countries have been affected in varying degrees. The decrease in demand from the leading apparel-importing countries has meant a decrease in apparel exporters' product volumes and values and their access to credit, resulting in employment declines and in factory closings. Buyers are requiring more for less from the suppliers they choose to buy from and are seeking to build long-term partnerships with the most capable suppliers. Governments have responded in a variety of ways, ranging from tax rebates to increasing technology and infrastructure investments. These key impacts are highlighted below.

Decreases in Employees and Factories: Survival of the Fittest

During the recession, buyers transferred business away from marginal suppliers to their core operations, which created job losses in countries that are highly dependent on the apparel industry (Birnbaum 2009). Lower demand from international customers put a large number of vulnerable garment manufacturers in developing countries out of business (Barrie and Ayling 2009; Driscoll and Wang 2009; International News Services 2009). Annex table 5A.4 includes employment figures and estimated job losses in the textile and apparel industries in developing countries. Upper estimates of number of jobs lost because of the economic crisis include China, 10 million; India, 1 million; Pakistan, 200,000; Indonesia, 100,000; Mexico, 80,000; Cambodia, 75,000; and Vietnam, 30,000 (Forstater 2010). Job losses are causing rising levels of poverty and geographical shifts from urban areas focused on export markets to rural areas focused on agriculture and traditional employment, thus reducing the number of skilled textile and apparel laborers available.

Decline in Export Volume and Value

Many surviving companies are experiencing a decline in exports in some product categories. By May 2009, apparel imports to the U.S. market dropped by 15.7 percent, with every major garment supplier reporting declines (WTO 2009). Most view the decline in U.S., EU, and Japanese consumption as temporary. However, the longer the effects of the recession are felt, the longer consumers become accustomed to living with less. If that decrease in consumption becomes permanent, the current slow shift toward domestic markets in developing economies will accelerate and production networks will become more national or regional in nature.

New Sources of Credit and Trade Finance

Perhaps the most lasting effect of the recession on existing and new suppliers is access to credit and finance. The recession brought the importance of suppliers' financial stability to the attention of all buyers. The crisis has made access to credit much more difficult, leading to new types of financial arrangements, and thus increasing suppliers' dependence on buyers. In the future, firms will have to prove their financial stability in order to become suppliers.

To make matters worse, some customers are delaying payments and banks are becoming stricter with credit access (just-style.com 2009a). The general decline in credit availability is affecting all suppliers, but particularly hard hit are small and medium-size firms and locally owned firms (Barrie and Ayling 2009; Driscoll and Wang 2009).

The credit crunch has spurred new financial arrangements. Some buyers fear that when demand returns, it may be difficult to find qualified suppliers (Driscoll and Wang 2009). Retailers such as Kohl's and Walmart are offering financial support to their suppliers. Kohl's offered 41 percent of its suppliers a "Supply Chain Finance" program that lets suppliers get paid quickly once their invoices are approved for payment; by mid-2009, 11 percent of suppliers had signed on to the deal (O'Connell 2009). Walmart also offered about 1,000 suppliers, primarily apparel manufacturers, an alternative to traditional means of financing: a new "Supplier Alliance Program," in which eligible suppliers can get payment for their orders within 10 to 15 days of Walmart's receipt of goods, compared with the more typical 60 to 90 days (O'Connell 2009). Li and Fung is also moving into financing by becoming a lender of last resort to factories and small importers whose credit was cut off during the global financial meltdown (Kapner 2009; O'Connell 2009).

Increasing Government Support

In the aftermath of the MFA quota phaseout and the recent recession, the governments of nearly all major apparel-exporting countries have provided various forms of support to local industry. During the recession, the actions of individual governments became critical steps to recovery. Government interventions in developing economies have taken various forms, for example, providing tax relief, suspending tariffs or export duties, and assuring financing and liquidity for enterprises (see annex table 5A.1).[3]

Forming Strategic Long-Term Relationships with Lead Firms

Strategic long-term relationships are beneficial for buyers and suppliers. Buyers benefit from these relationships by virtue of their ability to exert influence over a supplier in order to achieve efficiencies in the supply chain, including reducing lead times, standardizing production processes to suit the nature of the buyer's product (asset specificity and tacit knowledge—lead firm setting standards), establishing preferential logistics and transportation arrangements, and increasing the transparency of the supplier's inventory (Technopak 2007). Suppliers benefit because these relationships provide security in the form of guaranteed demand for the supplier's output.

The strategic-supplier relationship is likely to become increasingly prominent in the apparel GVC in the post-MFA and postcrisis era. As global supply chains become more rationalized and consolidated, lead firms are realizing that future efficiency gains will require closer, more integrated linkages among all parts of the chain. The question today cannot be limited to "how successful is my firm?" Instead firms must ask themselves, "How successful is my network, and what role does my firm play in the bigger picture?"

More Stringent Supplier Capabilities

The following factors have long been important in apparel-sourcing strategies, but the crisis has heightened the need for suppliers to meet all or most requirements, as opposed to just one or two:

- *Cost/price:* During the recession and since, consumers have been placing more emphasis on price, thus causing retailers and brand marketers to focus on reducing costs (MSN 2009; Tucker 2009).
- *Product quality:* Firms must provide quality in addition to low prices, flexible production, and services (Driscoll and Wang 2009).
- *Supplier flexibility:* Firms are under pressure to make multiple products in small runs in order to deal with decreased demand and niche markets (MSN 2009).
- *Visibility/transparency:* Growing consumer demand for higher social and environmental standards has increased the need for supply chain transparency in both the United States and the European Union. Lead firms want to know more about their suppliers to ensure that they uphold the principles of the brands (Sauls 2008).
- *Full-package capabilities:* Suppliers need to be able to offer a full package to buyers and expand their capabilities to other parts of the value chain—including design, inventory management, and transportation of goods—and adopt the appropriate technologies to facilitate this transition (Technopak 2007).

Since the expiration of quotas, the global apparel industry has been faced with overcapacity that is creating intense competition in low-cost countries. By restricting leading apparel country exporters, the quota system enabled too many factories in too many countries to enter the global apparel trade, and now more factories are competing for fewer orders. In the short term, this has significantly raised the bar to be a global competitor; manufacturers must be more creative and comprehensive in the development of their products and services (Technopak 2007). Buyers are placing stricter demands on manufacturers and are asking for better products (quality), more nonmanufacturing capabilities, and faster turnaround times, all for lower costs. Suppliers must meet buyer demands to keep orders, increase volume, and reduce costs (Talking Strategy 2008). When this is coupled with the ongoing consolidation in the retail sector, the result is more power in the hands of the global buyers (that is, retailers, global brands, and large manufacturers that have outsourced their production).

Recommendations for Economic Development

This section offers recommendations for economic developers, governments, and the private sector that can provide assistance to developing countries in facing the challenges and harnessing the opportunities created by the crisis. How can developing countries best use current circumstances to make critical reforms that will enable them to take part in global growth once the economy recovers?

Short-Term Crisis Strategies

- *Implement "furlough" days:* Firms should implement the equivalent of "furlough" days rather than lay off workers. By reducing the number of hours or wages, firms and countries can maintain the labor force and industry expertise that will be needed when production returns.
- *Encourage local-market production:* Firms and governments should encourage production for the local market to keep companies in business. For example, MOL Magazalari (Turkey) is a consortium of 38 local clothing manufacturers that have recently set up manufacturer-owned shops selling goods manufactured, designed, and marketed as "Made in Turkey." These Turkish firms have used the crisis as an opportunity to upgrade their skill sets in marketing and retailing, which is helping them survive the recession and become more competitive in the future (The Clothing Industry 2009).

Long-Term Postcrisis Suggestions to Foster Growth

- *Invest in education and training:* Education and training opportunities will help to overcome the skills deficits that could hinder economic upgrading. Whereas quotas helped to initiate a textiles and clothing industry in developing countries, maintaining or improving a country's position in the global apparel GVC requires a continuous dedication to workforce development by the government and local firms. In the long run, innovative capacities depend on suitable human capital. Education should include technical skills as well as soft skills in areas such as management, product development, design, and market research.
- *Create marketing and networking functions:* Firms and governments should work together to create organizations to market and network the country/region and

align firms with international organizations dedicated to standards development, industry advocacy, research and development, and best practices. Economic developers and governments should provide firms with assistance to attend and participate in international trade shows to increase visibility to potential buyers.

- *Promote foreign direct investment or joint ventures to develop vertical capabilities:* The government of countries without domestic textile production should market their countries as a favorable location to locate FDI. This is a good strategy in areas that are still dominated by assembly or CMT production models, such as Africa, Southeast Asia, and the Caribbean. This will help to establish backward linkages and to develop skills not in the country. Economic authorities need to provide a one-stop shop for any investor or supplier wishing to set up a new firm (Knappe 2008).
- *Invest in technology and flexible production systems:* Firms and governments with a long-range vision of recovery are prepared to invest in technology that enables more efficient and flexible business and production models. Investments are needed to upgrade production machinery as well as logistics and information technologies that enable suppliers to become more integrated into their buyers' networks. Enterprises willing to invest in creative solutions will come out ahead in the aftermath of the recession.
- *Develop full-package capabilities:* Firms must be able to—or have alliances with firms that can—provide a final product and additional services related to product development, design, logistics, and quality control. Global brands and retailers are starting to move product development and design divisions closer to regional manufacturing. Suppliers able to offer these services (strategic suppliers) can be indispensable to the buyer and are likely to maintain market share through tough economic times.
- *Develop standards to meet international and regional standard certifications:* Governments should encourage and provide assistance to firms with product and process standards required by international buyers, such as ISO 9000 and 14000, the Global Organic Textile Standard, and the European Union's REACH directive.
- *Promote sustainable production practice:* Surviving suppliers will be companies that chose to compete on their environmental credentials in addition to cost, quality, and other traditional factors. Whether legally enforceable or "voluntary," agreement to make adjustments to have a greener and more transparent firm and supply chain will be mandatory to compete in the future. Countries that develop policies that facilitate the transition to more sustainable practices will be the winners.
- *Diversify buyers, products, and end markets:* Firms need to diversify into multiple product lines and end-use markets as well as different geographic markets.

Equally important, suppliers should expand their export focus to emerging countries with growing disposable incomes. These markets are often less demanding than traditional export markets in the United States and the European Union, but they offer more opportunities to upgrade skills to higher value-adding functions such as product design, marketing, and branding. Bilateral and regional trade agreements can help facilitate this process and build future long-term relationships.

Conclusions

Developing countries in the global apparel GVC have been beset by two major crises in recent years: the WTO phaseout of the quota system in 2005, which provided access for many poor and small export-oriented economies to the apparel markets of industrialized countries, and the recent economic recession that has lowered demand for apparel exports and led to massive unemployment across the industry's supply chain. Beyond the need to adjust to these two crises, our analysis has also highlighted a longer-term process of global consolidation, whereby a handful of leading apparel suppliers (countries and firms) has strengthened their positions in the apparel GVC, which complicates the adjustment strategy of smaller or more vulnerable players who have lost ground in the crisis.

On the country side, China has been the big winner. It has increased its dominant position in all of the major industrial economies (the United States, the European Union, and Japan). It has also diversified its export reach by gaining ground in many of the world's top emerging economies as well, such as Russia for finished goods and India, Brazil, and Turkey for intermediate goods, like textiles. Other developing economies have also gained in the post-MFA era, such as Bangladesh, India, Vietnam, and Indonesia. But regional suppliers have been hard hit, especially Mexico and CAFTA-DR in North America, and East European and North African suppliers to the European Union.

On the firm side, the quota phaseout and economic recession have accelerated the ongoing shift to a rationalization of global supply chains. Major retailers, brand marketers, and brand manufacturers have been stressing their desire to work with fewer, larger, and more capable suppliers, strategically located around the world. In addition, there has been a consolidation among the lead firms, as the largest retailers (Walmart), traders (Li and Fung), brand marketers (Nike), and brand manufacturers (VF Corporation) are increasing their market shares through mergers, acquisitions, and bankruptcies within the textile and apparel chain.

Within the developing world, the dual crises outlined in this paper pose the biggest threat to two kinds of vulnerable actors. The "trade impact" will be most significant for the smaller countries that were privileged by the MFA quota system, who no longer have guaranteed access to developed country markets. Regional trade agreements can ameliorate, but not eliminate, this pressure from dominant global exporters. A more specific "recession impact" is likely to hurt the weaker manufacturers in large developing economies, such as India, China, and Bangladesh. This could lead to major unemployment in these economies as supply-chain consolidation occurs inside these economies. We have offered suggestions to apparel suppliers in developing economies for coping with these competitive pressures, but there is no quick fix or certain solution.

The ultimate impact of the economic crisis is likely to extend well beyond specific industries, such as apparel. It challenges the broader viability of export-oriented industrialization as a growth model for developing economies. The economic recession will probably push even the successful apparel-exporting countries, such as China and India, toward more emphasis on domestic markets, and less reliance on export-oriented development per se. This is not only because export demand has slackened, but also because the upgrading opportunities of domestic and regional markets are likely to be greater for suppliers in developing countries. While these issues are beyond the scope of any specific industry analysis, they highlight the importance of rethinking national models of development in light of what we have learned about global value chains and the crisis.

Annex: Examining the Apparel Industry

Annex tables and figures begin on the following page.

Table 5A.1 Leading Apparel Exporters: Government Support and Trade Agreements

Country	Government support and dates of initiation	Key trade agreements
China	**2009 (April 24): China's State Council Three-Year Textile and Clothing (T&C) Stimulus Plan.** The aim of the plan is to ensure stable development and to upgrade the T&C infrastructure. The plan will eliminate obsolete capacity, reduce energy consumption, improve efficiency, and encourage a shift to higher value-added products plus improvements in product quality and variety. The government is targeting average textile production growth of 10 percent each year and export growth of 8 percent annually to reach US$240 billion by 2011. They want the industry to invest in more advanced technology to increase productivity, nurture 100 domestic brands to make them account for 20 percent of all export volumes in three years, and to boost domestic consumption and improve access to credit and extend loan repayment deadlines to textile companies facing difficult times. Reports of massive lending sprees by Chinese banks to exporting companies to keep factories going despite customers delaying or defaulting on payments or demanding price reductions.	Association of Southeast Asian Nations (ASEAN) ASEAN–China (Jan. 1, 2010),
	2008–09: Increase in Value Added Tax (VAT) Export Rebates. China charges a VAT of 17 percent at every level of the production process and the final product, but firms exporting a product can receive VAT export rebates on finished and input products. Due to decreases in export demand and increasing domestic production costs (currency and labor), China progressively increased VAT export tax rebates a total of five times for T&C (three times in 2008 and twice in 2009). Chinese clothing manufacturers can now claim a rebate up to the 17 percent ceiling. Prior to increases in 2008, China had been taking measures to slow export growth by decreasing export rebates.	Free Trade Agreements (FTA): Pakistan, New Zealand, Hong Kong, China
Turkey	**2009: Strategic Action Plan for Textile, Ready-to-Wear, and Leather Sectors** (2009–14). This is a scheme recently unveiled by the government to alleviate problems with T&C production in the country. The plan provides support in the form of government finance, advice, and training for export-oriented clothing producers who wish to relocate factories from Istanbul and its surrounding areas to eastern provinces of Turkey where wages are lower. Incentives include exemptions from customs tax and reductions in VAT, corporation tax, and energy bills.	EU Customs Union; Active in China Safeguards

Table 5A.1 *continued*

Country	Government support and dates of initiation	Key trade agreements
	2003: Government Incentive program, Turquality (WTO-compliant). This is an accreditation and support program to strengthen the international image of the country and of the garments manufactured by a select group of approximately 30 T&C brand owners.	
Bangladesh	**2006: Government of Bangladesh assistance.** The government support measures to bolster the T&C industry include the provision of bonded warehouse facilities, technological upgrading (concessionary duty rates and tax exemptions for the import of capital machinery), cash subsidies for the use of local fabrics as inputs for exporting ready-made garments (RMG) enterprise, and an Export Credit Guarantee Scheme covering risk on export credits at home, and commercial and political risks occurring abroad. The government also supports market promotion efforts of the RMG exporters and subsidizes utility charges.	South Asian Free Trade Area (SAFTA), Generalized System of Preferences (GSP): EU Everything But Arms (EBA), FTAs: Canada, Australia, and Norway
India	**2006–11: Government Strategic T&C Development Plan.** Initiatives in the budget included the following: reduced the VAT on all goods; established the Scheme for Integrated Textile Parks in 2004 to encourage vertically integrated textile clusters with modern infrastructure; approved 40 parks and 4 are in operation. Also investing in handloom and handicraft clusters. **2009/10: India's National Budget includes supports.** The budget included several support mechanisms to help T&C manufacturers recover from the economic recession including a US$26 million financial aid package to help companies looking to develop new export markets. It is also increasing availability of low interest loans and tax incentives (extension of tax holiday arrangements) for export-oriented firms. **1999–2009: India's Textile Upgradation Fund Scheme.** The government offers financial incentives (low cost loans and special credits) for domestic manufacturers to upgrade their technology. This has been a very effective tool to foster new investment.	SAFTA, European Union: GSP (textile articles included, but textiles omitted)
Vietnam	**2010: Government Industry Plans.** The plans include restructuring production by moving textiles into industrial parks and apparel to rural areas, encouraging big firms to establish long-term relationships with overseas importers and retailers, adding value to products using fashion techniques, paying attention to local markets, and improving workers' quality of life.	ASEAN, ASEAN-Japan, ASEAN-Australia-New Zealand, ASEAN-China

(*continued next page*)

Table 5A.1 *continued*

Country	Government support and dates of initiation	Key trade agreements
	2009: Cotton Development Program. With the goal of tripling raw cotton production by 2020, the program includes free cottonseed to several provinces. **2008 (March): Vietnamese Government Development Strategy**. The government is seeking to encourage manufacturing value-added products by emphasizing the use of domestically grown raw cotton, promoting the production of high-quality woven fabrics by improving dye and finish operations, and focusing on training workers in management and design positions. The government asked Vinatex, one of the largest domestic firms, to increase the amount of local material from 36 to 50 percent. Efforts are under way to make the industry more fashion-oriented and to develop qualified fashion designers and Vietnamese fashion brands.	EU: GSP (footwear and headgear omitted)
Indonesia	**2009: Indonesian Government assistance.** The government approved a US$26.5 million state budget fund to support the country's T&C (82 percent) and footwear (18 percent) industries. In 2007, this fund supported 78 T&C manufacturers with approximately US$18.9 million; in 2008, US$23.1 million. In 2008, government set aside US$25.2 million to update textile machinery to meet Japan's high import standards. The subsidy for textile machinery upgrading was pulled back in 2010 due to a lack of interest and applicants.	ASEAN, ASEAN-Japan, ASEAN-Australia-New Zealand, ASEAN-China
Pakistan	**2009 (August): Government industry-specific five-year plan.** The government released details of a new five-year program to revitalize the textile industry. The policy allocates funds to companies to make investments necessary to compete in international apparel markets by increasing the local availability of Pakistan-made textiles, especially yarns and fabrics. The initiative focuses on gas and electricity supply, full refund of past R&D claims, availability of 5 percent export refinancing, relief on long-term loans, tax-free import of machinery, and subsidized credit. Mills that increase market share and earn more money for the country have been promised a higher rate of duty drawback. **2008/09: National Trade Strategy initiatives.** The trade plan has several textile-related initiatives including establishing new export clusters for weaving and textile processing and embroidery, funding productivity audits, hiring international consultants to develop the handicraft sector, providing tax incentives to facilitate imports of machinery and raw material inputs, and encouraging manufacture and export of recycled polyester.	SAFTA, GSP: EU, U.S. Reconstruction Opportunity Zone (similar to an Export Processing Zone), FTA: China, Malaysia, Sri Lanka

Table 5A.1 *continued*

Country	Government support and dates of initiation	Key trade agreements
	2006: Government support for upgrading. This support focused on technology upgrading and modernization as well as training institutes for skill development.	
Cambodia	**2001: Better Factories Cambodia: ILO Project.** The project grew out of a trade agreement between the United States and Cambodia. Under the agreement the United States promised Cambodia better access to U.S. markets in exchange for improved working conditions in the garment sector; the ILO project was established to help the sector make and maintain these improvements with lead firms.	ASEAN, ASEAN-Japan, ASEAN-Australia-New Zealand, ASEAN-China
	2000s: Government incentives. This support centered on encouraging foreign investment with generous incentives.	
Sri Lanka	**2006: Sri Lankan Government debt write-off.** The government wrote off the unpaid debt of the local textile manufacturers that had registered for restructuring the textile industry; initiated incentives for apparel productivity improvement through a grant of US$1 million to promote backward linkages; began setting up an industrial park with a waste and effluent treatment plant to facilitate fabric manufacturing. Another program was outlined aimed at developing a regional apparel hub in Katunayake, where both an EPZ and an international airport are located.	SAFTA, GSP+: EU
	Government attracts FDI. Government provides incentives, including special industrial zones, tax holidays, and import duty exemptions.	
	2002: Garments Without Guilt. This program is cofunded by the government and private sector to promote the country's image as an ethical T&C manufacturer, committed to labor rights and ethical sourcing. The campaign is a way for Sri Lankan producers to differentiate themselves from other Asian suppliers.	

Source: Authors.

Table 5A.2 Leading Apparel Exporters: Strengths and Weaknesses/Threats

Country	Strengths	Weaknesses/threats	Labor pay rate[a]
China	• **Labor:** high productivity, competency, and experience: China excels at improving productivity in light of rising inflation. • **Quality and reliability:** fabric and garments • **Technology investment** (logistics) • **Product diversity:** fabric and finished goods • **Mentality and management:** "can do" business approach	• **Inflation:** (increases producer prices) and **competition for workers** from higher paying, non-apparel-sector industries • **Labor costs and labor laws:** rising domestic wages, expected to increase further as a result of new labor laws • **Currency appreciation** • **Energy costs:** increasing • **Shipping cost:** major increases • **Product safety**	$1.44–1.88/hour
Turkey	• **Flexibility and speed:** domestic manufacturers investing in new production in Egypt	• **Labor costs** • **Intellectual property enforcement** • **Inflation in raw material costs** compared to competitors	$2.44/hour
Bangladesh	• **Low-cost production and firms' willingness to keep margins low** while investing in new technology to improve productivity and to reinforce relationships with buyers • **Improvements in terminal handling and customs:** Clearance has gone from 12–13 days as recently as last year to clear goods within 3 days • **Low labor costs and availability** • **Low energy costs** • **Currency depreciation:** coincided with post-ATC period. More of an advantage to knit exports. • **Growing textile industries:** Taiwanese and Korean investors are setting up fabric/fiber operations	• **Lack of design, soft skills, and technology** • **Currency fluctuation** (mainly euro) causing losses in previously arranged letters of credit • **Shortage of skilled workers and middle management** • **Human capital (poor)** and worker unrest and strikes over poor pay and conditions • **Energy reliability:** power interruptions in the national power grid are common, and stand-alone generators are often needed (more expensive) • **Inefficient infrastructure:** port and transportation	$0.31/hour
India	• **Product diversity:** most diversified exporter of T&C products in South Asia	• **Procedural hurdles** to international trade	$0.51/hour

Table 5A.2 *continued*

Country	Strengths	Weaknesses/threats	Labor pay rate[a]
	• **Low cost, flexibility, and speed:** strengths when compared to China. Flexibility: can cater to buyers' requirements for small, customized orders as well as large orders. Intricate, high-quality garments with flexibility and speed. • **Domestic market:** growing number of firms switching to supply domestic market	• **Lack of scale economies:** 80 percent of T&C units are small, cottage-like, typically employing fewer than 11 workers; only 6 percent have more than 49 employees • **Currency fluctuation** percent • **Inflation in raw material costs** compared to competitors • **Manufacturing costs:** power, operating, and transaction costs are higher compared to competitors	
Vietnam	• **Alternative to China:** FDI and sourcing • **Growing textile industries:** Taiwanese and Korean investors are setting up operations • **Growing exports to Japan** and domestic market; ASEAN trade pacts • **Relatively stable** business environment	• **Skilled workers:** Lack of skilled workers with experience in technology, fashion, and management • **Imported textiles:** Dependent on imported textiles • **Private capital:** Ability to allow private capital to operate freely	$0.38/ hour
Indonesia	• **Large domestic market** • **Large installed production capacity** • **Low labor costs** and relatively **low turnover** rates • **Long, refined textile tradition** (batik techniques, embroidery)	• **High energy costs** **Outdated** machinery **Inconsistency** • **General business climate:** unfavorable bureaucracy, taxes, corruption, security, cooperation	$0.44/ hour
Mexico	• **NAFTA** • **Proximity** to the United States	• **High labor cost**	$2.17/ hour
Pakistan	• **Low labor cost** • **Government support** and liberal **FDI policies** with incentives have been essential to development • **Currency depreciation** against the U.S. dollar and other Western currencies. This has helped exports, but has also raised the cost of imported inputs.	• **Energy access and reliability** • **Political instability:** security and safety issues • **Mediocre quality and color consistency** of textiles and clothing • **Labor:** low productivity • **Lack design** skills and global **market knowledge** as well as supporting **resources** (research and training centers)	$0.56/ hour

(*continued next page*)

Table 5A.2 *continued*

Country	Strengths	Weaknesses/threats	Labor pay rate[a]
Cambodia	• **Labor:** cost, availability, and standards • **Government support** • **Economies of scale** (2005): 7 percent of the garment manufacturing entities employ more than 5,000 people	• **Labor:** Unskilled, low productivity • All FDI; **lack local firms** Apparel export dependence Production flexibility and efficiency • **Lack upstream** textile industry • **Lack in transportation and communication infrastructure**	$0.33/ hour
Sri Lanka	• **Diversification** of product exports • **Focus on niche apparel** and enterprising nature of the private sector to position country in niche markets • **Quality, on-time deliveries and service** • Compliance and emphasis on **international labor and environmental standards**	• Higher labor costs • **Uncertainty** of EU-GSP benefits • **Dependence** on apparel exports	$0.46/ hour (2004)

Sources: Anson and Brocklehurst 2008; Jassin-O'Rourke Group 2008; and authors.
Note: a. Labor rates are for 2008 unless otherwise noted.

Table 5A.3 Apparel Country Exporter Capabilities

Country	Country capabilities	Firm ownership and size
China	• Full-package (ODM), vertical capabilities within country with full supply chain geographic clusters • Man-made fiber (MMF) and cotton: world's largest cotton producer, importer, and consumer. Upgrading to higher-end clothing. • Primary supplier to global buyers: major buyers have local sourcing offices. Strong domestic market as well (OBM).	Foreign direct investment (FDI) approx. 45 percent; state-owned enterprises (SOE) 2 percent
Turkey	• Full-package (ODM): vertical capabilities within country • Intricate, high-quality garments; cotton and MMF production. More knitted apparel, about 70 percent (t-shirts, pullovers, socks), than woven 20 percent (outerwear, shirts, blouses).	Many small- and medium-enterprise firms

Table 5A.3 *continued*

Country	Country capabilities	Firm ownership and size
Bangladesh	• Package contractors (OEM) (knit apparel only) • CMT assembly: woven apparel, woven fabrics; industry is not developed; import 85 percent of needed materials from China, India, Pakistan, and Hong Kong and Taiwan, China • Major buyers tend to have sourcing offices • Products: cotton apparel, about 50/50 knitted (t-shirts) and woven	FDI dominates
India	• Full-package (ODM): vertical: cotton to cut/sew final products • Strong design skills • Mostly cotton apparel: medium quality and relatively high-fashion, ready-made garments for export and domestic markets	Local dominates; foreign firms must be a joint venture. Small firm size
Vietnam	• CMT assembly, limited OEM: lack domestic textile industry • Major buyers tend to have sourcing offices • Products: low-cost, volume production • Cotton and cotton blends; primarily woven garments	FDI: 45 percent State-owned enterprise (SOE): 10 percent
Indonesia	• Package contractors (OEM): garment manufacturers source the bulk of fabrics from the United States and Europe. Do not take full advantage of domestic upstream production for apparel exports. • Vertical capabilities; strong, well-integrated materials and accessories base with strong textile and apparel export markets. • Products: low-cost, volume, synthetics; fabric and apparel; second strongest in MMF behind China	Foreign and local firms
Mexico	• OEM and CMT capabilities • Products: commodity cotton denim trousers, image-wear	Foreign and local firms
Pakistan	• Vertical production for cotton: spinning, weaving, knitting, finishing, and cut/sew; focus more on home textiles than apparel products • Cotton apparel, nearly 50/50 knitted and woven	Foreign firms important Woven apparel: small-scale firms
Cambodia	• CMT assembly; lack domestic textile industry • Less important supply country, mostly basics (t-shirts)	FDI: 90 percent Local: 7 percent
Sri Lanka	• Package contractors (OEM) and ODM for knitted apparel • Niche products: particularly women's underwear and bras; specialize in knitted intimate apparel and activewear • Several lead firms have long-term strategic relationships with firms (Victoria's Secret, Nike, Gap)	

Source: Compiled by authors from various trade journals and online sources.
Note: CMT = cut, make, and trim; FDI = foreign direct investment; MMF = man-made fiber; OBM = original brand manufacturing; ODM = original design manufacturing; OEM = original equipment manufacturing; SOE = state-owned enterprise.

Table 5A.4 Leading Apparel Exporters: Export Value, Markets, and Dependence, 2008

Country	Export value (US$, billions)	Export markets (percent)	Employment	Estimated employment loss and percent total	Apparel export dependence (percent)
China	120.0	**EU 15: 24** U.S.: 15 JPN: 15 HK: 6 RUS: 5	T&A: 30 million	10 million (33)	8.4
Extra-European Union 27	27.7	**RUS: 19** SWISS: 17 U.S.: 10	—	—	—
Turkey	13.6	**EU 15: 76** US: 2.3	—	—	10.3
Bangladesh	10.9	**EU 15: 59** U.S.: 32 CAN: 4	T&A: 3 million	0 (0)	71.1
India	10.9	**EU 15: 48** U.S.: 26 UAE: 8	T&A: 35 million	300,000–1 million (0.9–3)	6.1
Vietnam	9.0	**U.S.: 61** EU 15: 19 JPN: 9	T&A: 2 million	20,000–30,000 (1.0–1.5)	14.3
Indonesia	6.3	**U.S.: 58** EU 15: 24 UAE: 2	T&A: 1 million	41,000–100,000 (4–10)	4.5
Mexico	4.9	**U.S.: 97** CAN: 1 EU 15: 1	T&A: 750,000	36,000–80,000 (4–10)	1.7
Pakistan	3.9	**EU: ~30** U.S.: ~30 HK: ~4	T&A: 2.5 million	200,000 (8)	19.2
Cambodia	3.6	**U.S.: 70** EU: 22	A: 352,000	74,500–75,500 (20–22)	84.8
Sri Lanka	3.3 (2007)	**EU 15: 48** U.S.: 44 CAN: 2	A: 270,000	—	40.9

Source: Authors.

Note: Export dependence is percentage share of total merchandise exports. Geographic export markets: figures for Bangladesh, Cambodia, and Vietnam are for 2007. Employment information and loss for Bangladesh, China, India, Indonesia, Mexico, and Pakistan are from Forstater (2010). CAN = Canada; EU = European Union; HK = Hong Kong, China; JPN = Japan; SWISS = Switzerland; UAE = United Arab Emirates; RUS = Russian Federation; — = not available.

Table 5A.5 Functional Upgrading Trajectories, Governance, and Local Skills

Functional capabilities	Governance structure	Weaknesses and upgrading	Skills acquired
Assembly (CMT): the focus of the supplier is on production alone; suppliers assemble imported inputs following buyers' specifications.	Captive or market	Lack capital, expertise, direct access to buyers, local inputs Process or product upgrading	Local firms learn foreign buyers' preferences, including international standards for price, quality, and delivery.
OEM: the supplier takes on a broader range of tangible, manufacturing-related functions, such as sourcing inputs and inbound logistics in addition to production.	Captive or market	Lack design capabilities and strong managerial and technical skills. Functional upgrading to logistics and coordination	Production expertise increases over time and spreads across different activities. Suppliers learn the upstream and downstream segments of the chain from buyers. Can lead to substantial backward linkages in the domestic economy.
If the ability to codify transactions increases and supplier competencies remain high, degree of explicit coordination decreases.	Modular		
ODM: supplier carries out part of the preproduction processes, including design or R&D		Lack direct access to foreign consumers and marketing skills. Functional and product upgrading	Innovative skills related to new product development
If in collaboration with buyer	Relational		
If buyer attaches its brand to a product designed by the supplier	Captive or modular		
OBM: supplier acquires postproduction capabilities and is able to fully develop products under its own brand names.		Knowledge changing	Innovative skills related to marketing and consumer research

(*continued next page*)

Table 5A.5 *continued*

Functional capabilities	Governance structure	Weaknesses and upgrading	Skills acquired
If maintains relationship with and develops brands with buyer	Relational	Functional upgrading	
If no longer relies on buyer for any functions and establishes own distribution channels	Lead firm	Channel and functional upgrading	

Sources: Adapted from Gereffi (1999); Gereffi and Memedovic (2003); Humphrey (2004).
Note: The table assumes vertical integration is not present.

Table 5A.6 Mass Merchants: Private-Label Sourcing Strategies, 2008

Retailer	Sales (US$, billions)	Sourcing	Description and known countries
Walmart	302.6	Direct sourcing; intermediary: Li and Fung	80 percent from 3rd parties; <20 percent sourced directly from manufacturers (2009); Countries: China, about 90 percent; others incl. Mexico, Bangladesh, and Jordan
Target	64.9	Own intermediary	Target owns (subsidiary) a domestic agent, Associated Merchandising Corp. (AMC)
Sears	25.3	Direct sourcing	60–70 percent direct sourcing via 8 sourcing and 4 quality assurance offices worldwide (2005)
Macy's	24.9	Own intermediary; intermediary: AMC	Macy's owns (subsidiary) a domestic agent, MDSI, that has offices in 10 countries
JCPenney	18.5	Direct sourcing	16 overseas buying offices; concentrate on 15 countries including Bangladesh; Hong Kong, China; Pakistan
Kohl's	16.4	Intermediary: Li and Fung	Kohl's is currently Li and Fung's largest supplier
Marks & Spencer (UK)	15.3	Direct sourcing	Domestic importers: 70 percent provided from < 15 UK-based full-service importers/vendors. 30 percent direct sourcing with 120 suppliers via 7 owned sourcing offices; Turkey/Morocco office responsible for 12 percent (2006). Others are Bangladesh and Sri Lanka.

Source: Sales figures from Asaeda (2009).
Note: Sales represent all divisions, not just apparel.

Table 5A.7 Specialty Retailers: Sourcing Strategies, 2008

Retailer	Sales (US$, billions)	Private-label sourcing	Description and known countries
Gap	14.5	Direct sourcing	900 vendors in 60 countries. China, 27 percent; U.S., 3 percent. Others: Bangladesh, Sri Lanka, Pakistan, Philippines, Jordan, Vietnam, Cambodia (Gap largest buyer), Morocco, Turkey, and India
HandM (Sweden)	13.1	Direct sourcing	20 offices (10 each in Europe and Asia); relationships with 750 factories: 60 percent Asia (incl. Bangladesh, Pakistan, Cambodia) and 40 percent Europe (2007)
Limited Brands Inc.	9.0	Own intermediary	Own MAST Industries (agent, contract mfg., design): mfg. facilities in 35 countries in Asia (Sri Lanka), Europe, S. America, Africa
Abercrombie and Fitch	3.5	Direct sourcing	Domestic Importer: use MAST Industries; relationships with 38 countries: primarily Asia and Central and South America
Talbots	2.4	Intermediary: Li and Fung	
Aeropostale	1.9	Direct sourcing	>67 percent of business with five vendors
Gymboree	1.0	Intermediary: Li and Fung	

Sources: Sales for 2008 are from Apparel Magazine (2009); Talbot's (Euromonitor 2009).

Table 5A.8 Brand Marketers and Manufacturers: Sourcing Strategies, 2008

Brand firm	Sales (US$, billions)	Sourcing strategy	Description and known countries
Nike	19.2	Direct sourcing	Apparel from 38 countries. China, largest—others including Thailand; Indonesia; Malaysia; Vietnam; Turkey; Sri Lanka; Cambodia; Taiwan, China; El Salvador; Mexico; India; and Israel.
Inditex (Zara) (Spain)	15.1	Direct sourcing; manufacturer	50 percent owned manufacturing (Spain, "fashion items"); 50 percent sourced, with 40 percent from Asia (China, Bangladesh, basics, t-shirts); and 10 percent, Europe and Northern Africa (Morocco). 1990: Asia represented almost 0 percent.
VF Corporation	7.6	Direct sourcing; manufacturer	77 percent sourced: China largest; others including Bangladesh, Vietnam, Indonesia, Thailand, Cambodia, the Philippines, Pakistan, India, Sri Lanka, Egypt, Chile, Argentina, Tunisia, and Morocco. 23 percent owned manufacturers incl. Mexico, Nicaragua, Honduras, Poland, and Turkey.
Liz Claiborne	4.2	Intermediary: Li and Fung	
Hanesbrands	4.0	Direct sourcing; manufacturer	34 percent sourced from 3rd party manufacturing (FOB); 66 percent: owned facilities or 3rd party cut/sew contractors (CMT). Hanesbrands owns 52 manufacturing plants with locations in the United States, Vietnam, Thailand, Puerto Rico, Dominican Republic, El Salvador, and Honduras.
Phillips-Van Heusen (PVH)	2.5	Direct sourcing	175 manufacturing plants in 26 countries (including Bangladesh, Cambodia, United States) to firm specifications (FOB)
Timberland	1.5	Intermediary: Li and Fung License to PVH for some apparel	

Source: Authors; sales figures from Driscoll and Wang (2009).

Figure 5A.1 Shifts in Regional Structure of U.S. Apparel Imports, 1996–2008

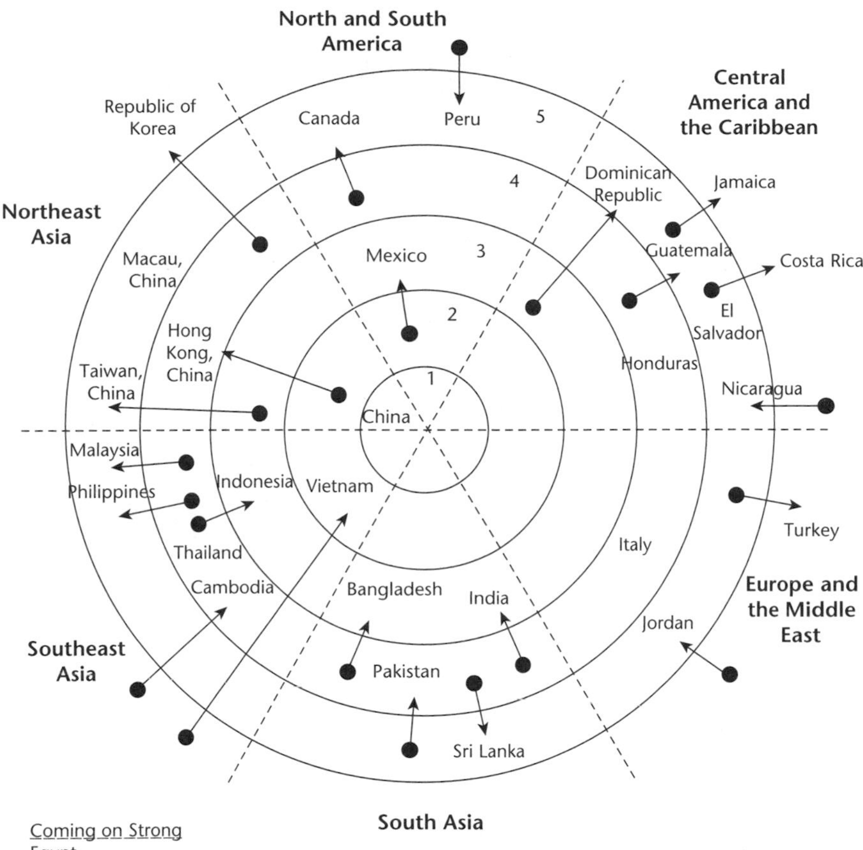

Coming on Strong
Egypt

Source: United States International Trade Commission (USTIC); U.S. imports for consumption, customs value: SITC 84, rev. 3.

Note: The rings indicate the share of total U.S. imports in U.S. dollars by partner country:

1. 10%+
2. 6.0% – 9.9%
3. 4.0% – 5.9%
4. 2.0% – 3.9%
5. 1.0% – 1.9%.

The 2008 position corresponds to the ring in which the country's name is located; the 1996 position, if different, is indicated by a small circle. The arrows represent the magnitude of change over time. Total value of U.S. clothing imports grew from $41.5 billion in 1996 to $78.8 billion in 2008. From 1996 to 2008, China's import share of the U.S. apparel market grew from 15.2 percent to 34.5 percent.

Figure 5A.2 Shifts in Regional Structure: EU 15 Apparel Imports, 1996–2008

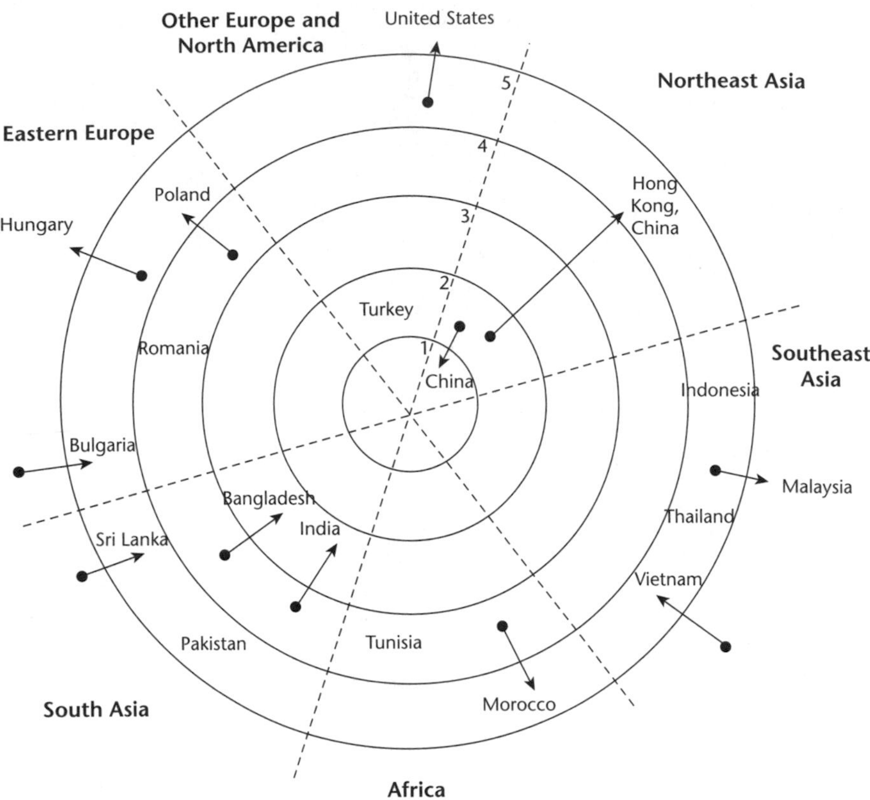

Source: Comtrade, SITC 84, Rev 3, imports to the EU 15.
Note: The rings indicate the share of total European imports in U.S. dollars by partner country:
1. 10%+
2. 6.0% – 9.9%
3. 4.0% – 5.9%
4. 2.0% – 3.9%
5. 1.0% – 1.9%.

Apparel imports are for the EU 15 countries only. The calculations include the value of intra-EU trade, but the chart excludes the names of the individual EU 15 countries (Austria, Belgium, Denmark, Finland, France, Germany, Greece, Ireland, Italy, Luxembourg, Netherlands, Portugal, Spain, Sweden, and the United Kingdom). The 2008 position corresponds to the ring where the country's name is located; the 1996 position, if different, is indicated by a small circle. The arrow represents the magnitude and direction of change over time. Total value of extraregional European clothing imports grew from $45.5 billion in 1996 to $203.4 billion in 2008.

Figure 5A.3 Industrial Upgrading by Asian Economies in the Apparel Value Chain

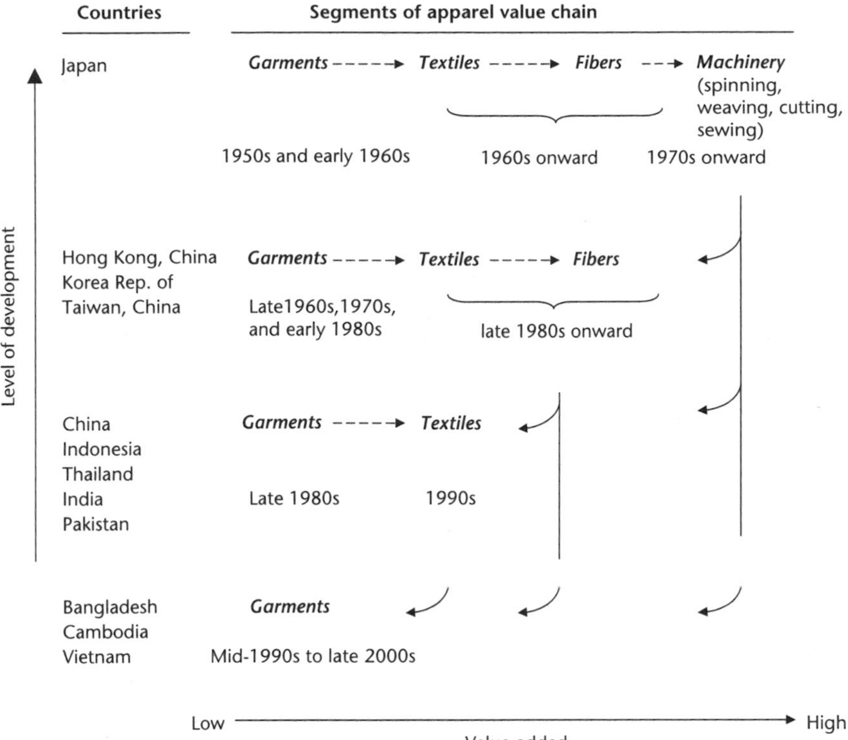

Source: Adapted from Gereffi 2005, 172.
Note: Dashed arrows refer to the sequence of production and export capabilities within economies. Solid arrows refer to the direction of trade flows or foreign direct investments between economies. Dates refer to a country's peak years for exports of specific products.

Notes

1. Costa Rica, El Salvador, Guatemala, Honduras, and Nicaragua.
2. See, for example, http://www.stanford.edu/~swinney/FastFashion.pdf.
3. For a more detailed review of protectionist actions in the textile and apparel industries, see Frederick and Gereffi (2009a; 2009b).

References

Adhikari, R., and C. Weeratunge. 2006. "Textiles and Clothing Sector in South Asia: Coping with Post-quota Challenges." In *South Asian Yearbook of Trade and Development 2006,* ed. B. S. Chimni, B. L. Das, S. Kelegama, and M. Rahman, 109–45. New Delhi, India: Center for Trade and Development and Wiley-India.

———. 2007. "Textiles and Clothing in South Asia: Current Status and Future Potential." *South Asia Economic Journal* 8 (2): 171–203.

Adhikari, R., and Y. Yamamoto. 2007. "Textile and Clothing Industry: Adjusting to the Post-Quota World." In *Industrial Development for the 21st Century: Sustainable Development Perspectives,* United Nations (UN-DESA). New York: United Nations.

Anson, R., and G. Brocklehurst. 2008. "Trends in World Textile and Clothing Trade." *Textile Outlook International* 138: 120–85.

Apparel Magazine. 2009. "Apparel's Top 50: Cover Story." July. pp. 6–16.

Asaeda, J. 2008. *Retailing: General.* New York: McGraw Hill.

———. 2009. *Retailing: General.* New York: McGraw Hill.

Audet, D. 2004. "A New World Map in Textiles and Clothing Policy Brief." Organisation for Economic Co-operation and Development (OECD), Washington, DC. Retrieved from http://www.oecd.org/dataoecd/43/14/33824605.pdf.

Bair, J. 2005. "Global Capitalism and Commodity Chains: Looking Back, Going Forward." *Competition and Change* 9 (2): 153–80.

———. 2006. "Regional Trade and Production Blocs in a Global Industry: Towards a Comparative Framework for Research." *Environment and Planning A* 38 (12): 2233–52.

Bair, J., and G. Gereffi. 2001. "Local Clusters in Global Chains: The Causes and Consequences of Export Dynamism in Torreon's Blue Jeans Industry." *World Development* 29 (11): 1885.

Barrie, L., and J. Ayling. 2009. "Apparel Industry Outlook for 2009." January/February Management Briefing. Aroq Limited, Bromsgrove, UK.

Birnbaum, D. 2009. "Sourcing: Marginal Suppliers Need a Radical Re-think." *Just-Style.Com.* August 21.

Clothesource. 2008. "The Great Apparel Sourcing Issues of 2008—And How to Deal with Them." Management Briefing (March). Aroq Limited. Worcestershire, UK.

"The Clothing Industry and the Economic Crisis—A just-style Review 2009." Management Briefing (September). Aroq Limited, Bromsgrove, UK.

Datamonitor. 2009. "Global Apparel Retail Industry Report." New York, NY: Datamonitor.

Driscoll, M., and P. Wang. 2009. *Apparel and Footwear: Retailers and Brands.* New York, NY: Standard and Poor's (S&P).

Euromonitor. 2009. "Clothing—U.S.: Country Sector Briefing Report." Euromonitor International.

Forstater, M. 2010. "Implications of the Global Financial and Economic Crisis on the Textile and Clothing Sector." International Labour Organization (ILO), Geneva.

Frederick, S. 2010. "Development and Application of a Value Chain Research Approach to Understand and Evaluate Internal and External Factors and Relationships Affecting Economic Competitiveness in the Textile Value Chain." (Ph.D. dissertation). North Carolina State University. www.lib.ncsu.edu/theses/available/etd-03132010-084518.

Frederick, S., and G. Gereffi. 2009a. "Protectionism in Textiles and Apparel." In *Effective Crisis Response and Openness: Implications for the Trading System,* ed. S. Evenett, B. Hoekman, and O. Cattaneo, 321–44. Washington, DC: World Bank and Centre for Economic Policy Research (CEPR).

———. 2009b. "Review and Analysis of Protectionist Actions in the Textile and Apparel Industries." In *The Fateful Allure of Protectionism: Taking Stock for the G8*, ed. S. Evenett, B. Hoekman, and O. Cattaneo, 321–44. London, UK: Centre for Economic Policy Research (CEPR). http://www.voxeu.org/index.php?q=node/3728.

Fung, V., W. Fung, and J. Wind. 2008. *Competing in a Flat World.* Upper Saddle River, NJ: Wharton School Publishing.

Gereffi, G. 1997. "Global Shifts, Regional Response: Can North America Meet the Full-Package Challenge?" *Bobbin* (November): 15.

———. 1999. "International Trade and Industrial Upgrading in the Apparel Commodity Chain." *Journal of International Economics* 48 (1): 37–70.

———. 2004. "Industrial Adjustment in the North Carolina Textile and Clothing Industry." Presentation at the Global Apparel/Clothing Europe Conference, University of North Carolina at Chapel Hill. October 15–16, 2004. http://www.unc.edu/depts/europe/conferences/04/global/papers.htm.

———. 2005. "The Global Economy: Organization, Governance, and Development." In *Handbook of Economic Sociology*, 2nd ed., ed. N. Smelser and R. Swedberg, 160–82. Princeton, NJ: Princeton University Press.

Gereffi, G., J. Humphrey, R. Kaplinsky, and T. Sturgeon. 2001. "Introduction: Globalization, Value Chains and Development." *IDS Bulletin* 32 (3): 1–14.

Gereffi, G., and O. Memedovic. 2003. "*The Global Apparel Value Chain: What Prospects for Upgrading for Developing Countries*?" Sectoral Studies Series. United Nations Industrial Development Organization (UNIDO), Vienna.

Humphrey, J. 2004. "Upgrading in Global Value Chains." Working Paper 28. International Labour Organization (ILO), Geneva.

International News Services. 2009. "Seven Macro Trends in the Textiles and Apparel Industry." Management Briefing. June. Aroq Limited, Worcestershire, UK.

Jakarta Globe. 2009. "Japan Mulls Importing More Indonesian Textiles." February 24.

Jassin-O'Rourke Group. 2008. "Global Apparel Manufacturing Labor Cost Analysis 2008." Textile and Apparel Manufacturers and Merchants. http://www.tammonline.com/researchpapers.htm.

just-style.com. 2009a. "Analysis: Do Stimulus Packages Help the Garment Trade?" April 20. http://www.just-style.com/article.aspx?id=103915andlk=dm.

———. 2009b. "Japan: China Sourcing Cuts Could Raise Costs for U.S., EU Buyers." March 4.

———. 2009c. "10 Ways to Develop a Balanced Sourcing Strategy." November 24.

Kapner, S. 2009. "The Unstoppable Fung Brothers." *CNN Money.* December 8.

Kilduff, P., and C. Ting. 2006. "Longitudinal Patterns of Comparative Advantage in the Textile Complex. Part 2: Sectoral Perspectives." *Journal of Fashion Marketing and Management* 10 (2): 150–68.

Knappe, M. 2008. "The Textiles and Clothing Value Chain: Write-Ups by ITC Panelists." UNCTAD XII: World Investment Forum Session II: Global Value Chains: Opportunities and Challenges for International and Domestic Firms, Accra, Ghana.

MSN (Maquila Solidarity Network). 2009. "How Will the Global Financial Crisis Affect the Garment Industry and Garment Workers?" Maquila Solidarity Network, Ontario, Canada.

O'Connell, V. 2009. "Wal-Mart Looks to Bolster Suppliers." *Wall Street Journal.* November 14.

Rasmussen, J. 2008. "Part I: State of the Industry 2008." *Specialty Fabrics Review* (May): 28–35.

Sauls, J. 2008. "Excellence in Sourcing: An Apparel Research Study and Analysis." A Supplement to *Apparel Magazine.* August.

"Talking Strategy: Expert Views on U.S. Apparel Sourcing." 2008. *Global Apparel Markets* (1): 5–9.

Technopak. 2007. "Strategies for Textile and Apparel Manufacturers in the Post-quota Era: Prospects to 2015." *Textile Outlook International* (July–August): 152–67.

Tewari, M. 2006. "Is Price and Cost Competitiveness Enough for Apparel Firms to Gain Market Share in the World after Quotas? A Review." *Global Economy Journal* 6 (4): 1–46.

Thoburn, J. 2009. "The Impact of the World Garment Recession on the Textile and Garment Industries of Asia." Seoul (Korea) Workshop: November 13–15: United Nations Industrial Development Organization (UNIDO).

Tucker, R. 2009. "Not Only the Recession: Industry Hit by Resizing, Trade Issues and More." *Women's Wear Daily* 197 (89): 1, 8–9.

U.S. Census Bureau. 2009a. "Apparel—Summary 2008 Report." Report MQ315A(08)-5. U.S. Department of Commerce, Washington, DC.

———. 2009b. "Socks Production—Summary 2008 Report." Report MQ315B(08)-5. U.S. Department of Commerce, Washington, DC.

Vernon, R. 1966. "International Investment and International Trade in the Product Cycle." *Quarterly Journal of Economics* 80 (2): 190–207.

WTO (World Trade Organization). 2009. *International Trade Statistics 2009.* World Trade Organization, Geneva.

———. 2010. *Time Series on International Trade*. World Trade Organization, Geneva. http://stat.wto.org/Home/WSDBHome.aspx?Language=E.

6

EFFECTS OF THE 2008–09 CRISIS ON THE AUTOMOTIVE INDUSTRY IN DEVELOPING COUNTRIES: A GLOBAL VALUE CHAIN PERSPECTIVE

Johannes Van Biesebroeck and Timothy J. Sturgeon

This chapter examines the impact of the 2008–09 economic crisis on global value chains (GVCs) in the automotive industry. The goal is to provide an overview of GVCs in this important industry, examine government responses to the recent economic crisis, and discuss where the industry is headed, particularly in light of the increasing importance of both production and consumption in large developing countries such as China and India.

The first section highlights three important ways in which the organization of automotive industry GVCs differs from that in other industries. First, export of finished vehicles to large mature markets is effectively limited by political constraints. Second, product architecture is of an integral nature, leading to thick "relational" linkages between lead firms and first-tier suppliers. In essence, the dense interaction of system elements within the vehicle is mirrored by dense interactions between automakers and key suppliers. For this and other reasons, the role of suppliers in the industry has become more important than in the past. Third, because of these features, the organization of production in the industry has remained more regional than global.

The chapter's second section summarizes government responses to the 2008–09 economic crisis, focusing on mature markets, especially North America and Europe. These interventions underscore the influence politics has on the industry, and vice versa. Government interventions will continue to affect the industry as market growth, and hence production, shift to less-developed countries (LDCs) and local firms begin to compete more directly with multinational firms in developing-country and world markets.

Section three analyzes the position and role of developing countries in automotive industry GVCs by comparing the development paths of China, Mexico, and India. While these three countries have relied to varying degrees on foreign direct investment to jump-start their industries, we see a gradual deepening of GVC integration in all three. However, outcomes and prospects for the future are variable. Two features of the Chinese industry—the leveraging of a well-developed supply base, both locally in Shanghai and abroad, and a domestic market large enough to justify the development of vehicles tailored to local tastes—position that country best for future development.

The fourth section summarizes our insights and provides policy recommendations for the automotive industry in developing countries.

Global Value Chains in the Automotive Industry

In previous publications[1] we have argued that the automotive industry is neither fully global, with interlinked, specialized clusters, as is the case in the electronics industry, for example; nor fully local, tied to the narrow geography of nation states or specific localities, as is the case for some cultural or service industries. Instead, the degree of global integration differs at various stages of the value chain. Global integration has advanced least at the design stage, as firms have sought to leverage engineering effort across products sold in multiple end markets. Because centrally designed vehicles are manufactured in multiple regions, however, lead firm–supplier relationships typically span multiple production regions. Increasingly, lead firms demand that their largest suppliers have a global presence and system design capabilities as a precondition to being considered as a source for a complex part or subsystem (Sturgeon and Florida 2004). As suppliers have taken on a larger role in design, they have established their own design centers close to those of their major customers to facilitate collaboration. On the production side, the dominant trend is regional integration, a pattern that has been intensifying since the mid-1980s for both political and technical reasons. In North America, South America, Europe, southern Africa, and Asia, regional parts production tends to feed final regional assembly plants that produce largely for regional markets. Political pressure for local production has driven automakers to set up final assembly plants in many of the major established market areas, such as the United States and Europe, as well as in the largest emerging market countries, such as Brazil, China, and India.

Within regions, there has been a gradual investment shift toward locations with lower operating costs: the southern United States and Mexico in North America, Spain and Eastern Europe in Europe, and Southeast Asia and China in Asia. Ironically, perhaps, it is primarily local lead firms that take advantage of such regional cost-cutting investments (for example, the investments of Ford, General Motors [GM], and Chrysler in Mexico, and Volkswagen and Peugeot in Eastern Europe). This is because the political pressure that drives the establishment of foreign assembly plants in large markets is only relieved when jobs are created locally; for example, Japanese and Korean (Republic of Korea) automaker investments in North America and Europe have been concentrated in the United States, Canada, and Western Europe, and not in Mexico or Eastern Europe. As a result, automotive parts are more heavily traded between regions than are finished vehicles. Within a country, automotive production is typically clustered in one or a few industrial regions. In some cases, these clusters specialize in specific aspects of the business, such as vehicle design, final assembly, or the manufacture of parts that share a common characteristic, such as electronic content or labor intensity. Because of large sunk investments in capital equipment and skills, regional automotive clusters tend to be very long-lived.

To sum up the complex economic geography of the automotive industry, global integration has proceeded furthest at the level of buyer-supplier relationships, especially between automakers and their largest suppliers. Production tends to be organized regionally or nationally, with bulky, heavy, and model-specific parts production concentrated close to final assembly plants to ensure timely delivery (for example, engines, transmission, and seats and other interior parts), and lighter, more generic parts produced at a distance to take advantage of scale economies (for example, tires and batteries) and low labor costs (for example, wire harnesses). Vehicle development is concentrated in a few design centers such as Tokyo, Detroit, and Stuttgart. As a result, local, national, and regional value chains in the automotive industry are "nested" within the global organizational structures and business relationships of the largest firms.

The Growing Role of Large Suppliers

One of the main drivers of global integration has been the consolidation and globalization of the supply base. In the past, multinational firms either exported parts to offshore affiliates or relied on local suppliers in each location, but today *global suppliers* have emerged in a range of industries, including motor vehicles

(Sturgeon and Lester 2004). From the mid-1980s through the 1990s, suppliers took on a much larger role in the automotive industry, often making radical leaps in competence and spatial coverage through the acquisition of firms with complementary assets and geographies. As automakers set up final assembly plants in new locations and tried to leverage common platforms over multiple products and multiple markets, they pressured their existing suppliers to move abroad with them. Increasingly, the ability to produce in all major production regions has become a precondition to being considered for a project. However, what is emerging in the automotive industry is more complex than a seamless and unified global supply base, given the competing pressures of centralized sourcing (for cost reduction and scale) and regional production (for just-in-time and local content). The need for full co-location of parts with final assembly varies by type of component, or even in stages of production for a single complex component or subsystem. Suppliers with a global presence can try to concentrate their volume production of specific components in one or two locations and ship them to their own plants close to their customers' final assembly plants, so that modules and subsystems can be built up and sent to final assembly plants as needed.

What should be clear from this discussion is that the economic geography of the automotive industry cannot be reduced to a set of national industries or a simple network of specialized clusters. Business relationships now span the globe at several levels of the value chain. Automakers and first-tier suppliers have certainly forged such relationships, and as the fewer, larger suppliers that have survived have come to serve a wider range of customers, these relationships have become very diverse. With further consolidation induced by the crisis, the staying power of smaller, lower-tier local suppliers is called into greater question, no matter how well supported they are by local institutions and interfirm networks, especially since many upstream materials suppliers, such as the automotive paint supplier PPG, are also huge companies with global operations.

Continuing Importance of Regional Production

Since the late 1980s, trade and foreign direct investment have accelerated dramatically in many industries. A combination of real and potential market growth with a huge surplus of low-cost, adequately skilled labor in the largest countries in the developing world—such as China, India, and Brazil—has attracted waves of investment, both to supply burgeoning local markets and for export back to developed economies. It is common with GVCs of this type that innovation and design functions remain in industrialized countries, while production functions migrate to developing countries, enabled and encouraged by the liberalization of trade and investment rules under an ascendant World Trade Organization (WTO). Yet regional production in some industries has remained very durable, especially in the automotive industry. The WTO notwithstanding, political pressure motivates lead firms to locate production close to end markets. This in turn creates pressure for supplier co-location within regional-scale production systems for operational reasons, such as just-in-time production, design collaboration, and the support of globally produced vehicle platforms. Because lead firms in the automotive industry are few in number and very powerful, they have been able to force their key suppliers to embrace the strategies of regional co-location and global expansion, what Humphrey and Memedovic (2003) call "follow sourcing."

While consumer tastes and purchasing power, driving conditions, and the nature of personal transportation can vary widely by country, local idiosyncrasies in markets and distribution systems are common in many industries. However, it is possible to feed fragmented and variegated distribution systems from centralized production platforms, as long as product variations are relatively superficial. The continued strength of regional production in the automotive industry is one of its most striking features (Lung, Van Tulder, and Carillo 2004),[2] standing in stark contrast to other important high-volume, consumer-oriented manufacturing industries, especially apparel and electronics, which have developed global-scale patterns of integration that concentrate production for world markets in a few low-cost locations.

Why is political pressure for local production felt so acutely in the automotive industry? The high cost and visibility of automotive products, especially passenger vehicles, among the general population can create the risk of a political backlash if imported vehicles become too large a share of total vehicles sold. This situation is heightened when local lead firms are threatened by imports. The case of Japanese exports to the United States in the 1960s and 1970s did much to set the regional pattern of automotive industry GVCs. In that period, Japanese (and to a lesser extent, European) automakers began to gain substantial market share in the United States through exports. Motor vehicle production in Japan soared from a negligible 300,000 units in 1960 to nearly 11 million units in 1982, growing on the strength of Japan's largely protected domestic market of about 5 million units, plus exports (Dassbach 1989). Excluding intra-European trade, Japan came to dominate global finished-vehicle exports by a wide margin, with the bulk of exports going to the United States (Dicken 2007).

As Japanese automakers' exports to the United States increased, the concomitant gain in market share came at the direct expense of the American "Big 3" automakers (General Motors, Ford, and Chrysler), sparking a political backlash that resulted in the setting of "voluntary" limits to market-share expansion via exports. A stark reality increased the political tension further: American automakers had been, and continue to be, unable to penetrate Japan's domestic market in any meaningful way. In response, Japanese automakers agreed to a set of "voluntary export restraints" that capped exports to the United States. As a way to continue their market share gains, Japanese automakers embarked on a wave of plant construction in the United States. By 1995, Japanese automakers were locally manufacturing two-thirds of the passenger vehicles they sold in the United States (Sturgeon and Florida 2004).[3]

As Japanese "transplant" production in North America ramped up after 1986, Japanese exports began a long decline. In 2009, transplants in North America had the capacity to assemble more than 6 million units, more than one-third of projected U.S. demand in 2011, and employed approximately 90,000 workers, just under one-third of North American assembly employment in 2005 (Sturgeon, Van Biesebroeck, and Gereffi 2007). Because of the high cost, large scale, and long life of assembly plant investments, there has been a cyclical pattern of rising finished-vehicle imports to the United States as market share shifted in favor of non-U.S.-based firms, followed by new assembly plant investments that effectively ratchet imports back down. In this way, plants in Japan are kept in full operation as new market share in the United States is absorbed by new capacity in North America. This pattern can be expected to continue if market share continues to shift away from the Big 3, but new plants will be added only if and when Japanese and other non-U.S. automakers are confident that their market share gains in North America will be long-standing.

This pattern reveals the political sensitivity to high levels of imports, especially of finished vehicles, in places where local lead firms are present, as they are in the United States and Europe. In our view, the willingness of governments to prop up or otherwise protect local automotive firms is comparable to that of industries such as agriculture, energy, steel, utilities, military equipment, and commercial aircraft. As a result, lead firms in these industries have adjusted their sourcing and production strategies to include a greater measure of local and regional production than can be seen in other industries. Political sensitivity also explains why Japanese, German, and Korean ("Korean" refers to Republic of Korea throughout) automakers in North America have not concentrated their production in Mexico, despite lower operating costs and a free trade agreement with the United States (Sturgeon, Van Biesebroeck, and Gereffi 2007).[4] Japanese automakers also shifted European production to Eastern Europe later and less aggressively than American and European lead firms, and have even moved to China later than their European and American competitors.[5]

Policy Interventions during the Crisis

The global financial crisis of 2008–09 severely deepened an ongoing global economic recession that had been under way since early in 2008. The impact of the crisis on the automotive industry has been more severe than for any other industry except housing and finance, which prompted large-scale government intervention around the world. This section provides background on the impact of the crisis, highlights the possible objectives of various government interventions, and discusses the different stages or degrees of intervention undertaken. (For a more detailed discussion of these issues, see Sturgeon and Van Biesebroeck 2009.)

The severity of the impact on the auto industry has several causes. First, the industry was in a dire state to begin with. The value chains led by the American Big 3 automakers were in particularly bad shape, with declining market share, global overcapacity, and rampant supplier bankruptcy. For companies already on life support, the freezing of credit markets meant canceled orders, unpaid supplier invoices, and "temporarily" shuttered plants. Huge debt loads, high fixed-capital costs, high labor costs, and immense pension and health care commitments to retirees added to the immediacy of the damage. Second, the high cost and growing longevity of motor vehicles prompted buyers to postpone purchases that they might otherwise have made. Consumers, especially in the world's largest national passenger vehicle market, the United States, found it difficult to obtain loans for purchase and, driven by fear of job loss, moved aggressively to increase their rate of saving. Vehicle sales plunged, and as a result, beginning in the fall of 2008, the industry fell into the most severe crisis experienced since the Great Depression.

Because of the co-location of assembly and parts plants in national and regional production systems, the effects of the crisis have largely been contained within each country or production region. For example, the largest sales decline was experienced in the United States. While this had a dramatic effect on parts imports, which declined at an average annual rate of 20.2 percent over the 2008–09 period (U.S. International Trade Commission), the more severe impact of the crisis in the United States was on assembly and parts plants within North America, some of which not only ceased importing parts, but temporarily or even permanently closed.

In this environment, the U.S. Congress, supported by a new administration unwilling to preside over the liquidation of the country's largest and most heavily unionized manufacturing industry, offered several waves of bailouts, but only after a series of humiliating congressional hearings where Big 3 CEOs made the case for government assistance and were aggressively cross-examined about management culpability. In the aftermath, General Motors' CEO resigned and the company was forced to file for Chapter 11 bankruptcy. Chrysler also filed for bankruptcy and narrowly avoided a break-up through partial liquidation and sale of its more lucrative assets to the Italian automaker Fiat, which provided technology and management support in an effort to restructure the company to make it viable again. While it is widely believed that Ford has not yet asked for or received government assistance, the company did accept a $5.7 billion "retooling loan" in June 2009 from the U.S. Department of Energy to develop more fuel-efficient cars and trucks.

In Europe, too, bailouts were provided, but in different ways. Credit support and loan guarantees were given directly to troubled firms. The scrappage, or environmentally motivated subsidies provided to consumers, helped firms indirectly by boosting industry sales. The different ways governments intervened are discussed in greater detail below.

Government Intervention in Developed Countries

During the 2008–09 economic crisis, many sectors saw reduced sales and firms teetering on the edge of, or falling into, bankruptcy, but only in the banking sector did the Western governments intervene on a larger scale than in the automotive industry. The systemic importance of the banking sector explains the motivations for interventions there. The reasons for the bailout of the automotive industry require a longer list of explanations as follows:

1. *Intervention was believed to be feasible and manageable.* The automotive industry is extremely concentrated at the top. Lead firms are very large and few in number and the value chain is structured in a clear, hierarchical way. As a result, government officials believed they could effectively assist the industry by propping up lead firms, which in turn generate business for thousands of the upstream suppliers.
2. *Political sensitivity is acute.* Large bankruptcies can create political reactions in any industry or country, but large, regionally concentrated employment in the automotive sector, the iconic status of passenger vehicles, and strong labor unions made it all the more difficult for politicians to let large firms in this sector fail, especially at a time when the aggregate labor market was very weak.
3. *Multiplier effects boost the rationale for automotive industry bailouts.* The notion of multiplier effects was frequently evoked as a justification for bailing out automakers. While it is misleading to present these as indirect job creation, bailouts can minimize the increase in cyclical unemployment over the short term.[6]
4. *Stimulating vehicle demand was seen as an effective way to stimulate aggregate demand.* Customers can alter the timing of vehicle purchases more easily than most other purchases. Purchasing a new vehicle is often a discretionary decision, usually made when the household still has a working vehicle. While this causes sales declines to be larger at the start of recessions (triggering calls

for intervention), it also makes demand-stimulus interventions quite effective, because consumers can move purchases forward.

5. *Stimulating vehicle demand has environmental side-benefits.* The high fuel prices of the summer of 2008, along with rising concern over carbon emissions, awakened politicians, once again, to the importance of reducing the consumption of fossil fuels. Policy measures have included CO_2 taxes, higher fuel efficiency standards, and R&D for technology development.
6. *Bailing out automakers helped solve the nation's credit problems.* In most countries, the bulk of vehicle sales are financed (90 percent in the United States). Tightening credit conditions for customers made it much harder to obtain vehicle financing than in normal circumstances. The operations of GM and Chrysler are deeply intertwined with their finance companies, often depending on them for profits. The difficulty for these firms to obtain credit themselves made it impossible for them to provide consumer financing and hampered their usual role in financing working capital (that is, vehicle inventories) in dealership networks.

Because the policy objectives, justifications, and motivations for interventions and bailouts have been so numerous and the actions taken so swift and complex, it is hard to evaluate them. No single criterion—the rescue of an individual firm, the slowing of unemployment, the repair of credit markets, the reduction of carbon emissions, or stimulation of aggregate demand—can be used as a measure of success. Clearly, policies that seek to achieve multiple objectives are laudable, but the debate has been muddied because different objectives and outcomes have been emphasized by different policy makers and with different constituencies. With so many possible goals and measures to choose from, it is easy to claim success or failure based on political expediency.

The Ladder of Government Intervention

While the examples above are drawn from the United States, virtually every Western government with a sizeable domestic automotive industry intervened in that industry in some way or another during the 2008–09 economic crisis. These policy measures are laid out here according to a "ladder of intervention," from less drastic and controversial to more so. As problems with individual companies worsened, governments have found themselves climbing this ladder quite rapidly.

1. *Credit warranties* are the least controversial form of intervention. Most countries have initiated schemes to guarantee or extend credit, and these are typically not limited to the automotive industry. A popular approach to support

the automotive industry is to earmark loans for R&D or vehicle development to boost fuel efficiency or to secure the loan with company land or buildings.

2. *Recapitalizing financing units* is similar to credit warranties and interventions in the banking sector, with an important difference that there is often very little or no equity participation by governments. The fall in both new and used vehicle demand forced large losses at financing units active in the leasing market. Compared with banks or other financial institutions, there are few retained earnings in an automaker's credit arm to strengthen the company's equity position, because earnings are passed on to keep manufacturing units afloat.
3. *Purchase subsidies paid directly to consumers* benefit automakers and suppliers, stimulate the broader economy, and are easily monitored. In most countries, rules were put in place to yield environmental benefits as well. The macroeconomic effect of these programs has been large, but they are proving to be a drag on sales recovery.
4. *Government provision of working capital* to specific companies is unlikely to come without policy makers gaining some influence over decision making, although governments have been at pains to stress that they were not interfering with the day-to-day operations of firms and that they plan to sell their stakes at the first opportunity.
5. *Takeover liabilities* are similar to the provision of working capital without the expectation that the loans will ever be repaid. In this case, governments become even more extensively involved in the management of the firm. While these cash infusions are technically structured as loans, there is often no real expectation of repayment.
6. *Quasi-nationalization of the industry* took place as part of the accelerated bankruptcy procedure of Chrysler and GM, wherein the U.S. (and Canadian) government took large equity stakes in the restructured companies in exchange for debtor-in-possession financing. At this point, government intervention in strategic decision making became more explicit: appointing new top management, demanding larger wage cuts, restructuring of the product portfolio, and insisting on additional plant closures. The stated objective is to sell government ownership shares as soon as possible, but before this can happen it will have to be clear that the companies are financially stable.

Accelerated Growth of the Industry in Developing Countries

This section analyzes the historic shift—accelerated by the 2008–09 economic crisis—of the automotive industry to large developing countries. The industry's rapid growth in these countries has permitted governments to limit the scope of their interventions during the crisis. Nevertheless, the crisis in the industry in industrialized countries has had important consequences for the industry in developing countries as well.

Despite the recent and dramatic effects of the economic crisis on the automotive industry, it is important to begin with a longer-term perspective. Recent events will serve to hasten long-term trends, most notably, (1) the shift of automotive production to developing countries, where sales growth is strongest; (2) consolidation in the global supply base and among automakers; and (3) the internationalization of automakers from developing countries (for example, the Chinese state-owned automaker Geely's current bid to take over Ford's Swedish car unit, Volvo).[7] Automakers are discussed first, followed by suppliers.

Table 6.1 lists the countries where more than 1 million vehicles were produced in 2007 (except France and the Islamic Republic of Iran, where data were unavailable), ranked by annual production growth rates over the 2007–08 period, which were negative for most countries. The table shows that the crisis-induced contraction

Table 6.1 Passenger Vehicle Production Levels and Growth in Countries Producing 1 Million or More Units in 2008

	Units (thousands)		Annual growth (percent)	Units (thousands)	Annual growth (percent)
Country	2002	2007	2002–07	2008	2007–08
Spain	2,855	2,891	0.25	1,940	–32.90
Canada	2,629	2,602	–0.21	2,068	–20.52
United Kingdom	1,821	1,770	–0.57	1,450	–18.08
United States	12,280	10,611	–2.88	8,746	–17.58
Italy	1,427	1,284	–2.09	1,085	–15.47
Germany	5,145	6,200	3.80	5,500	–11.29
Korea, Rep. of	3,148	4,085	5.35	3,830	–6.24
Mexico	1,805	2,254	4.54	2,154	–4.44
India	892	2,046	18.06	2,022	–1.20
Japan	10,258	11,596	2.48	11,564	–0.28
Turkey	340	1,097	26.40	1,147	4.57
China	3,251	8,890	22.29	9,340	5.06
Russian Federation	1,220	1,654	6.28	1,776	7.40
Brazil	1,793	2,960	10.55	3,210	8.45
Thailand	540	1,178	16.88	1,400	18.85

Sources: Data for 2002 and 2007 and for North American countries and Japan are taken from *Automotive News*. Other information comes from various Internet sources, mostly from newspaper reports and national industry associations.

Note: Two countries are missing: France (3.01 million vehicles in 2007) and the Islamic Republic of Iran (1.18 million in 2007); 2008 production volumes were not available for these countries.

of production has been most pronounced in countries that have experienced the slowest rate of production growth over the preceding five years. The table also shows China, where the rebound in sales has been particularly strong, surpassing the United States for the first time in 2008 as the number 2 auto producing country in the world. Looking at these trends and considering the pending plant closures in North America and Europe, we are led to the conclusion that some portion of the current production decline in mature markets will be permanent and that China is likely to occupy the top spot soon and keep it for the foreseeable future.

That said, the overall structure of the postcrisis industry is still taking shape, as many firms have yet to liquidate, fully complete their bankruptcy restructurings, or be certain of avoiding bankruptcy. Only after the announced plant closures and capacity reductions have been carried out will alterations in global market share and the relative weight of the industry in different regions become apparent. However, the likely four market-share leaders in size order, Toyota, Volkswagen, Ford, and Hyundai, will signal a remarkable break from the industry's recent past. Furthermore, the ascendance of Chinese companies and India's Tata into the top 20 could have far-reaching effects on the global automotive market.

It is important to note that the industry's growth in the developing world has been limited to a specific subset of countries. Political pressure to build vehicles where they are sold and effective caps on large-scale finished-vehicle exports, discussed earlier, combined with very high minimum economies of scale for truly "integrated" production, mean that market size dictates the potential for the industry's growth. The impact of market size is manifested in four ways. First, even when existing vehicle designs are used as a basis, it is only profitable for lead firms to tailor final products to fit consumer tastes in very large markets (Brandt and Van Biesebroeck 2008). This took place in Brazil, China, and India, but not in other developing countries. In these countries, lead firms have established local design, engineering, and regional headquarters facilities. Once automakers set up these local technical centers, they tend to pressure "global suppliers" to establish local engineering capabilities as well (Humphrey and Memedovic 2003; Sturgeon and Lester 2004). When this occurs, global suppliers can begin to source inputs locally, providing opportunities and support for local second-tier suppliers to develop. Over time, it is possible for local firms to start serving automakers directly, and international opportunities can grow from there. Thus, a virtuous cycle of development can develop only if the local domestic market is large enough to attract significant investment in the first instance.

A second dynamic has unfolded in a few midsize developing countries that are large and rich enough to support the assembly of vehicles without modification. Examples include South Africa, Thailand, and Turkey. These countries have become final assembly hubs for their wider regions. Because there are strong agglomeration economies in the automotive industry, the presence of final assembly plants can provide opportunities for local suppliers producing, especially, bulky, heavy, or fragile parts such as seats. Proximity to plants assembling existing vehicle designs can create export opportunities as well, even when supply contracts are based on existing blueprints, because identical vehicles are being produced elsewhere in the world. However, global suppliers are commonly present in these locations as well, limiting the opportunities for local firms.

A third dynamic has occurred in developing countries that are proximate enough to large markets in developed countries to supply parts on a just-in-time basis and within regional trade blocs—such as Mexico in the North American Free Trade Agreement (NAFTA), Hungary and the Czech Republic in the European Union (EU), and Thailand in the Association of Southeast Asian Nations (ASEAN) and in East Asia more generally. If they are geographically close to large existing markets, they can become hubs, especially, for the production of labor-intensive parts. Wire harness and automotive electronics assembly on Mexico's border with the United States is a longstanding example, and several Central and Eastern European countries have taken on a similar role for the industry in Western Europe. As some final assembly has developed in Mexico and Eastern Europe, these plants have been able to serve them, and plants for the production of more capital-intensive parts have been established as well. However, because of the proximity to developed economies, these activities tend to be carried out by global suppliers and few opportunities have arisen for local firms.

A fourth, nascent dynamic is for a local lead firm to leverage the new, relatively open local and global supply base to rapidly become more competitive locally and, perhaps, in world markets. Consider the case of Chery Automobile, a small state-controlled Chinese company based in Wuhu, some 200 kilometers west of Shanghai, that within a remarkably short time, has been able to develop and market a line of Chery-badged vehicles. While perhaps not world class, the Chery vehicles are nevertheless suitable both for the local market and for export to other developing countries. The first Chery prototype was built in December 1999, and volume production began in March 2001. By the end of 2007, plant capacity had grown to 600,000 units, and Chery was already China's largest vehicle exporter.

A few details are necessary to understand how remarkable is Chery's rise. Vehicle design and development are notoriously difficult tasks, typically the purview of companies that have been in the business for decades. New vehicle designs commonly require more than 30,000 engineering hours and take three to five years to complete, as well as several billion dollars of upfront investment (Sturgeon, Van Biesebroeck, and Gereffi 2008). Firms that do enter the business usually come from a field such as aircraft, where related design and engineering experience has been accumulated over a similarly long period (Mitsubishi, Subaru, BMW, and SAAB are examples).

Chery has been able to launch its own line of branded vehicles in a very short time by tapping the expertise of first-tier global suppliers with operations both in China and in the West to obtain a full range of inputs, from parts to processes to design expertise. For styling and engineering, Chery works with Italdesign, Pininfarina, and Torino in Italy. Additional engineering and development work is outsourced to Lotus Engineering and MIRA in the United Kingdom and to Porsche Engineering in Germany and Austria. Chery works with AVL in Austria on gasoline and diesel engines, and with Ricardo in the United Kingdom on hybrid power trains. Heuliez in France supplies a retractable hardtop for the Chery A3 coupe cabriolet, a car designed by Pininfarina. For critical parts and subsystems, Chery sources from global suppliers such as Bosch, ZF, Johnson Controls, Luk, Valeo, TRW, and Siemens VDO (Automotive News 2007). These sourcing arrangements, which have only recently become readily available for fledgling companies like Chery to piece together, show that Chery is nothing like a typical car company, especially because it is far removed from the most recent entrants to the mass market for cars, the vertically integrated and horizontally diversified national champions from Korea, Hyundai, Kia, and Daewoo. Companies that jump to the head of GVCs in this way, however, may still fail to develop deep design and system integration expertise that allows them to compete at the vanguard of fast-moving markets. More than any other motivation, it is access to the deep competencies in vehicle design and engineering that has driven local lead firms from China and India to acquire or attempt to acquire distressed auto companies in the West during the 2008–09 crisis and its aftermath.

What has been left unsaid so far, but should be clear from this discussion, is that small developing countries far from large existing markets have been and will likely continue to be unable to develop a domestic automotive industry. For most countries with small, easily saturated markets, it has been extremely difficult for local firms to develop a significant role in the industry.[8] Because of this, the geographic shift of the industry from developed countries (DC) to emerging markets has been the most dramatic in large developing countries such as Brazil, China, and India.

The investment patterns and strategies at the automaker level just discussed have direct analogs in the parts-making sector, not least because the strategies of buyer and suppliers tend to be tightly interwoven, as discussed earlier. In 1999 only four firms from developing countries (one each from Malaysia and China and two Indian firms) appeared on a list of automakers producing more than 100,000 vehicles annually (Automotive News 2007). By 2007, right before the global crisis, 12 additional developing-country lead firms joined the list, 1 from the Islamic Republic of Iran and 11 from China. As a result, developing-country lead firms' total share of world vehicle production increased from 1.9 percent to 7.5 percent from 1999 to 2007, an increase almost entirely attributable to Chinese firms.

Similarly, the list of the largest suppliers to the North American industry (top 150) and to the global industry (top 100) published annually by *Automotive News* reveals the limited importance of developing firms among first-tier suppliers. First, the number of developing-country suppliers on the global 100 list remained the same between 1999 and 2007. Only one Mexican firm moved significantly upward in the ranking. Of the top-150 suppliers to the North American industry, one of the two Mexican firms on the list in 1999 failed to make it in 2007. As Korean lead firms saw their production grow by 25 percent, almost identical to worldwide production growth, Korean suppliers also started to play an important role. Two Korean firms are now on the top-100 list worldwide and one Korean firm is on the top–North American list, prior to any Korean assembly plant's opening on the North American continent.

In contrast to many other industries, developing-country firms have not been able to establish a presence in the global automotive industry by moving from simple, labor-intensive components to capital- and technology-intensive components. Instead, local assembly is often the first step, and the development of a parts sector comes later. Sutton (2007) illustrates the difficulties faced by second-tier suppliers in China and India in meeting the quality standards set by foreign carmakers. Brandt and Van Biesebroeck (2008) show that China only started to run a trade surplus in parts in 2005. This is the usual pattern: as a local automotive industry develops, the country initially runs a trade deficit in parts because it does not have the local capabilities to produce advanced components or the quality standards to sell in advanced markets. Significant parts exports emerge only when final assembly capability is quite mature. In the context of GVCs, these exports might be dominated by global rather than local suppliers. This hypothesis is supported by table 6.2, which shows the top-10 developing-country exporters of automotive and motorcycle parts. Most of the countries listed have had substantial final assembly capacity for many decades, and host significant investment by global automotive suppliers.

Canadian Auto Industry before and during the Economic Crisis

The growing importance of developing countries as final goods markets and production platforms has prompted important changes in the way suppliers in the mature markets operate. Before describing the different development patterns in developing countries, we discuss the recent experience of Canadian suppliers. A recent survey by the Canadian Auto Parts Manufacturers (Asia Pacific Foundation of Canada 2005) demonstrates that the growing importance of markets in East Asia creates both opportunities and threats for home-based firms. Canadian suppliers are under pressure both to compete harder for domestic business and to establish manufacturing facilities overseas.

Table 6.2 Top-10 Developing-Economy Exporters of Intermediate Parts for Passenger Vehicles and Motorcycles

Economy	1988 (US$, billions)	2006 (US$, billions)	CAGR 1988–2006 (percent)
Mexico	790	27,930	21.9
China[a]	109	26,361	35.6
Brazil	417	7,855	17.7
Thailand	53	6,349	30.5
Taiwan, China	274	5,064	17.6
Turkey	57	3,365	25.4
Indonesia	17	2,904	32.9
Philippines	18	2,564	31.7
India	189	2,190	14.6
Argentina	25	1,579	26.0

Source: UN Comtrade, using modified Broad Economic Category (BEC) classification (see Sturgeon and Memedovic, forthcoming).
Note: The exporters are ranked by 2006 exports, with annual growth 1988–2006. CAGR = compound annual growth rate.
a. Includes Hong Kong, China.

Table 6.3 groups the answers to five survey questions that probe the firms about their own production activities, sourcing, investments, and customer demands. These responses illustrate the changing geographical activities of Canadian supplier firms before the crisis. Comparing the geographical distribution of three activities—production, sourcing, and investment—a clear trend away from Canada toward Asia is apparent. While almost 70 percent of the firms' production takes place in Canada, only 51 percent of inputs are currently sourced domestically and only 49 percent of greenfield investment occurs in Canada. In contrast, Asia is the production location for only 0.3 percent of current output, but the source of 4.7 percent of inputs. Most important for the future, 28 percent of all greenfield investment by Canadian automotive parts suppliers is made in Asia, ahead of even the United States.

An important impetus for Canadian suppliers to invest overseas is the explicit requests from current customers: 64 percent of suppliers report that they have received a request in the last three years to aid the overseas expansion of their customers by setting up overseas operations of their own. Some suppliers also indicated that they believe serving Japanese-owned firms in other countries will increase their chances of gaining new business to supply Japanese assembly in Canada.

The responses of Canadian suppliers to the 2008–09 crises can be gauged from a small survey of second-tier suppliers by Facey (2009), summarized in table 6.4. In this survey, cost-cutting is the item that appears time and again. While firms

Table 6.3 Changing Geographical Exposition for Canadian Suppliers
percentage of survey responses

Survey questions	Canada	United States	Europe	Latin America	Asia
Fraction of your firm's production taking place in facilities located in . . .	69.4	17.1	11.9	1.4	0.3
Fraction of supply needs that were sourced from . . .	51.1	33.3	9.0	1.9	4.7
Fraction of greenfield investments (past five years) made in . . .	49	18	4	1	28
In the last three years, has one or more of your major customers ever threatened to switch to overseas suppliers? Yes					71
In the last three years, has one or more of your major customers asked your firm to initiate or expand activities in new geographical markets in order to facilitate its own expansion agenda? Yes					64
Countries mentioned most frequently: United States (33), Korea (33), China (33), Mexico (22)					

Source: Asia Pacific Foundation of Canada 2005.

Table 6.4 Impact of the Crisis on Quality Initiatives of Second-Tier Canadian Suppliers, 2009
percentage of responses

Survey questions	Possible answers	Fraction answering "yes"
Is the area of . . . in your company affected by the recession?	Quality control	6
	Top answer: human resources	25
	Answered "all of the above"	37
Over the past six months, which of the following events have you noticed in your company?	Cut in quality program	13
	Top answers: cost reduction, layoffs, reduced working hours, waste reduction	100

Rate your company's involvement in the following programs before and during the recession	Fraction answering "active" or "very": Before	During
Cost reduction activities	50	100
Customer satisfaction	100	100
Supplier development	37	24
Continuous improvement	69	37
New product development	13	6
Process/product innovation	63	25

Source: Facey 2009.

report layoffs and other cost-cutting measures, they have clearly resisted cutting quality programs, even in difficult economic times. The top section shows that there were cuts in quality programs, but only as part of broader cost-cutting efforts. The bottom section ranks the programs that have seen changes in the firm's "active involvement." The areas are ranked from the largest increase at the top to the largest decrease at the bottom. Only 50 percent of firms indicated an active involvement in cost reduction activities before the crisis, while all firms did so during the crisis. Active involvement in process or product innovation declined from 63 percent of firms before the crisis to 25 percent during the crisis. Not surprisingly, cost reduction has moved to the top of the list. More interestingly, it also seems that suppliers have chosen to scale down activities related to innovation, product development, and continuous improvement before de-emphasizing customer satisfaction or supplier development initiatives. This is somewhat surprising since the bottom two areas on the list are likely to have a more immediate effect on product quality.[9]

Lead Firm Strategies toward Developing-Country Expansion: A Case Study in China

The impact of the 2008–09 economic crisis on developing countries can be seen through a comparison of two distinctive strategies that foreign lead firms in the automotive industry have followed in China. Because all the firms discussed here are huge multinational corporations (MNCs), with established brands and extensive international operations, their strategies share many elements. However, firms have sought to participate in the rapidly growing Chinese market in different ways.[10] Some firms have actively tailored their existing vehicle portfolios to local tastes, while others have focused on selling existing vehicles in upper market segments. The former strategy, while riskier because of the larger investment and supply-base support required, has led to greater success because it has allowed MNC lead firms to sell more vehicles and compete more directly with local carmakers.

This discussion draws on information the authors collected as part of a global automotive supplier benchmarking study of the International Motor Vehicle Program (IMVP), comparing practices, capabilities, and performance of automobile suppliers around the world. The assessment focuses on the production of seats, exhaust systems, and brakes at plants in China, Europe, Japan, Korea, and North America. Thus far, data have been collected at plants in China and Japan, as well as at a few European plants. A report on the interim findings of this project can be found in Brandt and Van Biesebroeck (2008).

Although the identities of the firms interviewed are confidential, observed differences fell largely along national lines, with clear differences between Asian and

Western automakers. The first strategy, "cautious localization," is favored by the Japanese and Korean producers interviewed. Vehicles are produced in China in large volumes, but designed entirely overseas. Most first-tier suppliers are joint ventures (JVs) between a local Chinese firm and a foreign partner responsible for manufacture and often the design of the part back in the home country. Some modules are supplied by wholly owned foreign subsidiaries (WOSs), which are allowed in China for parts but not for final assembly. Since the use of second- or even third-tier suppliers is typically blocked by headquarters for quality reasons, the majority of suppliers to cautious localizers tend to be either JVs or WOSs.

This sort of centrally coordinated GVC facilitates high product quality but raises costs because parts cannot be altered or easily outsourced to take advantage of lower-cost, lower-quality manufacturing. In the end, vehicles tend to cost too much to appeal to a large number of buyers, and it is more difficult to introduce products specifically aimed at the local market. While average income levels in the Chinese economy are rising rapidly, relatively wealthy customers have led the market, leaving the lower priced segments as the fastest-growing market segments. Japanese and Korean lead firms have sought to avoid competition with domestic lead firms selling low-quality/low-cost products, but the high costs associated with the cautious localization strategy have also *forced* them to pursue the upper segment of the market, which is becoming less important over time as vehicle ownership levels in China increase. One potential benefit of this strategy, however, is that it may enable lead firms, over time, to tap into lower cost JV and WOS sources for parts and components for export to higher cost production locations. Since vehicles produced in China are identical to those being assembled elsewhere, they may be creating a competitive export platform for the future.

It should be noted that designing vehicles at home for production overseas is the same approach described earlier that Japanese automakers took to penetrate markets in the United States and Europe, so the cautious localization strategy is compatible with the larger global strategies of these firms. The difference is that consumer preferences in China, as well as in other developing countries, are vastly different from the market in Japan, while the markets in the United States and Europe are similar enough to sell vehicles with only minor alterations, such as converting right-hand drive vehicles to left-hand drive. As a result, with a few exceptions, the vehicles produced by Japanese automakers in Japan, Europe, and the United States have proven too expensive to sell in large volumes in developing countries.

The second strategy pursued by automotive lead firm multinational enterprises (MNEs) in China can be called "aggressive localization." A select number of European and American JVs have taken an approach in which both lead firms and first-tier suppliers set up design and engineering centers in China. Parts, modules, and eventually complete vehicles are redesigned to better suit the tastes and purchasing power of local consumers. An important advantage of this approach is that modules can be redesigned to be compatible with the manufacturing capabilities of the domestic firms and meet local regulatory, that is, safety and environmental, requirements. In this way, larger fixed costs are incurred in terms of design and engineering, but variable costs fall because lower cost domestic suppliers and production processes can be used. As a result, vehicles can be produced in China at lower cost and compete directly with less expensive domestic offerings. The challenge is to find components of the vehicle for which this sort of localization is feasible and cost-effective, while at the same time ensuring that quality and fit are not so compromised that the company's brand image is damaged.[11]

It is notable that only a few automotive lead firm MNCs have chosen the second approach thus far, but this model could prove very disruptive for manufacturing in more-developed countries if prices fall and quality improves to the point where large-scale parts exports are possible. Moreover, intense competition in the domestic Chinese market and falling prices may be accelerating the process of local capability building. One major international lead firm described a five-year plan to lower its production costs in China by 40 percent by 2010.

An observable area of difference in the two strategies is in the composition of suppliers. The authors interviewed several final assembly plants, asking for the identity of first-tier suppliers for a wide range of major parts and systems (60–75 suppliers per firm). Table 6.5 reports the fraction of domestic, JV, and WOS first-tier suppliers, as well imports for two domestic, three Asian, two North American, and two European automakers operating in China. The results show that domestic Chinese lead firms are clearly localizing most aggressively and did not report any imports of major modules or systems. These firms were also much more likely to source from 100 percent domestically owned firms than from either joint ventures or foreign subsidiaries: 61 percent of the suppliers identified were domestic firms and the rest were JVs.

For the three Asian lead firms, on the other hand, only 5.5 percent of suppliers were domestic Chinese-owned firms, on average. In two of the three cases, the share was well below 5 percent. Imports also make up a nonnegligible share of components, accounting for almost 22 percent on average and even one-third of parts in one case. In contrast, for the American and European lead firms interviewed, the share of parts sourced from domestic firms was noticeably higher and imports were lower. For one U.S. lead firm, in particular, sourcing is almost as domestically focused as for Chinese lead firms.

While the two approaches to expansion in China have been apparent for some time, the effect of the crisis, by and large, has meant an acceleration of the observed precrisis differences, at least in the short term. For some firms, the

Table 6.5 Sourcing by Original Equipment Manufacturers in China from Three Possible Sources
percentage of first-tier suppliers

Lead firm	Domestic firms	Joint ventures and wholly owned foreign subsidiaries	Overseas (imported)
European	14.0	86.0	0
European	23.8	68.3	7.9
United States	14.3	57.1	24.5
United States	39.6	58.5	3.8
Average Western	15.4	69.7	14.5
Asian	2.2	64.4	33.3
Asian	4.8	85.5	9.7
Asian	9.4	67.9	22.6
Average Asian	5.5	72.6	21.9
Chinese	58.2	41.8	0
Chinese	63.4	36.6	0
Average Chinese	60.8	39.2	0
Average (all)	25.5	62.9	11.3

Source: Brandt and Van Biesebroeck 2008.

aggressive localization strategy has been driven by a scarcity of resources—either financial or in terms of management capacity. The greater toll of the crisis on American lead firms, in particular, has further encouraged a very aggressive expansion strategy in China; sales there accounted for the same number of vehicles as the U.S. market sold in the first nine months of 2009. Starved of funds for vehicle development, Western lead firms have relied on more global suppliers to tailor vehicles to local tastes. The need for cost savings has intensified the quest to utilize lower cost second- and third-tier suppliers in China as well.

On the other hand, the crisis has made firms pursuing a cautious localization strategy, in particular the Japanese, even more cautious. A common strategy for firms in a recession is to return to core markets and perceived comparative advantages. During a recession, there is even less incentive to deviate from strategies—centered on efficient production and high quality—that have served Japanese lead firms well in the past.

More generally, the aggressive localization strategy can be viewed as a more short-term, less patient strategy. The objective is to expand Chinese sales quickly without waiting for the Chinese middle class to grow even richer or technological capabilities in the local supply to rise even further, such that the same vehicles popular in developed countries can be sold in China as well. It is also a higher risk strategy, as there is a nonnegligible risk that the premium brand advantage will be eroded if low-quality local parts find their way too quickly into Chinese-made vehicles. Again, such a strategy appeals most to firms hit hardest by the crisis.

Development of the Industry before and during the Crisis in Mexico

Mexico's automotive industry is deeply integrated in the North American production system. It relies almost entirely on foreign lead firms and suppliers for vehicle designs and investment. The country's annual car sales are too small, given its population size and level of economic development, to warrant many models made specifically for the local market. Relatively low wages make Mexico an attractive export platform for the NAFTA market. In the four years from 2004 to 2007, Mexican production expanded by 35.5 percent, while U.S. production fell by 9.5 percent and Canadian production declined by 4.5 percent. Almost all of this expansion was due to exports to the United States. Table 6.6 shows very high export ratios—specifically to other NAFTA countries—for all assemblers in Mexico, though less so for Volkswagen and Nissan, which use their plants in Mexico to serve the local market and for export to other countries in Latin America.

Mexico has become an important export platform for automotive parts within North America as well. In 1990, Mexico ranked third as an exporter of automotive parts to the United States ($5.2 billion), well behind Japan ($10.2 billion) and Canada ($8.4 billion). By 2005, Mexico occupied the top position, with exports to the United States totaling $18.5 billion. For some labor-intensive parts, wiring harnesses perhaps being the best example, Mexico has a NAFTA market share of more than 90 percent. Note that most of these producers are global suppliers operating gigantic facilities in Mexico for both export and shipment to domestic assembly plants.

Production of auto parts, especially electronics and other labor-intensive parts, began in the border region of Mexico well before NAFTA, with investments and sourcing driven by American firms seeking to cut costs under the "Maquiladora" program, which allowed firms to pay tariffs only on value-added in Mexico. But after NAFTA these trade preferences were extended to the whole country and investments surged to the interior. Except for investments to support Nissan's final assembly plant in Aguascalientes, the only high-volume Japanese-owned assembly plant in Mexico, Japanese parts suppliers have announced only a few sizable investments in Mexico, such as Ahresty's $66 million foundry in Zacatecas and Bridgestone's $81 million lampblack plant in Tamaulipas.

This integration into the larger North American economy boosted production disproportionately in the good years, but it also exposed Mexico to the U.S.-originated crises and the collapse in demand centered on the American lead firms that made substantial investments there, Ford and GM. The greater

Table 6.6 Production, Sales, and Exports by Automakers with Assembly Plants in Mexico, 2004–07

Automaker	Domestic production (no. of units)	Domestic production sold in Mexico (no. of units)	Imports (no. of units)	Exports (no. of units)	Exports to United States and Canada (no. of units)	Total domestic sales (US$)
GM	1,884,730	385,665	585,989	1,499,065	1,483,965	971,654
Nissan	1,550,563	726,829	184,209	823,734	669,167	911,038
Chrysler	1,282,670	20,785	475,948	1,261,885	1,185,608	496,733
Volkswagen	1,282,314	261,979	329,356	1,020,335	568,750	591,335
Ford	909,480	165,007	527,052	744,473	730,110	692,059
Honda	89,753	29,734	133,309	60,019	52,713	163,043
Toyota	65,458	0	185,490	65,458	42,360	185,490
Total	7,064,968	1,589,999	2,421,353	5,474,969	4,732,673	4,011,352

Automaker	Share of domestic sales produced locally (percent)	Share of local production exported (percent)	Share of exports to United States and Canada (percent)	Exports CAGR 04-07 (percent)	Production CAGR 04-07 (percent)	Domestic sales CAGR 04-07 (percent)
GM	40	80	99	1	–1	–3
Nissan	80	53	81	34	16	–2
Chrysler	4	98	94	–7	–6	4
Volkswagen	44	80	56	27	22	–7
Ford	24	82	98	54	41	–5
Honda	18	67	88	3	–3	18
Toyota[a]	0[a]	100[a]	100[a]	—[a]	—[a]	40
Total	40	77	86	14	10	–1

Source: Associacion Mexicana de la Industria Automotriz (AMIA).

Note: No. of units refers to the cumulative total for the years 2004–07. CAGR = compound annual growth rate; — = not available.

a. Toyota began production in Mexico in 2006; production data are for 2006 and 2007 only. Figures for domestic sales are for 2004–07.

importance of smaller vehicles in Mexico's assembly plants, and drive by American automakers to concentrate closures in higher cost plants in the United States and Canada, has softened the blow to some extent. While North American production declined by 16.4 percent between 2007 and 2008, Mexican production increased slightly, by 3.9 percent. As a result, production of finished vehicles in Mexico surpassed Canadian production for the first time in 2008.

Clearly, the fate of an industry in a small, regionally embedded country like Mexico is tied to factors that lie largely outside the control of the state or of local firms. Ironically, the flagging prospects of the Big 3 automakers have created more risks for Mexico and Canada than for the United States.[12] These companies, even though based in the United States, have been more important in driving investment and industrial upgrading in Mexico than have Asian firms. Japanese and Korean automakers, with the exception of Nissan, have concentrated their North American investments within the United States (and to a lesser extent, Canada) for political reasons, while the Big 3, when they have made new North American investments at all, have sought to cut costs in North America by building and planning new capacity in Mexico. Now, with the crisis, we believe that the future of this most recent investment wave must be called into question by the severe crisis that has currently overtaken the Big 3.

Development of the Industry before and during the Crisis in China and India

China's strategy mirrored Mexico's initially, with the important difference that government policy insisted on joint ventures and other explicit policies to facilitate or even force technological transfer and greater involvement of local firms. While the long-term success of these programs is still unclear, they may have helped local assemblers compete with foreign firms producing in China. In the early years, the industry depended very strongly on investment by Western MNCs (lead firms and suppliers) and relied almost entirely on the advanced design and engineering expertise of these companies. Chinese firms were only responsible for the very simplest steps in the production process, and the parallel management structures (and the Chinese and Western plant manager, engineering manager, and so on) often required little from the Chinese side of the company. JVs only in name, the Chinese contribution to new investments often amounted to little more than the provision of real estate. However, over the course of 20 years, the JVs in assembly and component production have transferred many crucial production, engineering, marketing, and management skills to individuals and independent Chinese firms, a few of which are now operating successfully at each stage of the automotive value chain. Acquisition of final elements of technological knowledge, including vehicle design and system integration, will be hastened by the 2008–09 financial crisis, which has made some of these assets (for example, in companies such as SAAB, Volvo, Hummer) available for acquisition at "fire sale" prices.

In contrast, India has, even from the start, relied more than any other developing country on homegrown lead firms to propel its industry. A disadvantage of this approach is that the absorption of global best practices has been proceeding more slowly (Sutton 2007). Nevertheless, the development of the Indian automotive industry has accelerated very quickly in the past several years. This improvement in the breadth and depth of local capabilities has been aided, most notably, by foreign acquisitions.

Because per capita income growth is slower in India than in China, market potential was not perceived to be large enough to convince foreign lead firms to take the investment risks they did in China, even when investment restrictions were lifted. As a result, while growth in the Indian industry started earlier than it did in China, it has proceeded at a slower pace. Nevertheless, every aspect of vehicle development and production, including design and engineering, has been present in local firms from the beginning, and this has allowed the industry in India to make rapid progress.

To gauge the difference in initial development between China and India, it is instructive to compare the market shares of the leading automakers in both countries in 2001 (see table 6.7). In India, no leading multinational automakers were among the top four. Suzuki, a small Japanese firm with a controlling investment stake held by GM, was the number one producer in India. The company ranked 15th in the world when it began production in India, accounting for about 10 percent of GM's sales. Suzuki's Indian JV has operated with a great deal of independence and substantial input from the local partner, Maruti. Hyundai, India's number two producer, was only the eighth-largest producer worldwide at the time it began production in the country. The next two firms, Tata and

Table 6.7 Market Share of Leading Car Producers in India and China in 2001

Maruti Udyog Ltd. (JV with Suzuki)	62.2	SAIC-VW Joint Venture (JV)	32.7
Hyundai Motor India Ltd.	16.5	FAW-VW JV	18.9
		Dongfeng-Citroën JV	10.2
Tata Engineering and Locomotive Co. Ltd.	11.5	SAIC-GM JV	8.2
Hindustan Motors Ltd.	3.4	Guangzhou-Honda JV	7.2
		Tianjin Xiali-Daihatsu JV	7.2
Top four:	93.6	Top six:	84.4
Number of vehicles	529,947	Number of vehicles	597,074

Source: Sutton 2004.

Hindustan Motors, are independently owned Indian firms. In China, by contrast, all of the six largest producers were foreign JVs. Ford was the only one of the top-seven firms worldwide not producing in the country.[13]

The market share differences between China and Mexico in table 6.7 are mirrored by differences in the sourcing strategies of local assemblers. As the table shows, sourcing by Chinese lead firms is almost fully local. Chinese lead firms are piggybacking on the global supply chain that has emerged around the JV car assemblers, on one hand, and are providing some local first-tier suppliers with important "learning" opportunities on the other. As seen in the case of China's Chery, discussed earlier, local lead firms contract out much of their design work (and even some of the engineering and testing) to vehicle engineering companies. The "integral" design architecture of motor vehicles highlights the fact that these firms will have to master design and development capabilities to be independently successful.

Nevertheless, Chinese firms such as Chery and Geely are providing domestic suppliers, as well as JV suppliers, important opportunities to upgrade their capabilities and to become more deeply involved in the design, prototype development, testing, and mass production of important part and vehicle subsystems. Managers at several major JV suppliers interviewed as part of our field research expressed similar sentiments about the emerging "learning" opportunities provided by local lead firms, and described how they hoped to build on them. The process of capability building can be difficult and time consuming, and weaknesses in areas such as system integration on the part of domestic lead firms present a set of issues for suppliers that are distinct from those faced when they serve lead firms with deeper competencies. However, the first-tier suppliers interviewed for the study were nearly universally impressed with the speed of learning at firms like Chery. The rapid proliferation of models sold by these firms is testimony to the opportunities being provided.

In addition, competition with the most advanced domestic firms—Chery, Geely and SAIC (Shanghai Automotive Industry Corporation)—is proving to be a major stimulus for some foreign lead firms to pursue an aggressive localization strategy in China. Only by sourcing locally almost as much as Chinese lead firms have foreign automakers been able to compete for the middle of the market—a segment that is growing especially strongly (Brandt and Thun 2010).

These differences are reflected in the quality of the domestic supply base. The statistics in figure 6.1 illustrate the higher defect rates (in parts-per-thousand) for Indian versus Chinese suppliers. Because foreign automakers invested more aggressively in China to build up a local supply chain than in India, it is not surprising that Indian suppliers were lagging behind Chinese suppliers in productivity and quality, both at the time of our initial field research (2004) and in a follow-up study by Sutton (2007). Furthermore, an update of the Chinese data in

Figure 6.1 Supplier Defect Rates for New-Generation Lead Firms

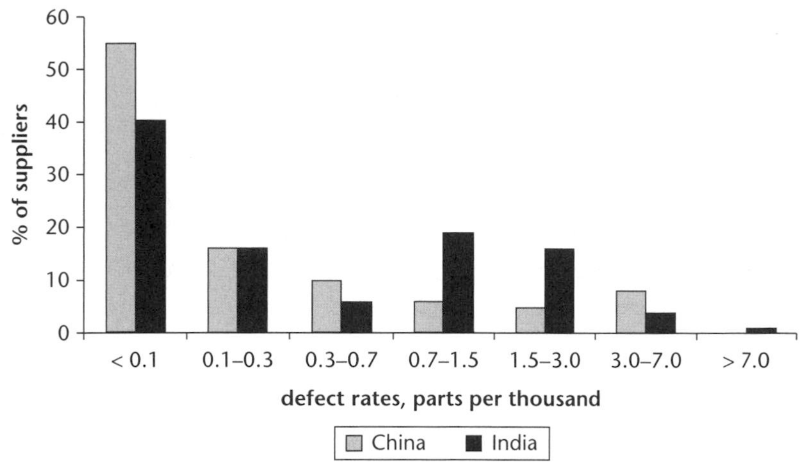

Source: Brandt and Van Biesebroeck 2008.

Brandt and Van Biesebroeck (2008) shows remarkable improvement that is unlikely to be matched by the Indian industry, which has been developing more slowly.

On the other hand, capabilities at the lead firm level show an opposite pattern. Because Indian industrial policy promoted local lead firms from the start, substantial domestic capabilities in development of design, product development, and engineering have developed. When local expertise was not available, the independent lead firms, such as Tata Motors, acquired Western companies or formed international JVs.

While Indian lead firms have remained focused on the domestic market, Chinese lead firms have begun to export finished vehicles, and to do so first to other developing countries. Geely has repeatedly postponed its plans to start exporting vehicles to North America, but it is likely to happen eventually. During its restructuring, DaimlerChrysler briefly contracted with Chery to manufacture and export compact cars to North America. SAIC—the joint-venture partner of General Motors and Volkswagen in Shanghai—has announced its intention to start exporting, a risky strategy since they will be competing with its joint-venture partners in their home markets. A new JV involving Honda in Guangzhou is already exporting small compact cars (the Fit/Jazz model) to Europe.

These trends are likely to continue to affect outcomes as the recent economic crisis winds down. The crisis has caused Western lead firms and global suppliers to shed assets that would not have been otherwise available for acquisition. Indian Tata Motors was the first lead firm from a developing country to purchase divisions of Western lead firms that were struggling for survival. In July 2007, Tata acquired the venerable British luxury vehicle brands Jaguar and Land Rover from Ford. The deal included the brand names, production facilities in the United Kingdom, design and engineering facilities, and compensation to Ford for the intellectual property tied up in existing models. This acquisition of know-how, especially on the design and development side, is by far the largest prize. These capabilities could provide the company with skills and technological knowledge necessary to satisfy consumers in the West and enable Tata-designed vehicles to meet the emissions and safety standards of mature markets.

Tata's acquisition of Jaguar and Land Rover has been followed by a flurry of deals or near deals involving Chinese companies. Most of these have been motivated by a desire to acquire foreign technology. The following deals have been noteworthy:

- *SAIC* entered into a joint-venture partnership to produce former Rover models in China in June 2004. After losing a legal battle over the brand name, it launched its own model on the Rover platform.
- *SAIC* invested US$500 million to acquire a controlling stake in Ssangyong, a Korean automaker, in October 2004. This followed a 2002 investment to buy a 10 percent stake in Daewoo, another Korean automaker controlled by GM.
- *Nanjing Automobile* acquired the British MG Rover and shipped production equipment to China in July 2005. The company restarted production of MGs in China in 2007.
- *SAIC* purchased Nanjing Automobile in December 2007 and restarted production of MGs in the United Kingdom in 2008.
- *SAIC* began talks with bankrupt German automotive design house and contract assembler Karmann in February 2008 for a future development and contract manufacturing project. Karmann was acquired by Volkswagen in November 2009.
- *Tengzhong Heavy Industrial Machinery*, a privately owned Chinese road equipment manufacturer, signed a memorandum of understanding with GM to purchase the Hummer unit in June 2009. The sale was subsequently abandoned.
- After *Beijing Automotive*'s (BAIC) bid for Opel was rejected, it signed a partnership deal with the Swedish Koenigsegg Group that had been negotiating to purchase Saab from GM in September 2009. Eventually, GM sold its Saab division to Spyker from the Netherlands. The connection between BAIC and

Koenigsegg is rumored to have been one contributing factor in the redirection of the sale.
- Geely is the sole remaining negotiator to purchase Volvo from Ford. A tentative agreement to complete the sale in the first quarter of 2010 was announced by Ford in December 2009.

Several other announcements illustrate that developing-country lead firms are claiming an increasingly important role in the global automotive industry. Again, Tata Motors is leading the way:

- *Tata* launched the Nano, a highly anticipated "one lakh" (100,000 rupees, approximately €1,800) car in January 2008. A version for Europe is anticipated in 2012.
- Berkshire Hathaway (the investment firm of Warren Buffett) invested $230 million to acquire a 10 percent stake in *BYD*, a Chinese battery maker from Shenzhen with aspirations to manufacture electric vehicles, in September 2008.
- *SAIC* took majority control (50 + 1) of Shanghai GM in December 2009, and teamed up with GM to enter the Indian market via a new joint venture. SAIC has also announced plans to produce 200,000 vehicles under its own brand name by 2010, of which 50,000 are intended for export. Much of this production will take place in a wholly owned plant (that is, without its joint venture partners GM or VW) in Yizhen, Jiangsu Province.
- Volkswagen announced a €2.5 billion investment to acquire a 20 percent stake in Suzuki in December 2009. Suzuki's dominant position in the Indian market through its JV with *Maruti* was cited as the prime motivation.

Conclusions and Policy Discussion

While much of our discussion has been framed in fairly general terms, it is important to bear in mind the tremendous heterogeneity in how different firms or industrial groups experienced the 2008–09 economic crisis. Experiences have ranged from an all-out collapse and radical restructuring at General Motors and Chrysler, to a retrenching of core strategies until demand picks up for Toyota and Volkswagen, to pursuit of opportunistic growth opportunities carried out either conservatively (Hyundai) or aggressively (SAIC, Geely, and Tata).

The recent crisis in the automotive sector taught the world many lessons, but left many questions unanswered as well. In particular, the question must be raised as to whether government interventions in North America and Europe positioned the companies based in these regions to compete effectively in the future.

Although the process of restructuring is still under way, several general observations can be noted, as follows.

- Economic nationalism cannot be ignored in the automotive industry. To a remarkable extent, relative to other consumer goods industries, governments are willing to put money on the line to support national champions, even at the risk of angering their trading partners and political allies. The strength of the German government's interest in supporting GM's European Division, Opel, may be due not only to the automaker's position as a major employer but also to its roots as a German company prior to its acquisition by GM in 1929. Deep historical roots like these drive political sensitivities, help to justify government bailouts, and strengthen the regional pattern of GVC organization of the industry. These same dynamics are likely to play a role if finished-vehicle exports from developing countries, such as China or India, increase substantially, or even if parts imports to Western economies increase suddenly after the crisis. For example, if history is any guide, companies such as Tata (India) and Geely (China) will have to establish or purchase substantial final assembly capacity in the (economic) heart of North America and Western Europe if they intend to sell large quantities of vehicles in these regions, just as Japanese and Korean firms have done in North America and GM and Volkswagen have done in China. The fact that most of the deals featuring Chinese firms purchasing well-known Western brands have fallen through underlines this point. At the same time, if market share losses continue, firms based in the United States and Western Europe are likely to continue to shift production to the low-cost peripheries of Eastern and Central Europe and Mexico to reduce operating costs. It is clear that the tendency for vehicles to be built where they are sold and to be manufactured in the context of regional production systems will not quickly fade away. Indeed, the political dynamics that underlie these GVC patterns have been dramatically exposed by the nationalistic government responses to the 2008–09 economic crisis.
- Chinese interests in purchasing struggling carmakers serve as just one illustration of the rising importance of developing countries in this industry (Thun 2006). An important motivation for these firms' acquisition efforts is to acquire advanced engineering and design expertise, which they have thus far largely outsourced to European-based automotive design firms (Whittaker et al. forthcoming).
- The (failed) bid of the Canadian global supplier Magna for the automaker Opel, on the one hand, highlights the increasing importance of suppliers and, on the other hand, the relative, regional, operational independence of the European arm of GM from its other operations. Many suppliers, especially in

North America, have been bankrupted even prior to the recession, by their weak bargaining position and the declining market shares of their core Detroit customers, but the lack of credit in the crisis made the situation for them far worse. It seems inconceivable that the group of surviving suppliers will make themselves as vulnerable again by aligning themselves to the same extent with a few clients. The solution, as before, is likely to be a wave of mergers and the rise of fewer, larger suppliers. In China, currently, the balance of power is tilted more toward global first-tier suppliers than in other places.

- From a GVC perspective, the intense political attention paid to automakers has further weakened the relative position of suppliers. Even though Delphi employed approximately the same number of workers as its former parent, GM, and filed for Chapter 11 bankruptcy in 2005, politicians paid little attention until GM itself inched toward bankruptcy in 2008. The decision by the Obama Administration to run the supplier support program through lead firms can only tie suppliers more tightly to old commercial relationships with firms that are losing market share.
- As work shifts to the supply base, value-added at the assembly stage falls, leading to a greater protectionist effect, even when import tariffs on finished vehicles are unchanged. This is particularly important in the automotive industry, where lead firms have disproportionate power in the chain. Lead firms can force their domestic supply base—which invariably faces lower levels of protection than they do—to compete vigorously with foreign firms, effectively enforcing world market prices for inputs manufactured at home.[14] All benefits of protectionism of the final product then accrue to lead firms. Effectively, lead firms are able to transfer the import tariff on the final good entirely onto components, which they purchase at world prices and which make up an increasing share of the final cost of a vehicle.

On the one hand, government bailouts can be considered protectionist because they discriminate against foreign producers by assisting domestic and quasi-domestic companies only. In contrast, a policy such as the U.S. government's extremely popular "cash for clunkers" program, which subsidized the purchase of new, higher-mileage vehicles, does not discriminate based on the nationality of the automaker. As long as certain criteria are met, the policy subsidized any vehicle, domestically produced or imported. However, such policies can favor specific firms in subtle and perhaps unintended ways. Ford's popular Focus model was a strong seller with this program, but so was the already popular Toyota Prius hybrid, which is produced in Tsutsumi, Japan.

Imports of high-mileage cars from Republic of Korea to North America actually increased during the fourth quarter of 2008 and first quarter of 2009

(Wilson 2009). In China, government incentives for vehicles with engine sizes below 1.6 liters boosted sales of domestic firms, such as Chery and Geely, which offer smaller cars at the low end of the market (Reuters 2009). On the other hand, this spike in small car sales may also be caused by the general economic slowdown. It may be part of a broader trend toward smaller cars, as traffic congestion worsens in large cities and the Chinese automotive market matures to include more owner-driven cars (many cars in China are chauffeur driven) and sales to individuals in cities with highly constrained parking opportunities.

However, if a central motivation of protectionist legislation is to retain domestic jobs, as opposed to companies, the strong regional structure of GVCs in the automotive industry complicates the picture. Even if the American Big 3 were to fail completely (unlikely, since the worst-case scenario would most likely lead to a breakup and sale of large companies rather than broad-based liquidation), it is very likely that the vast majority of vehicles in the United States would continue to be produced locally, by "foreign" transplant factories owned by Asian and European automakers. American suppliers would certainly be hurt, but the largest have already diversified their customer lists to include all the world's major automakers, and it is conceivable that smaller, domestically focused suppliers could find work with transplants, since market share would quickly swing in their direction and orders would increase.

So now, when U.S. and EU policy makers provide bailouts to save "the car industry," they are really moving to save (in the U.S. case) the Big 3, their suppliers, and United Auto Workers' jobs, not aggregate U.S. auto employment, which, barring huge increases in finished-vehicle trade, will certainly recover to some degree when sales inevitably rebound and stabilize. There is, of course, some logic to this scenario: the GVC perspective highlights the possibility of a global division of labor, where vehicle and technology development (and R&D and engineering jobs) stay largely at home, in places such as Japan, Korea, China, and Italy. While bailouts could save U.S. design and engineering jobs, this is not an argument that has been made by policy makers.

Moreover, we have to ask if nationalistic policies will always be followed. Efforts by lead firms from China and India to acquire assets and skills in the higher value-added portions of the supply chain would have been vehemently opposed in normal times. However, in the crisis climate, the desire to save jobs, seemed, at least temporarily, to trump those concerns. In the short run, the nationalistic stance of Western governments may have made it harder for lead firms from developing countries to penetrate mature markets, but this is not the end of the story. In the crisis, firms with the comparative advantage of making smaller vehicles, such as Hyundai and Suzuki, have been hurt the least and have gained market share. At the very least, the crisis has provided good marketing opportunities for firms producing lower quality and lower priced vehicles, such as the Dacia Logan from Romania or the Tata Nano from India, extremely low cost vehicles that have garnered much attention, at least in the news media.

Market differences limit the options available to policy makers seeking to support the automotive industry in the developing world. The extremely large development cost of country-specific or region-specific vehicles, as well as the tendency for co-location of suppliers and lead firms, puts the goal of a viable, independent, national industry beyond the reach of all except the very largest less-developed countries (LDCs). As discussed in this chapter, the options are to become a regional assembly hub or to specialize in labor-intensive tasks in the context of regional production. Both options do provide growth possibilities for local suppliers and opportunities to move up in the value chain. However, both take a very long time to develop, as the selection of new suppliers is tied to new vehicle programs, which have a four- to six-year life cycle, and increasingly require co-location of engineering work in or near the world's automotive design centers.

In the long run, however, the close collaboration and co-location of lead firms with suppliers could begin to work to the advantage of LDCs.[15] Global suppliers have been concentrating an increasing share of product development in the industry's traditional design centers, and when virtually all development work took place in the United States, Germany, and Japan, developing-country firms were excluded. Now that some LDC markets have grown sufficiently to warrant market-specific vehicles, lead firms and suppliers are setting up local design centers. Once these reach sufficient scale, more suppliers will follow, and opportunities could open up for local firms. Once established, such industry clusters, based as they are on industry-specific labor markets and skills, tend to be very long-lived.

If the experience of the Korean industry is any guide, it is likely that the increasing production capacity in developing countries will be followed, albeit with a long lag, by the emergence of important supplier firms. This process is far from automatic, however. Our research evidence from China and India underscores the importance of satisfying and exceeding quality standards set by foreign lead firms and first-tier suppliers. The large minimum-scale requirements and high technical barriers in this industry make it nearly impossible to succeed with a strategy that seeks to advance inexperienced national champions. Several countries that have tried, through the expenditure of enormous resources, to develop independent industries have lately changed course and opened up more to foreign investment. The automotive industries in the Russian Federation, the Islamic Republic of Iran, and Malaysia stand a chance only if foreign lead firms are welcomed rather than discouraged.

The experience of the Mexican industry—or, similarly, that of Turkey or Thailand—highlights further that success by independent suppliers is extremely difficult as well. The experiences of successful suppliers in developing countries suggest that three objectives must be achieved in turn. The first goal is to achieve worldwide quality standards. This is a necessary condition to start providing internationally competitive supply chains. The second goal is to improve productivity. Achieving quality standards already requires a great deal of automation. In order to be a viable automotive supplier, productivity levels must be sufficiently high and must improve at the same speed as the global average technological progress in the sector; otherwise, it is impossible to match continuous price declines that are the norm in the industry. Third, firms should acquire design capabilities, which is a necessary step to greater independence and also a precondition to become lead supplier on a part when new vehicle programs are started. To achieve the first two goals, working in the value chains of foreign-owned firms accelerates the process. To achieve the third goal, it is often extremely valuable to also work for domestic lead firms because they tend to give local suppliers greater opportunities.

Notes

1. See Sturgeon, Van Biesebroeck, and Gereffi (2008) for a more elaborate discussion of the GVC perspective on this industry.
2. Of the three major vehicle-producing regions, regional integration is the most pronounced in North America. In 2004, 75.1 percent of automotive industry trade was intraregional there, in contrast to 71.2 percent in Western Europe and 23 percent in Asia (Dicken 2007, 305).
3. Around the same time, starting with Nissan in 1986 in the United Kingdom, Japanese firms constructed assembly plants in Europe to avoid import quotas in France and Italy and import tariffs in most other EU countries.
4. Volkswagen is an exception in that it has concentrated all of its North American production in Mexico, and Nissan is the sole Japanese automaker that has built up large-scale, export-oriented final assembly there.
5. The large U.S. trade deficit with China might have influenced Honda's decision to export the Honda Jazz to the European Union from China, while the almost identical Honda Fit for North America is shipped from Japan.
6. To the extent that governments are concerned with slowing the pace of layoffs during a recession, making sure automakers keep operating is indeed a sensible strategy, especially when multiplier effects are invoked. However, if we take a long-term view that includes stable unemployment rates, there is no evidence that governments are able to boost aggregate employment by propping up specific firms in specific industries. Any job that is preserved in a country's automotive industry, directly or indirectly, means one less job filled somewhere else in the economy. However, job quality may be degraded in this process of job churn, and with massive deindustrialization, regional unemployment can remain high for long periods, even as aggregate unemployment stabilizes.
7. Ford named Geely as its preferred bidder for Volvo in October 2009. After the two sides agreed on terms for intellectual property transfer, production and manufacturing commitments, and management structure in December 2009, Ford announced that the sale would be completed in the second quarter of 2010 (Bennett and Dolan 2009).
8. An exception is Taiwan, which has developed a significant export industry supplying standardized parts for use in aftermarket repair (Cunningham, Lynch, and Thun 2005).
9. In some instances, funding for continuous improvement projects was refused because downsizing had left firms too short-staffed to carry them out.

10. These differences are not limited to China: in Europe and Latin America some firms have always followed a much more engaged strategy. The chosen strategy in China for a given firm seems to carry over well to its operations in different parts of the world.

11. Some automotive lead firms are pursuing global strategies that lie somewhere between cautious and aggressive localization by trying to increase the share of parts common among global vehicle families but maintaining high degrees of product differentiation across global markets.

12. In 2005 the automotive assembly and parts sectors accounted for 1.05 percent of Canada's total private sector employment and 1.07 percent of Mexico's, but only .77 percent of the United States' (based on calculations using data from International Labour Organization, U.S. Bureau of Labor Statistics, National Institute of Statistics and Geography [Mexico], and Mexican Association of Automotive Distributors).

13. Citroën is part of PSA, the number 6 firm globally, and Daihatsu is part of Toyota, number 3 globally at the time. DaimlerChrysler (55) is not on this short list but was in fact the first firm entering the Chinese market with a production joint venture in Beijing.

14. For evidence on component price convergence, see Thun 2006.

15. For China, the tremendous success of the SAIC joint ventures with GM and VW has made Shanghai a world-class hub of the global auto industry. Two of the most successful private firms, Chery and Geely, are located in adjacent provinces. GM built a $250 million technical center there, which employs 2,500 employees. Other production centers exist—fully 27 of 30 provinces have their own assembly plants—but the supply base in and around Shanghai, especially, is unrivaled in China (Thun 2006). The activity in India is less concentrated, which makes it less advantageous for suppliers to establish large local operations. Tata Motors and Mahindra & Mahindra have their headquarters in Mumbai, Maruti-Suzuki near Delhi, GM India is located near Vadodara in Gujarat, Hyundai Motor India in Chennai, and Kirloskar, the joint-venture partner of Toyota, is headquartered in Pune, Maharastra.

References

Asia Pacific Foundation of Canada. 2005. "The East Asian Automobile Industry: Opportunity or Threat? Results of a Survey of Canadian Auto Parts Manufacturers." Asia Pacific Foundation of Canada, Vancouver, BC.

Automotive News. various years. *Automotive News Market Data Books*. http://www.autonews.com/section/datacenter.

Bennett, Jeff, and Matthew Dolan. 2009. "Ford Aims to Complete Volvo Sale to Geely in 2Q '10." *Wall Street Journal Online*, December 23. http://www.easybourse.com/bourse/automobile/news/777468/update-ford-aims-to-complete-volvo-sale-to-geely-in-2q-10.html.

Brandt, Loren, and Eric Thun. 2010. "The Fight for the Middle: Upgrading, Competition, and Industrial Development in China." *World Development* (forthcoming).

Brandt, Loren, and Johannes Van Biesebroeck. 2008. "Capability Building in China's Auto Supply Chains." Working paper prepared for Industry Canada, Ottawa, Canada.

Cunningham, Edward, Teresa Lynch, and Eric Thun. 2005. "A Tale of Two Sectors: Diverging Paths in Taiwan's Automotive Industry." In *Global Taiwan: Building Competitive Strengths in a New International Economy*, ed. Suzanne Berger and Richard Lester. Armonk, NY: ME Sharpe.

Dassbach, Carl. 1989. *Global Enterprises and the World Economy: Ford, General Motors, and IBM, the Emergence of the Transnational Enterprise*. New York: Garland Publishing.

Dicken, Peter. 2007. *Global Shift: Reshaping the Global Economic Map in the 21st Century*, 5th ed. London: Sage Publications.

Facey, Lisa-Joy. 2009. "The Effects of the Recession on Top and Bottom Line Quality Improvement Initiatives of Tier 2 Part Suppliers in Southern Ontario." MBA dissertation, University of Leicester, UK.

Humphrey, John, and Olga Memedovic. 2003. "The Global Automotive Industry Value Chain: What Prospects for Upgrading by Developing Countries?" UNIDO Sectoral Studies Series Working Paper, United Nations Industrial Development Organization, Vienna.

Lung, Yannick, Rob Van Tulder, and Jorge Carillo, eds. 2004. *Cars, Carriers of Regionalism?* New York: Palgrave Macmillan.

Reuters. 2009. "China's Chery Auto Aims for 18 pct Car Sales Growth." Feb 16. Accessed August 19, 2009. http://www.reuters.com/article/rbssConsumerGoodsAndRetailNews/idU.S.SHA932232009026.

Sturgeon, Timothy, and Richard Florida. 2004. "Globalization, Deverticalization, and Employment in the Motor Vehicle Industry." In *Locating Global Advantage: Industry Dynamics in a Globalizing Economy,* ed. Martin Kenny with Richard Florida. Palo Alto, CA: Stanford University Press.

Sturgeon, Timothy, and Richard Lester. 2004. "The New Global Supply-base: New Challenges for Local Suppliers in East Asia." In *Global Production Networking and Technological Change in East Asia,* ed. Shahid Yusuf, Anjum Altaf, and Kaoru Nabeshima, 35–87. Washington, DC: World Bank and Oxford University Press.

Sturgeon, Timothy, and Olga Memedovic. Forthcoming. "Measuring Global Value Chains: Intermediate Goods Trade, Structural Change and Compressed Development." UNIDO Working Paper, United Nations Industrial Development Organization, Vienna.

Sturgeon, Timothy, and Johannes Van Biesebroeck 2009. "Crisis and Protection in the Automotive Industry: A Global Value Chain Perspective." In *Effective Crisis Response and Openness: Implications for the Trading System,* ed. Simon J. Evenett, Bernard Hoekman, and Olivier Cattaneo, 91–118. Centre for Economic Policy Research–World Bank, Washington, DC.

Sturgeon, Timothy, Johannes Van Biesebroeck, and Gary Gereffi. 2007. "Prospects for Canada in the NAFTA Automotive Industry: A Global Value Chain Analysis." Industry Canada Research Report, Ottawa, Canada.

———. 2008. "Value Chains, Networks, and Clusters: Reframing the Global Automotive Industry." *Journal of Economic Geography* 8 (3) (May): 297–321.

Sutton, John. 2004. "The Auto-Component Supply Chain in China and India: A Benchmarking Study." Mimeo. London School of Economics.

———. 2007. "Quality, Trade and the Moving Window: The Globalisation Process." *The Economic Journal* 117 (524): 469–98.

Thun, Eric. 2006. *Changing Lanes in China. Foreign Direct Investment, Local Governments, and Auto Sector Development.* New York: Cambridge University Press.

Whittaker, D. Hugh, Tianbao Zhu, Timothy Sturgeon, Monhan Tsai, and Toshie Okita. Forthcoming. "Compressed Development." *Studies in Comparative International Development.*

Wilson, Duncan. 2009. "Impacts of the Economic Crisis on the Port of Vancouver." Remarks before the Directorate for Science, Technology and Industry, Committee on Industry, Innovation and Entrepreneurship; Working Party on Globalisation of Industry; Organization for Economic Co-Operation and Development (OECD). October 28, Paris, France.

7

GLOBAL VALUE CHAINS IN THE ELECTRONICS INDUSTRY: WAS THE CRISIS A WINDOW OF OPPORTUNITY FOR DEVELOPING COUNTRIES?

Timothy J. Sturgeon and Momoko Kawakami

The electronics hardware industry is the world's most important goods-producing sector. Not only does it employ more workers and generate greater revenue than any other sector, its products also enhance productivity in other activities and stimulate innovation across entire economies (Mann and Kirkegaard 2006). It is what Hirschman (1958) calls a "propulsive sector." Consider the case of the United States, where innovation in electronics hardware, which employed 1,105,900 in 2009, has helped spawn a host of downstream service industries, including the computer systems design services, telecommunications, as well as data processing, hosting, and related information services, which together employed 2,697,200.[1] The heavy use of computers and information technology in other sectors, including retail and wholesale trade, transportation, finance, real estate, education, professional services, and industrial production, makes it clear how pervasive the changes made by electronics hardware have been.

The goal of this chapter is to delineate the central characteristics of global value chains (GVCs) in the electronics hardware sector, describe how they have evolved to incorporate newly developed and developing countries, and discuss how they have been affected by the 2008–09 economic crisis. As is common in GVC analysis, we focus on the key actors in the chain of value-added activities, where various activities are located geographically, and how information and knowledge flow within the chain.

This chapter first presents evidence for the importance of electronics GVCs in the global economy, then discusses the effects of the recent economic crisis on the industry. The third section focuses on how information is exchanged in electronics GVCs, introducing the concept of "value chain modularity." The next section identifies three key firm-level actors: lead firms, contract manufacturers, and platform leaders, and discusses their development, or "coevolution." A series of company, cluster, and country case studies are then presented to illustrate how supplier capabilities in various places have developed in the context of electronics GVCs. The sixth section identifies some of the persistent limits to upgrading experienced by even the most successful firms in the developing world. Four models used by developing-country firms to overcome these limitations are then presented: (1) global expansion through acquisition of declining brands (emerging multinationals), (2) separation of branded product divisions from contract manufacturing (ODM spinoffs), (3) successful mixing of contract manufacturing and branded products (platform brands) for contractors with customers not in the electronics hardware business, and (4) the founding of factoryless product firms that rely on GVCs for a range of inputs, including production (emerging GVC leaders).

Some of the cases presented here suggest that the 2008–09 economic crisis presented a window of opportunity, in particular, for firms based in Taiwan, China, which represent a key point of transformation in the industry and appear to be gaining more leverage in the industry in the wake of the crisis. The conclusion states the case that firms in the developing world will, in one or all of the ways described, soon come to play a more central role in driving the innovative trajectory of the industry by leveraging the full complement of resources that have become available in GVCs.

The Electronics Industry's Role in Global Value Chain Formation

Each year, the electronics industry generates a mushrooming array of products and services increasingly used in nearly every human endeavor.[2] Now deeply entwined in our social fabric, electronics products and systems support critical aspects of communication, education, finance, recreation, and government. Thousands of companies from dozens of countries contribute to the industry on a daily basis. Even a single product can contain work carried out by dozens of firms in multiple countries. Because there is less need for co-location of engineers than in other technology-intensive sectors, such as with the co-location of design with manufacturing, it is relatively easy for electronics firms to engage in the twin strategies of outsourcing and offshoring. Global sourcing is common. Factories can be relocated with relative ease and produce a wide variety of end products. As a result, GVCs in the electronics industry are more geographically extensive and dynamic than in any other goods-producing sector.

Evidence of the importance of the electronics industry in GVC formation can be found in statistics on intermediate goods trade. Trade in intermediate goods is indicative of GVCs because fragmented production processes require that parts, components, and partially manufactured subassemblies cross borders—sometimes more than once—before finished goods are shipped to final markets (Feenstra 1998; Dean, Fung, and Wang 2007; Brülhart 2008). Table 7.1 shows the relative importance of various goods-producing industries in GVCs: intermediate electronics and automotive goods dominate total trade in the top-50 manufactured intermediate products (a combined 64.7 percent in 2006). Next important is a group of undifferentiated materials including metal stock (copper, aluminum, and steel), wood, and paper (8.4 percent in 2006), followed by chemicals and plastics, manufactured metal parts, gold and diamonds, aircraft parts, and so on. The share of electronics intermediates (including semiconductors, printed circuit boards, and so on) has grown dramatically since 1988, from 24.4 percent of the top-50 products to 43.3 percent in 2006. The share of automotive intermediates fell from the top spot in 1988 (25.1 percent) to the number two spot in 2006 (21.4 percent). As a result, the growth rate of electronics intermediates was the highest in the top-50 product groupings (13.8 percent per year).

As the data show, the electronics industry accounts for a growing share of intermediate goods trade and, by extension, of GVC formation. Trade in automotive and motorcycle intermediates is also very important, but strong incentives for local content have undoubtedly dampened their growth. Somewhat surprisingly, given the attention paid to the industry in the GVC literature (for example, Gereffi and Korzeniewicz 1994; Gereffi 1999), intermediate inputs to the apparel industry appear to be far less important in terms of the value of total intermediate goods trade than inputs to the electronics and passenger vehicle industries.[3] Of course, this probably reflects the low unit value of textiles and other inputs to apparel and footwear relative to inputs to electronics and motor vehicles, as well as the establishment of fiber and fabric production within the world's largest major apparel and footwear production centers, including China, Mexico, and Bangladesh. In fact, the unit value of intermediate goods is likely to have a great effect on the composition of table 7.1. For example, while GVCs in the aircraft industry are important drivers of global integration (see Kimura 2007), the high unit value of

Table 7.1 Industries in Manufactured Intermediate Goods in 1988 and 2006 Ranked according to 2006 Total Trade

	1988			2006			1988–2006
Industries and product groups	**MIG trade (US$, millions)**	**Share of top-50 MIG (percent)**	**Share in total MIG trade (percent)**	**MIG trade (US$, millions)**	**Share of top-50 MIG (percent)**	**Share in total MIG trade (percent)**	**Annual growth rate (percent)**
Top-50 MIG product list							
Electronics	162,980	24.4	8.1	1,670,940	43.3	17.4	13.8
Automotive and motorcycle	167,506	25.1	8.3	824,392	21.4	8.6	9.3
Basic materials (metal/wood/paper)	116,339	17.4	5.8	325,676	8.4	3.4	5.9
Chemicals and plastics	62,954	9.4	3.1	254,523	6.6	2.7	8.1
Manufactured metal parts	40,328	6.0	2.0	215,085	5.6	2.2	9.7
Gold and diamonds	47,596	7.1	2.4	203,064	5.3	2.1	8.4
Aircraft parts	37,131	5.6	1.8	184,575	4.8	1.9	9.3
Construction equipment & general industrial machine parts	20,166	3.0	1.0	78,688	2.0	0.8	7.9
Pharmaceuticals	0	0.0	0.0	66,503	1.7	0.7	NA
Propane	0	0.0	0.0	35,946	0.9	0.4	NA
Textiles (and hides)	12,657	1.9	0.6	0	0.0	0.0	NA
Total top-50 MIG	667,657	100.0	33.1	3,859,393	100.0	40.3	10.2
Total MIG for three industries							
Electronics MIG total	231,295		11.5	1,942,283		20.3	12.5
Automobiles and motorcycles	212,961		10.6	974,278		10.2	8.8
Apparel and footwear	73,610		3.6	239,866		2.5	6.8
Total MIG for three industries	517,866		25.7	3,156,427		32.9	10.6
Total MIG trade	2,018,297		100.0	9,579,710		100.0	9.0

Sources: Sturgeon and Memedovic (forthcoming) from UN Comtrade Standard International Trade Classification (SITC) Rev. 1 data. To identify commodities as consumption, capital, and intermediate goods, the conversion table Broad Economic Category (BEC) to SITC Rev. 1 from World Integrated Trade Solution (WITS) was used. In order to calculate constant price data, National Accounts data from the United Nations Industrial Development Organization (UNIDO) Statistics Unit and a GDP deflator were applied.

Note: MIG = manufactured intermediate goods.

aircraft parts likely elevates their ranking in table 7.1. Gold and diamonds also rank high in the table.

Turning to a comparison of *total* manufactured intermediates, rather than just the top 50, the increasing importance of the electronics industry in GVCs is evident in both absolute and relative terms. The lower portion of table 7.1 shows that the share of total manufactured intermediate goods trade accounted for by the electronics industry increased from 11.5 percent in 1988 to 20.3 percent in 2006, and the average annual growth rate of electronics intermediates was the highest (12.5 percent per year) of the three industries most often discussed in the literature on GVCs. Inputs to apparel and footwear accounted for only 3.6 percent of manufactured intermediates in 1988, a share that fell to 2.5 percent in 2006 (see the lower portion of table 7.1).

The Shift of Electronics Production to China

In the past 20 years, East Asia in general and China in particular have become increasingly important in electronics as well as other industries, both as production locations and final markets. This is reflected in the flow of intermediate goods. As table 7.2 shows, "greater China" (mainland China, Hong Kong, and Taiwan) accounts for 33.1 percent of world imports of intermediate electronics goods and 29.4 percent of exports. Growth since 1988, especially on mainland China, has been extraordinarily high. The tendency for trade to be interindustry, that is, for countries to specialize in imports and exports in the same industry, is also striking. All 15 countries in table 7.2 appear on both the top importer and exporter lists, albeit in a slightly different rank order after the top four: China; Hong Kong, China; the United States; and Singapore. While strong interindustry trade can be a function of transshipment (for example, importing and exporting materials and parts via Hong Kong, China, and perhaps Singapore), the tendency for specific countries to both import and export intermediate products in the same industry reveals the highly integrated nature of the global economy and, for developing countries, the rich opportunities for industrial upgrading, even when parts imports are high.

While the importance of the electronics industry in GVC formation is undeniable, note that the trade statistics presented here contain no information about trade in services or the ownership of physical or intellectual assets. As a result, GVCs can exist without strong growth in intermediate goods trade.[4] Nevertheless, while current trade statistics cannot capture the more "intangible" aspects of GVCs with any degree of specificity, the scale and rapid growth of intermediate goods trade in the electronics industry are certainly indicative of its importance and dynamism in GVC formation.

Table 7.2 Top-15 Intermediate-Goods Importers and Exporters in the Electronics Industry, 2006

Electronics intermediate importers	US$, millions	Percentage of total	Percentage change 1988–2006	Electronics intermediate exporters	US$, millions	Percentage of total	Percentage change 1991–2006
China	186,294	18.9	15,219.0	China	109,433	11.7	21,649.1
Hong Kong, China	104,856	10.6	1,452.2	Hong Kong, China	101,873	10.9	2,580.0
United States	94,466	9.6	194.0	United States	101,807	10.9	179.4
Singapore	73,040	7.4	590.5	Singapore	97,278	10.4	942.2
Germany	51,569	5.2	236.3	Japan	88,994	9.5	160.8
Japan	45,639	4.6	422.5	Taiwan, China	63,824	6.8	834.0
Malaysia	44,695	4.5	466.8	Korea, Rep. of	55,028	5.9	543.2
Taiwan, China	35,899	3.6	405.6	Germany	52,685	5.7	235.5
Mexico	35,705	3.6	3,048.9	Malaysia	43,966	4.7	512.9
Korea, Rep. of	35,486	3.6	365.8	Netherlands	30,637	3.3	520.2
Netherlands	26,868	2.7	392.9	United Kingdom	22,538	2.4	121.1
Philippines	23,685	2.4	1,052.6	Philippines	22,024	2.4	1,186.4
United Kingdom	23,130	2.3	79.5	France	19,148	2.1	131.3
France	19,577	2.0	118.8	Thailand	15,756	1.7	438.6
Thailand	18,607	1.9	423.3	Mexico	13,115	1.4	3,594.1

Sources: UN Comtrade Standard International Trade Classification (SITC) Rev. 1 data. To identify commodities as Consumption, Capital, and Intermediate goods, the conversion table Broad Economic Category (BEC) to SITC Rev. 1 from World Integrated Trade Solution (WITS) was used. In order to calculate constant price data, National Accounts data from United Nations Industrial Development Organization (UNIDO) Statistics Unit and a GDP deflator were applied.

Effects of the Economic Crisis on Electronics Industry GVCs

As with almost all other sectors, the electronics industry was deeply affected by the economic crisis of 2008–09. The scale of the crisis in trade is reflected in figures on overall ocean transport traffic, which carried all but the most lightweight and expensive electronics shipped over long distances. The combined results of the 16 largest ocean container carriers publishing quarterly figures—including Maersk Line, Hapag-Lloyd, China Shipping, "K" Line, and NYK Line—showed revenue declines of 40 percent for the first nine months of 2009, $56 billion, in comparison to figures from a year earlier, $94 billion (Barnard 2009).

Aggregate international trade statistics for 2008 and 2009 are still being finalized at this time, and preliminary estimates are unreliable. Nevertheless, past patterns are a reasonable indicator of recent and future patterns. Figure 7.1 shows world export growth from 1962 to 2006 in terms of intermediate, capital, and consumption goods, as well as capital and consumption goods combined into a "final goods" category. As the figure indicates, trade in intermediate goods appears to be much more volatile than trade in capital or consumption goods. This supports the notion of "bullwhip" effects of recessions and business cycles, where slowdowns and downturns affect part and component shipments more than final goods shipments because final goods producers tend to draw down parts inventories and delay reordering during periods of uncertainty (Escaith, Lindenberg, and Miroudot 2010). In addition, intermediate goods trade usually grows notably after recessions, especially U.S. recessions—U.S. company outsourcing has been one of the most important drivers of GVC expansion—but also following sectoral bubbles (for example, the 1985 PC bubble and the 2001 dot.com bubble), regional crises (the East Asian financial crisis), and worldwide slowdowns (the oil shocks of 1972 and 1979).

It is well documented that companies tend to be reluctant to hire new workers after the trough of recessions until demand improvements are sustained, making employment a lagging indicator of recovery. Related to this, however, and less well documented, is a reluctance to invest in new production capacity and a carryover from efforts during recession to cut costs, leading to more aggressive implementation of outsourcing and offshoring strategies. This pattern is in line with the findings of qualitative research (Sturgeon 2003) that lead firms in the electronics industry increase outsourcing and offshoring following recessions because demand uncertainty makes investments in internal capacity seem more risky. Then, as the cycle continues, firms report expanding outsourcing relationships that proved successful during the recession because there is insufficient time to install new capacity to meet rapidly growing demand.

Figure 7.1 World Imports of Intermediate, Capital, and Consumption Goods, 1962–2006

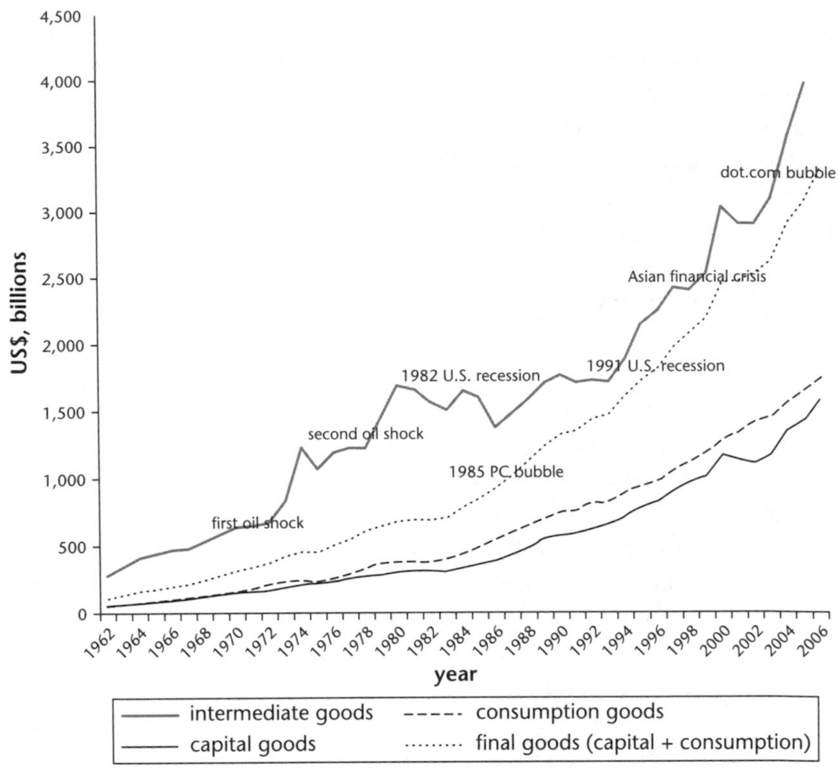

Sources: Sturgeon and Memedovic (forthcoming) from UN Comtrade Standard International Trade Classification (SITC) Rev. 1 data. To identify commodities as Consumption, Capital, and Intermediate goods, the conversion table Broad Economic Category (BEC) to SITC Rev. 1 from World Integrated Trade Solution (WITS) was used. In order to calculate constant price data, National Accounts data from United Nations Industrial Development Organization (UNIDO) Statistics Unit and a GDP deflator were applied.

In the case of the United States, where up-to-date trade statistics are available (table 7.3), the value of electronic component imports decreased at an average rate of 11 percent per year during the crisis period 2008–09 after being relatively stable during the period 1996–2007 at about $70 billion per year. Remarkably, imports of final products decreased much less. While these declines are significant, declines in imports of automobiles (–23.0 percent) and auto parts (–20.2 percent) were more dramatic. The value of electronic component exports also decreased during the crisis period, by 9 percent per year, which is even more remarkable since component exports increased at an average annual rate of nearly 6.7 percent per year during the 1996–2007 period, regaining in 2007 the

Table 7.3 Average Annual Change in Imports and Exports: Final and Intermediate Goods in Three Industries in the United States, 1997–2009
percent

	Average annual change — value of trade	
Final and intermediate goods	**1997–2007**	**2007–09**
Imports		
Electronics final goods	8.7	–3.8
Electronic components	*–0.4*	*–11.0*
Motor vehicles	5.8	–23.0
Motor vehicle parts	*7.1*	*–20.2*
Apparel	4.9	–7.4
Textiles and fiber	*1.6*	*–15.8*
Total nonpetroleum Imports	7.3	–10.1
Exports		
Electronics final goods	8.0	–17.3
Electronic components	*6.7*	*–8.9*
Motor vehicles	0.5	–9.5
Motor vehicle parts	*0.6*	*–14.7*
Apparel	–8.7	–3.8
Textiles and fiber	*4.2*	*–11.7*
Total nonpetroleum exports	4.8	–6.2

Source: U.S. International Trade Commission, http://dataweb.usitc.gov.

peak of $50 billion reached in 2001, the height of the technology bubble (see table 7.3).

Because electronics hardware and systems are rightly perceived as having a "propulsive" effect on other industries, and because deep expertise has tended to be concentrated in only a few places (for example, in Silicon Valley, California, and in large firms based in the United States, Europe, and Japan), politicians and policy makers have been loath to put too much pressure on firms to produce locally or to put up barriers to trade, even during economic crises. Intense competition, at first between American and Japanese producers, is what pushed early fragmentation of electronics GVCs, rather than trade barriers and local content rules. Producing electronics hardware in low-cost locations lowers prices, which speeds adoption of information technologies at home and leads to productivity spillovers (Mann and Kirkegaard 2006). Because trade barriers have been minimal in this industry worldwide, the main impact of the economic crisis has been to sharply reduce demand, driving the full absorption of operating inventories and accelerating existing trends toward consolidation and low-cost geographies discussed throughout this chapter. However, the crisis may have hastened the long-standing trends of consolidation and supplier learning and GVC upgrading that are discussed at length in subsequent sections of the chapter.

Value Chain Modularity

Why is it that before and likely after the crisis, GVCs in the electronics industry are more extensive and dynamic than in any other goods-producing sector? One reason is that electronic parts and most final products have a high value-to-weight ratio that makes long-distance shipping relatively inexpensive. For the high-value components and some final products, such as notebook computers and mobile phone handsets, air shipment is common. Obviously, low transportation costs and the option for rapid delivery support the movement of goods within GVCs and allow companies to engage in operating cost arbitrage based on geographic variations in operating costs. Moreover, the industry's propulsive nature has motivated a host of national policies to encourage its development, though not at the expense of liberal import policies to ensure access to advanced products, systems, and services. Given the fast pace of technological development in the industry, import substitution policies have rarely been implemented. More often, the industry has seen incentives for investment, including by multinational firms, and other industry supports.

Another reason for the global character of electronics production is the nature of the industry's product and value-chain architecture, which can be characterized as highly "modular." The industry's roots in large, highly complex military systems developed in the United States and Europe during the 1950s and 1960s (Principe, Davies, and Hobday 2003), and the myriad of commercial and consumer applications and product variations that followed during the 1970s and 1980s, led to the development of explicit de facto and de jure standards for describing components, system features, and production processes. Since then, the ability to codify electronic systems and system elements has been greatly enhanced by the advent of computer-aided design (CAD) technologies, and the shift away from hard-to-quantify analog systems toward digital systems that can be fully characterized in terms of unambiguous binary codes consisting of ones and zeros. Not only does digitization expand the scope of what can be achieved with electronics and information technology, but the codification and standardization it allows enhance interoperability and allow components and other system elements to be substituted without the need to redesign the entire product (Ulrich 1995). This "product modularity" has, in turn, enabled a high level of "value chain modularity," in which multiple firms can contribute to the realization of specific products and where component producers and other firms in the supply chain can be substituted without a need for thoroughgoing engineering changes (Langlois and Robertson 1995; Balconi 2002; Langlois 2003).

The key business processes in the electronics industry that have been formalized, codified, standardized, and computerized are product design (for example, computer-aided design), production planning and inventory and logistic control (for example, enterprise resource planning), as well as various aspects of the production process itself (for example, assembly, test and inspection, materials handling). Furthermore, because it is "platform independent," that is, not tied to any specific computing platform, the Internet has provided an ideal vehicle for sharing and monitoring the data generated and used by these systems. These technologies and practices are at the core of value chain modularity. It is the formalization of information and knowledge at the interfirm link and the relative independence of the participating firms that gives value chain modularity its essential character: flexibility, resiliency, speed, and economies of scale that accrue at the level of the industry rather than the firm.

One of the most important implications of value chain modularity is that it makes it easier to accomplish work across great distances. This has created opportunities for developing countries as production locations both for multinational firms and for local firms seeking to participate in the industry as suppliers and contract manufacturers. Once a local supplier has gained a role in a GVC, rapid product innovation and short product life cycles keep opportunities for learning and industrial upgrading coming. A handful of recent developers have taken particular advantage of these opportunities to compress their development experience (Whittaker et al. forthcoming). The following stand out as examples: Singapore; Taiwan, China; the Republic of Korea; and, more recently, mainland China and the "ASEAN four" (Indonesia, Malaysia, the Philippines, and Thailand—members of the Association of Southeast Asian Nations).

Lead Firms, Contract Manufacturers, and Platform Leaders in Electronics GVCs

In the electronics industry's hardware "ecosystem," there are three principal actors: lead firms, contract manufacturers, and platform leaders. Of course, dozens of other entities play important roles in the broader industry, including software vendors, production equipment manufacturers, distributors, and producers of more generic components and subsystems. Nevertheless, an analysis of how these three firm-level actors interact in the industry's GVCs provides a useful if simplified portrait of the global electronics industry. The value captured by the most powerful firms in GVCs—lead firms with global brands and component suppliers with strong positions of "platform leadership"—can be extremely high.

Lead Firms

Lead firms in GVCs carry brands and sell branded products and systems in final markets to individual consumers, other businesses, or government agencies.

These firms initiate, or "lead," the GVC's activities by placing orders with suppliers, giving them market power over suppliers. This "buyer power" is earned, if not by technological leadership and large investments in brand development, then by the financial risk taken on between placing orders and selling products.[5] Of course, the size of the orders matters. Large orders in the supply base are driven by the expectation of large sales in end markets, and this connects lead firm power derived from market performance to their buyer power in GVCs.

Because the electronics industry has diversified as it has grown, lead firms compete in a widening array of end markets. Table 7.4, showing nine major end markets, reveals the remarkable breadth of the electronics industry. Each product example in the second column represents a significant and diverse market in its own right, with dozens of competitors. Examples of important firms are listed in the third column, but there are many more companies, large and small, competing in each of these markets and detailed product segments. Table 7.4 is necessarily incomplete and static. Applications for electronics technology have grown almost too numerous to list, with new companies formed and new products introduced almost daily. Moreover, many of these market segments contain companies that resell hardware products by integrating them into larger systems, adding software and offering after-sales services that tailor the systems for use in specific situations and settings.[6] The electronics and wider information technology "ecosystem," therefore, is vast.

As the nationalities of the well-known firms listed in table 7.4 suggest, most important lead firms in the electronics industry are based in industrialized countries, especially the United States, Western Europe, and Japan. Of newly industrialized countries, Korea stands out as a base of important lead firms, especially Samsung and LG. Because of their role as production platforms and contract manufacturing centers, only a handful of important lead firms have emerged from developing countries, including Acer, a PC company based in Taiwan, China; Huawei, a Chinese manufacturer of networking equipment; and Lenovo, a Chinese PC company that leapt onto the world stage with the acquisition of IBM's PC division in 2004. Later in the chapter, we discuss the possibility that lead firms from developing countries are finding new ways to compete successfully in global markets, and that the recent economic crisis has provided lead firms based in Taiwan, China, with new opportunities to move into more important roles as lead firms in the electronics industry.

Contract Manufacturers

Contract manufacturers make products for lead firms and sometimes provide design services as well. The popularity of contract manufacturing in the electronics

Table 7.4 Main Electronics Markets, Products, and Lead Firms

Main market segments	Examples	
	Products	**Lead firms**
Computers	Enterprise computing systems, PCs (desktop, notebook, netbook), embedded computers	IBM, Fujitsu, Siemens, Hewlett-Packard, Dell, Apple, Acer, Lenovo
Computer peripherals and other office equipment	Printers, fax machines, copiers, scanners	Hewlett-Packard, Xerox, Epson, Kodak, Cannon, Lexmark, Acer, Fujitsu, Sharp
Consumer electronics	Game consoles, television, home audio and video, portable audio and video, mobile phone handsets, musical equipment, toys	Toshiba, NEC, Vizio, Sony, Sharp, Apple, Nintendo, Microsoft, Samsung, LG, NEC, Matsushita, Hitachi, Microsoft, HTC, Philips
Server and storage devices	Portable, internal, external, backup systems, storage services	Toshiba, Western Digital, EMC, NetApp, Hewlett-Packard, Hitachi, Seagate, Maxtor, LeCie, Quantum
Networking	Public telecommunications, private communications networks, Internet, mobile phone infrastructure	Alcatel, Nortel, Cisco, Motorola, Juniper, Huawei, Ericsson, Nokia, Tellabs
Automotive electronics	Entertainment, communication, vehicle control (braking, acceleration, traction, suspension), vehicle navigation	TomTom, Garmin, Clarion, Toyota, General Motors, Renault, Bosch, Siemens
Medical electronics	Consumer medical, diagnostics and testing, imaging, telemedicine, meters and monitoring, implants, fitness	General Electric, Philips, Medtronic, Varian
Industrial electronics	Security and surveillance, factory automation, building automation, military systems, aircraft, aerospace, banking and ATM, transportation	Diebold, Siemens, Rockwell, Philips, Omron, Dover
Military and aerospace electronics	Ground combat systems, aircraft, sea-based systems, eavesdropping and surveillance, satellites, missile guidance & intercept	L-3 Communications, Lockheed Martin, Boeing, BAE Systems, Northrop Grumman, General Dynamics, EADS, L-3 Communications, Finmeccanica, United Technologies

Source: Authors.

industry is a direct result of value chain modularity, which enables a clear technical division of labor between design and manufacturing at multiple points in the value chain, most notably between the design and assembly of final products and the design and fabrication of integrated circuits, or ICs. At the product level, some lead firms still assemble products in their own factories, but the use of contract manufacturers has been a strong trend since the late 1980s. Production services alone—comprising component purchasing, circuit board assembly, final assembly, and testing—are referred to in the industry as electronics manufacturing services (EMS), and also known as original equipment manufacturing (OEM) firms in Taiwan, China. Historically, the largest EMS contract manufacturing firms have been based in the United States and Canada (see table 7.5.); for example, Celestica was spun off from IBM in 1997. These firms tend to have global operations and produce for lead firms in most of the product segments listed in table 7.4. In recent years, Foxconn (Hon Hai), based in Taiwan, China, but with very large production facilities in China, Vietnam, and the Czech Republic, has emerged as the industry's largest player, in part on the basis of huge orders received from Apple for the production of the iPod and iPhone product lines. A number of firms based in

Table 7.5 Top-Five Electronics Contract Manufacturers, Various Regions, 2009

Top-five contract manufacturers	Primary service	2009 revenue (US$, millions)
Taiwan, China		
Foxconn/Hon Hai	EMS	44,065
Quanta Computer	ODM	23,265
Compal Electronics	ODM	19,424
Wistron	ODM	16,226
Inventec	ODM	12,349
North America		
Flextronics (United States & Singapore)	EMS	30,949
Jabil Circuit (United States)	EMS	11,685
Celestica (Canada)	EMS	6,092
Sanmina-SCI (United States)	EMS	5,177
Benchmark Electronics (United States)	EMS	2,089
Other locations		
Venture (Singapore)	EMS	2.428
Elcoteq (Luxembourg)	EMS	2,090
SIIX (Japan)	EMS	1,360
Beyonics (Singapore)	EMS	1,120
Zollner Elektronik (Germany)	EMS	970

Sources: Digitimes (Taiwan, China) and company annual reports.
Note: EMS = electronic manufacturing services; ODM = original design manufacturing (services).

Singapore have also risen in the EMS ranks, including Venture and Beyonics, ranked 7th and 12th in the world, respectively, in 2009.

Manufacturing plus product design services are known collectively as original design manufacturing (ODM) services. Nearly all of the large ODM contract manufacturers are based in Taiwan, China, with manufacturing now concentrated in China. These firms (top of table 7.5) have historically focused on producing for lead firms in the personal computer (PC) industry. Because manufacturing process technology, especially at the circuit board level, is quite generic, EMS contract manufacturers can aggregate business from lead firms in many electronics subsectors. Design expertise is far less generic, however, which explains why ODM contract manufacturers have historically been confined to the PC industry (Sturgeon and Lee 2005).

It has proven to be a powerful combination for U.S.-based "global" EMS contract manufacturers to have facilities both at home, to work out the manufacturing details of new product designs in collaboration with lead firm design groups, and abroad, to perform high-volume production in locations with lower costs and proximity to promising new markets. In some cases, the offshore affiliates of these large suppliers have challenged developing-country contract manufacturers on their home turf. In other cases, a complementary pattern emerged where global suppliers rely on "second-tier" developing-country suppliers for components, services, and as subcontractors. A third pattern is for developed-country suppliers to specialize in products and services that require the initial co-location described above.

Despite these differences, both the EMS and ODM contract manufacturing segments have been characterized by rapid growth and geographic expansion, making them key actors in electronics GVCs. Because of this rapid expansion, they now purchase the bulk of the world's electronic components, albeit on behalf of their lead firm customers. Even with large market shares in specific product segments (for example, Taiwanese ODM contract manufacturers produce more than 90 percent of the world's notebook computers), their market power (and profitability) have generally remained low because they are highly substitutable. Even though they purchase billions of dollars worth of components, the buying power of contract manufacturers is limited because components are purchased specifically on behalf of their customers. Contracts for key components, such as high-value microprocessors and application-specific integrated circuits (ASICs) are negotiated directly between lead firms and semiconductor companies; contract manufacturers are provided allocations at set prices. Markups on generic parts are also low or nonexistent, since the pricing for these inputs is well known to lead firms. As a result, the electronics contract manufacturing sector has long been characterized by intense competition, low profitability, and dramatic consolidation, even as it has experienced rapid growth.

Most recently, revenues of ODM contract manufacturers based in Taiwan, China, have surged ahead of EMS contractors. Because of their expertise in small form factor (that is, portable) product design, ODMs have been able to capture the lion's share of new business for burgeoning product categories like portable computers, smart phones, and navigation devices.

Whatever the competitive battles and complementarities that have emerged among developed- and developing-country suppliers, the most important change is that increasing supplier capability is allowing lead firms to implement global production strategies in ways that were unimagined 20 years ago. Sustained efforts by the largest lead firms to expand and consolidate their sourcing networks have helped to create a new class of huge, globally operating suppliers in the electronics industry, and supplier consolidation has meant that there are larger, more capable suppliers to choose from. Suppliers have collected bundles of capabilities and can now provide one-stop shopping for lead firms seeking regional and global supply solutions. This new class of global supplier has internalized many of the most difficult and costly aspects of cross-border integration such as logistics, inventory management, and the day-to-day management of factories (Sturgeon and Lester 2004).

Platform Leaders

In some industries, such as PCs, mobile phones, and a few industries unrelated to electronics such as bicycles, platform leaders play a crucial role (Galvin and Morkel 2001; Fixson and Park 2008). Platform leaders are companies that have been successful in implanting their technology (in the form of software, hardware, or a combination) in the products of other companies. In extreme cases, platform leaders can capture the bulk of industry profits and retain tight control over the innovative trajectory of the industry. In the electronics industry, the notebook PC and mobile phone handset cases show why the term "lead firm" does not necessarily imply that branded product firms such as Dell and Motorola are the dominant and, in many cases, the most profitable actors in the chain.

Using the language of Baldwin and Clark (2000), it can be said that Intel, as the dominant platform leader in the PC industry, has the technological capability and market power to unilaterally change the location of key "pinch points" in the GVC. In other words, Intel can decide how to bundle tacit, proprietary activities and where to locate the points in the chain where codified handoffs can occur and open standards can begin. It is logical to think that PC producers, if they were able to develop a viable substitute for Intel chipsets, would seek to protect and enhance their profitability by abandoning Intel. In fact, many have tried in the past. IBM's late 1980s Microchannel PC architecture and the 1990s IBM/Motorola/Apple

PowerPC CPU (central processing unit) alliance are examples of how branded PC companies have tried, and failed, to supplant Intel's platform leadership in the PC industry. In most industries, however, lead firms, not component suppliers, define system architecture. Personal computers and mobile phone handsets are important and well-known cases of industries where platform leaders dominate, but it is important to note that such cases are in fact quite unusual.

Apple is an interesting case of a lead firm that is also a platform leader. The system architecture of Apple products is proprietary, even though most parts and many subsystems are purchased from outside companies. Most notably, Apple has successfully created a vibrant "ecosystem" of third-party vendors to supply software applications and hardware add-ons by carefully limiting the scope of its products and publishing specifications for the creation of Apple-compatible products. Note here that fully open systems, such as the Linux PC operating system, are a rarity, even in the electronics industry, where many firms claim to provide them.

Very few platform leaders have as yet emerged from the developing world. In the electronics industry a notable exception is MediaTek, a "fabless" semiconductor design house founded in 1997 in Taiwan, China. The company has moved along with the market, providing chipsets for reading compact disks (CDs), digital video disks (DVDs), digital video recorders (DVRs), and high-definition televisions (HDTV). Most recently MediaTek mastered the difficult art of combining fundamentally different technologies, such as analog and digital signal processing on the same chip, in what is known in the industry as "system-on-chip" (SOC) technology. Using SOC capabilities, the company began offering single-chip "platform solutions" with the advantages of lower cost, smaller size, and lower power consumption, while sacrificing, to some degree, the ability to customize platforms in the interest of product variety. In the years 2004 and 2005, MediaTek leveraged its experience in audio, imaging, and video to develop chipset solutions for mobile phones with functionality for audio capture (voice recording), music playback (MP3), and image capture and playback (camera and video phones). MediaTek chipsets have played a central role in supporting the development of low-cost phones suitable for the Chinese market, covered in detail later in this chapter.

The Rise of Supplier Capabilities in Electronics GVCs

East Asia has contributed to the development of GVCs for a long time and in different ways. Japanese trading companies were some of the earliest sources of low-cost consumer goods for the West, such as footwear and apparel produced for large retailers in the United States and consumer electronics produced for branded lead firms such as RCA and Philips. When wages rose in Japan, Japanese trading companies became intermediaries in more complex "triangle manufacturing" arrangements that brought factories in Korea; Taiwan, China; and Hong Kong, China into a system that had previously consisted of Japanese factories exporting directly to countries in the West (Gereffi 1999). Eventually, global buyers in the West learned how to buy directly from factories in developing East Asia, or through local intermediaries in places like Hong Kong, China.

As firms in Korea and Taiwan, China, began to supply more technology-intensive products like electronics with help from the state, their paths diverged. By and large, Korean firms followed in Japan's footsteps. During the 1980s Korean *chaebol* (business family) emerged as large, diversified enterprise groups with a vertically integrated stance toward product development, manufacturing, and marketing. Today, using their own brand names, Samsung, LG, and Hyundai Motors compete head to head with firms based in the United States, Japan, and Europe in global markets for technology-intensive products, such as mobile phone handsets, flat-panel television sets, and passenger vehicles.

In Taiwan, China, however, local manufacturers began by supplying components and subassemblies, rather than finished products, but sought—and indeed were asked and in some cases forced by de-verticalized "manufacturers" in the West—to move up the value chain. As a result, they began to assist in the design process and take full responsibility for component purchasing, final assembly, and the organization of multicountry value chains in East Asia. Taiwanese contract manufacturers had long hoped to leverage this learning process to become full-blown original brand manufacturers (OBMs), selling their own branded products on markets (Weiss and Hobson 1995). Few have been successful, however, in large part because OBM activity brought them into direct competition with their customers (small in number and very powerful), and put future orders at risk.[7] The fallback strategy for Taiwan-based suppliers was to remain within the expanding set of value chain niches that had been made available, and to increase their range of competencies in contract manufacturing and design services, while expanding geographically into mainland China in an effort to respond to customer demands for ongoing cost reductions. As a result, a different business model and path to development, separates Taiwanese firms, such as TSMC, Quanta, and Hon Hai, from their Korean "national champion" counterparts, such as Samsung and LG.

The reasons for the different paths of Korea and Taiwan, China, are complex. They include the more fragmented industrial structure of Taiwan, China, noted by Feenstra and Hamilton (2006), the larger home market in Korea, different capabilities in the customer base (retailers versus de-verticalizing manufacturing companies), and different state policies (the Korean state actively promoted vertical and horizontal integration). Korea's earlier insertion into GVCs also played a role. From more arms-length relationships, GVC coordination and governance evolved. Taiwan's buyers were more circumspect about offloading full design and product conception responsibilities to suppliers, in part because they had observed how Japanese and Korean suppliers had overtaken their customers with their own brands in consumer electronics (televisions) and home appliances (microwave ovens). The differences between Korea and Taiwan, China, then reflect differences in strategy, developed in a coevolutionary manner with a set of de-verticalizing customers, and not just different starting points in industrial structure. As a result, we see Taiwan, China, as transitioning toward the new "compressed development" model rather than simply a variant of "late development."

The success of the ODM contract manufacturing model eventually shifted Taiwan, China's industrial policy away from efforts to create full-blown, vertically integrated, globally competitive national industries through a process of sequential value chain upgrading. Eventually, most ODM contract manufacturers and other Taiwan-based suppliers in electronics GVCs realized that it was better to spin off their branded product divisions to compete in end markets and, as seen later in the chapter, a few of these ODM spinoffs have met with some success.

As mentioned previously, the prevalence of GVC modularity in the electronics industry has played a critical role in enabling the industry to spread geographically and, by extension, to include developing and newly developed countries in the industry's GVCs. Even though the specifications and information handed off between value chain functions in the electronics industry tend to be highly complex, the combination of information technology and well-known standards means that specifications can be codified and temporarily simplified, creating a pinch point in the flow of tacit information that allows data to be transmitted across vast distances and to other firms (Baldwin and Clark 2000).

Obviously, even with product modularity and value chain modularity, this sort of outsourcing would be impossible without suppliers with the capabilities to accept the work and efficiently meet the requirements of lead firms. Such firms exist today, but it was not always the case. Following are a few examples from Singapore; the United States; Mexico; and Taiwan, China of how these capabilities emerged, including several firm-level examples, a cluster-level example from a regional production hub in Mexico, and a summary of the trajectory of contract manufacturers from the United States and Taiwan, China, as they have developed and set up international operations. These cases show how supplier capabilities have coevolved with lead firm outsourcing strategies in the electronics industry to help create the extensive GVCs seen today.

Singapore and Southeast Asia

In the early 1970s, American semiconductor firms located “back-end” (post-production) semiconductor assembly, which was very labor intensive at the time, in East and Southeast Asia, and Japanese companies located low-cost transistor radio production in Taiwan, China, and Hong Kong, China (Grunwald and Flamm 1985; Sayer 1986).[8] Over time, semiconductor assembly was automated, with the Philippines becoming a favored location; more labor-intensive processes, including circuit board and final product assembly, were shifted to developing East Asia as well. At first, most of these capabilities were contained within the affiliates of multinational firms, but local capabilities gradually developed. This was especially true for suppliers serving the affiliates of American multinationals, which have proven to be more willing to encourage local suppliers to take on additional responsibilities than their Japanese counterparts (Borrus, Ernst, and Haggard 2000). Singapore was a favored location for multinational firms in the disk-drive industry (McKendrik, Doner, and Haggard 2000), but production and subassembly work gradually spread to local firms that soon outgrew the small land and labor markets in Singapore and set up operations throughout Southeast Asia (Deitrick 1990; Vind and Fold 2007). Because rates of unionization were very low in the U.S. electronics industry, and because modularity allowed design and innovation functions to remain at home, these moves were not strongly resisted by politicians or the general public.

The important role of multinational affiliates in driving supplier upgrading in Southeast Asia is illustrated in the case of Beyonics, an EMS contract manufacturer based in Singapore. In 1981, two Singaporean engineers decided to start their own company after they were laid off from the Singaporean subsidiary of the German camera manufacturer Rollei. Seeing that the local tool-and-die business in Singapore was underdeveloped—because most foreign firms tended to bring in their own tooling—the two set up their own tool-and-die shop on a chicken farm owned by one of the founder's parents. From their experience at Rollei they knew that advanced lathes for precision metal cutting could be stopped quickly to make rapid setup changes. The two retrofitted some inexpensive lathes with motorcycle brakes to achieve the same effect. The company, which was initially called Uraco, generated $700,000 in revenues during its first year of operation, mostly by supplying precision metal parts to American disk drive producers, which were investing heavily in manufacturing in Singapore and Malaysia at the time (Business Times 1995).

As Uraco grew, it began to supply a wider range of products to the disk drive industry, including precision metal stampings and assembled electronic circuit boards. Most of the company's business was with Seagate, the leading American disk drive manufacturer at the time, but the company also exported precision parts to Hitachi's disk drive operations in the Philippines. Because of the extreme volatility in disk drive and PC markets, in 1987 management began the first of many efforts to diversify the company's customer base by distributing electronic components, eventually winning distributorships from Motorola, Harris Semiconductor, and Siemens.[9] In the mid-1990s the company took these efforts at diversification a step further. The idea was to leverage experience with electronic components, contract manufacturing, and warehouse management to manufacture and sell products of its own design, including connectors, crystals, automated warehouse vehicles, electronic ballasts for fluorescent lamps, light bulbs, and telecommunications products. Ultimately, these attempts were not successful, and the bulk of Uraco's business remained in providing EMS contract manufacturing services and precision-engineered metal parts to foreign firms operating in the Southeast Asian region. As traditional distribution networks in the region matured, the need for the company's distribution services waned as well.

Nevertheless, in 1995 the company underwent a successful initial public offering on the Singapore stock exchange. In 1996, as annual revenues were approaching $53 million, Uraco won an important contract to manufacture flatbed scanners for Hewlett-Packard (Business Times 1996a). In 1997 the firm reorganized its business into three divisions: precision machining, contract manufacturing, and investment (Business Times 1996b, 1997). The company's troubles were not over, however, and flagging profitability led to a management reshuffling in 2000 and a name change to Beyonics in 2001. The company returned to profitability in 2001, when it generated nearly $300 million in revenues, with 62 percent coming from contract manufacturing services, 29 percent from precision engineering, and 9 percent from distribution (Geocities 2004).

The company's current product and service offerings are electronics manufacturing services (that is, contract manufacturing), medical and consumer plastic injection molding and assembly, precision engineering services, precision metal stampings, and precision tooling design and fabrication services. This is a highly focused and complementary product portfolio, covering many of the processes and a few of the basic products required to produce a wide variety of electronics and closely related goods. The company has followed the rest of the electronics contract manufacturing industry into the bundling of services to enable the production of complete products through its acquisitions of precision plastic moldings suppliers, Techplas (in 2000) and Pacific Plastics (in 2002). In 2003 the company merged with a similar Singaporean contract manufacturer, Flairis Technology Corporation, to achieve additional economies of scale and scope. The company's distribution activities and attempts at selling its own branded products have been dropped entirely.

With this tighter focus, the company has expanded dramatically. As shown in table 7.5, the company now ranks 12th on a list of the world's largest EMS electronics contract manufacturers. Through a combination of internal expansion and acquisition, Beyonics has developed a solid regional manufacturing footprint, most notably by establishing "vertically integrated" electronics contract manufacturing campuses in Kulai, Malaysia, in 2005; Suzhou, China, in 2006; and Batam, Indonesia, in 2007. In all, the company currently operates 16 facilities: 3 in Singapore, 6 in Malaysia, 3 in China, 2 in Thailand, and 2 in Indonesia.

While Beyonics may have grown much larger than most local firms in East Asia that started as suppliers to multinational corporations (MNCs), there are several lessons to be drawn. First, Beyonics' managers demonstrated the use of dynamic capabilities (Teece 2009) for sensing opportunities, seizing them, and transforming the company as needed. Second, they stumbled by trying to diversify and develop their own products, which required end-user marketing competencies they had not yet developed, but recovered when they refocused on providing producer services to MNCs in the region. Third, like most large electronics contract manufacturers, Beyonics has struggled to remain profitable, even as the company has grown rapidly. Fourth, as the company expanded, it chose a variety of lower cost locations within Southeast and East Asia, balancing its investments in China with locations in Malaysia, Thailand, and Indonesia. What the Beyonics case illustrates most dramatically, however, is how, with enough time (a 28-year span in this case), local firms with extremely humble roots have been able to grow, master advanced technologies, and set up multiple locations in Asia, largely by serving American MNC affiliates in the region.

The United States

In the U.S. electronics industry, a combination of globalization, outsourcing, and vertical bundling at suppliers in the 1990s helped to push a small but elite set of supplier firms to quickly move beyond their traditional cluster- or national-scale footprint to become global in scope. Vertically integrated lead firms with global operations based in both the United States and Europe, including Lucent, Nortel, Alcatel, Ericsson, and Apple Computer, sold off most, if not all, of their in-house manufacturing capacity—both at home and abroad—to a cadre of large and highly capable U.S.-based contract manufacturers (table 7.5), including Flextronics/Solectron, Jabil Circuit, Celestica, and Sanmina-SCI (Sturgeon 2002; Sturgeon and Lee 2005).

Solectron (acquired by Flextronics in 2007) provides an example of how U.S.-based EMS contract manufacturers overexpanded during the 1990s. The company was concentrated in a single campus in Silicon Valley (California) from its founding in 1979 through the 1980s. In 1991 Solectron's key customers in Silicon Valley, including Sun Microsystems, Hewlett-Packard, and Cisco Systems, demanded that Solectron provide global manufacturing and process engineering support. The company went on an acquisition-fueled binge of global expansion and revenue growth; by 2001 the company's footprint had expanded to more than 135 facilities worldwide (see annex) and annual revenues had increased from $265 million to $12 billion. In the process of this expansion, the company acquired competitors, customer facilities, and an array of specialized firms with capabilities that allowed the company to offer a much broader package of services.

An example of a global electronics contract manufacturer that emerged as a lead firm spinoff is Celestica, an in-house manufacturing division of IBM that was spun off as an independent company in 1996. At the outset, the firm had only two production locations, a large complex near Toronto, Canada, and a small facility in northern New York State, since closed. By 2001, after completing 29 acquisitions of customer and competitor facilities, Celestica had accumulated nearly 50 facilities in North America, South America, Western and Eastern Europe, and Asia, and annual revenues had soared to more than $10 billion (see map 7.1).

In the round of consolidation that followed the technology bubble bursting in 2001, Flextronics (listed in Singapore, but managed from San Jose, California)

Map 7.1 Celestica's Global Operating Footprint, 2001

Source: Celestica.

emerged as the world's largest electronics EMS contract manufacturer, a position that was further solidified through its acquisition of number 2-ranked Solectron in 2007. Flextronics' 2009 revenues were slightly less than $31 billion. Aside from dozens of stand-alone factories and technology centers around the world, Flextronics, with its strategy of "vertical integration," operates nine huge "industrial parks," where it has "invited" many of its most immediate suppliers of product-specific components (bare printed circuit board and plastic enclosures) to co-locate with its final assembly plants for rapid response in regional markets. Flextronics has one industrial plant in Poland and two each in Brazil, China, Hungary, India, and Mexico. In a pattern typical of many goods-producing industries, facilities located in developing countries tend to be significantly more vertically integrated than those in industrialized countries, where existing local suppliers and component distributors can be relied on for inputs.

The sale and spinoff of in-house manufacturing and parts operations in the American and European electronics industries underline the structural shift that has been occurring in the electronics industry from in-house production to global outsourcing. The accumulation of this offloaded capacity within a relatively small number of huge suppliers shows the dramatic consolidation and increasing integration of the global supply base. However, outsourcing, as such, does not tell the entire story. In the electronics industry, fast-growing lead firms with little if any in-house production capacity, such as EMC, Sun Microsystems, Cisco, and Silicon Graphics, also demanded that suppliers provide global support. And, in some key locations, lead firms did not necessarily have plants to sell or spin off, especially in newer locations like China and Eastern Europe. As a result, a great deal of the global expansion of suppliers in the 1990s was either "organic" in character, involving the enlargement of existing facilities and the establishment of new "greenfield" plants,[10] or achieved through the acquisition of regional suppliers, in what some industry participants refer to as the "rolling up" of regional supply bases to create a global footprint.

Global coverage allows the largest EMS contract manufacturers to produce high-volume, price-sensitive products for global markets from plants in China, and higher-value, medium-volume products in regional production facilities such as Mexico and Eastern Europe. It also enables them to produce a variety of products locally for regions containing large developing countries such as India, Brazil, and China, and to work closely on lowest-volume, highest-value products with customers in industrialized countries, in places like Silicon Valley.

However, expansion in the 1990s was so rapid that the largest EMS companies quickly became overextended. Integrating diverse plants acquired from customers and competitors left these firms with excess capacity, facilities with incompatible factory and information systems, and too many plants in high-wage locations.

Efforts at consolidation are ongoing, but overexpansion and poor management left certain companies, especially Solectron and SCI, with too much inventory in the system and in very weak financial position, making them ripe for acquisition. After the 2001 technology bubble burst, contractors made a strong push to increase capacity in low-cost geographic areas, especially China, and, as shown in the next section, to transform regional production hubs in Mexico and Eastern Europe to produce higher-value, lower-volume products previously manufactured in the United States and Western Europe.

Guadalajara, Mexico

Economic downturns can have obvious negative effects on workers, companies, industrial clusters, industries, and entire national and regional economies.[11] But they can also provide an impetus for positive change, adaptation, better prospects for sustainable development for the long term, and an improved ability to weather future downturns. One example is the electronics cluster in Guadalajara, the capital of Jalisco State in southwest Mexico. The 2001 technology bubble bursting in 2001 was felt acutely across electronics GVCs, and the Guadalajara electronics cluster was no exception. Companies and facilities there went through a wrenching and rapid decline, but recovered through a remarkable process of industrial upgrading. This involved a move to new products and processes, as well as changes in work organization and training as high-volume production lines were transformed into high-mix production cells to accommodate a greater variety of higher-value products.

The Guadalajara electronics cluster is deeply embedded within electronics GVCs. With few exceptions, electronics goods produced in Guadalajara are designed and sold by U.S.-based lead firms. Most are produced by affiliates of U.S.-based global EMS contract manufacturers using imported components and equipment, especially from East Asia (see figure 7.2). Almost all output is exported, the vast majority going to the United States.

Until 2001 Guadalajara's factories competed directly with those in China in the production of high-volume, price-sensitive items such as mobile phone handsets and notebook computers. Because global suppliers dominate the landscape of electronics GVCs, competition between locations often occurs within the global footprint of contract manufacturers. Thus, decisions to shift work from one location to another are taken by the managers of contract manufacturing firms, carried out at the request of lead firm customers, or some combination. During the period 1994–2000, the value of electronics exports from Jalisco State, which contains the Guadalajara metropolitan area, on average, increased at a rate of 35.4 percent per year. During the period 2000–05, the average annual export

Figure 7.2 Position of the Guadalajara Electronics Cluster in Electronics GVCs

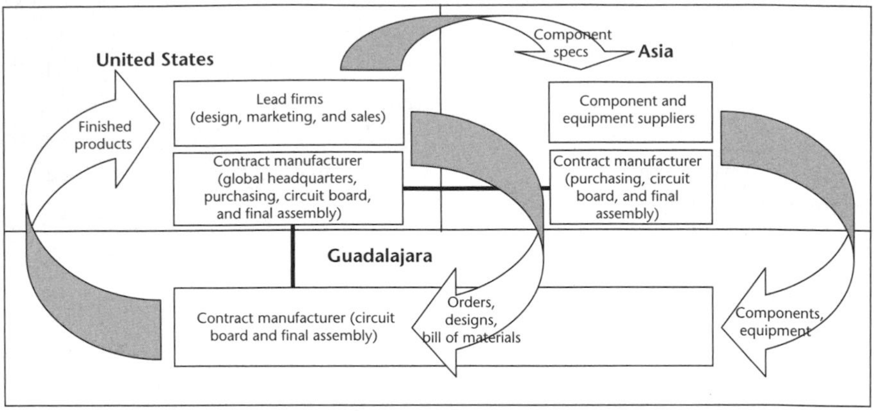

Source: Authors' drawing.
Note: Guadalajara, Mexico.

growth rate declined to only 1.3 percent per year, falling in absolute terms for several years (see figure 7.3). While a few foreign electronics firms (for example, Hewlett-Packard and IBM) had been operating in Guadalajara since the 1970s, a new wave of foreign direct investment (FDI) peaked at $611 million in 1998 as the affiliates of global EMS contract manufacturers expanded in the area as part of the worldwide expansion strategy described earlier. Flextronics, Jabil Circuit, Solectron, Sanmina-SCI, Benchmark, and Foxconn (Hon Hai) all established facilities in Guadalajara, along with a handful of multinational component manufacturers and a few component distribution companies to manage the increased inbound flow of components. Because the decline in output after 2001 followed these huge investments, capacity utilization dropped precipitously and remained low for several years. As figure 7.3 shows, the nadir for both employment and exports was 2003.

With new, large, state-of-the-art production facilities sitting idle, the stakes were very high in 2001–03. Employment had grown to about 10,000 workers each at several of the largest plants, and total high-tech employment in Jalisco State peaked at 76,666 in 2000. After the technology bubble burst in 2001, employment dropped by 40–60 percent at some plants, with total high-tech employment in Jalisco falling by 40 percent to 45,877. This downturn was more than a temporary drop in demand. In an effort to lower costs, global contract manufacturers were shifting high-volume work to their plants in China. There was no expectation that this work would come back to Mexico when the crisis abated. Failure to find new business would likely have meant further stagnation, decline, and possible plant

Figure 7.3 Guadalajara "High-Tech" Employment and Exports, 1996–2009

Source: CADELEC 2010.

closures. In an effort to utilize their state-of-the-art investments in Guadalajara, the global firms provided the electronics cluster there a new role in the global industry: produce higher-priced, lower-volume products, often on a direct-ship, rapid replenishment basis to retail outlets in the United States.

This strategy led to a dramatic transformation and gradual recovery to precrisis levels of employment and exports. Very few of the products made in Guadalajara in 2000 are still made there. The assembly of high-volume, price-sensitive products has been shifted to other locations, mainly China. Products produced in Guadalajara after the 2001 crisis tend to have the following characteristics:

- *Products with high transport costs:* For example, 20 percent of the final costs of video game consoles are for transportation. Large and heavy products, obviously, are well suited for production in Mexico.
- *Products with complex logistics:* These products require last-minute configuration, very responsive logistics, and short transit times. Transportation costs also rise with low-volume, rapid-response shipments.
- *Products needing intensive development:* These are products with requirements for intense interaction between design, research and development (R&D), engineering, configuration, testing, and prototype development. Such products

typically require close engineering collaboration and often call for multiple engineering changes during new product introduction. In some cases, lead firm engineers contact the production facility engineers every four hours and even every hour. U.S.-based engineers sometimes spend days or weeks onsite to solve problems. Long distances and vastly different time zones, as is the case with Asia, make this type of manufacturing very difficult.
- *Very expensive products:* These include, for example, items for industrial or IT infrastructure applications in which labor is not a determinant cost.
- *Regulated products:* Regulations sometimes specify tariffs or come with other "rules of origin." For example, the 18 percent U.S. tariff on cellular phones produced outside of NAFTA (North American Free Trade Agreement) has kept some higher-value cellphone handset production in Mexico, even though they are produced in high volumes that would otherwise render them more suitable for production in China.

Prior to 2001 most production of products with the above characteristics had been done in the United States, where costs are high. Mexico offered a potential low-cost "near-shore" solution for more expensive products made in small batches, but first a series of challenges needed to be met. During the 2001–03 period contract manufacturers in Guadalajara undertook the following measures:

- Employment and new investment were dramatically cut.
- The remaining workers and managers went through an intensive period of retraining.
- New systems were developed to maintain product quality in the context of higher product complexity and diversity. These changes impacted procedures for product testing, inventory management, and work processes.
- New systems were developed to configure and customize products for small orders. This required an increase in engineering employment.
- "Hard tooling," that is, inflexible tooling dedicated to a single product, was replaced with "soft tooling." This transformation often meant less automation and greater labor intensity and worker skill, especially in final assembly.

At the level of circuit board assembly, where individual electronic components are mounted and affixed to bare circuit boards to create the major functional elements of electronics systems, highly automated robotic equipment can be reprogrammed with relative ease, making the work highly geographically mobile. In final assembly, however, automation is more difficult because of the radically different size and shape of finished products and poor flexibility of the equipment used. Assembly personnel, therefore, have had to adapt to a much more complex and challenging production environment. Instead of performing one or a few operations on the same product for months at a time, line workers must frequently perform new and different operations as a variety of products move down the line. Such work is much less geographically mobile.

Materials management, for both circuit board and final assembly, is also much more complex, and many plants are working to adopt the most advanced "lean production" methods for maintaining quality in the face of product variety. While circuit board assembly machines still feed final assembly stations in a linear fashion, final assembly has been reorganized into "cells" that hold very little inventory and where workers perform several tasks rather than a single task. Finally, new logistics functions have been added to ship small lots, often by air, directly to retailers for distribution. Materials management, testing, and quality assurance systems have all been upgraded dramatically to accommodate the vast increases in product variety.[12]

The retraining and new process development specified here were implemented in 2001–02 for a small number of old and new products that fit the target profile of the plants. These new capabilities in turn provided a platform to win new low-volume, high-mix business in the period 2003–05. Since then, the Guadalajara electronics cluster has solidified its new role and employment has rebounded to pre-2001 levels, with a higher ratio of engineering and other skilled occupations. This is reflected in figures on exports per worker, which rose from 128,610 in 2000 to 226,723 in 2008. Due to the sudden drop in demand during the most recent economic crisis, this figure fell to 188,143 in 2009 (authors' calculations, CADELEC 2010). Because of the new product mix, high investment in worker training, and decreased portability of the work now performed in Guadalajara, contract manufacturing firms have apparently been more reluctant to engage in massive layoffs during the recent economic crisis than they were in 2001, at least so far (see year 2009 in figure 7.3). While the growth of high-tech employment in Jalisco State did decrease in 2009, employment remained stable at about 78,500 workers, 83 percent of whom were in manufacturing (CADELEC 2010).

The changes in Guadalajara's electronics industry since 2001 are a striking example of "industrial upgrading" (Humphrey and Schmitz 2002), in which the industry shifts to higher-value products and more advanced processes, and adds a host of new functions and services. However, it is important to note that many of the techniques that support these changes were developed outside of Guadalajara. In this way, global contract manufacturers can provide a powerful mechanism with which to disseminate best practices. On the other hand, our field research also found that local officials, plant managers, and workers played a powerful role in the transformation of the region. Finally, while employment at foreign-owned contract manufacturing facilities is now back to 2001 levels, local suppliers have not made the transition to the new high-mix product profile of production in Guadalajara, and employment has not recovered at most of these firms.

The case of the transformation of the Guadalajara electronics cluster provides some lessons for the concept of GVC upgrading and for the prospects for economic transformation in locations where modular GVCs touch down. First, any neat partition between product, process, and functional upgrading as specified by Humphrey and Schmitz (2002) seems problematic because of the powerful complementarities that flow from product upgrading. The shift to higher-value, lower-volume products, in this case, *required* firms to upgrade processes to accommodate rapid changeover and to add new functions to control a much more complex inventory basket and to develop new engineering inputs to support changes. Second, rapid upgrading was possible in part because the skills to do so had been developed within the larger global structure that the facilities in Guadalajara are part of. Finally, the authors' research found that local firms have not been able to adapt to the new requirements of the cluster, in part because the resources and knowledge to transform their plants are not available locally. Nevertheless, the upgrading achieved after the technology bubble burst in 2001 may have provided the Guadalajara electronics cluster with some protection during the current economic crisis.

Taiwan, China

Taiwan-based ODM contract manufacturers have come to dominate world production of PCs, but have historically had difficulty selling their own branded products to consumers.[13] However, the recent economic crisis may have created new opportunities for Taiwan-based firms to overcome these barriers, as is discussed in this section on the evolution of electronics hardware production in Taiwan, China.

While there are significant PC components, subsystems, and peripheral devices in which Taiwan-based firms are not active—namely, software, printers, hard disk drives, and higher-value semiconductors such as microprocessors and memory—Taiwan, China, has developed what is arguably the world's most capable and agile supply base for the design, manufacture, and delivery of PCs and related products, especially notebook computers (Dedrick and Kraemer 1998). Initially working in close geographic proximity, mostly along the Taipei-Hsinchu corridor in Taiwan, China, this supply base grew to constitute an extremely efficient system that could respond rapidly to orders from lead firms. Notebook computers, which generally have a high enough value-to-weight ratio to make air shipment viable, can be shipped from Taiwan, China (or now from mainland China plants owned by Taiwan-based contractors) to end users in the United States and Europe within two to three days of incoming orders.

This powerful productive engine has developed, almost in its entirety, in response to orders from lead firms based in the United States, and, more recently, Japan (Sturgeon 2007). At the same time, the development of contract manufacturing in Taiwan, China, and elsewhere has provided lead firms with an increasing range of sourcing options. This process of coevolution means that Taiwan's electronics industry has been able to develop without a significant cadre of local lead firms. From the late 1970s to the present day, sourcing from Taiwan, China, has expanded from computer monitors, to various components and subsystems, to complete desktop and notebook PC systems.

Firms from the American PC industry have played an especially important role in the development of Taiwan's electronics contract manufacturing sector. In the early 1980s, IBM began sourcing PC monitors from Tatung, a television producer in Taiwan, China, for its new line of PCs. As the demand expanded rapidly and the open architecture of the IBM-compatible PC became firmly established in 1984 with the IBM model AT, some entrepreneurial firms in Taiwan, China, including Acer and Mitac, recognized the opportunities and moved aggressively to develop the capability to design PCs and peripheral devices based on the emerging standard. IBM's modular PC system architecture relied on a central processing unit (CPU) supplied by Intel and on an operating system from Microsoft, and because the contracts famously did not block Intel and Microsoft from selling to IBM's competitors, a bevy of new entrants, intense price competition, and a series of boom and bust cycles soon followed. These conditions caused contract manufacturing to become a popular strategy for lead firms in the United States seeking to cut costs and limit investments in fixed capital in the face of severe market uncertainty. The surging demand for contract manufacturing services encouraged existing Taiwan-based contract manufacturers producing consumer electronics and electronic component companies to develop capabilities to assemble PCs.

Then, in the late 1980s, a set of firms that had been focused on the design and manufacture of handheld calculators entered the field. These firms—including Quanta, Compal, and Inventec—eventually became the dominant notebook computer producers, in part because the design and assembly competencies that drove miniaturization in calculators were well suited to notebook computers, where small size, light weight, and efficient power consumption are key factors for success. In addition, calculators, while much simpler, are similar to PCs in that they are built around a CPU whose product architecture determines product functionality.

The modular system architecture of PCs, and the dominant role of the CPU and operating system software in setting system architecture, along with intense competition and short product life cycles, created the conditions for the emergence of a set of firms to specialize in the iterative, postarchitectural portions of product design, including the board-level operating system (BIOS), which determines how the machine handles the input and output from its main board to the other elements of the system, such as storage and displays. However, because most functionality resides in chipsets and software—system elements that computer producers do not design—control over the innovative trajectory of the industry has continued to reside in "platform leaders" such as Intel and Microsoft, which have traditionally worked closely with branded PC firms on future requirements. However, as the notebook format has come to dominate consumer PC sales, and branded PC firms have either left the business (IBM), changed their business focus to bundling services with PCs (Hewlett-Packard), or tried to move up-market to servers and storage systems (Dell), Intel has begun to work more closely with Taiwanese firms on the requirements for next generation CPU design for mobile computing (Kawakami, forthcoming).

The migration of Taiwan's electronics production to mainland China began to accelerate in the mid-1990s, following a sharp drop in desktop PC prices (some models fell below $500). The migration started with components and peripherals and then spread to assembly of desktop PCs and motherboards, with the latest stage being notebook computers in the period 2001–06, when notebook PC ODMs moved nearly all of their manufacturing from Taiwan, China, to mainland China. As sales of notebook PCs expanded rapidly, surpassing desktop units in the early 2000s, production in Taiwan, China, soared from 2.3 million units in 1995 to a peak of 14.3 million in 2002. However, after 2002, notebook PC production in Taiwan, China, dropped just as rapidly, even as Taiwanese firms produced a larger share of the world's output, reaching 92 percent in 2008 (see figure 7.4). This migration contributed to the dramatic expansion of two industry clusters for electronics manufacturing, one in the Pearl River Delta near Hong Kong, China, focused on the assembly of desktop PCs, PC main boards, and peripheral products, and the second in the Yangze River Delta near Shanghai, focused on notebook PC assembly. Smaller Taiwanese contract manufacturers and component suppliers were not able to make this move, leading to a dramatic consolidation among firms specializing in notebook PC production: the number of Taiwanese notebook PC producers fell from 45 in 1993 to only 21 in 2006, with market share shifting dramatically in favor of the largest five producers (Kawakami forthcoming).

The coevolution of lead firms, suppliers, and platform leaders outlined here reveals a recursive dynamic of outsourcing, upgrading, and further outsourcing; the enabling role of open standards and modular product architecture in the PC sector; the intense competition and rapid product life cycles that drove lead firms to seek to spread risk and lower costs through outsourcing; and the entrepreneurial

Figure 7.4 Taiwan, China's Production of Desktop and Notebook PCs, 1986–2006

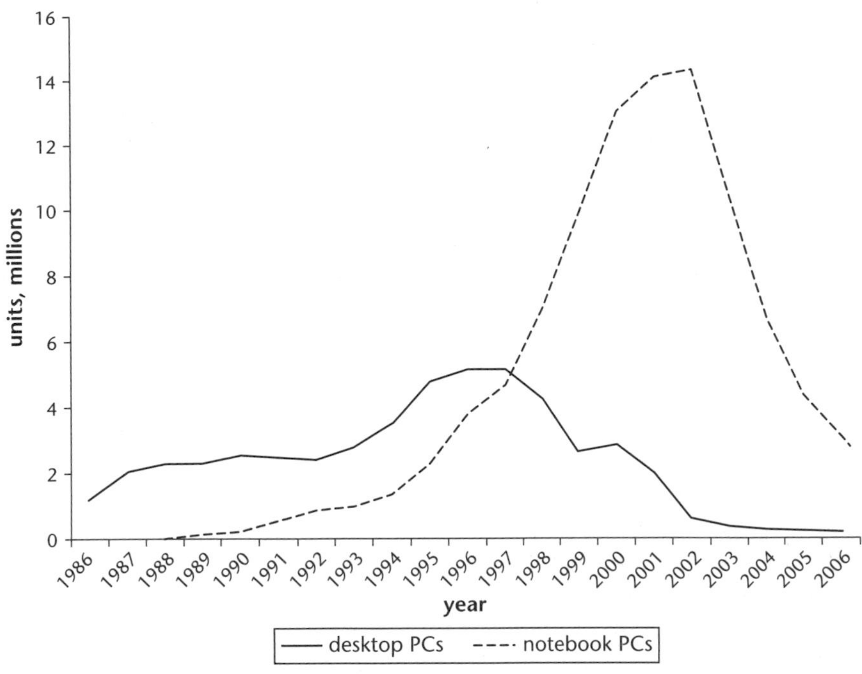

Source: Kawakami (forthcoming) from the Internet Information Search System, Department of Statistics, Ministry of Economic Affairs, China.
Note: PCs = personal computers.

agility displayed by Taiwanese firms to recognize and quickly seize new opportunities to specialize in narrow segments of the value chain.[14]

Upgrading: Pluses and Minuses for Developing-Country Firms

The advantages of incumbent lead firms with deep technological expertise, in terms of value extraction in GVCs, as well as the limitations for firms based in developing countries, are illustrated by the well-known case of Apple Computer Inc. Linden, Kraemer, and Dedrick (2007) estimate that only $4 of the $299 retail price of an Apple 30 gigabyte video iPod MP3 player is captured in China, where they are assembled and tested by the Taiwan-based ODM contract manufacturer Inventec. The share captured by domestic Chinese companies is even less; probably limited to packaging and local services. This is, in part, because iPods are assembled from components made mostly in other countries, such as the United States, Japan, and Korea. But more important, it is because Apple—which conducts high-level design work and software development in-house and orchestrates the product's development, production, marketing, and distribution—is estimated to capture $80 of the sale price. This study also estimates that $83 is captured in the United States by Apple's technology suppliers and by retailers. Clearly, assigning the $183 per unit wholesale price of exported iPods (as would be reported in trade statistics) to the Chinese economy misrepresents where value is created in the global economy. Similarly, a "teardown analysis" of the recently released iPad tablet computer by the consulting firm iSuppli estimated Apple's gross margin for the product (the $499 sale price less the component costs) to be $270, or 54 percent (Hesseldahl 2010). Assembly costs for the iPad may be higher than for the iPod, but it can still be assumed that very little of the product's value is captured in China, and even less by mainland Chinese companies.

For developing-country lead firms involved in product innovation, the solution in technologically intensive product areas like electronics is to purchase highly modular design solutions from platform leaders. This allows quick market entry, but can also lead to several traps. First, as already mentioned and to be covered in more depth later, there are the high costs associated with acquiring highly functional components and subsystems, as well as the royalties that must be paid, directly or indirectly, to the platform leaders and other standard setters in the industry. Second, there is the "modularity trap," as identified by Chesbrough and Kusunoki (2001), where the highly integrated off-the-shelf components and subsystems provided by platform leaders reduce product distinctiveness. By and large, the world's major contract manufacturers have been trapped in low value-added segments of the electronics GVC: manufacturing and iterative, detailed design. In the PC industry, most of the industry's profits have been captured by branded lead firms such as Dell and Hewlett-Packard, and especially by platform leaders in software operating systems (Microsoft) and CPU chipsets (Intel).

Intel's Platform Strategy for Taiwan, China's ODMs

In consumer electronics products like the iPod or video game consoles, lead firms can control product architecture and extract the lion's share of profits from GVCs; but in other industries, platform leaders dominate. For example, in her analysis of major players in the notebook PC value chain, Kawakami (forthcoming) shows the highest profit (more than 50 percent, measured by the ratio of gross margin to net sales) made by Intel—the platform leader that supplies most of the central processing chipsets to the notebook PC industry—while profits are much lower at Dell, one of the most important lead firms in the PC industry (less than 20 percent), and extremely low (below 5 percent after 2001 and dropping) at the Taiwan-based contract manufacturer Quanta, which assembles the largest share of Dell-branded notebook PCs in China (see figure 7.5). This measure of profitability, which in fact does *not* take Intel's huge capital investments into account, clearly shows the dominance of Intel in terms of value capture, the relatively modest performance of Dell, as well as the declining profitability of Quanta, despite its apparent success in capturing a growing share of global notebook PC design and production.

Such disparities have led to a series of conflicts between Intel and branded-PC lead firms over the expropriation of value-added. In the early 1990s, lead firms, especially the Japanese firms Toshiba and NEC that dominated the notebook PC market at the time, enjoyed high profits. The capability of Japanese lead firms to develop Intel CPU-inclusive chips sets in-house and to verify those developed by

Figure 7.5 Value Capture in Notebook PC GVC in Three Competitors

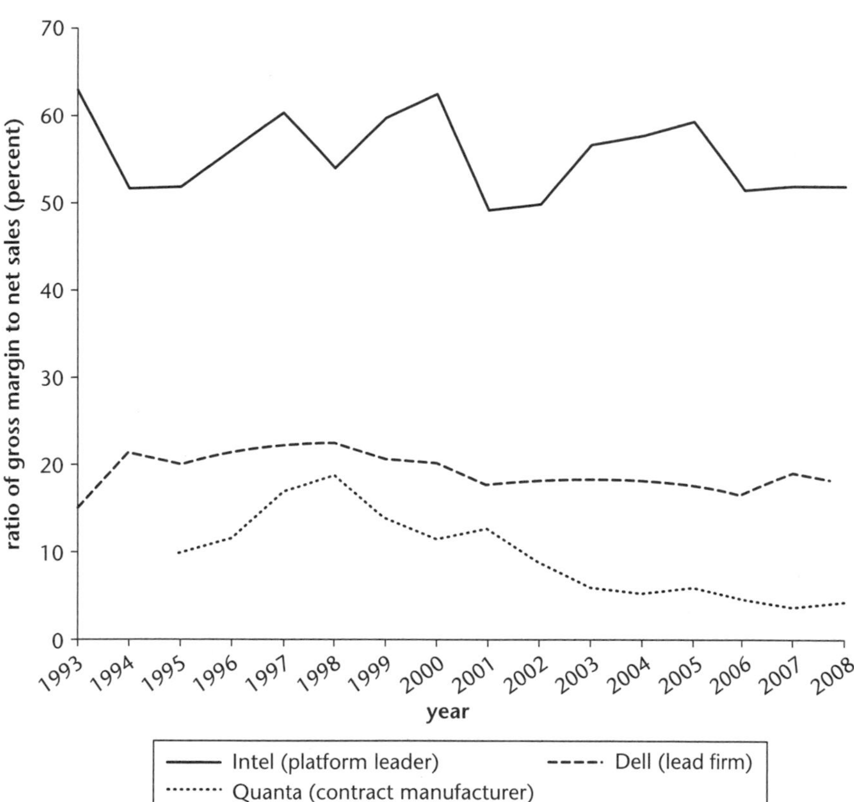

Source: Kawakami (forthcoming), based on annual reports.

third-party vendors, constituted a core competitive advantage. However, in 1997, Intel, following a strategy it had employed to dominate the desktop PC industry (Gawer and Cusumano 2002; Tatsumoto, Ogawa, and Fujimoto 2010), began to offer highly integrated chipsets and launched "mobile modules" that integrated CPUs and chipsets for the notebook PC industry as well.[15] This provided a turn-key solution (integrated platform) for latecomer firms. Intel also exercised its market power by controlling the flow of information. The company stopped disclosing technological information necessary for developing chipsets, and kept the internal structure of its products as a proprietary black box. By doing so, Intel successfully negated the previously scarce and valuable engineering know-how of lead PC firms (Ogawa 2007). In addition, the emergence of the 3D-CAD system for developing molds and the launch of thermal modules that could deal with the problem of heat dissipation in small notebook PC enclosures negated the valuable know-how about product miniaturization and heat treatment that Japanese lead firms had accumulated earlier.

Lead firms were affected by Intel's platform strategy in different ways. American PC firms—Dell, Gateway, and Compaq—embraced the new platforms as a way to increase their market share in notebook PCs. Exploiting the increased modularity of the product, these firms stepped up their use of Taiwanese ODMs to reduce costs and speed product life cycles. The market for notebook computers expanded rapidly as a flood of relatively inexpensive machines hit the market. By contrast, Japanese firms, which had based high profitability on superior R&D and production capabilities, resisted the commoditization of the product. Toshiba, the world's leading notebook PC company in 1997, faced not only a sharp decrease in market share, but also mounting losses from its notebook PC unit. NEC, the world's second-largest notebook PC brand firm at the time, and other Japanese firms suffered similar fates. This led to a rapid increase in orders from Japanese lead firms to Taiwanese ODMs, but only for their lower-cost models (see Sturgeon 2007). As time wore on, high-cost notebook PCs made in-house by Japanese lead firms were increasingly restricted to the Japanese market. In this way, lead firms across the notebook PC industry started to specialize in concept creation, brand marketing, and the management of suppliers and to contract out mass production, product development, logistics, and after-service to Taiwanese firms.

In 2003, Intel again used its power as a platform leader to "encapsulate" another bundle of hard-to-integrate PC functions. This time their "Centrino" chipset added key power management features that made it suitable for mobile applications. Taiwanese ODMs provided the design expertise needed to generate a flow of new products based on the chipset, and soon dominated world production of notebook PCs.

To summarize, Intel has repeatedly used its platform leadership position in the PC GVC to capture a larger portion of the industry's profits. The emergence of readymade technological solutions with well-defined external interfaces encapsulated the most difficult electrical engineering problems, and the rewards for solving them, within Intel, and created a swarm of low-cost competitors to Japanese producers. Intel's platform strategies have repeatedly devalued the core competencies of lead firms in the notebook PC industry, especially Japanese lead firms, which have developed and relied on in-house system integration competencies more than U.S. firms have. A secondary effect, intended or not, was to create a larger role for Taiwanese ODMs in the industry, along with an ongoing set of opportunities for them to expand their competencies. Less system-level design work was required to create notebook PCs overall, but Taiwanese ODMs have taken on many new tasks, gained many new competencies, and grown rapidly—if not profitably.

China: Modularity and Competitive Outcomes in the Mobile Phone Handset Industry

Despite China's attempts to nurture a group of former state-owned enterprises as national champions (or a "national team": cf. Nolan 2001; Sutherland 2003),[16] and recent announcements of a renewed focus on government purchases of "indigenous technology," little progress has been made. Rather, China's development in technologically intensive sectors such as electronics has been driven by close engagement in GVCs, with its export sector dominated by foreign financial, technological, and organizational resources. The success of this approach is underscored by the fact that nearly two-thirds of China's manufactured exports come from foreign-invested firms.[17] But what does this reliance on outside capabilities mean for development? On one hand, it has resulted in an unprecedented acceleration of industrialization. However, as was the case with Taiwan, China, once engaged, it can be difficult to move beyond low-value niches and to gain the autonomy and profits that can come with lead firm or platform leader status in GVCs. Song (2007) has shown how profits in China's electronics industries have become very thin, despite massive increases in labor productivity, in what he calls a "Chinese-style modularity trap."[18]

Imai and Shiu (forthcoming) provide an example of this from the domestic Chinese mobile phone handset industry. From 1999 to 2003, the market share of local firms soared from 5 to 55 percent, but subsequently—and very suddenly—local handset firms lost this ground to multinational brands, notably Motorola and Nokia, as consumers began to expect products with color LCDs and increased functionality, such as MP3 music playback and cameras with both still and video capabilities. Local handset design houses did not have the competencies needed to bundle these new technologies in larger, more integrated design platforms, reopening the window for the multinational brands, whose deep internal design and system integration capabilities, built up over many decades, allowed them to rapidly retake market share.

This case provides an example of how the three GVC governance variables of complexity, codifiability, and supplier competence can contribute to explanations of competitive outcomes (Gereffi, Humphrey, and Sturgeon 2005). The introduction of new features, such as color screens, cameras, and audio playback, raised the technological requirements for mobile phone design and drove rebundling in the value chain for the low-cost mobile phones popular in China. Technological change shifted the location of key pinch points in the value chain, which, in short order, created and eliminated opportunity for different firms. On the one hand, rising competency requirements favored multinational firms, with their deep in-house design competence, but also the Taiwan-based IC design house MediaTek, which provided highly integrated chipsets that encapsulated much of the new functionality demanded by Chinese consumers. Losers were local handset firms and the independent design houses they relied on for system design.

As table 7.6 shows, China has suddenly become the world's largest producer, exporter, and consumer of mobile phone handsets. In 1998, a negligible 2.2 million

Table 7.6 China's Mobile Phone Handset Production, Export, and Consumption, 1998 and 2005

Indicator	1998	2005	CAGR (percent)
Production			
World handset production (millions of units)	174	816	25
China handset production (millions of units)	4	304	86
China share of world production (percent)	2.3	37.2	
Exports			
China mobile phone exports (millions of units)	2	228	94
Export share of production (percent)	55.0	75.2	
Consumption			
China mobile phone subscriptions (millions of units)	25	400	49
China handset sales[a] (millions of units)	3	88	59
China handset imports (millions of units)	2	13	35
Import share of sales (percent)	47.1	14.5	

Source: Imai and Shiu 2007.
Note: CAGR = compound annual growth rate.
a. Sales figures for 2003 and 2004 were 109 million and 100 million, respectively. While annual sales may have leveled off or even declined since the 2003 peak, because of saturation in urban markets, the figures for handset sales in domestic consumption probably underestimate the real total due to undercounted sales of illegal and quasi-legal handsets.

handsets were assembled in China, just over 2 percent of world output. By 2005, production surged to at least[19] 300 million units, more than 37 percent of world output. This increase in production reflected three trends: (1) a worldwide boom in mobile phone sales, (2) the rise of China as a primary location for mobile phone handset production, and (3) the emergence of China as the largest single national market for mobile phones. From 1998 to 2005, worldwide mobile phone sales increased 25 percent per year, from 174 million to 816 million units. As China's share of world production increased, the share of handsets produced for export increased from 55 percent to more than 75 percent. But the domestic Chinese market was also booming. According the Chinese Ministry of Information Industry, the number of mobile phone subscribers in China soared from about 25 million in 1998 to about 400 million in 2005. As handset sales surpassed 100 million units in 2003 and 2004, increased domestic production, along with import restrictions, caused imported handsets to fall as a share of sales.

Handset sales in China's domestic market rose from 3.4 million units in 1998 to an astonishing 109 million units in 2003. The most successful multinational brands in China—market leaders Nokia (Finland), Motorola (United States), and Samsung (Korea)—account for 95 percent of exports and quickly came to dominate domestic sales as well. Local Chinese brands held just a 5 percent market share in 1999, while together Nokia and Motorola controlled 70 percent of the market. As the domestic market took off, however, dozens of local handset brands appeared and were able to capture 55 percent of the market by 2003.

As Imai and Shiu (forthcoming; 2007) argue, the success of local firms can be explained by a combination of market opportunity and government policy. Multinational handset producers could not simply divert a share of export production to the local market. The feature-rich phones produced for export were too expensive for Chinese consumers, and those produced for export to the United States are incompatible with China's dominant mobile phone standard (GSM) in any case. While even the older GSM phone models sold by multinational firms in China were too expensive for most of the Chinese market, the more fundamental problem for multinational firms was the lack of variety in their lower end product lines. High costs and low product variety created a market opportunity for local cell phone handset companies, and local brands did well by selling simpler, less-expensive handsets with a wide variety of exterior designs and other technologically superficial features.

On the policy side, in 1999 the Chinese government, through its Ministry of Information Industry, placed limits on imports by creating a licensing system for the production and marketing of mobile phone handsets. The dominant multinational firms were able to secure licenses through their joint ventures with China's major state-owned telecommunications operating companies, Eastcom and Capital, but these came with strict minimum export ratios and high local content requirements. The dozens of small local companies that were granted licenses did not face these requirements, but did face a different challenge, a lack of mobile phone design expertise.

Technical barriers in fast-moving and technologically complex products like mobile phones are high, but not as high as they might be, were there not so many options for purchasing mobile phone handset technology. While system-level mobile phone design requires a high level of competence, there are a variety of market solutions in the industry, from semiconductor "chipsets" that encapsulate key features of the phone to fully designed (ODM) phones. Price pressure and the need for high product variety favor system-level designs that add features and appealing exterior design to standard chipsets that perform the basic functions of the phone, such as converting voice to digital signals and back again and sending and receiving signals. This demand for system-level design and integration created an opportunity for a new cadre of Chinese independent design houses (IDH).

The largest Chinese IDH is Techfaith, a Shanghai-based company founded in 2002 by Motorola China's former sales manager; 11 of 13 executive directors were previously employed by Motorola China. Other IDHs, such as CEWC, SIM, Longcheer, and Ginwave, were formed by engineers from state-owned ZTE, Konka, and Cellon, a Silicon Valley IDH. Estimates vary, but Imai and Shiu (2007) estimate that up to 50 percent of the handsets sold by local producers are designed by local IDHs. Customers of the top-five Chinese IDH firms shipped 31 million phones in 2005, a year when total reported handset sales were 88 million.

The largest local Chinese handset brands—Bird, Amoi, Lenovo, TCL, and Konka (together accounting for about 20 percent of the market in 2005)—have in-house design groups, but the dozens of other smaller players use IDHs exclusively. The advantage of IDHs is that they can pool design elements across horizontal segments. The IDH SIM, in its 2005 annual report, claimed that it sold 152 models based on 12 main boards (Imai and Shiu 2007, 19). IDHs are also suppliers, either directly or indirectly, to "guerrilla" handset makers (illegal or quasi-legal handset companies) that purchase complete motherboards to produce simple imitations of models sold by well-known brands. By 2005, the market share of legal local brands had fallen to 40 percent (Imai and Shiu 2007, 6) and the Chinese IDHs were in deep trouble. Techfaith, for example, has retreated from contract design services and now survives mainly on contract assembly services. Guerrilla handset makers are the only domestic firms in the sector that have continued to thrive after 2005. Concentrated in Shenzhen and Guangdong, they accounted for approximately one-fourth of the total production of handsets in China in 2009. They are highly dependent on MediaTek chipset platforms that encompass communication and multimedia functions and survive on extremely thin profit margins (Kawakami, forthcoming).

The GVC governance dynamics of the Chinese mobile phone handset case are quite clear: competitive outcomes in the Chinese industry shifted as the GVC governance variable of complexity went up (see Gereffi, Humphrey, and Sturgeon [2005] for a discussion of key GVC governance variables, complexity, codifiability, and supplier competence). Rising complexity altered where the codified links in the chain had to be positioned. Local firms were forced to bundle new technologies in larger, more integrated platforms, which raised the competence level required to deliver handset design services. This was something that local design houses could not do, and MediaTek stepped into the breach with their own integrated platform. The competitive problem this posed for local handset makers was that the larger, more integrated platforms could not be as easily customized to create the differentiation on which the local handset firms based their competitive positioning. The local Chinese handset industry has been caught in a classic modularity trap.

Overcoming the Limits to Industrial Upgrading in Electronics GVCs

Such examples as the Chinese mobile phone handset industry reveal the opportunities, but also the challenges and limits to industrial upgrading in electronics GVCs. On the other hand, there are a growing number of important exceptions that suggest that new models of learning through close engagement in GVCs could be emerging, with broader lessons for developing countries (see Yeung 2009). As mentioned at the start, there are four identifiable models that electronics companies from the developing world are using to escape these limitations: (1) global expansion through acquisition of declining brands (emerging multinationals), (2) separation of branded product divisions from contract manufacturing (ODM spinoff), (3) successful mixing of contract manufacturing and branded products (platform brands) for contractors with customers not in the electronics hardware business, and (4) the founding of factoryless product firms that rely on GVCs for a range of inputs, including production (emerging GVC leaders). The analysis in this final section is derived from the authors' ongoing research and secondary sources covering very recent events and nascent trends. As such, it is more speculative and forward-looking and less certain.

Emerging Multinationals: An Updated, Global National Champion Model?

The case of Lenovo, a partially state-owned Chinese PC company, shows one way in which lead firms from developing countries have been able to overcome traditional barriers to upgrading their positions in GVCs.[20] In the mid-1990s Lenovo, benefiting from a protected market, emerged as the largest domestic producer of

PCs in China. As import restrictions were lifted, however, Lenovo struggled to remain competitive, as have most developing-country national champions in technology-intensive sectors. After the technology bubble burst in 2001, persistent low profitability in the global PC industry, for the reasons described earlier, led some of the largest multinational producers to exit the industry, precipitating a wave of acquisitions, most notably Lenovo's purchase of IBM's huge PC division in 2004.

The IBM purchase gave Lenovo a new headquarters in the United States with a large R&D center in North Carolina; an advanced notebook computer development facility in Japan; three final assembly plants in China and one in India; regional distribution facilities in the Netherlands, Dubai, Florida, Australia, and India; and an important corporate planning, finance, and business process development group in Singapore. The deal also came with a dense set of ongoing supply relationships, mainly with Korean, Taiwanese, and American component producers and contract manufacturers, the largest with global operations, to provide main boards, microprocessors, memory, disk drives, monitors, LCD screens, keyboards, and contract manufacturing services.[21] Lenovo's new American CEO, based in Singapore, was a former Dell Computer executive. He led a management team with top executives from China, the United States, Europe, and India. While it would be wrong to portray Lenovo as something other than a China-based company, the structure, geography, ownership, leadership, supply base, and sources of innovation at the new Lenovo were vastly different from the national champions that emerged in Japan and later in Korea.[22]

Lenovo can be seen as an example of a small but dynamic set of emerging multinationals (Bonaglia, Goldstein, and Mathews 2007), also called "dragon multinationals" by Mathews (2002) in the context of Chinese East Asia. Additional examples of emerging multinationals include other Chinese firms such as Huawei (communications infrastructure equipment) and Haier (home appliances and consumer electronics), as well as firms from countries as diverse as Mexico (Mabe, home appliances) and Turkey (Arçelik, home appliances). As Bonaglia, Goldstein, and Mathews (2007) put it, "These new [multinational enterprises] did not delay their internationalization until they were large, as did most of their predecessors, and often become global as a result of direct firm-to-firm contracting. Many *grow large as they internationalize;* conversely, *they internationalize in order to grow large*" (p. 3, emphasis in the original). These companies have sometimes become global by "rolling up" (purchasing) smaller regional producers with well-known but declining brands using funds generated not so much by selling products or services in their home markets but by acting as suppliers to existing multinationals, tapping into international capital markets, and producing and selling globally.

What remains to be seen is whether these examples are exceptions that prove the rule or the vanguard of a new wave of multinationals with roots in the developed world. It is notable that all of the emerging multinationals mentioned here, with the exception of Huawei and perhaps Lenovo, work in relatively mature product areas. It also remains to be seen whether companies from the developing world can prosper in the lead firm position without building up deep internal expertise in market and product definition organically or whether such expertise will continue to develop once it has been captured through acquisition.

ODM Spinoffs: Settling for Scraps or Setting the Agenda?

During the recent economic crisis, the authors identified a set of significant successes for a set of Taiwan, China–based ODM spinoffs, branded factoryless lead firms that have become legally independent from their former ODM contract manufacturing arms. Acer pioneered this model when it separated its branded PC business from its ODM contract manufacturing (Wistron) and PC peripherals (BenQ) businesses in the early 2000s. By so doing, the company successfully avoided competing with their ODM customers in final markets and put Wistron into position to compete with pure-play (that is, contract manufacturing only) ODMs such as Quanta and Compal, which had been winning huge contracts at the expense of Acer. In order to create viable conditions for the contract manufacturing business, spun-off lead firms typically make aggressive moves to use nonaffiliated ODMs for contract manufacturing services. For example, today Acer uses Quanta and Compal for the bulk of its contract manufacturing services; Wistron now ranks a distant number three. ASUSTeK, founded by former employees of Acer in 1990, followed suit when it spun off Pegatron in 2008.

One case is the successful launch of "netbook" computers, the ultra-low-cost portable PCs, by Taiwanese branded firms. ASUSTeK first developed the idea for simple-to-use and ultra-low-cost portable PCs in 2006 and launched its first product, the "EeePC" netbook computer, in 2007 (Shih et al. 2008). The quick success of the EeePC set new expectations for PC consumers regarding PC prices and disrupted Intel's product roadmap, as well as those of competitors in the notebook PC market. Intel had promoted the development of low-price PCs for educational purposes in developing countries, but it had not envisioned or encouraged the netbook product space in *developed* countries. Intel responded by quickly adapting a newer processor, the Atom, developed primarily for embedded products and mobile devices, for use in netbook computers and other low-cost mobile electronics. Traditional branded PC lead firms like Dell and HP were not developing ultra–low-cost machines, not least because price erosion was a perennial concern. In response to the success of EeePC, these firms decided to enter the netbook market as well. Among them, Acer is by far the most successful follower; and a sharp increase in netbook shipments helped them surpass Dell to become the world's second-largest-selling PC brand by the third quarter of 2009.

Even while moving away from formerly affiliated contract manufacturers, ODM spinoffs are well positioned to leverage ODMs' deep expertise in product definition and design. Proximity, both spatial and cultural, allows them to effectively collaborate with ODMs. For example, Acer's rising competitiveness may stem from its ability to bargain with ODMs over terms of trade and to leverage their extensive knowledge of current business conditions, especially component availability and costs. Acer has good intelligence about the current business conditions and cost structures of individual ODM firms, and ODMs have difficulty hiding profits from Acer, in part because of the dense labor market in Taiwan, China's technology sector (for example, several ex-employees of Quanta and Compal now hold key positions at Acer). Proximity to ODMs and easy access to the flow of information within Taiwan, China's electronics cluster may be enough to sustain and even expand Acer's competitive advantage in the PC industry.

During the economic crisis of 2008–09, the arrival of new platform solutions for low-cost mobile devices—Intel's Atom chipset and Google's Android operating system discussed below—has created new opportunities for ODM spinoffs to identify and fill underserved market niches, especially for low- to mid-range products that established multinationals previously deemed unattractive. In a dynamic similar to that in the China mobile phone handset case—where local firms used MediaTek platforms to fill underserved low-cost and rural mobile phone handset market niches in China—Taiwan-based ODM spinoffs are having success in low-end markets in both developed and developing countries. But instead of being easily pushed aside when consumers demand more sophisticated products, they appear to have the technological capabilities, and the close working relationships with ODMs, to move up-market into more lucrative segments for existing "mainstream" products.

The case of low-cost PCs recently developed by local companies from mainland China provides a useful contrast. Inspired by the success of MediaTek, an IC design house based in Taiwan, China, called Via Technologies, entered the netbook market with their own platform and by marketing their own low-cost PC chipset platform to a set of small "guerrilla" PC makers in China. As with the China mobile phone handset case discussed previously, the problem for these firms is an inability to respond when consumers begin to ask for more sophisticated products. The guerrilla PC makers cannot add new features fast enough; preliminary analysis suggests that consumers in China are moving to products from HP, Acer, and Lenovo when they upgrade.

Platform Brands: Leveraging Modularity to Define New (Low-End) Product Categories

As shown earlier, competing with customers has proven to be a poor strategy for ODM contract manufacturers. Most ODMs have either given up their brand aspirations or legally separated their branded product business from their contract manufacturing business. A few, however, have been successful in selling branded products, based on highly integrated platforms, in markets that are of little interest to their main contract manufacturing customers. One such company is ASUSTeK, which has long had a successful business selling branded PC motherboards to "value-added resellers" that assemble custom desktop PCs for individual end users and small companies, an especially popular sales channel in Europe. Overall, this sales channel has remained small and is of little interest to dominant PC brands.

A more current example is HTC, a Taiwan, China–based mobile phone handset ODM founded in 1997. At first, HTC developed handsets branded with the logos of carriers such as Orange, 02, T-Mobile, Vodafone, Cingular, Verizon, Sprint, and NTT DoCoMo (company Web site). More recently, HTC won the ODM contract for the G1 Smartphone, based on Google's Android software operating system. Shortly after the G1 hit the market, HTC began selling its own Android-based phone using the HTC brand. In this case, mixing ODM contract manufacturing with the selling of branded products has not created a conflict because Google is not interested in generating profits from selling phones under its own brand. In fact, the opposite is true. The G1 was launched with the intention of gaining platform leadership in smartphones and other Internet-enabled portable electronic devices. Even Android licensing is of little interest to Google as a revenue-generating business. Their main goal is to provide more mobile users with easy access to the Internet, where Google's search engine and other online Google services expose them to Web advertising, Google's main source of revenue. In the context of Google's business model, HTC branded phones are welcome. If Android takes hold in mobile electronics, opportunities for HTC and other firms with the design capabilities to become platform brands could expand rapidly.

Emerging GVC Leaders: Moving into the Driver's Seat?

Recently, a few firms from developing countries have been able to engage in pure systems integration, assembling system elements purchased through the global supply base. An example from the automobile sector is Chery, a small state-controlled Chinese automobile company based in Wuhu, some 200 kilometers west of Shanghai. The company has been able to develop and market a line of

Chery-badged vehicles within a remarkably short time by making use of the supply base, both within China and in the West, for a full range of inputs, from parts to process technology to design expertise.[23] These sourcing arrangements, which have only recently become readily available for fledgling companies like Chery to piece together, show that Chery is nothing like a typical car company, and that it is far removed from the most recent entrants to the mass market for cars, the vertically integrated and horizontally diversified national champions from Korea: Hyundai, Kia, and Daewoo.

Similar cases from the electronics industry can be found in the area of portable global positioning (GPS) and portable navigation devices (PNDs). Until the early 2000s, the mobile navigation market was dominated by Japanese manufacturers such as Pioneer, Panasonic, and Clarion. These firms supplied automakers with very sophisticated systems with rich functions. Because U.S. government policy limited the accuracy of global positioning system (GPS) signals prior to 2000, the systems developed by Japanese electronics firms relied on comparisons of measured distance and direction traveled to on-board map databases. While some of these systems were sold as aftermarket products, many were supplied directly to automakers for inclusion as optional in-dash original equipment on new cars. These firms worked closely with automakers to customize products and meet strict quality standards. Their products had integral system architectures based on proprietary technologies developed in-house and were extremely expensive, as much as one-tenth of a car's sale price.

In the early 2000s, the availability of more accurate GPS signals allowed a set of start-up PND makers to enter the market with ultra-low-cost aftermarket products that quickly began to erode the profits and market share of traditional car navigation makers. Among the market share leaders today are Netherlands-based TomTom, U.S.- and Taiwan-based Garmin, and Mitac, based in Taiwan, China. These emerging GVC leaders are able to produce affordable products by making heavy use of Taiwanese ODMs' capabilities in designing and manufacturing portable electronics. In contrast to the integral architecture of in-dash car navigation systems, PNDs have highly modular architecture, which lowers development costs. PNDs initially cost only $500–$1,000, but today TomTom's lowest cost model sells for less than $100. This affordability opened up new markets, such as handheld GPS, and world shipment of PNDs grew from less than 1 million units in 2004 to more than 10 million units in 2006 (Nikkei Electronics 2007). While not all of these companies are fully based in Taiwan, China, they are all making heavy use of Taiwan-centered supply-base capabilities. TomTom outsources to Inventec and Quanta. Garmin was founded in the United States by a Taiwanese immigrant entrepreneur; R&D and production are both located in Taiwan, China. Mitac itself is a Taiwanese IT hardware company.

Companies that jump to the head of GVCs in this way are quite common in the industrialized world. Many are started in Silicon Valley each year, for example. But without the backdrop of a cluster with the capital and intellectual resources of Silicon Valley, emerging GVC leaders may be unable to develop the deep design, system integration, and market-defining expertise that would allow them to compete at the vanguard of fast-moving markets. On the other hand, having close relationships with the world's most dynamic set of EMS and ODM contract manufacturers, it seems inevitable that an increasing number of these firms will meet with success over the long term.

Crisis and Convergence

The recent economic downturn has created a seemingly conducive climate for the implementation of these new models, as shown by the following scenarios. First, traditional Intel customers, the branded PC lead firms, were displeased with the sudden arrival of small, portable netbook computers selling for less than $300, but Intel's quest for business during the crisis may have allowed it to overlook the objections of its traditional customer base. Even without Intel's cooperation, the appearance of excess Celeron stock in distribution channels provided the first opportunity for ASUSTeK's EeePC. Second, the economic downturn introduced a new cost-consciousness among consumers in developed countries that made netbooks and PNDs attractive options. The downturn also heightened the search for new markets, and those with the greatest potential for growth are in developing countries, where netbook computers and PNDs may serve as ideal entry-level machines.

In the past, PC standard platforms were largely used in PC-related products, and ODMs were mostly confined to that market. Very recently, the arrival of highly functional but low-cost platforms like the Intel Atom chipset and Google's Android operating system is driving product convergence in netbooks, smartphones, and PNDs. Intel's Atom chipset, for example, is being used in netbooks, PNDs, embedded systems, and the new Google TV platform. This may be disrupting the status quo and improving the competitive position of ODMs. The introduction of new software-based platforms from companies with no direct prior involvement in the PC industry, such as Google, may be opening up new strategic space for ODMs. By combining new platforms with the capabilities of ODMs, lead firms appear to be able to quickly launch products that cross traditional product boundaries. In this way, convergence is creating a broader market for both ODM contract manufacturing services and new opportunities for platform brands and ODM spinoffs. These trends may finally steer Taiwan, China's electronics industry out of the (albeit very large and expanding) cul-de-sac of PC design and manufacturing and into the larger innovation system of the electronics industry.

Conclusions

This chapter has summarized the evolution of GVCs in the electronics industry and highlighted some recent developments that have come into focus during the 2008–09 economic crisis. It shows the increasingly important role the electronics industry has played in GVC formation since 1988. One enabler of this, the authors argue, is value chain modularity, which allows firms and work groups to collaborate on relatively complex projects from a distance. As companies have learned how to instigate, sustain, and expand these cross-border collaborations, electronics GVCs have expanded rapidly. The result is an industry that is both spatially dispersed and tightly integrated. Three key actors were identified in electronics hardware GVCs: lead firms, contract manufacturers, and platform leaders. Modularity, in the realm of both product architecture and industrial organization, has opened strategic space for all three of these GVC actors. In particular, modularity has allowed the industry's most successful platform leaders to continually stake out and hold key territory in the industry's technological landscape. The strategic moves of platform leaders such as Intel, therefore, can trigger changes across large swaths of the industry.

A key to GVC development, as argued here, is the emergence of deep supplier capabilities, most recently in contract manufacturers based in Taiwan, China; the United States; and Singapore. Consolidation, both organizational and geographical, has cemented the position of these firms as critical actors in electronics GVCs. Since the largest contract manufacturers have established facilities throughout the world and are purchasing huge volumes of electronic components on behalf of their customers, their investment and purchasing decisions influence industry trends in less-developed countries such as Malaysia, the Philippines, Thailand, Vietnam, and Mexico. Clearly, the crisis is causing GVCs in the electronics industry to undergo further consolidation, both organizationally and geographically. It may be that the firms in the Taiwan/China nexus are joining firms based in places like the United States, Japan, and Europe as key players in the global innovation system of the electronics industry—not just the production system.

The experiences of electronics contract manufacturers provide examples of both the limits and opportunities for suppliers in electronics GVCs, and thus serve as important lessons for latecomer firms from developing countries. However, given the integrated nature of the global electronics industry, latecomer firms have to consider global suppliers not only as examples but as potential dominant competitors as well. While the barriers created by recent developers are substantial, there are few zero-sum games in an industry as dynamic as electronics hardware. As this chapter argues, new models for GVC participants may be emerging that will allow latecomer firms to leverage, rather than seek to supplant, the deep capabilities that have built up in the global electronics supply base over the past 20 years.

If we are to draw any lessons from the long history of GVC development discussed, it is a lesson against stasis and for continuous change and opportunity. Assumptions about industry life cycles, where product segments stabilize as the industry matures, do not seem to apply to the electronics industry. At the same time, long exposure to the industry's rapid but volatile growth and the sudden emergence of immense new market opportunities (for example, the PC, the mobile phone, and the Internet) has allowed electronics companies in the developing world to build up extraordinary capabilities. We need to ask not how emerging economies can repeat the experiences of successful recent developers like Taiwan, China, and Singapore, but what roles might be available in electronics GVCs in the future. Newcomers should seek to avoid the pitfalls and limits of GVC engagement and supplier-led upgrading outlined here, certainly; however, in an integrated global industry, this has proven to be exceedingly difficult, even for firms with established roles in the industry and deep expertise in their GVC niche.

Looking forward must instead consider the possibilities of using the same palette of globally distributed capabilities that firms in the industry see, as well as acknowledging the expanding potential for new combinations. The combination of value chain modularity and deep capabilities in multiple locations will continue to create huge opportunities for both suppliers and lead firms in electronics GVCs. Lead firms have options to assemble and reassemble GVC elements in new ways for new markets and products that did not exist even a few years ago. Dynamic change is nothing new in the electronics industry (see Brown and Linden 2009). However, going forward, new industries and value chain combinations will inevitably include more firms—lead firms, contract manufacturers, component suppliers, and even platform leaders—based in newly developed and developing countries. We can anticipate, if nothing else, a spate of new lead firms born in developing countries without the expectation that they will need to move up the contract manufacturing ladder in their efforts to become branded companies. Today, more GVC elements are available than ever before, either for sale or for hire, and it is only a matter of time before one, and then several new, world-beating electronics companies arise from the developing world to dominate some as-yet-unknown product area in the ever-expanding electronics industry. We may look back on the crisis of 2008–09 as an inflection point where firms from the developing world began to lead, rather than follow, the development of the global electronics industry.

Annex: Solectron's Operations at the Height of Global Expansion

Table 7A.1 Solectron's Operations, 2001

Region	Regional headquarters	Manufacturing	Materials management	New product introduction	After-sales service	Technology development
Asia Pacific						
Taipei, Taiwan, China	X					
Singapore		X	X	X		
Johor, Malaysia		X	X	X		
Penang, Malaysia		X	X	X		X
Suzhou, China		X	X			
Penang, Malaysia		X	X			
Wangaratta, Australia		X				
Singapore			X			
Liverpool, Australia				X		
Bangalore, India						X
Tokyo, Japan	X					X
Kanagawa, Japan			X	X	X	
Europe and Middle East						
Reading, U.K.	X					
Bordeaux, France		X	X	X		X
Herrenberg, Germany		X	X	X		
Munich, Germany		X	X	X		X
Östersund, Sweden		X	X	X		X
Istanbul, Turkey		X	X	X	X	
Dublin, Ireland		X	X			
Carrickfergus, Northern Ireland		X	X			
Dunfermline, Scotland		X	X			
East Kilbride, Scotland		X	X			
Timisoara, Romania		X	X			
Longuenesse, France		X		X		X
Pont de Buis, France		X			X	
Cwmcarn, Wales		X				
Norrköping, Sweden			X	X		
Tel Aviv. Israel			X			
Port Glasgow, Scotland				X		

Table 7A.1 *continued*

Region	Regional headquarters	Manufacturing	Materials management	New product introduction	After-sales service	Technology development
Irvine, Scotland						X
Stockholm, Sweden						X
Americas						
Milpitas, CA, U.S.	X	X	X	X	X	
Fremont, CA, U.S.		X	X	X		
Austin, TX, U.S		X	X	X		X
Charlotte, NC, U.S.		X	X	X		X
Columbia, SC, U.S.		X	X	X		
San Jose, CA, U.S.		X	X	X		
Atlanta, GA, U.S.		X	X	X	X	
Westborough, MA, U.S.		X	X	X		
Suwanee, GA , U.S.		X	X	X	X	
Fremont, CA, U.S.		X	X			X
Everett, WA, U.S.		X	X			
Raleigh, NC, U.S.		X		X		
Aguadilla, Puerto Rico, U.S.		X				
Aguada, Puerto Rico, U.S.		X				
Los Angeles, CA, U.S.					X	
Austin, Texas, U.S.					X	
Memphis, TN, U.S.					X	
Louisville, KY, U.S.					X	
San Jose, CA, U.S.						X
Vaughn, Canada					X	
Calgary, Canada		X				
Guadalajara, Mexico		X	X			
Monterrey, Mexico		X	X	X		
São José dos Campos, Brazil		X	X	X	X	
Hortolândia, Brazil		X			X	

Source: Solectron company Web site.

Notes

1. U.S. Bureau of Labor Statistics Current Employment Statistics program, http://www.bls.gov/data/#employment, accessed Janurary 15, 2010.

2. This section draws from Sturgeon and Memedovic (forthcoming).

3. In 1988, only two products likely to be inputs to apparel and footwear products appeared in the top 50, bovine hides and skins (SITC 46) and cotton yarn (SITC 48), comprising 1.9 percent of the value of the top 50 and 0.6 percent of total trade in all manufactured intermediates. By 2006 no apparel inputs ranked among the top 50. The four highest ranked apparel inputs in 2006 were knitted and crocheted fabrics (#94), nonwoven fabrics (#109 out of 1,600), impregnated (waterproof) fabrics (#129), and parts of footwear (#175).

4. For example, in the automotive industry a pattern of regional production has been intensifying since the mid-1980s for both political and technical reasons. This has undoubtedly dampened trade in both final and intermediate goods. Nevertheless, global integration has proceeded at the level of buyer-supplier relationships, especially between automakers and their largest suppliers, which have plants in multiple regions. As a result, local, national, and regional value chains in the automotive industry are "nested" within the global organizational structures and business relationships of the largest firms (Sturgeon, Van Biesebroeck, and Gereffi 2008). These relationships structure not only the flow of physical goods, but also the flow of information, instructions, payments, and investment that characterize GVC development. The stable share of automotive parts in total manufactured intermediate goods trade, despite the establishment of dozens of final assembly plants in developing countries over the period (Sturgeon and Florida, 2004), probably reflects the strong drive for local content in this industry, both for regulatory and operations reasons (see Sturgeon, Van Biesebroeck, and Gereffi [2008] for an extended discussion). Similarly, apparel GVCs are highly dynamic, extensive, and robust, even though inputs (for example, fabric, fiber, and other footwear and apparel parts) make up a small fraction of total intermediate goods trade and none of the top 50. While the capacity to produce inputs and final products in developing countries has been growing strongly, orders are highly specific in terms of fabric and other accessories such as buttons and zippers. Design features are most often dictated by global buyers and change constantly as fashions and seasons vary, and deliveries are very timely, coordinated with the needs of retailers. In some cases, store pricing and barcode labels are attached to garments in the factory prior to direct delivery to retail stores. This type of explicit coordination is an important driver of industrial upgrading in developing countries, as suppliers expand their capabilities to meet the demands of global buyers, and is an important determinant for where value is captured in the industry: largely by the brand-carrying firms and large retailers based in industrialized countries.

5. While this risk-taking is a source of lead firms' advantage over suppliers, lead firms often seek to pass on as much financial exposure to suppliers as possible. One such mechanism is "vendor managed inventory," where suppliers own the parts until the moment they pass onto the factory floor.

6. Markets associated with specific industrial settings are sometimes referred to as "vertical markets," including banking, legal and accounting services, airline security, shipping, and so on.

7. Exceptions include Giant Bicycles, which began as a supplier of "private label" bicycles to U.S. retailers like Montgomery Ward and eventually developed its own line of high-quality branded products, and to some extent Acer, which recently surpassed Dell as the number 2 PC brand in the world after Hewlett-Packard, the first brand not based in the United States or Japan to achieve this high market share (Vance 2009). Full success with this supplier-driven upgrading model, however, has been elusive (Sturgeon and Lester 2004).

8. This section draws from Sturgeon, Humphrey, and Gereffi (forthcoming).

9. The opportunity for electronic component distribution in Singapore and Malaysia stemmed from the lack of an adequate conduit to connect local chip assembly and test operations with the growing subassembly and product-level manufacturing that foreign firms were doing in the region. Offshore affiliates of both semiconductor and product-level firms had increased their Asian operations, and Uraco's new distribution arm helped to connect the dots.

10. At Celestica, for example, 40 percent of global capacity expansion was "organic" in nature.

11. This section draws from Sturgeon and Dussel-Peters (2006).

12. Increases in product variety vary by firm, but in general it has increased by several orders of magnitude, that is, from tens to thousands. As a result, the number of components in use have increased even more dramatically.

13. This section draws on Sturgeon and Lee (2005) and Kawakami (forthcoming).

14. Another important factor that has not been discussed here is the role of Japanese technology partners, which provided critical technologies and components, such as disk drives, that came as "black boxes" or with licensing restrictions that inhibited Taiwanese firms from building up fully independent technological capabilities. Restrictive licensing agreements have continued to be important, for example in Taiwan, China's flat-panel display industry (see Akinwande, Fuller, and Sudini 2005).

15. The initial product offering coupled Pentium CPUs with second-level cache memory on a single circuit board module.

16. This section is drawn from Imai and Shui (2007 and forthcoming).

17. Four Asian economies—Japan; Korea; Taiwan, China; and Hong Kong, China— account for 70 percent of foreign direct investment in China (Hamilton and Gereffi 2009, 145). We should not forget that many mainland Chinese firms are small and localized. They produce a portfolio of highly commodified goods and services and engage in intense price competition with other local firms (Steinfeld 2004).

18. Linden, Kraemer, and Dedrick (2007) estimate that China captures only a few dollars of the $300 retail price of every Apple video iPod exported to the United States.

19. Imai and Shiu (2007, 5) note that this number likely undercounts production in 2005. A significant number of handsets in China are produced illegally, which could be a contributing factor.

20. This section draws from Whittaker et al. (forthcoming).

21. The IBM PC Division was in many ways the vanguard of "de-verticalization" at IBM, and the focus on design and marketing and select critical technologies and capabilities (e.g., integrated mouse pointer technology and notebook design in its Japanese "Thinkpad" design facility) is a prime example of what leading U.S. "manufacturing" firms had become during the 1990s through the process of coevolution with their global (mostly Asian) supply base.

22. In 2007 Lenovo had 27,000 employees worldwide: 18,400 in China; 2,780 in the United States; 2,040 in Europe, the Middle East, and Africa; and 3,800 elsewhere. In terms of ownership, 45 percent of the company's shares were publicly traded; 6 percent were held by IBM, 7 percent by investment banks, and 42 percent by its parent company Legend Holdings. The Chinese Academy of Sciences maintained 27 percent ownership of Lenovo through its 65 percent share of Legend Holdings (Ling 2006).

23. For styling and engineering, Chery works with Italdesign, Pininfarina, and Torino in Italy. Additional engineering and development work is outsourced to Lotus Engineering and MIRA in the United Kingdom and to Porsche Engineering in Germany and Austria. It works with AVL in Austria on gasoline and diesel engines, and with Ricardo in the United Kingdom on hybrid powertrains. Heuliez in France supplies a retractable hardtop for the Chery A3 coupe cabriolet, a car designed by Pininfarina. For critical parts and subsystems, Chery sources from global suppliers such as Bosch, ZF, Johnson Controls, Luk, Valeo, TRW, and Siemens VDO (Whittaker et al. forthcoming).

References

Akinwande, Akintunde, Douglas Fuller, and Charles Sodini. 2005. "Leading, Following or Cooked Goose: Explaining Innovation Successes and Failures in Taiwan's Electronics Industry." In *Global Taiwan: Building Competitive Strengths in a New International Economy.* ed. Suzanne Berger and Richard Lester, chapter 3. Armonk, NY: ME Sharpe.

Balconi, Margherita. 2002. "Tacitness, Codification of Technological Knowledge and the Organisation of Industry." *Research Policy* 31: 357–79.

Baldwin, Carliss, and Kimberly Clark. 2000. *Design Rules; Unleashing the Power of Modularity*. Cambridge, MA: MIT Press.

Barnard, Bruce. 2009. "Container Carrier Losses Reach $11 Billion." *The Journal of Commerce Online* Dec. 22, 2009. Accessed at http://www.joc.com/maritime/container-carrier-losses-reach-11-billion on January 15, 2010.

Bonaglia, Frederico, Andrea Goldstein, and John Mathews. 2007. "Accelerated Internationalization by Emerging Multinationals: The Case of the White Goods Sector." *Journal of World Business* 42: 369–83.

Borrus, M., D. Ernst, and S. Haggard, eds. 2000. *International Production Networks in Asia*, London and New York: Routledge.

Brown, Clair, and Greg Linden. 2009. *Chips and Change: How Crisis Reshapes the Semiconductor Industry*. Cambridge, MA: MIT Press.

Brülhart, Marius. 2008. "An Account of Inter-industry Trade, 1962–2006." Research Paper Series in Globalisation, Productivity, and Technology, 2008/08, Leverhulme Centre for Research on Globalisation and Economic Policy, University of Nottingham, UK.

Business Times On-line. 1995. "Precision Engineering Group Uraco Plans Expansion in Jahor." July 14, p. 3. http://www.businesstimes.com.sg.

———. 1996a. "Uraco Aims to Boost Revenue to US$400m." April 22. http://www.businesstimes.com.sg.

———. 1996b. "Uraco Tops Actives with 16.7m Shares Traded." December 12. http://www.businesstimes.com.sg.

———. 1997. "Uraco Managing Director Quits; 3 Executives Replace Him." January 23. http://www.businesstimes.com.sg.

CADELEC. 2010. "Jaliso High Tech Industry: Suppliers Development for the Jalisco Electronics Industry." Slide presentation. *Cadena Productiva de la Electrónica, A. C.* March. cedelec@cadelec.com.mx.

Chesbrough, Henry, and Kenichi Kusunoki. 2001. "The Modularity Trap: Innovation, Technology Phase Shifts, and the Resulting Limits of Virtual Organizations." In *Managing Industrial Knowledge*, ed. L. Nonaka and D. Teece, 202–30. London: Sage Press.

Dean, J. M., K. C. Fung, and Z. Wang. 2007. "Measuring the Vertical Specialization in Chinese Trade." U.S. International Trade Commission, Office of Economics Working Paper, No. 2007-01-A.

Dedrick, Jason, and Kenneth Kraemer. 1998. *Asia's Computer Challenge: Threat or Opportunity for the United States and the World*. Oxford, UK: Oxford University Press.

Deitrick, Sabina. 1990. *Linkages between Manufacturing and Services; A Case Study of the Semiconductor Industry in Singapore*. Ph.D. dissertation. Department of City and Regional Planning, University of California, Berkeley.

Escaith, Hubert, Nannette Lindenberg, and Sébastien Miroudot. 2010. "International Supply Chains and Trade Elasticity in Times of Global Crisis." Working paper, Economic Research and Statistics, World Trade Organization, Geneva.

Feenstra, Robert. 1998. "Integration of Trade and Disintegration of Production in the Global Economy." *Journal of Economic Perspectives* 12 (4): 31–50.

Feenstra, Robert, and Gary Hamilton. 2006. *Emerging Economies, Divergent Paths: Business Groups and Economic Organization in South Korea and Taiwan*. New York: Cambridge University Press.

Fixson, Sebastian, and Jin-Kyu Park. 2008. "The Power of Integrality: Linkages between Innovation and Industry Structure." *Research Policy* 37: 1296–316.

Galvin, Peter, and Andre Morkel. 2001. "The Effect of Product Modularity on Industry Structure: The Case of the World Bicycle Industry." *Industry and Innovation* 8 (1): 31–47.

Gawer, Annabelle, and Michael Cusumano. 2002. *Platform Leadership: How Intel, Microsoft, and Cisco Drive Industry Innovation*. Cambridge, MA: Harvard Business School Press.

Geocities. 2004. "Beyonics Technology." Company profile. http://www.geocities.com/fa_book/Benyonics_181201.html. Accessed January 23, 2004.

Gereffi, Gary. 1999. "International Trade and Industrial Upgrading in the Apparel Commodity Chain." *Journal of International Economics* 48: 37–70.

Gereffi, Gary, John Humphrey, and Timothy Sturgeon. 2005. "The Governance of Global Value Chains." *Review of International Political Economy* 12 (1): 78–104.

Gereffi, Gary, and Michael Korzeniewicz, eds. 1994. *Commodity Chains and Global Capitalism.* Westport, CT: Praeger.

Grunwald, Joseph, and Kenneth Flamm. 1985. *The Global Factory.* Washington, DC: Brookings Institution.

Hamilton, Gary, and Gary Gereffi. 2009. "Global Commodity Chains, Market Makers, and the Rise of Demand-Responsive Economies." In *Frontiers of Commodity Chain Research,* ed. Jennifer Bair, chapter 7. Stanford, CA: Stanford University Press.

Hesseldahl, Arik. 2010. "The iPad: More Than the Sum of Its Parts; $270 More, Actually." *Bloomberg Business Week,* February 22, p. 24.

Hirschman, A. 1958. *The Strategy of Economic Development.* New Haven, CT: Yale University Press.

Humphrey, John, and Hubert Schmitz. 2002. "How Does Insertion in Global Value Chains Affect Upgrading in Industrial Clusters?" *Regional Studies* 36 (9): 1017–27.

Imai, Ken, and Jing Ming Shiu. 2007. "A Divergent Path of Industrial Upgrading: Emergence and Evolution of the Mobile Handset Industry in China." Institute of Developing Economies Discussion Paper 125, IDE, Chiba, Japan.

———. Forthcoming. "Value Chain Creation and Reorganization: The Growth Path of China's Mobile Phone Handset Industry." In *The Dynamics of Local Learning in Global Value Chains; Experiences from East Asia,* ed. Momoko Kawakami and Timothy Sturgeon, chapter 2. Basingstoke, UK: Palgrave Macmillan.

Kawakami, Momoko. Forthcoming. "Inter-firm Dynamics of Notebook PC Value Chains and the Rise of Taiwanese Original Design Manufacturing Firms." In *The Dynamics of Local Learning in Global Value Chains; Experiences from East Asia,* ed. Momoko Kawakami and Timothy Sturgeon, chapter 1. Basingstoke, UK: Palgrave Macmillan.

Kimura, Seishi. 2007. *The Challenges of Late Industrialization: The Global Economy and the Japanese Commercial Aircraft Industry.* London: Palgrave Macmillan.

Langlois, R., and P. Robertson. 1995. *Firms, Markets and Economic Change.* London: Routledge.

Langlois, Richard. 2003. "The Vanishing Hand: The Changing Dynamics of Industrial Capitalism." *Industrial and Corporate Change* 12 (April): 351–85.

Linden, Greg, Kenneth Kraemer, and Jason Dedrick. 2007. "Who Captures Value in a Global Innovation System? The Case of Apple's iPod." University of California at Irvine, Personal Computing Industry Center (PCIC) working paper, June.

Linden, Greg, and Deepak Somaya. 2003. "System-on-a-Chip Integration in the Semiconductor Industry: Industry Structure and Firm Strategies." *Industrial and Corporate Change* 12 (3): 545–57.

Ling, Zhijun. 2006. *The Lenovo Affair: The Growth of China's Computer Giant and Its Takeover of IBM-PC.* Singapore: Wiley.

Mann, Catherine, and Jacob Kirkegaard. 2006. *Accelerating the Globalization of America: The Next Wave of Information Technology.* Washington, DC: Institute for International Economics.

Mathews, John. 2002. *Dragon Multinational: A New Model for Global Growth.* Oxford, UK: Oxford University Press.

McKendrick, David, Richard Doner, and Stephen Haggard. 2000. *From Silicon Valley to Singapore: Location and Competitive Advantage in the Hard Disk Drive Industry.* Stanford, CA: Stanford University Press.

Nikkei Electronics. 2007. "Kanabi Shijo wo Sekken suru PND" (PNDs Sweeping the Car-navi Markets), May 21.

Nolan, Peter. 2001. *China and the Global Business Revolution.* Basingstoke, UK: Palgrave Macmillan.

Ogawa, Koichi. 2007. *Wagakuni erekutoronikusu sangyo ni miru purattofomu no keisei mekanizumu: akitekucha-besu no purattofomu keisei niyoru erekutoronikusu sangyo no saiko ni mukete* (Mechanism of platform formation in the Japanese electronics industry: towards a resurgence of the electronics industry based on the formation of an architecture-based platform). MMRC Discussion Paper 146. Manufacturing Management Research Center, Tokyo.

Principe, A., A. Davies, and M. Hobday, eds. 2003. *The Business of Systems Integration.* Oxford, UK.

Sayer, Andrew. 1986. "Industrial Location on a World Scale: The Case of the Semiconductor Industry." In *Production, Work, Territory,* ed. A. Scott and M. Storper, 107–24. Boston: Allen and Unwin.

Shih, Willy, Chintay Shih, Hung-Chang Chiu, Yi-Ching Hsieh, and Howard H. Yu. 2008. "ASUSTeK Computer Inc. EeePC (A)." Harvard Business School Case Study 9-609-111, Harvard Business School, Cambridge, MA.

Song, Lei. 2007. "Modularization, Modularity Traps and Competitiveness: Towards an Architecture Analysis of China's AV Industry." ITEC workshop presentation, October 24, Kyoto, Japan.

Steinfeld, Edward. 2004. "Chinese Enterprise Development and the Challenge of Global Integration." In *Global Production Networking and Technological Change in East Asia,* ed. S. Yusuf, A. Altaf, and K. Nabeshima. Oxford, UK: Oxford University Press.

Sturgeon, Timothy. 2002. "Modular Production Networks: A New American Model of Industrial Organization." *Industrial and Corporate Change* 11 (3): 451–96.

———. 2003. "Exploring the Risks of Value Chain Modularity: Electronics Outsourcing during the Industry Cycle of 2001–2002." MIT IPC Working Paper 03-002, May. Massachusetts Institute of Technology, Cambridge, MA.

———. 2007. "How Globalization Drives Institutional Diversity: The Japanese Electronics Industry's Response to Value Chain Modularity." *Journal of East Asian Studies* 7 (1) (January–April): 1–34.

———. 2009. "From Commodity Chains to Value Chains: Interdisciplinary Theory-Building in an Age of Globalization." In *Frontiers of Commodity Chain Research,* ed. Jennifer Bair, chapter 6. Palo Alto, CA: Stanford University Press.

Sturgeon, Timothy, and Enrique Dussel-Peters. 2006. "From High Volume to High Mix and Beyond: The Changing Role of the Guadalajara Electronics Cluster in Global Value Chains." Unpublished manuscript: Main Findings and Preliminary Policy Recommendations, Industrial Upgrading in Mexico project. Center for Globalization, Governance, and Competitiveness, Duke University, Durham, NC.

Sturgeon, Timothy, and Richard Florida. 2004. "Globalization, De-verticalization, and Employment in the Motor Vehicle Industry." In *Locating Global Advantage; Industry Dynamics in a Globalizing Economy,* ed. Martin Kenny and Richard Florida. Palo Alto, CA: Stanford University Press.

Sturgeon, Timothy, John Humphrey, and Gary Gereffi. Forthcoming. "Making the Global Supply-base." In *The Market Makers; How Retailers Are Reshaping the Global Economy*, ed. Gary Hamilton, Ben Senauer, and Misha Petrovic, chapter 8. Oxford and London: Oxford University Press.

Sturgeon, Timothy, and JiRen Lee. 2005. "Industry Co-evolution: A Comparison of Taiwan and North American Electronics Contract Manufacturers." In *Global Taiwan: Building Competitive Strengths in a New International Economy*, ed. Suzanne Berger and Richard K. Lester. Armonk, NY: M.E. Sharpe.

Sturgeon, Timothy, and Richard Lester. 2004. "The New Global Supply-base: New Challenges for Local Suppliers in East Asia." In *Global Production Networking and Technological Change in East Asia,* ed. Yusuf Shahid, M. Anjum Altaf, and Kaoru Nabeshima, chapter 2. Oxford, UK: Oxford University Press.

Sturgeon, Timothy, and Olga Memedovic. Forthcoming. "Measuring Global Value Chains: Intermediate Goods Trade, Structural Change and Compressed Development." UNIDO Working Paper, United National Industrial Development Organization,Vienna.

Sturgeon, Timothy, Johannes Van Biesebroeck, and Gary Gereffi. 2008. "Value Chains, Networks, and Clusters: Reframing the Global Automotive Industry." *Journal of Economic Geography* 8: 297–321.

Sutherland, Dylan. 2003. *China's Large Enterprises and the Challenge of Late Industrialization.* London: Routledge Curzon.

Tatsumoto, Hirofum, Koichi Ogawa, and Takahiro Fujimoto. 2010. "The Effects of Technological Platforms on the International Division of Labor: A Case Study of Intel's Platform Business in the PC Industry." In *Platforms, Markets and Innovation*, ed. Annabelle Gawer, 345–67. UK: Edward Elgar.

Teece, David. 2009. *Dynamic Capabilities and Strategic Management: Organizing for Innovation and Growth.* New York: Oxford University Press.

Ulrich, K. 1995. "The Role of Product Architecture in the Manufacturing Firm." *Research Policy* 24: 419–40.

Vance, Ashlee. 2009. "Acer's Everywhere. How Did That Happen?" *New York Times*, June 28.
Vind, I., and N. Fold. 2007. "Multi-level Modularity vs. Hierarchy: Global Production Networks in Singapore's Electronics Industry." *Danish Journal of Geography* 107 (1): 69–83.
Weiss, Linda, and John Hobson. 1995. *States and Economic Development: A Comparative Historical Analysis*. Cambridge, UK: Polity Press.
Whittaker, D. H., T. Zhu, T. Sturgeon, M. H. Tsai, and T. Okita. Forthcoming. "Compressed Development." *Studies in Comparative International Development*.
Yeung, Henry Wai-chung. 2009. "Regional Development and the Competitive Dynamics of Global Production Networks: An East Asian Perspective." *Regional Studies* 43 (3) (April): 325–51.

8

WHAT HAPPENS WHEN THE MARKET SHIFTS TO CHINA? THE GABON TIMBER AND THAI CASSAVA VALUE CHAINS

Raphael Kaplinsky, Anne Terheggen, and Julia Tijaja

Chapter 4 of this volume, "Global Value Chains, the Crisis, and the Shift of Markets from North to South," showed that our understanding of the positioning of producers in global value chains (GVCs) and their capacity to upgrade efficiency necessarily requires a focus on final markets. It was argued in chapter 4 that when the final market shifts from a high-income to a low-income environment, the result would be a diminution of the role played by standards in the GVC. This is because the use of standards reflects a combination of meeting the differentiated needs of more demanding consumers, responding to the demands for consumer protection by states in high-income economies, and responding to the pressures for ethical production generated by civil society organizations. It was also argued that whereas there would be a complementary division of labor in the South-North trade of commodities, it was at least a possibility that the South-South trade in commodities would lead to a more competitive and less complementary division of labor.

The discussion of these two hypotheses in chapter 4 was unevidenced. This chapter focuses on two southern commodity-exporting economies. The first is Thailand, which exports cassava-based products, and the second is Gabon, which exports timber and timber-based products. In both cases, the final market has witnessed a significant shift over the past two decades from Europe to China. In both cases we explore the impact of this market shift on the standards intensity of production and in the intercountry division of labor in the GVC.

The Thai Cassava GVC

Cassava is cultivated widely all over the globe because it grows on poor-quality land and is relatively drought resistant, thus serving as a food crop of last resort in many countries. But it is also an important intermediate product channeled into the animal feed, bioethanol (biofuel), and starch markets. Since raw cassava is poisonous to humans, bulky, and perishable, cassava is usually traded in processed form. In 2008, global trade in cassava products was $1.124 billion and although Brazil and Nigeria were the largest producers, Thailand was the world's largest cassava exporter (see figure 8.1), accounting for around 80 percent of global trade in both major product families ($910 million) (Comtrade 2009).

Cassava plays an important role in the Thai economy. In 2007, it was the second most important crop after rice in terms of value and the third after sugarcane and rice in terms of volume (FAOSTAT Nov. 2009). At $948 million in 2007, combined dried cassava and cassava starch exports were its third biggest agricultural export after rubber and rice (FAOSTAT 2009). Unlike the case with other major

Figure 8.1 Thailand's Share in World Cassava Exports, 1961–2007

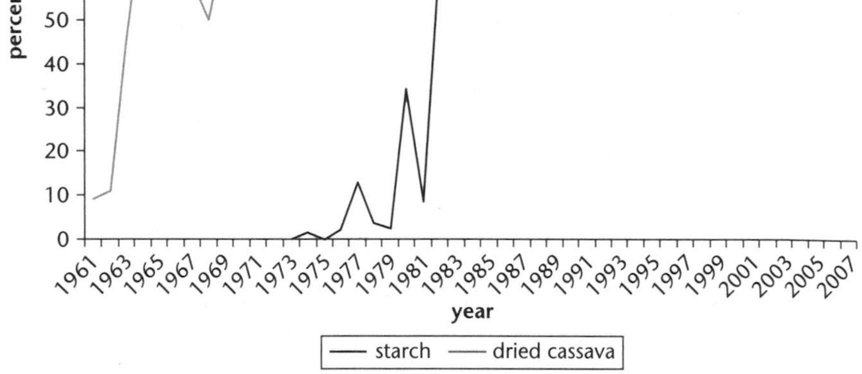

Source: FAOSTAT Agriculture TradeSTAT 2009.

producers of cassava, there is little domestic direct consumption of cassava as a food product in Thailand; almost all output is used as an intermediate product in other sectors. In 2008, an estimated 66 percent of all Thai cassava was exported, 26 percent was used domestically, and the rest was kept as stock (TTSA 2009).This represents a somewhat unusual story of an "alien" food crop being introduced into a low-income economy (in this case, dating back to the 1950s) and initially thriving solely as an exported intermediate product used in the food industry in the economies of other countries.

Thailand's rapid expansion of cassava exports reflects two factors. The first is the well-developed external marketing capabilities of Thailand's Chinese trading community. The second is the heavy investment in infrastructure in the northeastern region during the 1960s and 1970s, designed to counter the political influence of communist insurgents. The northeast has become the major cassava-growing region in the country.

The two families of products in the Thai cassava sector (figure 8.2) are dried cassava (comprising dried chips and cassava pellets) and starch, comprising two GVCs.

Figure 8.2 Domestic Dried Cassava and Cassava Starch Value Chains in Thailand

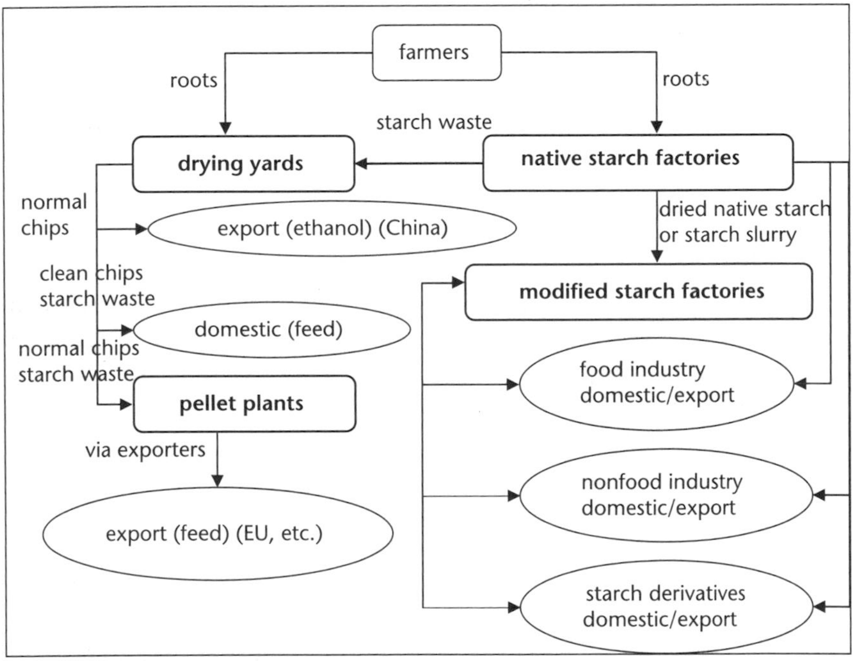

Source: Author's fieldwork interviews.

Cassava chips are inputs into both the animal feed and biofuel industries. They are produced by sorting root tubers that are then crudely cut and dried in open-air drying yards. Lower-grade "normal chips" are fed into the cassava pellet and biofuel industries. The higher-grade "clean chips" are used directly as domestic animal feed, but require the peeling and cleaning of tubers, necessitating rudimentary forms of mechanization (using rotating drums or a screen filter) and an additional day of drying. They have a lower sand and fiber content than "normal" chips.

Cassava pellets are made out of "normal chips" or low-grade wastage from the starch industry, or a mixture of both. These inputs are ground and steamed, sometimes mixed with starch residue, and then molded into pellets. The manufacturing process embodies some limited scale economies, and more skilled labor and capital than are required in the production of either clean or normal chips. Typically, an average pellet plant processes around 575 root-tonnes per day, compared to an average of 70 root-tonnes in the drying yards.

The second value chain, starch, also comprises two subproducts: "native" and "modified" starch (although a small quantity of sago is also produced). These starches have industrial uses, with modified starch feeding into more technologically intensive value chains. Modified starch involves a further step of processing after the production of native starch, reflected in the fact that while roots constitute 70–75 percent of the total production cost for native starch, they account for only around 46 percent of the costs of modified starch (author's fieldwork interviews; Titapiwatanakun 1994). In addition to being used in other industrial sectors, some of the native starch waste is sold to the pellet plants where they are combined with "normal" cassava chips to produce animal feed. The typical starch factory processes around 850 tonnes of cassava root per day.

Market Requirements for Cassava-Based Products

There are two established export markets and one emerging market for Thailand's dried cassava (chips and pellets)—the European Union (EU) and China, and, in recent years, the Republic of Korea. Each of these markets has particular trajectories and requirements. The smaller starch export market is more diversified.

The origin of Thailand's dried cassava industry can be traced back to the introduction of the EU's Common Agricultural Policy (CAP) in 1962, which artificially increased domestic cereal prices in Europe. Demand for Thai cassava pellets expanded rapidly after the introduction of the CAP in 1962, where the resulting high domestic cereal price triggered the search by EU feed manufacturers for cheaper alternative feed ingredients. Cassava exports to the EU expanded rapidly, reaching a peak of almost 9 million tonnes in 1989. Initially, these exports were cassava chips, but for a number of reasons, pellets became the dominant, and then the exclusive, cassava product exported to the EU. Since dried cassava was used in compound-feed production, cleanliness and uniformity of shape and size were important to ease the large-scale mechanized mixing of dried cassava with other feed ingredients. In addition, the distance between the EU and Thailand required less bulky products, favoring pellets over chips. Moreover, the transportation of chips is dusty, and in 1978 EU environmental regulations mandated the introduction of a less dusty form of dried cassava, again favoring pellets over chips. Finally, as cassava pellets are used in feed production, imports are governed by the EU farm-to-fork policy, which requires traceability. Hazard Analysis and Critical Control Points (HACCP) and Good Manufacturing Practice (GMP) certifications became mandatory for entry into the EU, and pellet production lent itself more favorably to this form of certification (see box 8.1).

However, the attractiveness of Thai cassava as an animal feed input for EU livestock producers was undermined by a series of trade restrictions introduced in the 1980s and early 1990s, and then, in particular, by the 1992 reform of the CAP. EU domestic cereals became increasingly competitive with cassava pellets. By 2005, pellet exports to the EU had collapsed to 250,000 tonnes, compared to a peak of more than 9 million tonnes in 1989 (Comtrade Nov. 2009; TTTA 2009) and price pressure grew. In 2008, pellet exports to the EU had regrown to 989,000 tonnes, still only 10 percent of the 1989 peak (Comtrade Dec. 2009).

China's cassava imports

The demand for imported cassava chips into China reflects the related desire by the Chinese government for food self-sufficiency, the growth in the demand for meat by consumers, and the development of its biofuels sector. As we saw above, Chinese policy privileges the production of food grains for domestic consumers, which means that the requirements for animal feed and feedstock for biofuels have increasingly had to be met via imports. This has led to the growing importation of soya products from Latin America and cassava from Thailand. Alternative feedstocks into biofuels such as molasses have been discouraged because of environmental concerns (OAE 2006).

The bulk of Thailand's cassava exports to China occurs in the form of dried cassava (cassava chips rather than pellets) and is used as an input in the production of biofuels (table 8.1). These imports began on a small scale in the mid-1990s but grew rapidly in the 2000s, following a wheat harvest failure in 2001 and the liberalization of trade barriers in agricultural products under the China-ASEAN (Association of Southeast Asian Nations) Free Trade Agreement (FTA) in 2003. The Early Harvest Programme of this FTA necessitated the removal of a 6 percent tariff previously imposed by China on Thai cassava products, boosting their price competitiveness.

Box 8.1 Standards Governing Production in the Thai Cassava GVC

Hazard Analysis and Critical Control Points (HACCP) and Good Manufacturing Practice (GMP) certification are required for exports to the European Union (EU).

Minimum export standards required by the Thai Ministry of Commerce: For both pellets and chips, the Thai Ministry of Commerce (MoC) requires a number of technical export standards based on Notification of MoC B.E.2545 (2002) for sale into the domestic animal feed market. The main ones are minimum starch content of 65 percent, maximum crude fiber of 5 percent, maximum moisture of 14 percent, maximum sand of 3 percent, and free from foreign materials. However, despite these export standards, some exports (including residue pellet exports to the Republic of Korea) are shipped to a lower starch content (see below).

Standards governing product entry into the EU: The EU's "farm-to-fork" policy, introduced in 2000, requires the traceability by buyers of products used in food and feed production. Compliance for traceability and hygiene requirements is obtained through HACCP and GMP certifications on the pellet plants, as follows:

- HACCP certification is required as cassava pellets are part of the animal feed food chain.
- GMP relates to the sanitary and processing requirements necessary to ensure the production of wholesome food.

The requirement for HACCP is based on European Council Directive 89/397/EEC of June 14, 1989, on the official control of foodstuffs, and Council Directive 93/43/EEC of June 14, 1993, on the hygiene of foodstuffs. The HACCP system has to be implemented in relation to products and production processes.

Standards governing product entry into China: No official standards govern product entry into China. However, since cassava chips are used as a biofuel feedstock, Chinese buyers customarily specify a 67 percent starch content, compared to the 65 percent level required to meet Thai Ministry of Commerce export standards. This also tends to be higher than the starch levels required by EU and Korean buyers, where cassava exports are sold to the animal feed market.

Standards governing product entry into Korea: No distinct standard certification is required for entry into the Korean market, but there are technical standards specified by buyers (notably, a 55 percent starch content).

Table 8.1 Thai Cassava Exports to China, 2002–08

Exports	2002	2003	2004	2005	2006	2007	2008
Total (US$, millions)	109.02	137.44	236.74	329.87	474.81	417.62	288.30
Dried cassava (percent)	94.10	94.66	90.04	89.44	87.61	83.26	72.57
Cassava starch (percent)	5.90	5.34	9.96	10.56	12.39	16.74	27.43

Source: Comtrade 2009.

China's demand for starch as an intermediate input into nonfood industries has increased rapidly in recent years and the share of starches in cassava imports from Thailand grew from only 6 percent in 1998 to 27 percent in 2008.

Korea's cassava imports

Korea imports mostly residue pellets made out of starch waste with a low starch content of 55 percent, compared to the pellets imported by the EU, which are made mostly (70–80 percent) from chips and which have 65 percent starch content. Korea is a very new entrant into the Thai export market, importing virtually nothing until 2007, and then taking 16 percent of dried cassava imports (mostly low-grade, that is, residue pellets) in 2008.

Changes in Market Destinations and Product Composition

There have been two major changes in the export composition of Thai cassava products over the past 10 years. The first is a change in destination. The Thai dried cassava industry—essentially a "creation" of the EU CAP after 1962—could potentially have been devastated after the reforms to EU agricultural policy in the early 1990s. This reform of the cereal price support system reduced the price competitiveness of cassava pellet imports as an animal feed. Fortuitously for the Thai industry, the Chinese market began to grow rapidly soon after the EU market began falling. This changed balance in export destination is shown in figure 8.3. Total export volume hovered around 4 million t during the 1990s, but the share to the EU fell from almost 95 percent in 1999 to less than 10 percent in 2005, subsequently reviving somewhat to around 30 percent in 2008. The share of dried cassava (pellets) exports to Korea grew rapidly from a mere 2 percent in 2004 to 16 percent in 2008 (Comtrade 2009; TTTA 2004, 2009).

Given the different demand patterns in the EU and China, this shift in export destination resulted in changes in the product composition of Thai cassava exports[1] (figure 8.4). The major change was from pellet to chip exports. But an important subsidiary change in Thai exports has been the growth of cassava starch exports to China: from 6 percent of Thailand's cassava exports to China in 2002 to 27 percent in 2008. However, there has been a marked shift in exports to China from modified to native starches (figure 8.5).

Consequences of Market Shifts

What have been the consequences of these shifts in the related market and product composition of Thai cassava exports over the past decade? Here it is helpful to distinguish between the implications for dried cassava exports and starch exports, as illustrated in figure 8.2.

Figure 8.3 Thai Dried Cassava Exports to Main Destinations, 1999–2008

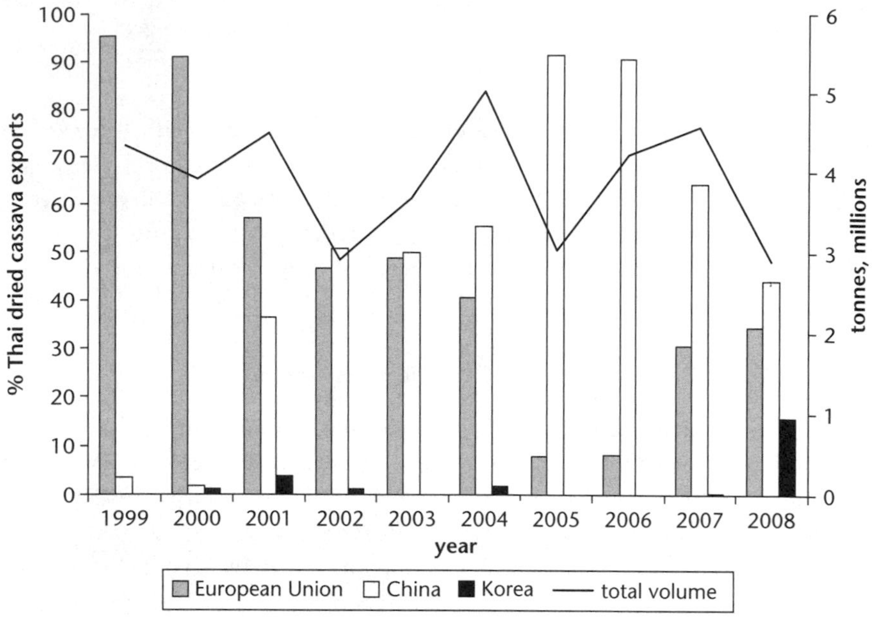

Sources: Comtrade 2009; TTTA 2004, 2009.

Dried cassava exports: from pellets to chips

The transition from pellets to chips has essentially knocked out a stage of processing. Chip production is a labor-intensive operation occurring in open-air drying yards—the raw cassava is cut, sorted, placed in the sun to dry, and then aggregated and exported in bulk containers. Pellet production builds on cassava chip production, adding value by steaming and molding the semiprocessed cassava chips in a factory. It is a more technologically complex operation, involving greater operational and managerial skills, not as a substitute for but as a complement to chip production. This change in product therefore represents a move down the technological chain, and at the margin pushes Thai producers backwards into an agricultural rather than a manufacturing comparative advantage, although the implications for revenues and profits are ambiguous.

This has implications for factor utilization. Table 8.2 simulates the employment and capital costs that would result if all of Thailand's cassava production in 2008 (29 million t of cassava root) were to be exported as either chips, pellets, or starches (as reflected in the current mix of exports). It shows that the additional stage of pellet production over chip production would lead to an additional 9,357 jobs (an increment of 51 percent in employment), but at a higher capital cost of \$6 million (increasing capital costs by 30 percent). The capital cost per job created

Figure 8.4 Thai Cassava Export Composition, 1976–2009

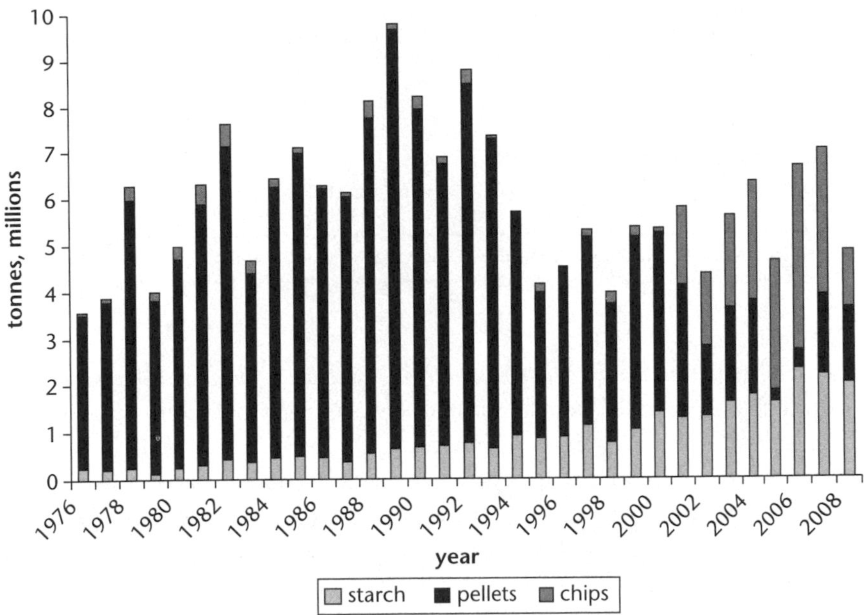

Sources: TTTA 2004, 2009.
Note: The graph represents the volume of final products.

Figure 8.5 Composition of Thai Cassava Starch Exports to China, 2001–06

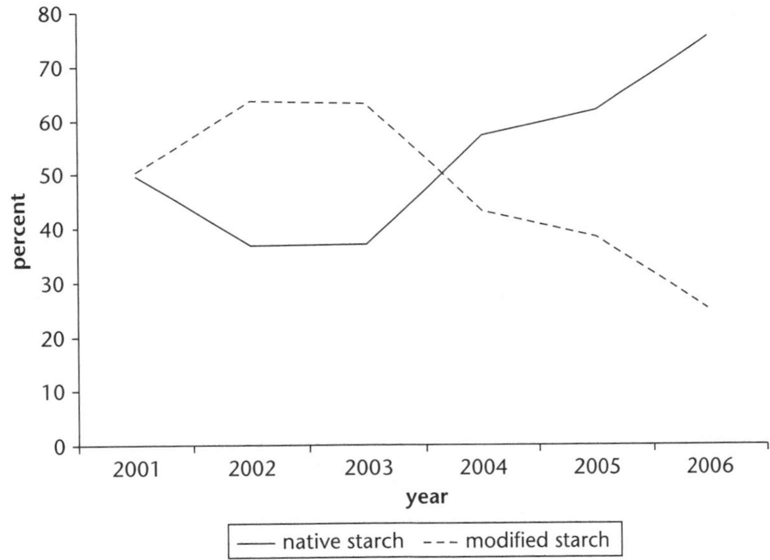

Source: TTSA 2008.

Table 8.2 Factor Utilization and Number of Establishments If All Cassava Produced as Chips, Pellets, or Starches

Economic factor	Chips	Pellets (including chips)	All starches
Employment	18,270	27,627[a] (of which 9,357 in pelletization)	29,725
Capital cost (US$, millions)	19.97	25.96	44.73
Number of firms	1,373	168 pelletization plants 1,373 drying yards	114

Sources: Capital cost calculated from Roonnaphai (2006); all other data from author's fieldwork interviews.
a. Assumes all pellets are made from chips; actually, many pellet factories also use starch residue as an input.

in pellet production is only $640. It would also add an additional 168 production units, contributing to the diversification of entrepreneurship and to the potential geographic diversification of production.

A further consequence of the transition from the EU pellet market to the Chinese chip market is the removal of the part that standards play in production processes and in product specification requirements. As shown in box 8.1, cassava chips exported to China are required to have only a minimum starch content. By comparison, pellet exports to the EU are required to satisfy demanding EU farm-to-fork GMP and HACCP standards. Arguably, the achievement of these standards requires more sophisticated managerial processes and higher labor skills, contributing to the growth of capabilities in the Thai economy.

Finally, there are knock-on effects that can be broadly understood as GVC governance issues. Pellet exports to the EU occur in bulk and in long-haul, 50,000-tonne ships and are controlled by four northern-based commodity traders (including Cargill and Toepfer) that assemble consignments of 6,000–7,000 tonnes from individual Thai exporters.[2] These exports occur mostly through long-term forward contracts, which provide a predictable income stream for producers and local aggregators. By contrast, in general, chip exports to China are sold on a spot-price basis and provide for far less predictability; for example, since prices fell suddenly in 2008, many Chinese importers reneged on agreed prices. As a consequence, many Thai firms continue to supply to the EU, even though margins on this trade have fallen in recent years as the changing agricultural price support system in the EU has led to increasing price competition from other animal feeds.

Starch exports: Trend toward lower value starches

If the transition from the EU pellet market to the Chinese chip market represents a downgrading of value addition and capability building, the same results are not true when Chinese demand for starches is compared with EU demand for pellets.

Starch production is considerably more technologically intensive than either chip or pellet production. This is especially true in the case of modified starches—as shown above, modified starch involves considerably greater processing than does native starch. Thus, in this case, the transition from the EU to the Chinese market would be reflected in an increase in technological complexity and skill requirements that is greater than that involved in the jump from cassava chip to pellet production. Moreover, it would lead to an increase of around 7 percent in total employment, since the packaging stage in starch production is particularly labor intensive. Moreover, starch production requires a higher skill level than dried cassava production. This increase in employment would, however, come at a considerable capital cost: more than double the investment of chip production (122 percent, an additional $24 million), a 72 percent increase ($18.8 million) over the cost of pellet production, and a capital cost per job of $1,505, still comparatively low by contemporary industrial production standards, but more than double the cost per job in pellet production.

So, on one level, the transition from the EU pellet to the Chinese starch market might suggest an augmentation of capabilities. However, within starch production, there has been an important shift in recent years that mirrors the pellet versus starch story. Whereas Chinese starch imports from Thailand constituted around a 50-50 split between modified and native starches in 2001, the share of the more processed modified starches produced in more technologically complex production processes had fallen to only 25 percent in 2006 (TTSA 2008). China's declining demand for modified starch might reflect the building of China's own starch modification capacity rather than a decline in demand. Modified starch (made from all starches, not just cassava) production in China has increased consistently from just 20,000 t in 1991, to 60,000 t in 1994, 330,000 t in 2001, and to almost 650,000 t in 2006 (W. Wang 2002, 34; X. H. Wang 2007). If this trend continues, Thailand might be relegated to a supplier of native starch, with the more sophisticated modification taking place in China. The Thai industry hopes for a more complex future, with premium-grade native starches and the most complex modified starches being produced in Thailand and intermediate grades of modified starches produced in China. On the basis of past trajectories, however, their ability to achieve this outcome is doubtful.

The Gabon Timber GVC

The development of timber and timber-related sectors is one of the primary stages of industrial growth, partly because timber products (such as furniture and housing) have high income elasticities of demand at low levels of income, partly because timber-related sectors are labor intensive (and hence encourage production at low wage levels), and partly because timber processing is closely related to the agricultural sectors that dominate low-income economies.

The trajectory of the timber sector mirrors this transition in macroeconomic structure as depicted in the "forest transition" model, which describes the changing patterns of wood utilization and forest resource exploitation over time (Mather 1992; Grainger 1995; Mather and Needle 1998; Rudel et al. 2005). During the preindustrial phase, forests in the now-mature northern economies were predominantly used for grazing and the collection of fodder, fuelwood, and nonwood forest products, as well as for timber (Farrella et al. 2000; Mather 2001). Until the 18th century, European forests were a hybrid of agricultural and timber production. During the following industrial phase, trees were "mined" to produce inputs for other industries.

But as forests were depleted, the remaining forest areas increasingly required more management. This led to new forms of ownership, with privately owned enclosures replacing communal forests (Mather and Needle 1999; Humphreys 2006). For most of the 19th and 20th centuries, forests in Europe and North America were "industrialized," and the timber was fed into related industries. As a result of timber shortages in Europe (and later its "newly depleted" outposts in North America), colonies in Africa and Asia were drawn on to fill the domestic wood gaps. Colonies were often treated as so-called resource taps (Jorgenson 2008).

After the 1950s, northern forestry industries moved into the postindustrial phase. Technological change in agriculture led to yield increases, making land available for forest expansion (Victor and Ausubel 2000; Rudel et al. 2005; Kauppi et al. 2006). At the same time, societal perspectives on the functions of forests began to change, and an increasingly affluent urban population exerted pressure on domestic forest management to cater to their needs for recreation and regeneration. They also focused on the need to avoid the loss of biodiversity in forests (Nilsson 1999; Bazett 2000), and in recent years they have become increasingly concerned that deforestation will lead to the erosion of the carbon-sinks that mitigate against climate change.

In southern economies, much of the tropical deforestation of the late 19th and the 20th centuries can be attributed to export-directed logging activities, as wages in northern economies grew and as they ran out of sustainable forests. The overwhelming majority of logging took place through an expansion of the extensive margin, with little attention being paid to sustainable cultivation. Forests increasingly came under state authority, with the primary objective of maximizing timber extraction, and forest land was taken by new settlers for agricultural purposes, thereby replacing traditional communal stewardship and common property systems (White and Martin 2002; Humphreys 2006).

Evolution of Gabon's Timber Industry

Situated on the West Coast of Africa, Gabon is a resource-rich economy with relatively high levels of per capita income, currently around four times the Sub-Saharan African average. It is a major exporter of oil, with a population of only 1.5 million. Gabon possesses more than 200,000 square kilometers of forests, as well as extensive deposits of manganese and iron ore that are only now being opened up for exploitation. Rents derived from the oil sector are substantial, and even though they are very unevenly spread, the contribution of nonoil sectors to GDP is small. The forest sector accounts for less than 3 percent of GDP (Melhado 2007; OECD 2009).

Gabon's forests are part of the second largest tropical ecosystem after the Amazon, namely, the Congo Basin, which covers 1.8 million square kilometers, stretching across six countries.[3] Nearly 85 percent of Gabon's total landmass is covered with forests, making it the second most heavily forested country in Africa (FAO 2005, 2007). Gabon is the 13th-largest tropical log producer globally, and the third-largest log exporter, with 16 percent of total exports in 2008 (FAOSTAT, ForestSTAT data, 2009). While Gabon's forests comprise 300 to 400 tree species, one—Okoumé—dominates. Around 70–80 percent of its forests contain Okoumé, and this species exists in comparatively smaller volumes only in parts of Cameroon, Equatorial Guinea, and Republic of Congo (ITTO 2006; UNEP and WCMC 2009). Okoumé is particularly favored because when fresh, it can be easily peeled without prior steaming. Between 1987 and 1996, more than 70 percent of log exports were Okoumé (Collomb, Mikissa, and Minnemeyer 2000), but since then, this proportion has fallen to around half of total exports (SEPBG 2009).

Gabon's timber GVC is shown in figure 8.6. A small proportion of harvested trees is converted into finished products that are consumed domestically (c). But the overwhelming bulk is exported either directly as logs (a), or as sawnwood (b.i), veneer sheets (b.ii), or plywood (b.iii). A very small proportion of timber is used to manufacture railway sleepers, both for domestic consumption and for export.

Until very recently, Gabon's timber sector was unregulated and out of the political focus. But with the growth of environmental concerns about climate change and mounting domestic economic problems, the timber industry has become a subject of increasing regulation, both within and outside Gabon. In light of decreasing oil production and following pressure from external donors that Gabon regulate this key resource to use it as a primary driver of industrial diversification, the state introduced a sector program for forests, fisheries, and the environment (Programme Sectoriel Forêt, Pêche et Environnement), involving major reforms of the forestry sector (Wunder 2003; Leigh and Olters 2006; Söderling 2006). Reforms included the abolition of the state-owned export

Figure 8.6 Domestic Timber GVC in Gabon

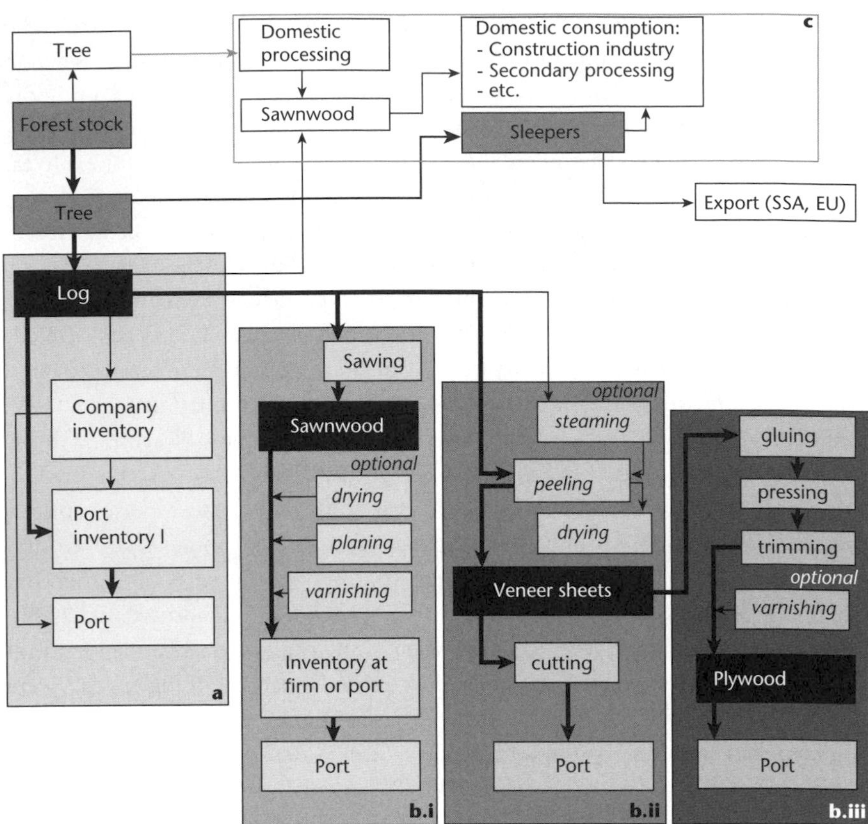

Source: Author.
Note: Bold arrows symbolize major raw material and product flows. EU = European Union; SSA = Sub-Saharan Africa.

monopoly (SNBG) and the introduction of a new legislative framework, the Forestry Code, in 2001. The overall focus shifted from raw material extraction toward the industrialization of the forestry sector through increasing domestic processing of sustainably managed forests (Methot and Ndongou 2009). The new rules imposed by the Forestry Code include the following:

- Redesign of the concessionary allocation system using a closed auction system to increase transparency
- Introduction of new types of concessions, with two types of commercial concessions, each with a total maximum surface area and a minimum duration of exploitation

- Reform of the tax system to stimulate local processing capacities, and to promote resource transfers to rural populations
- Introduction of local processing requirements to stimulate the processing of at least 75 percent of wood before exporting by January 2012
- Production quotas that are assigned to individual companies and tied to the concession type.

Explicit targets to deepen processing were set up, built on the trajectories of a few large European-owned companies that had established plants to manufacture primary processed wood products during the 1990s. Complemented by the requirements of the 2001 Forestry Code to process logs domestically, this has led to a rapid increase in Gabon's production of sawnwood, veneer sheets, and plywood (see figure 8.7). Nevertheless, in 2007 the major share of Gabon's timber (87 percent) was exported as raw logs, and given current trends, there is little hope of meeting the Forestry Code objective of 75 percent domestic raw material processing by 2012.

Two external pressures have had a major impact on Gabon's timber industry. The first, resulting from direct pressure by external donors on the Gabonese government, was to promote greater transparency in the management of the forestry sector in order to facilitate the sustainable management of this key global resource and to widen the distribution of benefits from the exploitation of the forests. The second set of pressures were indirect in that they were not aimed directly at Gabon. They involved a series of standards that global buyers set to ensure the sustainable management of the forests and the legality of wood products that they

Figure 8.7 Production Volumes of Selected Wood Products in Gabon, 1990–2007

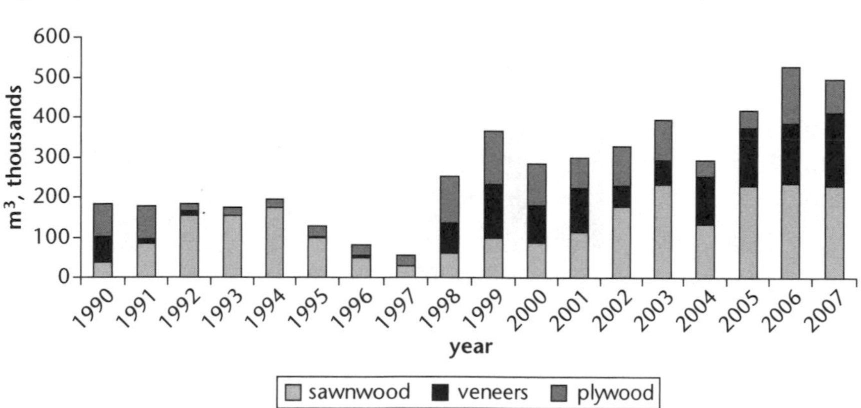

Source: FAOSTAT ForesSTAT data 2009.

sourced. This led to a combination of both private and public standards governing the procurement of wood from Gabon and other sources of tropical hardwoods.

Market Requirements for Gabon's Timber Products

The export markets for Gabon's timber products are the EU, to which Gabon has exported timber products for some years, and China, a relatively new market for Gabon's timber products.

The EU timber market

Gabon's timber exporting industry is a "creation" of French industry, reflecting the industrial phase in the Forest Transition trajectory in which northern firms—squeezed out of domestic sources of timber supply—identified cheap sources of raw material supply in former colonies. Timber exports from Gabon to France (the major external market) started with colonial settlements during 1850–90, and persisted after independence when French interests shifted to mining (Wunder 2003). Over time, total export volumes to France have risen from around 300,000 cubic meters in 1989 (from when reliable records are available) to nearly 600,000 cubic meters in the peak year of 2002 (figure 8.8). But as processing capacities rose in Gabon, these log exports were complemented by exports of sawnwood, veneers, and plywood, jointly reaching a roundwood equivalent of 230,000 cubic meters, exceeding the export of logs to France in 2006, which was 220,000 cubic meters.

Figure 8.8 Gabon's Exports of Logs and Processed Wood Products to France, 1997–2006

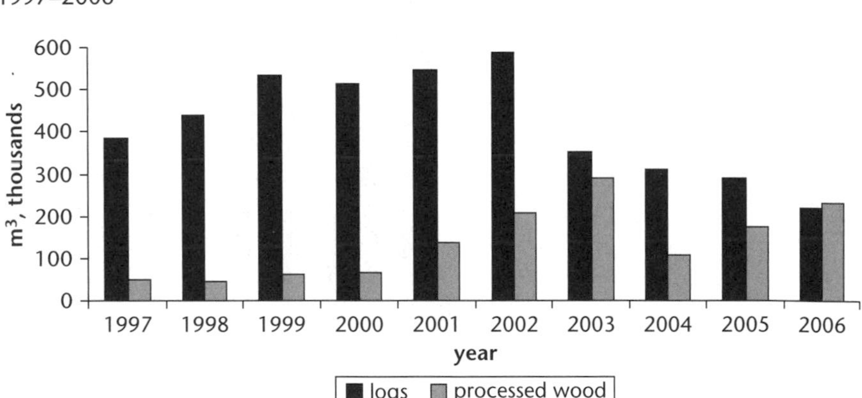

Sources: FAOSTAT Forestry Trade Flow data 2009; Collomb, Mikissa, and Minnemeyer 2000.
Note: The unit is roundwood equivalent in thousands of cubic meters.

The EU market for timber products has undergone four important changes since the 1980s. First, the EU's long-term dominance of global wooden furniture exports was eroded, particularly by expanding exports from China. In 1992, Chinese furniture exports were only 14 percent of Italian and 19 percent of German exports (the two leading global furniture exporters). In 2008, Chinese furniture exports were 2.3 times those of Italy and 2.6 times those of Germany (Comtrade 2009). Second, as wage levels rose in the EU, the competitiveness of its wood-processing industries fell in comparison with that of low-income economies, which at the same time, had developed their capabilities significantly in these processing sectors. This led to a migration of wood-processing activities out of high-income economies as the timber furniture GVC extended. Third, governments became increasingly aware of health and safety, and regulations were instituted in many sectors to ensure higher levels of safety for consumers. Finally, the growth of per capita incomes led to greater consumer concerns with the environment and with ethical standards in GVCs. In the timber sector, organizations such as the World Wildlife Fund and Friends of the Earth increasingly exerted pressure on producers to promote biodiversity and sustainability in forestry (Gulbrandsen and Humphreys 2006; Stringer 2006).

The growing prevalence of these standards in the EU market is reflected in box 8.2, which summarizes the major trends in preferences of European timber buyers and the government standards governing access to EU markets.

China: Gabon's New Export Market

China has replaced France as the dominant export market for Gabon's timber sector, particularly for its log exports. China is relatively poor in wood resources, with a per capita density of forest of 0.13 hectare compared to a world average of 0.65 hectares. Further, many of its forest reserves were depleted by extensive logging beginning in the late 1950s (Démurger, Yuanzhao, and Weiyong 2007), which led to the Chinese government's imposition of logging restrictions to stop deforestation and environmental degradation (Bowyer et al. 2004; White et al. 2006; Zhang and Gan 2007). At the same time, Chinese industry has increased its use of wood in the furniture and wood panel industries, as well as in massive housing and infrastructure investments. Chinese government officials reported an estimated gap of 140 million–150 million cubic meters in 2006 alone (Canby et al. 2008).

At the same time as China's demand for timber has grown so rapidly, its competencies in wood-using industries have also expanded (table 8.3). Thus, the shortfall in the supply of timber as an input has translated into the import of logs as opposed to processed wood. This is evident in figure 8.9, which shows that while

Box 8.2 Standards Governing Access to EU and Other Markets in the Organisation for Economic Co-operation and Development

Three sets of buyer requirements affect the entry of timber products into high-income markets such as those in the EU as follows.

The critical success factors of buyers: Importers acquire timber as a raw material or as an intermediate product for processing in other sectors. They trade off a series of critical success factors, the most prominent of which for logs are price, volume, quality, species, and environmental compliance. For processed wood, the dominant critical success factors are price, volume, quality, product specifications, and environmental considerations.

Industry-specific standards: Responding to concerns from civil society, two major sets of standards have emerged to protect forest ecosystems and the resource sustainability. European buyers increasingly require legality certification. In particular, the OLB (Origine et Légalité des Bois) certifies that the particular logging company is the legal owner of the concession and has the right to sell the specified logs. This includes verifying that the concession-holder has met its statutory obligations, such as paying all relevant taxes. Legality certification is increasingly under the umbrella of the EU FLEGT programme (Forest Law Enforcement, Governance and Trade), whose purpose is to eradicate illegal timber trade.

Sustainability certification is designed to promote the sustainable use of forests. The primary standard here is the Forest Stewardship Council scheme, which provides the systematic recording of sustainable production standards and a chain-of-custody certificate tracing timber all the way through the value chain; it also has wide-ranging requirements that include the protection of the rights of indigenous peoples. The ISO 14000 standards are also protective of the environmental impact of the timber value chain.

Public standards: Mandatory public standards affect health and safety concerns in the timber GVC. There are technical standards, for example, regarding formaldehyde emissions arising from the adhesives used to produce plywood, chemicals used in the production of medium-density fiberboards, and pollution from paint. Phytosanitary requirements ensure that "the producer has been capable of cleaning, sanitizing, sterilizing or by other means to render the offered commodity free from unwanted dirt, seeds, pests or germs" (Tissari 2009, 3). In the case of sawnwoods, for example, the cut edges are treated with a special paint to prevent infestation as well as decay. Other technical standards are building codes and product testing requirements (Pro Forest 2009; Sun et al. 2008).

Increasingly, where a government agency is the direct procurer of wood and wood products, EU countries have set Green Public Procurement standards for suppliers. These standards restrict market access. Frequently private standards such as FSC are incorporated into governments' purchasing policies. In other cases, the usage of tropical timber might be banned altogether.

sawnwood imports increased gradually, there was a much larger decline in the volume of imports of both veneer sheets and plywood and a very rapid increase in imports of raw unprocessed logs. An importer of plywood in the past, China became a net exporter after 2001 (Adams and Ma 2002; Changjin et al. 2008; Kozak and Canby 2007; White et al. 2006). However rapidly it developed over the past

Table 8.3 China's Growing Share of Global Exports in Timber-Processing Industries
percent

Product	1992	2008
Furniture	2.7	24.7
Veneer	0.7	7.9
Plywood	0.2	32.2
Fiberboard	0.5	11.4

Source: Comtrade 2009.

Figure 8.9 China's Imports of Logs and Selected Wood Products, 1970–2007
m³, thousands

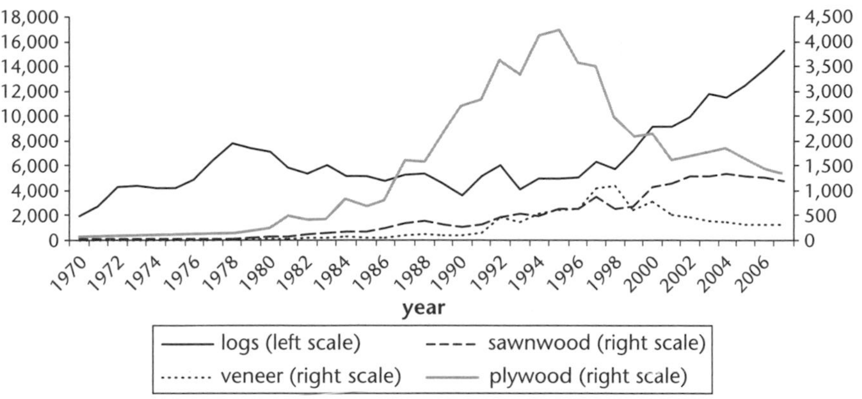

Source: FAO ForesSTAT 2009.

decade, the Chinese wood-processing industry is still not as developed as that industry in countries in the North. Consequently, whereas northern-based producers possess the technology to process wood of smaller diameter and with differing fiber characteristics (for example, plantation wood grown in temperate climates), Chinese industries continue to demand large-diameter logs from first- or second-growth natural forests (grown in subtropical and tropical climates) (Bowyer et al. 2004). Thus, China consumes timber from natural forests rather than smaller dimensioned and more rapidly grown timbers from plantation forests.

There is little evidence that access to the Chinese market is affected by the sorts of standards imposed on Gabon's exports of timber to the EU. Instead, given the large number of Chinese companies, low barriers to entry and exit, little product differentiation, the result is that competition in the Chinese wood-processing GVC is intense, often leading to an erosion of profit margins. Many processing mills are thought to survive only due to state subsidies such as value-added tax rebates (Changjin et al. 2008; TFT 2007). With the exception of some large foreign enterprises or joint ventures, wood-processing companies largely follow a low-cost/low-price competitive strategy with a focus on quantity rather than quality. For example, furniture and other wood products are usually of low to medium quality (Castaño 2002; Changjin et al. 2008).

Chinese civil society does not seem to be exerting the sorts of pressures evident in northern countries, where NGOs (nongovernmental organizations) actively lobby to ensure high environmental standards in the timber GVC. There is compelling evidence that a significant (but unknown[4]) share of Chinese log imports are "illegally sourced,"[5] including those from Gabon (EIA 2005; ITTO 2005; Stark and Cheung 2006). China is widely believed to be at the center of illegal log trade and processing (Global Timber 2009; Katsigris et al. 2002; White et al. 2006).[6] Insofar as the Chinese market shows any distinct preferences for wood products, Chinese consumers appear to like dark wood characteristics, as do Indian consumers. Chinese producers favor Okoumé and darker hardwoods, in contrast to European preferences for lighter-colored woods.

EU and China: Market Changes and the Importance of Standards

The contrast between the drivers of consumption and the determinants of market access in the EU and China surfaces in the preferences of global buyers operating in Gabon. Buyers from China tend to place a premium on low price and large volume. They are generally less concerned with specific varieties than are the EU buyers, and they also show particularly low preferences for environmental compliance and the quality of the logs they are purchasing (figure 8.10). Specifically

Figure 8.10 EU and Chinese Buyers' Requirements: Wood Logs

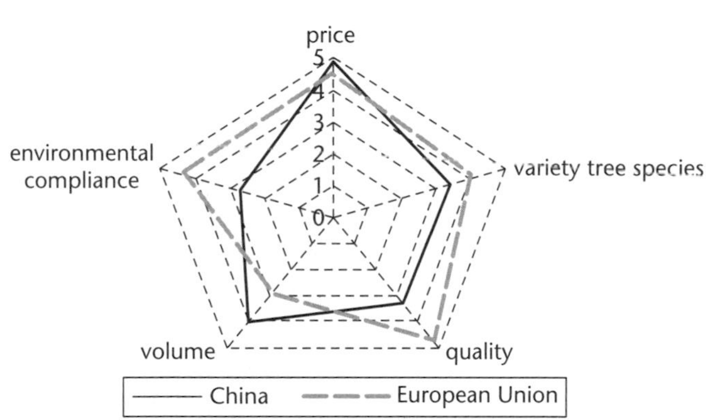

Source: Author's fieldwork interviews.
Note: The scale is 1 = not important and 5 = very important.

with respect to environmental standards, Chinese buyers make very few demands from Gabonese suppliers, particularly in comparison to EU buyers (figure 8.11).[7]

Changes in Market Destinations of Gabon's Timber Exports

The evolution of the EU and the Chinese markets has had major consequences for the direction and nature of Gabon's timber exports. In Gabon's exports, China (and India) have now become the dominant global importers of tropical hardwoods, as EU economies have moved to importing processed woods and have become increasingly concerned about the sustainability of global hardwood reserves. Between 1990 and 2007, China's share of global imports rose from 14 percent to 68 percent (and India's from 5 percent to 17 percent), while the share of all economies in the Organisation for Economic Co-operation and Development (OECD) collapsed from 78 percent to 11 percent (table 8.4). With 1990 as the base-year, in 2007 China's imports of tropical hardwood had more than quadrupled in volume terms; in the same period, EU and wider OECD imports had fallen by more than 90 percent.

This shift in the share of global tropical log imports is reflected in the destination of Gabon's timber exports. China became a significant importer of timber from Gabon in the mid-1990s (figure 8.12). In volume, Chinese imports of the roundwood equivalent of sawnwood, veneers, and plywood are currently more

Figure 8.11 EU and Chinese Buyers' Requirements: International Regulations and Standards

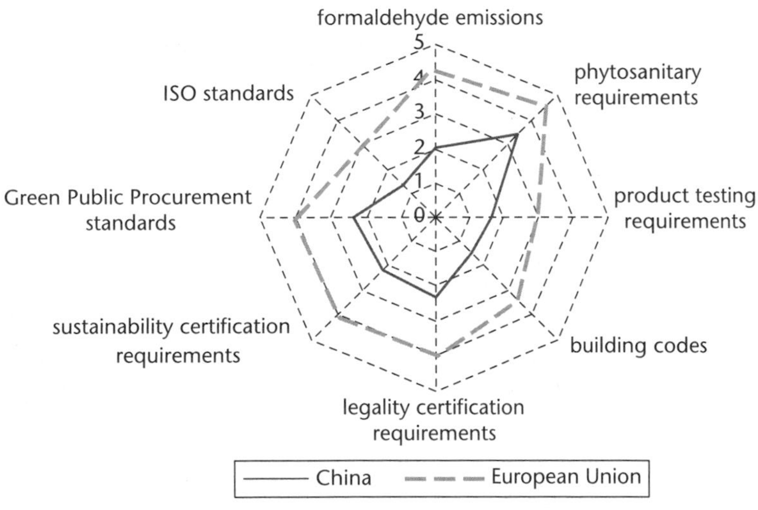

Source: Author's fieldwork interviews.
Note: The scale is 1 = not important and 5 = very important.

Table 8.4 Share of Global Tropical Log Importers for Selected Countries: 1990, 1997, and 2007
percentage of global market

Importer	1990	Importer	1997	Importer	2007
Japan	39.5	Japan	32.3	*China*	*68.2*
Korea, Rep. of	16.1	*China*	*29.2*	India	17.2
China	*13.9*	Korea, Rep. of	6.5	Japan	3.8
Thailand	8.1	India	5.5	France	2.1
India	4.7	Thailand	4.5	Thailand	1.3
France	3.6	France	3.7	Spain	0.9
Italy	2.9	Philippines	3.7	Korea, Rep. of	0.8
Portugal	2.1	Norway	2.2	Italy	0.8
Spain	2.0	Pakistan	1.9	Turkey	0.7
Germany	1.4	Portugal	1.8	Portugal	0.6
OECD	*78.29*	*OECD*	*53.23*	*OECD*	*10.99*

Source: FAOSTAT ForestSTAT data 2009.
Note: OECD = Organisation for Economic Co-operation and Development.

Figure 8.12 Chinese and French Tropical Wood Product Import Structures from Gabon: Log and Wood Product Volumes, 1997–2006

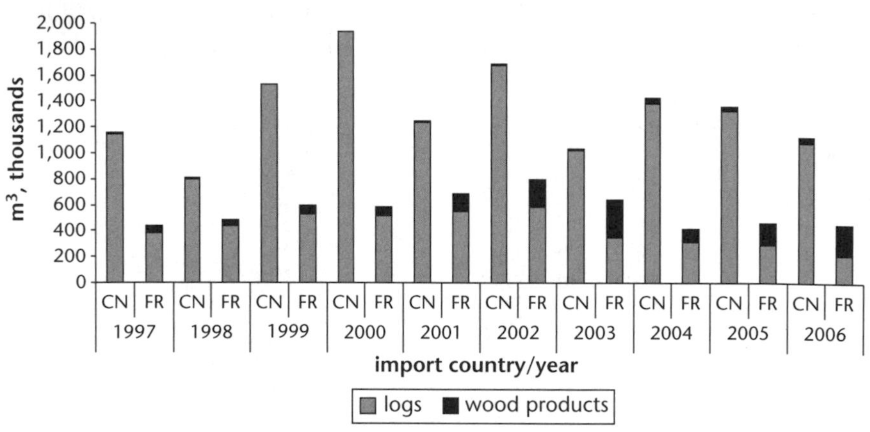

Source: FAOSTAT Forestry Trade Flow Data 2009.
Note: The unit is roundwood equivalent in thousands of cubic meters. Calculation of the roundwood equivalent uses the following conversion factors, based on the responses of firms in Gabon: for the EU, including France—the sawnwood ratio is 2.5:1, veneer sheets 1.82:1, and plywood 2.3:1. For China, the sawnwood ratio is 2.05:1 (reflecting the lower quality requirements of buyers). Veneer sheets and plywood have the same conversion factor as exports to the EU, including France. CN = China; FR = France.

than three times those of French imports, but in value, China imports roughly the same value of timber products from Gabon. The difference between value and volume shares is accounted for by the fact that, as is shown below, the Chinese market is almost exclusively a market for unprocessed logs, whereas an increasing (albeit still small) share of the EU market is serviced by processed timber products which have a higher unit value. Although China has been the dominant importer of Gabon's timber by volume, its dominance in Gabon's timber trade is a little atypical of the global picture, where its share of imports is even higher. The high relative share of France in Gabon's exports reflects its close historical links with France and the long presence of French timber companies operating in Gabon.

Consequences of Market Shifts

What have been the consequences for Gabon of the shift in the market for its timber exports, and what are the implications for the trajectory of its timber industry? Two major developments that have taken place—the nature and extent of standards imposed on producers and the accretion of value-added to harvested logs—are described as follows.

Importance of standards in the EU and Chinese markets

We emphatically state that the transition in market destination from the EU to China has led to a collapse in the standards required of producers (table 8.5). These standards have important implications for capability building. Greater demands for quality require enhanced skills and the capacity to improve quality over time. Instead, Gabonese timber suppliers can basically sell any timber product to China, irrespective of the quality of cutting, sawing, or finishing, as long as the price is low and volumes are large. Environmental standards that influence health and safety in the treatment of forest products are an important safeguard for the welfare of the workforce. Certification of logs helps to ensure that the sustainability of the forests is maintained, and environmental certification such as FSC accreditation helps to maintain biodiversity and to promote social cohesion. Virtually none of these standards apply to products exported to China; virtually all apply to products exported to the EU.

EU and China: Comparative value-added in exports

A combination of factors, particularly the growth of its own wood-processing industries, have resulted in China almost exclusively importing raw logs. In addition, China's low wages and lax environmental regulations make it a direct competitor to Gabon's processing industry. This is not the case in its trade with the EU, where high wages make for uncompetitive processing in labor-intensive industries that are often also polluting. While the bulk of Gabon's timber is still exported as raw logs, in recent years Gabon producers have begun to export an increasing volume of sawnwood, veneers, and plywood. From figure 8.13, it is evident that China shows little inclination to import either veneers or plywood. (In addition, this figure underestimates the value of this shift in export composition: since it

Table 8.5 Summary of Preferences and Buyer Standards of Chinese and EU Buyers of Gabon Timber Products

	Buyers	
Preference/standard	**Chinese**	**European Union**
Critical success factors in purchasing decision		
Stage of processing	Logs	Logs and processed wood
Species variety	Wide range, limited selection	Narrow range, selective
Quality	Medium	High
Volume	Large	Small
Product specifications (e.g., cut specificity)	Moderate importance	Important, intricate
Price	Critical	Critical
Environmental compliance	Minor importance	Important
Industry-specific and public standards		
Formaldehyde emissions	Not important	Important
Phytosanitary certificate	Basic entrance criteria	Important
Building codes	Not important	Moderate importance
Product testing requirements	Not important	Moderate importance
Labor standards	Not important	Moderate importance; few applications
Legality certification	Not required	Important, OLB dominates
Sustainability certification	Not required	Important, FSC dominates
Green public purchasing	Minor importance	Important; few applications
ISO 14001	Not required	Moderate importance

Source: Authors.
Note: FSC = Forest Stewardship Council; OLB = Origine et Légalité des Bois.

reflects export volumes rather than export value, the unit price of processed wood is higher than that of unprocessed logs.)

The development impact: Factor utilization

Since one of the major consequences of a shift in the final market from the EU to China is that the degree of processing has fallen, what are the consequences of this for factor utilization in the Gabonese economy? Table 8.6 simulates factor utilization if the same quantity of wood is exported in the form of logs, sawnwood, veneer sheets, and plywood. It calculates the resultant earnings of foreign exchange and the derived utilization of labor and capital, taking into account processing loss in the conversion of logs as well as the unit prices in global markets in 2006. It is necessarily a crude exercise, but nevertheless, the exercise does shed some light on the developmental consequences of alternative uses of forest resources, as reflected in different destinations of final markets.

Figure 8.13 Log and Wood Product Demand Distribution for China, France, and the EU 27 Countries, 1997–2006

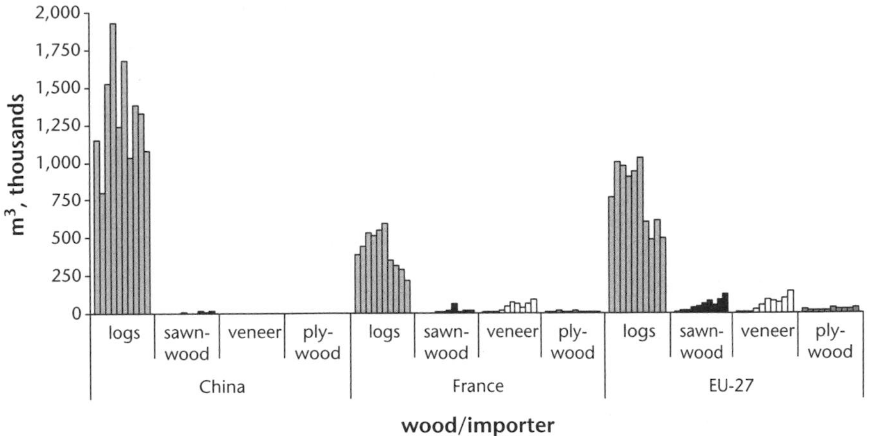

Source: FAOSTAT Forest Trade Flows data 2009.

Table 8.6 Gabon Log Output Channeled into a Single Chain, at Gabon Wood Utilization Rates

Item	Logs	Sawnwood	Veneers	Plywood
Output real (1,000 cubic meters)[a]	3,400	1,370	1,750	1,490
Foreign exchange[b]	1,050	750	1,170	1,190
Employment (including employment in earlier stages of processing)[c]	9,200	26,300	28,100	58,800
Capital cost ($1,000)[d]	40,000	75,000	429,000	730,000
Producer margins (FOB value minus cost) (indexed to ex-forest cost of log)[e]	107	–28	–23	23

Sources: Author's fieldwork data and Odyseé Développement 2005.

Note: The information in this table assumes a log input of 3.4 million cubic meters. The Gabon log production volume is the rounded average for 2003–07. FOB = free-on-board.

a. Converted using wood utilization rates in meeting EU buyer requirements regarding species and product specifications, that is, 2.22:1 (EU Okoumé sawnwood), 2.77:1 (EU other hardwood sawnwood), 1.96:1 (veneers), and 2.3:1 (plywood).

b. Species weighted average using 2006 prices based on UNCTAD Commodity Price Statistic (tropical logs and plywood), and FAO ForesSTAT (sawnwood and veneer export unit price, own calculations).

c. Based on author's fieldwork data collected November 2008–March 2009, and employment figures in Nguema (2007).

d. Based on 2003 capital depreciation costs across chains in Odyssée Développement (2005) converted into U.S. dollars using the average 2003 exchange rate from the UN Statistical Division.

e. Based on author's fieldwork data.

The table shows that there is a substantial gain in employment to be achieved by the downstream processing of logs into sawnwood, veneer, and plywood. Employment is more than doubled if the logs are converted into sawnwood, trebled with the extension to producing veneer sheets, and quadrupled if these veneer sheets are then incorporated in the production of plywood. Foreign exchange earnings are also enhanced with further processing, by 25 percent in the case of veneer and 12 percent in the case of plywood. However, this is not the case in sawnwood, in which there is a value and foreign exchange loss in processing because the Gabon sawmill industry is inefficient and has low conversion rates. Veneer firms also lose money in processing. The reason firms invested in sawmilling and veneer production is purely a function of the Forestry Code, where firms that were unable to afford the high capital entry costs into the production of plywood and/or veneer, deepened their value-added in the expectation of meeting the 2012 Forestry Code target. These loss-making firms manage to stay in production as a result of the profits earned through their log exports. This augmentation of value, employment, and foreign exchange earnings through processing comes at a very considerable cost of capital, particularly in the production of plywood and veneer, and constitutes a major obstacle for local firms in meeting the Forestry Code's 2012 target requiring the deepening of log-processing.

Another area of concern from a developmental perspective is the competitiveness of Gabonese producers at various points in the timber GVC. It is clear that Gabon possesses a significant resource rent in tropical hardwoods in general and Okoumé in particular. Table 8.6 shows that the free-on-board price of a log is approximately double that of the cost of extraction; however, at current prices and with current levels of processing efficiency, the surplus generated in plywood manufacture is much smaller, both as an absolute sum and as a proportion of costs. And at current prices, all of the resource rents are dissipated—indeed, more than dissipated—if logs are sawn or transformed and exported as veneer. Thus, the "retrograde" transition from processed to raw timber reflected in the shift from the European to the Chinese market may arguably be developmentally positive, at least in terms of static comparative advantage and at current prices.

But neither of these two conditions is a given. With appropriate policy support and in competitive markets, it is possible that processing efficiency in Gabon's timber value-adding sectors (especially in sawmills) could be improved. Moreover, it is also possible that Chinese producers will increasingly have to internalize some of the environmental costs that are currently not reflected in either the timber prices or the prices of processed wood products. This may lead to an increase in the relative price of sawnwood, veneer, and timber that will enable Gabonese producers to appropriate a larger portion of its timber rents in the processing stages of the timber and wood products GVC.

Conclusions

Chapter 4 showed that the growth agenda in many low-income countries has focused disproportionately on the development of supply capabilities, rather than on the role played by the nature of demand. The hypothesis in that chapter is that demand from low-income economies affects the organization of GVCs in two particular respects—the importance of process and product standards and the extent to which low-income exporting economies are constrained in their capacity to deepen value-added in their chains. The context is one of a global economy where China and India—both low-income economies—are likely to be the major drivers of global demand, particularly in soft commodity sectors (producing foods like cassava and intermediate products like timber) and in hard commodity sectors that produce the inputs required for the massive investments in infrastructure and housing as the very large Chinese and Indian economies urbanize rapidly (Kaplinsky and Farooki 2010).

This chapter explored the two hypotheses raised in chapter 4 by addressing the impact of a switch in demand from southern to northern economies. This was evidenced in relation to the cassava GVC in Thailand and the timber GVC in Gabon. In both cases, China's demand is becoming increasingly dominant, reflecting the very rapid growth of a very large, low-income economy. In the cassava sector, Chinese demand for food and energy has led to a derived demand for cassava, substituting for a rapidly declining EU market. In Gabon's case, northern demand for tropical logs has collapsed, while Chinese demand has mushroomed. In the case of timber, the associated shift from differentiated to undifferentiated product demand is particularly clearly evidenced. Northern importers are focused on a narrow range of species, and buyers are much more demanding on log specifications, variety, and quality than are Chinese buyers, who basically want large volumes at low prices.

With regard to the derived implications of this market shift for standards, it is clear that in both cases, value chains feeding into a southern market are much less likely to be standards intensive than those feeding into northern markets. This is very clearly evidenced in the timber sector in relation to both government-imposed standards focusing on health and safety and civil society–induced standards focusing on the environment. Although cassava production is less standards intensive, it too shows clear evidence that the move from a northern to a southern market leads to a significant reduction in the standards intensity of global value chains.

With regard to the move from a win-win North-South division of labor to a win-lose South-South division of labor, similar trends are observed in both Thailand's cassava GVC and Gabon's timber GVC. The change in final market from the

EU to China effectively wiped out a key value-added link in the Thai cassava GVC, as Chinese demand for raw chips substituted for EU demand for processed pellets. On the other hand, China also increased its demand for starch imports from Thailand, starch having a higher level of value-added than either cassava chips or pellets. However, within starch products, Chinese firms are seeking to command the higher value-added and more technologically demanding niches, relegating Thai firms to the production of simple native starches. A similar story is revealed for Gabon, where the Chinese market demands only unprocessed logs, whereas exports to the EU have increasingly comprised logs processed into sawnwood, veneers, and plywood. This is clear evidence of the competitive nature of industrial trajectories in southern trading economies, which are more likely to have win-lose outcomes in specialization, than in the case of win-win trade with northern economies.

So what are the wider implications of these findings? First, the growth implications are mixed and somewhat analogous to those associated with declining barter terms of trade. That is, the unit value-added per price of commodity exports to China may fall (that is, the barter terms of trade are affected), but augmented demand may increase total export incomes (that is, the income terms of trade are increased). Similarly, the challenge facing commodity exporters forced down the value-added chain as Chinese demand grows is similar to that faced by developing-country exporters in general who specialized in static dynamic comparative advantage. In this case, incomes may grow, but at the cost of declining capabilities. Chinese demand appears to force both the Thai cassava and the Gabon timber sector into low-technology, low-skill niches in their chains. This is reinforced by the lower requirement for standards in these value chains. Although standards also have their negative side (see below), they do promote managerial and skill competencies in production. Another positive consequence of standards in production is that they most often reflect the need to compensate for nonprice externalities arising in production (for example, the loss of biodiversity) rather than just embodying ethical concerns (for example, in relation to minimum wages or child labor).

A further negative consequence of trade with China, India, and other southern economies is that insofar as it involves lower degrees of value-added, there will be a loss in employment and, in some cases, in investment surpluses.

On the other hand, the substitution of a southern for a northern driver of demand has many advantages for low-income countries and for participants in their value chains. Particularly in the context of a sustained economic crisis in the North, it provides a dynamic and particularly rapid source of demand, allowing exporting economies and firms to reap scale economies and to reduce their costs. And, insofar as their previous trajectory may have been costly (as is arguably the case in Gabon's timber industry where industrial ambitions may be forcing the country to waste its resource rents in inefficient processing), being driven back into comparative advantage through trade with China and other southern economies may provide unintended benefits. Further, it is not axiomatic that all standards are developmentally beneficial in the context of low per capita incomes. The tradeoffs in terms of lost employment and value-added may be too high, for example, to justify the higher safety standards driving much legislation in the North, or, indeed, to meet the ethical concerns of northern civil society. Finally, there will be complex and differentiated implications for different participants in southern value chains. For example, small firms and farmers that are currently largely excluded from participating in global value chains by the need to encompass high standards in their production for northern markets may now find that these barriers to entry are removed.

Notes

1. There are major differences in the data on production and trade provided by the TTTA and Comtrade. To facilitate a comparative analysis of Thai export trade, Comtrade was used here as a data source on exports. But since Comtrade data do not distinguish between pellets and chips, TTTA was used as the source of the product composition of the dried cassava trade.
2. Thai "exporters" to the EU are actually just assemblers: they only handle paperwork on the Thai side, port handling, and off and on loading from lighters (small boats) to big long-haul vessels, usually organized by the agricultural commodity traders.
3. Congo Basin comprises parts of Cameroon, Central African Republic, Democratic Republic of Congo, Republic of the Congo, Equatorial Guinea, and Gabon.
4. The share of illegally sourced logs of total log trade volumes is estimated to be around 10 percent (EIA 2005).
5. Illegal logging occurs when timber is harvested, transported, bought, or sold in contravention of national laws (EIA 2005; Greenpeace 2009).
6. "China's sources for hardwood log imports reads like a who's who of countries with problems with illegal logging" (EIA 2005, 3).
7. See box 8.2 for details on standards.

References

Adams, M., and H. O. Ma. 2002. "ITTO Tropical Forest Update: China's Plywood Industry Takes Off." Yokohama, Japan: International Tropical Timber Organization.

Bazett, M. 2000. "Long-Term Changes in the Location and Structure of Forest Industries." Washington, DC: World Bank/World Wildlife Fund Project.

Bowyer, J. L., J. Howe, P. Guillery, and K. Fernholz. 2004. "Trends in the Global Forest Sector and Implications for Forest Certification." Dovetail Partners, Inc., Minneapolis, MN.

Canby, K., J. Hewitt, L. Bailey, E. Katsigris, and S. Xiufang. 2008. "Forest Products Trade between China and Africa: An Analysis of Import and Export Statistics." Forest Trends, Washington, DC.

Castaño, J. 2002. "The Booming Furniture Industry in China." *Bois et Forêts des Tropiques* 277 (3): 85–87.

Changjin, S., C. Liqiao, C. Lijun, H. Lu, and S. Bass. 2008. "Global Forest Product Chains: Identifying Challenges and Opportunities for China through a Global Commodity Chain Sustainability Analysis." International Institute for Sustainable Development, Winnipeg, Manitoba, Canada.

Collomb, J.-G., J.-B. Mikissa, and S. Minnemeyer. 2000. "A First Look at Logging in Gabon." World Resources Institute, Washington, DC.

Comtrade (United Nations Commodity Trade Statistics Database). Access dates as stated, from http://www.comtrade.un.org.

Démurger, S., H. Yuanzhao, and Y. Weiyong. 2007. "Forest Management Policies and Resource Balance in China: An Assessment of the Current Situation." Groupe d'Analyse et de Théorie Economique, Ecully Cedex, France.

EIA (Environmental Investigation Agency). 2005. "Chinese Involvement in African Illegal Logging and Timber Trade." Committee on International Relations, Subcommittee on Africa, Global Human Rights and International Operations, U.S. House of Representatives, Washington, DC.

FAO (Food and Agriculture Organization of the United Nations). 2005. "Global Forest Resources Assessment 2005: Progress Towards Sustainable Forest Management." Food and Agriculture Organization of the United Nations. Rome, Italy.

———. 2007. "State of the World's Forests 2007." Rome: Food and Agriculture Organization of the United Nations.

FAOSTAT (FAO Statistical Database). Access dates as stated, from http://faostat.fao.org/.

Farrella, E. P., E. Führer, D. Ryana, F. Andersson, R. Hüttl, and P. Piussi. 2000. "European Forest Ecosystems: Building the Future on the Legacy of the Past." *Forest Ecology and Management* 132 (1): 5–20.

Gereffi, G. 1994. "The Organization of Buyer-Driven Global Commodity Chains: How U.S. Retailers Shape Overseas Production Networks." In *Commodity Chains and Global Capitalism*, ed. G. Gereffi and M. Korzeniewicz. London: Praeger.

Global Timber 2009. *Info: China*. http://www.globaltimber.org.uk, accessed August 2009.

Grainger, A. 1995. "The Forest Transition: An Alternative Approach." *Area* 72 (3): 242–51.

Greenpeace. 2009. "Partners in Crime: The UK Timber Trade, Chinese Sweatshops and Malaysian Robber Barons in Papua New Guinea's Rainforests." Greenpeace International, Amsterdam.

Gulbrandsen, L. H., and D. Humphreys. 2006. "International Initiatives to Address Tropical Timber Logging and Trade." The Fridtjof Nansen Institute, Oslo, Norway.

Humphreys, D. 2006. *Logjam: Deforestation and the Crisis of Global Governance*. London: Earthscan Publications Ltd.

ITTO (International Tropical Timber Organization). 2009. "Annual Review and Assessment of the World Timber Situation 2008." ITTO, Yokohama, Japan.

———. 2005. "ITTO Mission in Support of the Efforts by the Government of the Gabonese Republic to achieve the ITTO 2000 Objective and Sustainable Forest Management." [Decision 2(XXIX)]. ITTO, Yokohama, Japan.

———. 2006. "Status of Tropical Forest Management 2005: Gabon Country Profile." ITTO, Yokohama, Japan.

Jorgenson, A. K. 2008. "Structural Integration and the Trees: An Analysis of Deforestation in Less-Developed Countries, 1990–2005." *The Sociological Quarterly* 49: 503–27.

Kaplinsky, R. 1994. *Easternisation: The Spread of Japanese Management Techniques to Developing Countries*. London: Frank Cass.

Kaplinsky, R., and M. Farooki. 2010. "Global Value Chains, the Crisis, and the Shift of Markets from North to the South." Chapter 4 in this volume.

Kaplinsky, R., and M. Morris. 2001. *A Handbook for Value Chain Research*. International Development Research Centre (IDRC). http://asiandrivers.open.ac.uk/documents/Value_chain_Handbook_RKMM_Nov_2001.pdf.

Katsigris, E., G. Bull, A. White, C. Barr, K. Barney, Y. Bun, F. Kahrl, T. King, A. Lankin, A. Lebedev, P. Shearman, A. Sheingauz, Y. Su, and H. Weyerhaeuser. 2002. "The China Forest Products

Trade: Overview of Asia-Pacific Supplying Countries, Impacts, and Implications." Forest Trends, Washington, DC.

Kauppi, P. E., J. H. Ausubel, J. Fang, A. S. Mather, R. A. Sedjo, and P. E. Waggoner. 2006. "Returning Forests Analyzed with the Forest Identity." *PNAS* 103 (46): 17574–79.

Kozak, R., and K. Canby. 2007. "Why China Prefers Logs—Explaining the Prevalence of Unprocessed Wood in China's Timber Imports." Forest Trends, Washington, DC.

Leigh, D., and J.-P. Olters. 2006. "Natural-Resource Depletion, Habit Formation, and Sustainable Fiscal Policy: Lessons from Gabon." International Monetary Fund, Washington, DC.

Mather, A. 1992. "The Forest Transition." *Area* 24 (4): 367–79.

———. 2001. "Forests of Consumption: Post-productivism, Post-materialism, and the Post-industrial Forest." *Environment and Planning C: Government and Policy* 19 (2): 249–68.

Mather, A., and C. Needle. 1998. "The Forest Transition: A Theoretical Basis." *Area* 30 (2): 117–24.

———. 1999. "Development, Democracy and Forest Trends." *Global Environmental Change* 9: 105–18.

Melhado, O. 2007. "Optimal Taxation in the Forestry Sector in the Congo Basin: The Case of Gabon." International Monetary Fund, Washington, DC.

Methot, P., and A. Ndongou. 2009. *Atlas Forestier Interactif du Gabon*. Washington, DC: World Resources Institute; New York: Oxford University Press.

Nguema, V. M. 2007. "Case Study on the Impacts of Forest Investment Policies and Practices—The Case of Gabon." International Tropical Timber Organization, Yokohama, Japan.

Nilsson, S. 1999. "Do We Have Enough Forests?" IUFRO Occasional Paper, International Union of Forestry Research Organizations, Vienna, Austria.

OAE (Office of Agricultural Economics). 2006. "A Study on the Export Potential of Thai Cassava Chips Export to China after Thailand—China Free Trade Agreement"(translated from Thai). *Agricultural Economic Research* 114, Ministry of Agriculture and Cooperatives, Bangkok.

Odyssée Développement. 2005. "Étude de la contribution du secteur forestier à l'économie gabonaise." Unpublished report. Agence Française de Développement, Paris.

OECD (Organisation for Economic Co-operation and Development). 2009. "African Economic Outlook 2009: Country Profile, Gabon." OECD, Paris.

Piore, M. J., and C. Sabel. 1984. *The Second Industrial Divide: Possibilities for Prosperity.* New York: Basic Books.

Pro Forest 2009. "Guidance on Effective Ways to Work with Chinese Officials and Suppliers." Oxford: Pro Forest.

Roonnaphai, N. 2006. "Pathways Out of Poverty through Cassava, Maize and Soybean in Thailand." CAPSA Working Paper 93, United Nation Economics and Social Commission for Asia and the Pacific, Bangkok.

Rudel, T. K., O. T. Coomes, E. Moran, F. Achard, A. Angelsenm, and J. Xu. 2005. "Forest Transitions: Towards a Global Understanding of Land Use Change." *Global Environmental Change Part A* 15 (1): 23–31.

SEPBG (Libreville Société d'Exploitation des Parcs à Bois du Gabon). 2009. "Evolution des volumes exportes de 2000 à 2008 par essence." SEPBG, Libreville, Gabon.

Söderling, L. 2006. "After the Oil: Challenges Ahead in Gabon." *Journal of African Economies* 15 (1): 117–48.

Stark, T., and S. P. Cheung. 2006. "Sharing the Blame: Global Consumption and China's Role in Ancient Forest Destruction." Greenpeace International and Greenpeace China.

Stringer, C. 2006. "Forest Certification and Changing Global Commodity Chains." *Journal of Economic Geography* 6: 701–22.

Sun, C., L. Chen, L. Han, and S. Bass. 2008. "Global Forest Product Chains: Identifying Challenges and Opportunities for China through a Global Commodity Chain Sustainability Analysis." International Institute for Sustainable Development (IISD), Winnipeg, Manitoba, Canada.

TFT (Tropical Forest Trust). 2007. "China Wood Products Supply Chain Analysis: Helping Chinese Wood Producers Achieve Market Demands for Legal and Sustainable Timber." TFT, Southampton, UK.

Tissari, J. 2009. "Report on the Study of the Technical and Environmental Standards of Tropical Timber Products in International Markets." International Tropical Timber Council, International Tropical Timber Organization, Yokohama, Japan.

Titapiwatanakun, B. 1994. "Thai Cassava Starch Industry: Current and Future Utilization." Paper presented at the International Meeting on Cassava Flour and Starch, Jan.11–15, The International Center for Tropical Agriculture (CIAT), Cali, Colombia.

TTSA (Thai Tapioca Starch Association). 2008. "Annual Report 2007." TTSA, Bangkok.

———. 2009. "Thai Ethanol Industry: the Opportunities and the Challenges." TTSA, Bangkok. http//tapiocathai.org, accessed Dec.14, 2009.

TTTA (Thai Tapioca Trade Association). 2009. "Annual Report 2008." TTTA, Bangkok.

———. 2004. "Annual Report 2003." TTTA, Bangkok.

UNEP and WCMC Species Programme. 2009. United Nations Environment Program and World Conservation Monitoring Centre. http://www.unep-wcmc.org/, accessed Oct. 2009.

Victor, D. G., and J. H. Ausubel. 2000. "Restoring the Forests." *Foreign Affairs* 79 (6): 127–44.

Wang, W. 2002. "Cassava Production for Industrial Utilisation in China: Present and Future Perspectives." 17th Cassava Regional Conference Proceedings, Oct. 28–Nov. 1. Bangkok.

Wang, X. H. 2007. "China's Corn Processing Industry: Its Future Development and Implications for World Trade." Presentation, National Grain and Oils Information Centre, China, April 2007. Beijing, China.

White, A., and A. Martin. 2002. "Who Owns the World's Forests? Forest Tenure and Public Forests in Transition." Forest Trends, Washington, DC.

White, A., X. Sun, K. Canby, J. Xu, C. Barr, E. Katsigris, G. Bull, C. Cosslater, and S. Nilsson. 2006. *China and the Global Market for Forest Products; Transforming Trade to Benefit Forests and Livelihoods.* Washington, DC: Forest Trends.

Womack, J. P., and D. T. Jones. 1996. *Lean Thinking: Banish Waste and Create Wealth in Your Corporation.* New York: Simon & Schuster.

Wunder, S. 2003. "When the Dutch Disease Met the French Connection: Oil, Macroeconomics and Forests in Gabon." Report prepared for the CIFOR-CARPE-USAID project, The Impact of Macroeconomic and Agricultural Policies on Forest Conditions in Gabon. Bogor: Center for International Forestry Research, Bogor, Indonesia.

Zhang, J., and J. Gan. 2007. "Who Will Meet China's Import Demand for Forest Products?" *World Development* 35 (12): 2150–60.

9

THE OFFSHORE SERVICES VALUE CHAIN: DEVELOPING COUNTRIES AND THE CRISIS

Gary Gereffi and Karina Fernandez-Stark

Over the past decade, the offshore services industry has experienced tremendous growth, emerging as a dynamic global sector that involves both developed and developing nations. Structural changes in the global economy precipitated by the information and communication technology (ICT) revolution have allowed emerging nations for the first time to contribute significantly to the world's services industry. No longer relegated to manufacturing and natural resource–intensive industries, developing countries now have an important opportunity to advance both their economic and social conditions. The global economic crisis of 2008–09 highlighted an important characteristic of the offshore services industry for developing countries: the industry demonstrated significant resilience to downturns as a result of its principal raison d'être—to lower costs for all industries around the world, which leads to a constant search for lower-cost destinations. This dynamic thus opens up opportunities for new countries to enter this global value chain (GVC).

The offshore services industry, incorporating the trade of services conducted in one country and consumed in another, has transformed the way companies do business by allowing for the separation of the production and consumption of services. The scope of the industry has evolved over time, and increasingly sophisticated activities are being exported. What began with the outsourcing of basic information technology (IT) services to external firms now includes a wide array of activities known as business process outsourcing (BPO), knowledge process outsourcing

(KPO), and other advanced activities in the GVC such as research and development (R&D) that were previously considered core functions of the firm.

As a result of cost arbitrage advantages, developing nations are leaders in many of these offshore services, and the industry has become an important source of employment and economic growth around the globe. Early market entrants rapidly specialized in service areas in which they have a competitive advantage. As they upgraded to higher-value activities, new countries joined the industry at lower points in the value chain. This shift provides emerging economies with an opportunity to drive sustainable growth through the expansion of the knowledge economy and to reduce their traditional dependence on manufacturing and natural resource industries.

The recent economic crisis highlighted the weaknesses of economies based on commodities and sent an urgent call for structural changes in order to attain development (Bárcena 2009). Unlike many other industries, offshore services are typically business-to-business and based on multiyear contracts that buffer the sector to a certain extent from slumps in consumer demand and the accompanying negative macroeconomic factors. This delayed the impact of the economic crisis on offshore services, which first registered lower demand during the last quarter of 2008 and the first three quarters of 2009. This sustained growth is essential for developing economies to protect the development gains they have achieved.

The economic crisis had two key effects on the offshore services industry. First, during the recession, the "demand effect" resulted from a contraction of demand for services from existing customers as business slowed around the world. This effect led annual growth rates in offshore services to decrease significantly. Second, there was a simultaneous "substitution effect," which involved the substitution of lower-price services (for example, those contracted in India) for the higher-price services originally carried out inside companies in developed economies. The "substitution effect" mitigated the negative impact of demand contraction as new clients began to adopt offshoring practices in order to lower costs and improve efficiencies. The response of the offshore service providers was to diversify both service center locations and client bases, improve cost structures, and provide innovative solutions. The net result was that while demand for offshore services dipped in response to the crisis, annual growth rates remained above 15 percent in large developing-nation providers such as India and the Philippines.

This chapter describes the development of the offshore services industry using the GVC framework to identify the opportunities for market entry for developing nations. It examines the structural changes that were taking place in business services prior to the crisis and provides an analysis of the effects of the crisis on the industry and on the various segments of the value chain.

The Offshore Services Industry: A GVC Approach

Having emerged rapidly in the past decade, offshore services now encompass an array of activities ranging from call centers to research and development services. The various segments and activities of the industry are identified and categorized here using a GVC framework. While the lack of official data makes it difficult to quantify the size of the industry, it has become clear that more companies are unbundling corporate activities, including services, using a variety of business models.

Key Concepts

The first stage in disaggregating the global services market is to categorize services based on the categories "outsourcing" and "offshoring." These concepts distinguish the location of and control over the organizations contracted to perform the tasks. Outsourcing is the act of contracting a function or service from a legally separate unit outside the boundaries of the company, rather than using the company's own internal resources and capabilities (in-house transactions). Offshoring is providing all or part of a function or service by entities outside national, rather than firm, boundaries. Offshoring is particularly important for policy makers and firms in developing countries.[1] Figure 9.1 shows different business models or trajectories that may develop in the outsourcing and offshore services industry (Sako 2005).

The first scenario (arrow 1) illustrates a firm's decision to outsource services locally. Arrow 2 shows the decision to outsource to a foreign provider instead of a

Figure 9.1 Business Models in Outsourcing and Offshore Services

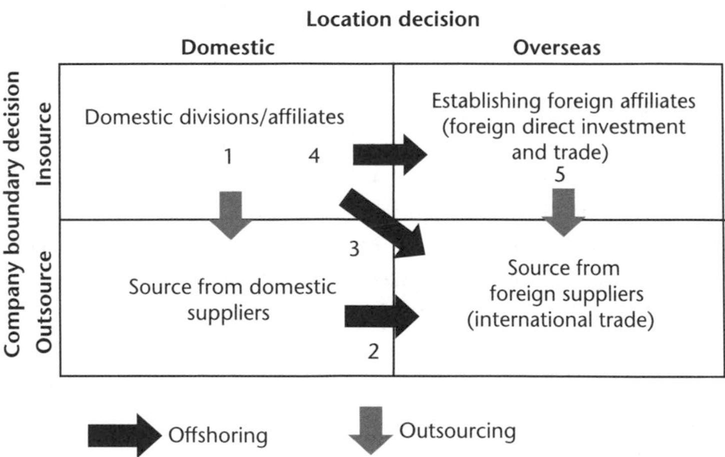

Source: Sako 2005.

domestic supplier (as in arrow 1). Arrow 3 shows the trajectory for a firm's decision to outsource services to a foreign supplier. Arrow 4 shows the firm's decision to move its service provision to a foreign affiliate or subsidiary. The final scenario (arrow 5), shows the shift from a foreign affiliate or subsidiary to provision of services by a foreign supplier (third-party providers). The most beneficial spillovers for host economies in terms of technology and higher-skilled jobs tend to occur in the process of changing from "captive offshoring" (upper right quadrant) to "third-party offshoring" or "offshore outsourcing" (lower right quadrant), as indicated by arrow 5 (Sako 2005).

The complex process of choosing an appropriate business model, that is, determining a firm's geographic location and level of control, depends on the nature of the service, size of investment required, entrepreneurship, local knowledge of the firm, and internal experience (BCG 2007). Governance patterns within this value chain[2] are beginning to emerge based on business models and supplier selection, and future research in this area will likely provide insight into the growing power of multinational offshore providers from developing countries like India.

Classification of the Offshore Services GVC

The services industry has evolved continuously since its inception, making efforts at categorization challenging. Despite these complexities, a fairly comprehensive, yet flexible, classification of the industry has emerged employing the global value chain (GVC) framework (Gereffi and Fernandez-Stark 2010). The GVC framework uses firm-level analysis to determine the different stages of production of a good or service and the value of each component (Gereffi et al. 2001). For manufacturing and extractive industries based on goods, value-added is determined by the difference between the cost of the inputs and outputs at each stage of the chain. In the case of the offshore services industry, measuring value is complicated by the lack of reliable company-level data and trade statistics for services (Sturgeon and Gereffi 2009). To partially address this problem, the value of different services can be related to employee education level and work experience (Gereffi and Fernandez-Stark 2010). By indicating the human capital required at different levels of the offshore services GVC, this classification system provides decision makers in developing countries with an instrument to determine where they may be best suited to enter the GVC in order to achieve their desired outcomes.

Figure 9.2 illustrates the GVC for the offshore services industry (Gereffi and Fernandez-Stark, 2010). This classification scheme makes it possible to identify the various types of offshore service activities, to show which firms participate in

Figure 9.2 The Offshore Services Global Value Chain

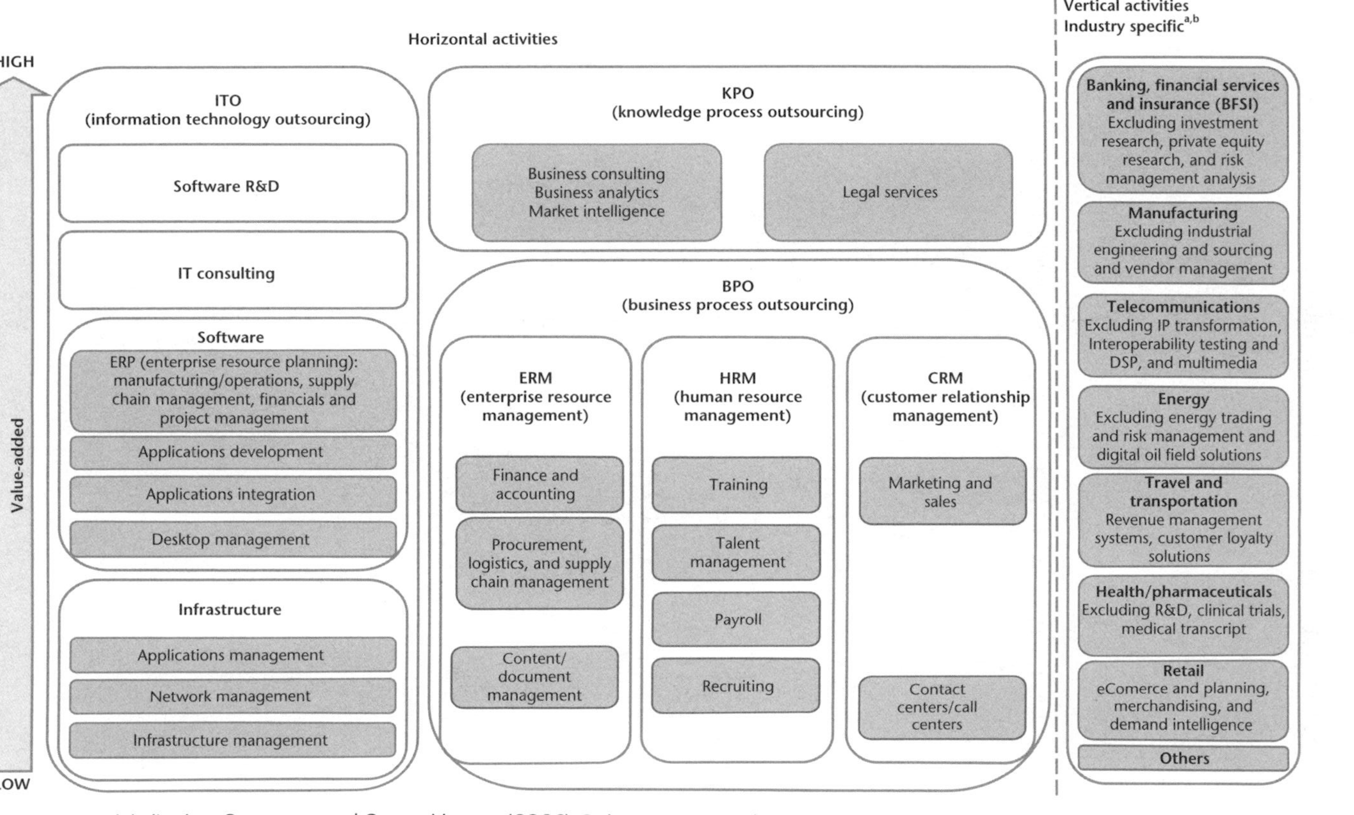

Source: Center on Globalization, Governance and Competitiveness (CGGC), Duke University, Durham, NC.

Note : DSP = digital signal processor; IP = intellectual property.

a. Industry-specific vertical activities: Each industry has its own GVC, within which associated services can be offshored.

b. This graphical depiction of vertical activities does not imply value levels. Each industry may include information technology outsourcing, knowledge process outsourcing, business process outsourcing, and other advanced activities.

which industry segments, and in turn, to locate the most important regions of the world in the industry's development.

The classification system works as follows. The first division is services that can be provided across all industries (horizontal activities), including information technology outsourcing (ITO), business process outsourcing (BPO), and knowledge process outsourcing (KPO). The second division refers to services that are industry specific (vertical activities). Firms operating in the horizontal services tend to be process experts, while those in the vertical chains must have industry-specific expertise and their services may have limited applicability in other industries. In horizontal services, all activities are related to supporting generic business functions, such as network management, application integration, payroll, call centers, accounting, and human resources. In addition, they include higher-value services, such as market intelligence, business analytics, and legal services (referred to as KPO in this chapter).

Within horizontal services, ITO contains a full spectrum of low-, middle- and high-value activities of the offshore services chain; BPO activities are in the low and middle segments, while KPO activities are in the highest-value segment of the chain. The value of each activity is correlated with human capital (education level), that is to say, lower value-added services are performed by people with fewer years of formal education. Call centers or routine BPO activities, for example, can be performed by employees with a high school diploma. Market research or business intelligence is typically carried out by employees with a minimum of a bachelor's degree, while the highest-level research and analysis is carried out by employees holding specialized masters degrees or PhDs.

This categorization can provide development agencies with an instrument for market entry based on the current educational level of their workforce. It also provides an initial blueprint for economic upgrading strategies within the industry. Developing countries that aim to provide services within certain segments of the GVC must evaluate their workforce development strategies and implement policies to build human capital for those segments, be it language skills for the call center market or promoting a doctoral program or advanced training for R&D activities in a specific industry.

Size of the Industry

The global offshore services industry is growing substantially, and no consensus has been reached on how to collect data that correspond to appropriate definitions of services. The rapid evolution of the industry has impeded attempts to categorize it, complicating the measurement of the offshore services themselves, and official statistics do not provide accurate quantitative assessment either (ECLAC

2009; UNCTAD 2009). Generally, countries do not collect data for these service exports, there is a relatively small number of trade classification codes to accurately identify service activities, and companies have little incentive to disclose this information (Sturgeon and Gereffi 2009). In addition to this dearth of available and reliable data, the different methodologies adopted to quantify the size of the offshore services industry have resulted in widely varying estimates from disparate sources.

Table 9.1 provides a list of estimates from private consulting firms, business associations, and international organizations. Two clarifications must be made at this stage:

1. *Outsourcing versus offshoring:* Some organizations, such as the global consulting firm Gartner, have measured the entire outsourcing industry, with respect to both domestic outsourcing and offshore outsourcing. These numbers for outsourcing are generally higher because they include both outsourcing and offshoring services. Another set of organizations, Organisation for Economic Co-operation and Development (OECD), Boston Consulting Group (BCG), and NASSCOM[3]-Everest, have measured only offshore services (their estimates range from US$101 billion to $157 billion for 2008).
2. *Activities included:* This chapter analyzes three industry segments: ITO, BPO, and KPO, along with more specialized, higher value-added service activities, such as engineering services and R&D. The size estimates in table 9.1 differ in the segments they include. Some provide estimates for just the ITO and BPO segments (for example, the McKinsey estimate), while others include higher value-added services in the BPO category (this is the case for the Gartner and BCG estimates). Generally, the high-value services segment is the most difficult to quantify; thus, it may be underrepresented here since some of the activities may not be included.

According to OECD (2008) estimates, the size of the offshore services market will reach $252 billion in 2010. The OECD stresses, however, that growth rates will be different in each segment of the GVC (see figure 9.3). The OECD study, published before the economic crisis began in early 2008, projected that the global demand for BPO services, especially those related to call centers, along with those in the financial services industry, was expected to triple between 2005 and 2010, and IT services were expected to continue growing at a similar pace. The demand for other high-value service activities was expected to reach $31 billion by 2010. This growth translates into a compound annual growth rate for the KPO segment of 58 percent between 2005 and 2010, much more than the expected growth rates for the demand of the BPO (25 percent) and ITO (26 percent) segments.

Table 9.1 Global Offshore Services–Market Size Estimates, 2005–10

			Revenue (US$, billions) Year						
Source	Market	Activity	2005	2006	2007	2008	2009	2010	Comments
OECD (2008)	Global offshore services		81.4	100.8	125.6	**157.4**	198.6	252.4	Includes ITO-BPO and other high-value service activities
NASSCOM (2009)	Global offshore services		44.25	59	78.3	**101**	117.5		Includes ITO-BPO and other high-value service activities. "Derived from a 40% share of market from India."[a]
BCG (2007) Based on IDC data	Global offshore services	ITO	19.2	22.7	26.9	31.9	37.3	43.2	BPO includes other high-value service activities.
		BPO	27.4	42.3	65.1	100.3	154.5	238.1	
		Total	46.6	65.0	92.0	**132.2**	191.8	281.3	
Gartner (2009b)	Global outsourcing and offshoring services	ITO					268		BPO includes other high-value service activities.
		BPO					156		
		Total					424		
NASSCOM & Everest (2008)	Global offshoring BPO	BPO					26–29		

McKinsey & Company (2006)	Global offshoring ITO-BPO	ITO BPO Total	16.7–19.6 9.8–12.3 26.5–31.9		McKinsey calculates the offshoring market potential with a range. They state that the market has captured only 10% of its full potential. ITO: $147 billion–$178 billion (captured only 11%) BPO: $122 billion–$154 billion (captured only 8%) From these estimates we have calculated the real market size in 2005.
A.T. Kearny (2009b)	Global offshoring BPO	BPO		30	22% of the global BPO market is offshore.

Source: Center on Globalization, Governance and Competitiveness (CGGC), Duke University, Durham, NC; based on A.T. Kearney 2009; Chakrabarty, Ghandi, and Kaka 2006; Harris 2009; NASSCOM 2008, 2009; OECD 2008; BCG 2007; Young et al. 2008.

Note: BPO = business process outsourcing; ITO = information technology outsourcing; KPO = knowledge process outsourcing: OECD = Organisation for Economic Co-operation and Development.

a. Based on the reports from BCG (2007) and the NASSCOM-Everest study in 2008. BCG estimated that Indian market share was 46 percent in 2007, while the NASSCOM-Everest estimate lies between 41 and 46 percent (NASSCOM 2008).

Figure 9.3 Global Demand for Offshore Services, by Activity, 2005–10

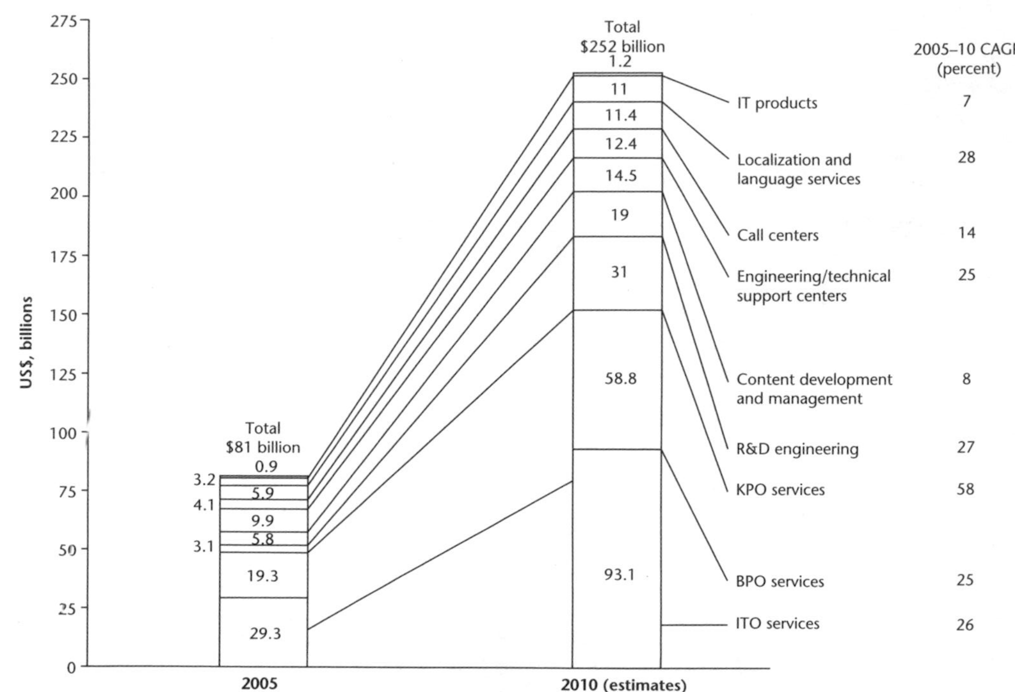

Source: OECD 2008.

Note: BPO = business process outsourcing; CAGR = compound annual growth rate; IT = information technology; ITO = information technology outsourcing; KPO = knowledge process outsourcing; R&D = research and development.

At the country level, as can be seen in map 9.1, the most mature providers of offshore services are India and the Philippines, with more than 50 centers in each country, followed by emerging nations, including Chile, the Czech Republic, and Malaysia. In addition, new locations are beginning to compete in the industry, such as the Arab Republic of Egypt, Morocco, and South Africa.

The supply of global services is highly concentrated among a small group of firms from a handful of countries. As shown in table 9.2, 13 of these firms are headquartered in North America, 4 in India, and 3 in Europe. The large global service providers operating in the offshore industry—Accenture, Capgemini, Computer Sciences Corporation (CSC), EDS (HP Enterprise Services), and IBM—are principally dedicated to serving large multinational corporations and governments (Datamonitor 2009). All these firms have operations in developing countries that serve as platforms for services exports. In 2007, Accenture employed more people in India than anywhere else in the world.[4] By 2006, IBM had 60,000 employees in India, and Capgemini employees there had reached 12,000 (Dossani and Kenney 2007).

The Offshore Services Industry's Potential for Developing Countries

The offshore services industry has emerged just within the past 20 years. The ICT revolution at the end of the 20th century allowed developing countries to enter this market with great success. India and the Philippines have already reached market maturity, while countries in Eastern Europe and South America are in the early to middle stages of development. In many of these nations, offshore services have been the fastest-growing industry in recent years. This has led to significant positive externalities for local economies, such as knowledge transfer, more and better jobs, access to new markets, and infrastructure improvements.

The offshore services industry provides opportunities for many developing countries that are striving to diversify and upgrade their economic activities. The global industry is still in its nascent stages, and the vast majority of its potential remains largely untapped. The McKinsey Global Institute's labor supply report in 2009 estimated that up to 161 million workers' jobs can be performed remotely. It states that "any task that requires no physical or complex interaction between an employee and customers or colleagues, and requires little or no local knowledge, could be performed anywhere in the world by a suitable qualified person" (McKinsey Global Institute 2009).

Figure 9.4 illustrates the significant growth potential of the offshore services industry. The shaded bars represent the adoption of offshore practices in the years 2003 (darker) and 2008 (lighter). In just five years (2003–08), this industry

Map 9.1 Global Supply and Demand for Offshore Services

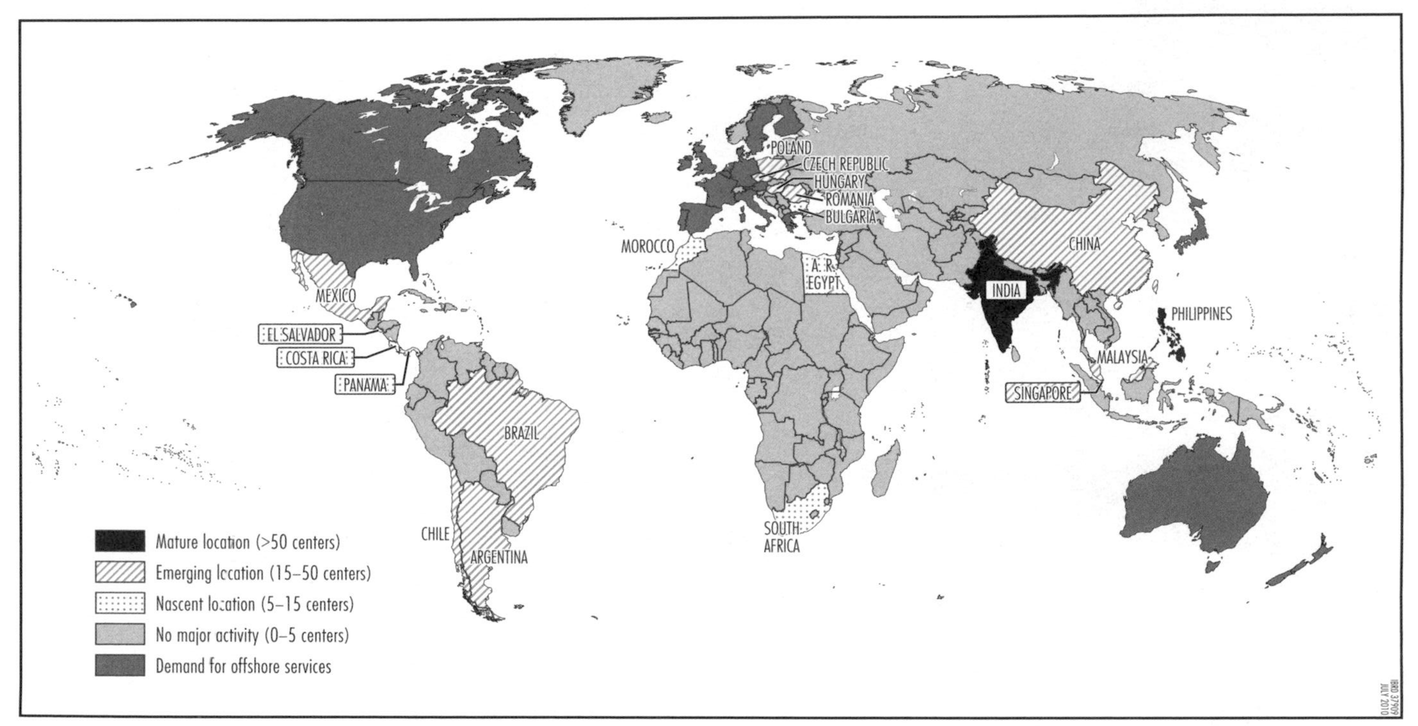

Source: Center on Globalization, Governance and Competitiveness (CGGC), Duke University, Durham, NC; based on data from Everest 2009 and Datamonitor 2009.

Table 9.2 Top-20 Offshore Services Providers

Rank	Company/country	Total sales, 2008 (US$, millions)	Total employees	Total services sales, 2008 (US$, millions)	Main services activities
1	IBM—United States	103,630	398,455	58,892	Consulting, IT services, application, and outsourcing services
2	Accenture—United States	23,171	177,000	23,171	Consulting, IT, and outsourcing services
3	Electronic Data Systems Corporation (EDS, now HP Enterprise Services)—United States	22,100	139,500	22,100	IT, applications, and BPO services
4	Computer Sciences Corporation (CSC)—United States	16,740	92,000	16,740	IT services (software management), BPO in customer relationship management (CRM), supply chain management, and KPO in legal matters
5	Capgemini—France	12,740	89,453	12,740	Consulting, IT, and outsourcing services
6	Automatic Data Processing (ADP)—United States	8,867	45,000	8,867	BPO (human resources, payroll, tax, and benefits outsourcing)
7	Affiliated Computer Services—United States	6,523	76,000	6,523	ITO and BPO in CRM and human resources management; also e-Government
8	Logica (formerly LogicaCMG)—United Kingdom	6,577	39,525	6,320	Business consulting, IT, and BPO services
9	Tata Consultancy Services—India	6,048	111,407	5,824	Consulting, IT, engineering, and BPO (includes KPO) services
10	Infosys Technologies —India	4,717	105,453	4,533	IT, engineering, consulting, and BPO services (knowledge and legal services)

(continued next page)

Table 9.2 *continued*

Rank	Company/country	Total sales, 2008 (US$, millions)	Total employees	Total services sales, 2008 (US$, millions)	Main services activities
11	Wipro Technologies—India	5,645	98,521	4,234	Consulting, IT, and BPO services
12	CGI Group—Canada	3,673	25,500	3,673	Consulting, IT, BPO, and systems integration services
13	Hewitt Associates—United States	3,228	23,000	3,228	Human resource consulting and outsourcing
14	Cognizant Technology Solutions—United States	2,816	68,000	2,816	Consulting, IT, and BPO services
15	Convergys Corporation—United States	2,786	75,000	2,786	BPO (customer care—call centers)
16	Perot Systems—United States	2,779	23,100	2,779	Consulting, IT, and BPO services
17	Teleperformance Group—France	2,605	102,186	2,605	BPO (customer care—call centers)
18	SITEL—United States	1,700	66,000	1,700	BPO (customer care—call centers)
19	Ceridian Corporation—United States	1,695	8,776	1,695	Payroll services and human resources management solutions
20	Genpact Ltd.—India	1,041	36,200	1,041	IT and BPO services
Total		240,210	1,815,519	192,267	

Source: Center on Globalization, Governance and Competitiveness (CGGC), Duke University, Durham, NC; based on OneSource, companies' Web sites and companies' annual reports.

Note: BPO = business process outsourcing; CRM = customer relationship management; HRM = human resources management; IT = information technology; ITO = information technology outsourcing; KPO = knowledge process outsourcing.

Figure 9.4 Actual and Potential Adoption of Offshore Practices

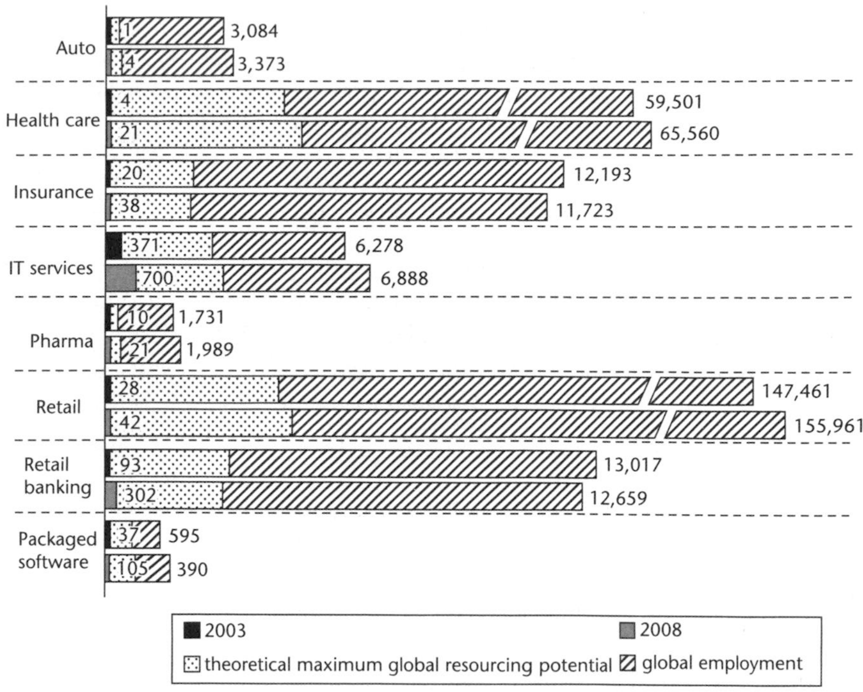

Source: McKinsey Global Institute 2009.
Note: Adoption of offshoring assesses the current and projected levels of offshoring to low-wage countries within a sector. *Theoretical maximum global resourcing potential* describes the percentage of a sector or function that may be performed remotely. *Global employment* is measured in thousands of jobs.

has demonstrated rapid growth. However, the dotted bar presents the vast opportunities that still exist to offshore activities across different industries. The graph also highlights the emergence of new segments in the GVC, including industry-specific offshoring in retail banking and the health care industry.

Nonetheless, global employment in offshore services had already reached 4.1 million by 2008 (McKinsey Global Institute 2009). This growth is being driven by an increasing number of business procurement services abroad to improve their efficiency levels in the global economy, enter new markets, and gain access to strategic assets in other countries (Lopez, Ramos, and Torre 2008). They are attracted to developing countries by competitive advantages, such as low human resource costs, technological skills, and language proficiency (AT Kearney 2007), as well as time zones and geographical and cultural proximity to major markets (ECLAC 2008).

Operating in the same time zone helps facilitate connections between companies, optimizing time and accelerating decision making. In addition, as more sophisticated jobs, such as new product development, R&D, and other knowledge-intensive activities, are performed abroad, the supply of scientific, engineering, and analytical talent offered by developing countries becomes more important (Duke Offshoring Research Network and Booz&Co. 2007).

Structural Changes Facilitating Offshore Services Growth

As the offshore services industry continues to expand—based to a large degree on low-cost yet educated labor forces around the world—developing nations have the opportunity to emerge as important players. Structural changes in the world economy during the past decade have facilitated this explosive growth and suggest that this shift of offshore service work to the developing world will be permanent. These changes are summarized as follows.

- Information technology (IT) now allows for quick and easy information transfer, eliminating the need for on-site operations. This has allowed many developing countries with basic IT infrastructure to enter the global economy and export services all over the world. India has updated its IT infrastructure and now is able to perform remotely almost every service requested.
- Companies looking to reduce costs have unbundled their corporate functions, such as human resources management, customer support, accounting and finance, and procurement operations, and have offshored these activities (Gospel and Sako 2008). This reduces the burden of support activities and allows firms to focus on their core business. These support activities are mainly IT and BPO activities; for example, many multinational corporation (MNC) customer support operations are being offshored to the Philippines.
- In recent years, core activities have also begun to move offshore. Many firms today look beyond low cost to talent in order to drive R&D activities. For example, many pharmaceutical contract research organizations from India and China are offering their services to giant pharmaceutical MNCs, such as GSK, Lilly, Merck, and Novo, among others (Gupta 2008; Wadhwa et al. 2008). This reflects the capabilities of developing countries entering the GVC, not only at the production level but also in creating the knowledge behind the products.

Developing countries have recognized this economic opportunity, and many are actively encouraging the development of the offshore services industry. Countries are offering different services according to their skill level. For example, Chile is working to position itself as an innovation center; already one-third of the country's offshore services are in engineering services (IDC Latin America 2009). Other countries in Latin America, such as El Salvador and Honduras, focus on call centers.

Impact of the Economic Crisis on the Offshore Services Industry

The global economic crisis of 2008–09 has had a tremendous negative effect on almost every industry in the world. Its impact, however, has been less severe for the offshore services industry. Two opposing effects have been seen: some companies have frozen offshore contracts, while other companies have offshored additional services in order to remain competitive by lowering their costs. Perhaps most significantly, demand slowed from financial service institutions, the offshore industry's key client, requiring suppliers to lower costs and improve efficiency to bolster sales. These two conflicting effects are explained in the next section.

Further, the economic crisis has affected distinct segments of the GVC to different degrees. In horizontal activities, IT and BPO services have been affected more than KPO services. Vertical activities reflect the level of impact of the economic crisis in their respective industries. The impact of the economic crisis in the offshore services GVC is analyzed later in the chapter. The overall effect reveals an industry that is still growing, although at a slower pace than previously and showing signs of recovery.

A recent Forrester report explains that companies react differently in their IT plans during an economic slowdown, depending on the model adopted in each organization. Some companies will face more cost pressure; others will react according to their business or may encounter more pressure to innovate and be competitive in their industry. Figure 9.5 illustrates the different categories of firms and the strategies that companies can consider, depending on their business model[5] (Andrews 2008).

According to Duke University's Offshoring Research Network (ORN) findings, companies are continuing to implement their plans to offshore some of their functions, despite the global economic crisis, and may even accelerate these strategies (Lewin et al. 2009). Figure 9.6 illustrates the changes identified by ORN in the key drivers of offshoring decisions as a result of the economic crisis. The results of the survey conducted in November 2008 show that the most significant driver in decision making about offshoring is "taking out costs," in other words, labor cost savings (see figure 9.6). Reducing labor cost in companies from developed countries directly boosts the competitiveness of developing countries in the offshore services industry.

The second most important change in offshoring services reported by ORN is the decision to offshore in order to enhance efficiency by redesigning business

Figure 9.5 How Firms Respond to the Economic Crisis

Archetype	Company's approach		
	Key priority in recession	Importance for service providers	Key positioning consideration
Solid utilities	Reducing IT costs Creating new operational efficiencies Providing stable operations for the business	Value-added services and consulting capabilities will be less attractive Deals take longer to close due to internal cost pressures	Lead with the pricing value Be willing to explain operational efficiencies Plan for longer deal-closing cycles
Trusted suppliers	Reacting to changing and uncertain business needs Reducing risk	Flexible pricing, billing, and payments options become priorities Financial health and longevity of providers are scrutinized	Clearly identify services that can be guaranteed Provide flexible payment options for the rest Prove your financial viability
Partner players	Driving innovation Differentiating the business from the competition	Potentially, this is the least price sensitive and most willing to invest in value-added services like consulting	Prove your long-term strategic value and innovation capabilities Target with strong business messaging like ROI

Source: Andrews 2008.
Note: ROI = return on investment.

Figure 9.6 Changes in Key Drivers of Offshoring Decisions, November 2008

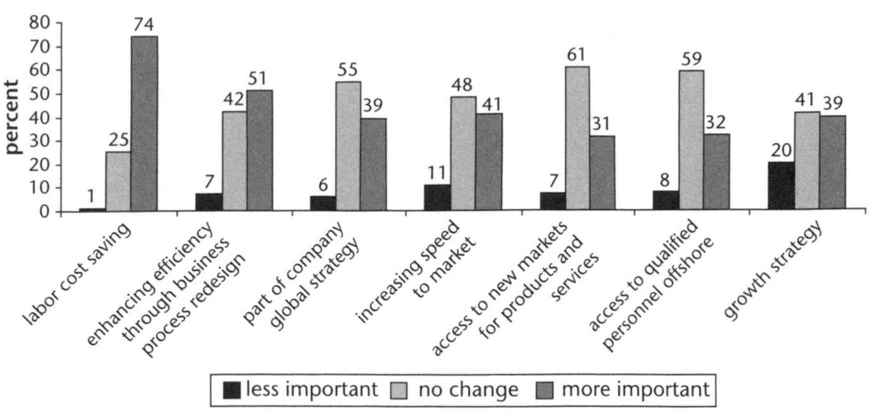

Source: Center on Globalization, Governance and Competitiveness (CGGC), Duke University, Durham, NC; based on Lewin et al. 2009.

processes and to strengthen existing organizational capabilities for managing offshoring strategies. To achieve this goal, the ORN study suggests that companywide strategies should be developed to help increase organizational flexibility, service quality, and above all, to achieve further cost savings.

Although access to qualified personnel continues to be an important driver, during the crisis, this factor had lower relative effects compared to cost (Lewin et al. 2009). The economic crisis is temporarily offsetting the search for global talent as a major driver for offshore services. However, the ORN study also argues that the slowing demand for talent can be explained by increased unemployment fueled by the economic crisis, which has made such talent more available domestically.

On the supply side, the economic crisis has also forced service providers to reduce prices, which has decreased both annual hires and salaries. The recession has increased the motivation of providers to improve the efficiency and quality of their services. Some providers have found new opportunities as a result of the crisis by engaging in innovative solutions for their clients. Providers are reevaluating their value proposition to their customers, and they have been forced to develop out-of-the-box services (NASSCOM Newsline 2009).

Table 9.3 shows the revenue growth of offshore service providers both before and during the economic crisis. The largest decline in provider revenues was during the April–June 2009 trimester. Almost all companies show negative growth rates compared to the same period in 2008. Accenture's revenues dropped 16 percent in that period, while those of IBM declined by 13.3 percent. Providers from developed countries show a sharper decline than providers from India (Tata

Table 9.3 Offshore Services Revenues by Provider, July 2007 to September 2009

percent, year-to-year comparison

						Economic crisis			
Provider	**Jul–Sep 07**	**Oct–Dec 07**	**Jan–Mar 08**	**Apr–Jun 08**	**Jul–Sep 08**	**Oct–Dec 08**	**Jan–Mar 09**	**Apr–Jun 09**	**Jul–Sep 09**
Accenture	27.0	18.1	17.2	18.9	17.7	6.0	–6.6	–16.0	–16.1
IBM	6.6	9.9	11.2	12.8	4.9	–6.4	–11.4	–13.3	–6.9
Computer Sciences Corporation	11.3	14.3	10.9	15.6	5.5	–5.0	–8.3	–12.1	
Automatic Data Processing	13.5	14.7	11.8	10.4	9.5	2.5	–2.2	–4.5	–3.6
CapGemini		21.00		14.4		0.2		–12.7	
Logica		27.60		16.3		–1.0		–20.1	
Affiliated Computer Services	7.8	5.9	7.1	6.2	7.5	6.7	4.4	5.1	4.5
Tata Consultancy Services	40.3	37.4	30.3	23.4	17.1	0.5	–5.3	–4.3	–3.2
Wipro	55.6	54.7	45.8	41.3	22.3	0.2	–8.4	–10.5	–3.7
Infosys Technologies	36.1	34.9	33.6	27.8	22.2	9.7	–0.9	–4.0	–6.7
CGI Group	14.6	15.1	19.0	13.1	3.3	–9.6	–17.8	–13.6	
Hewitt Associates	5.6	9.8	7.6	7.0	7.3	–3.1	–3.5	–6.4	
HCL Infosystems	26.6	27.7	13.6	–5.5	–8.8	–21.9	–19.8	–9.5	–10.9
Cognizant Technology Solutions	48.0	41.4	39.7	32.7	31.5	25.5	16.0	13.3	16.2
Convergys Corporation	0.1	–0.9	–0.5	–2.5	–3.9	–1.4	–3.0	–1.0	13.2

Source: Center on Globalization, Governance and Competitiveness (CGGC), Duke University, Durham, NC; based on OneSource, Hoovers, companies' Web sites and annual reports.

Consultancy Services, Wipro, Infosys Systems). The July–September 2009 trimester showed signs of recovery.

Many leading services providers from the developed world have more employees in emerging nations than in their own countries. This trend has accelerated during the recession. In order to mitigate the effects of the economic crisis, large providers have decided to expand their operations to developing countries and to reduce their personnel located in rich economies. These actions will help cut provider costs because salaries in emerging economies are just a fraction of those in developed countries. For example, IBM laid off more than 4,000 U.S. workers in January 2009 and moved these positions to developing economies, including Brazil, China, the Czech Republic, India, Mexico, the Russian Federation, and South Africa. To reduce negative social effects, the company created Project Match, in which laid-off U.S. workers with strong employment records could be relocated to the countries mentioned above, although with local salaries and employment conditions (McDougall 2009). Table 9.4 shows a select list of offshore services providers from the United States, Europe, and India that have reported layoff and hiring activities during the economic crisis.

The hiring and layoff activities reported in table 9.4 include changes implemented at the global level; however, hiring trends have been concentrated in the developing countries, with most retrenchments and layoffs occurring in developed economies. For example, Accenture announced they will hire 8,000 people in India during 2010, and Wipro added 3,500 workers in India and the Philippines between 2008 and 2009. Genpact hired almost 3,000 people in Guatemala, India, Morocco, the Philippines, Poland, Romania, and South Africa during 2009, and the company was planning to hire an additional 10,000 workers in early 2010. On the other hand, in November 2009, Logica, the British offshore services company, laid off 2,200 workers in the United Kingdom from their 40,000-worker labor force. Some of the growth effects noted for these leading companies reflect the acquisition of a large number of small companies, absorbing additional employees. This consolidation is one of the main effects of the economic crisis and was expected to continue in 2010.

The consolidation of this industry as a result of the economic crisis has also had an impact on the two most mature destinations: India and the Philippines. By the end of 2009, India controlled approximately 45 percent of the offshore services market, while the Philippines saw impressive growth in the five years leading up to the crisis. The section below highlights this impact on service supply in these developing nations, focusing in particular on the decline in attrition rates.

High employee attrition is one of the most pressing problems of the industry, specifically in India, and it is also affecting the market in the Philippines. In the Philippines, a survey carried out in mid-2009 revealed that 79 percent of the offshore

Table 9.4 Select Offshore Services Provider Hiring and Layoff Actions during the Economic Crisis, Late 2008 to Early 2010

Company	Date	Laid off	Hired	Action	Location
Accenture United States (Ranking: 2)	Mar 2009	500		Crisis effect	Manila, Philippines
	Aug 2009		100	Rehiring some of the people laid off	Philippines
	Aug 2009	300		Crisis effect and restructuring	Worldwide
	Oct 2009		NA	Acquisition to serve new sector	United States
	Feb 2010		NA	Acquisition	Rio de Janeiro, Brazil
	2010		8,000		Mostly in India
CSC United States (Ranking: 4)	Late 2008		20		India
	Nov 2008		5	Acquisition to serve local customers	Tianjin, China
	Early 2009	98			East Greenbush, NY, U.S.
	Aug 2009		550	Acquisition to serve local customers and strengthen existing sector	Brazil
	Sept 2009		65	New center to offer shared services	Albany, NY, U.S.
Capgemini France (Ranking: 5)	April 2009	56		Layoff of managers	Irving, CA, U.S.
	May 2009	100		Layoffs of middle management	Chennai, India
	Jun 2009		45	New center to perform IT help desk support and business continuity work	Iasi, Romania
	Nov 2009	85		Layoffs of middle management	Dallas, TX, U.S.
	Nov 2009		10	New center	Bangalore, India
	Jan 2010		200	New BPO to serve local customers	Katowice, Poland

Logica United Kingdom (Ranking: 8)	Apr 2009		NA	New International Utilities Competence Center	Portugal
	Oct 2009		NA	New center on IT-based solutions	Chennai, India
	Nov 2009	2,200		Laid off for restructuring	United Kingdom
Wipro India (Ranking: 11)	Sept 2008	1,000		Laid off for restructuring	India
	Dec 2008		2,500	Acquisition to follow customer	India
	2009		1,000	New center	Philippines
	Q3 2009	630			
	Nov 2009		100	New center, IT and BPO	Chengdu, China
	Jan 2010	85		Layoffs in telecom R&D sector	Finland
Genpact India (Ranking: 20)	2009		2,400	New center	Guatemala, South Africa, Philippines, Romania, Morocco, India
	Mar 2009		500	New center to serve customers in EU	Lublin, Poland
	Oct 2009		70	New remote operations center	Hyderabad, India
	2010		10,000		Worldwide
	Feb 2010		1,200	Acquisition	India and United States

Source: Center on Globalization, Governance and Competitiveness (CGGC), Duke University, Durham, NC; based on company Web sites, company press releases, news articles, and reports from consulting firms.
Note: Ranking refers to the top-20 offshore services companies (see table 9.2). BPO = business process outsourcing; EU = European Union; IT = information technology; R&D = research and development.

services providers had noted attrition rates as the "same," "decreasing," or "decreasing significantly" (Philippine Daily Inquirer 2009). During the crisis, India saw a reduction in the attrition rates, to levels similar to those of three years ago. According to a survey by IDC and Dataquest, India's average IT sector attrition rate decreased from 18 percent to 15 percent in 2009 (Business Standard 2010). For the last quarter of 2008, the attrition rates for TCS, Wipro, and Infosys were 11.9 percent, 11.9 percent, and 11.8 percent, respectively. Just one year earlier, the rates were 11.5 percent, 20.1 percent, and 13.7 percent, respectively, for the three IT majors (AbhiSays.com 2009). There was general consensus among senior management from the Indian offshore services providers that the highlight of the difficult 2008 crisis year was the decline in attrition rates. Alok Aggarwal, chairman and cofounder of Evalueserve, a KPO firm, noted that "attrition in the offshore outsourcing industry came down significantly and Indian employees became more realistic about their expectations and about their careers. The current expectations will be able to provide a more sustainable, long term growth for the Indian offshore-outsourcing industry" (BPOWatch India 2008).

Overall, the economic crisis has had various effects on offshore services. Some clients have frozen contracts, while others have demanded additional services in order to reduce costs. Providers have responded to the changing demands by employing a number of different strategies to reduce their own costs, including lowering salaries, opening offices in cheaper locations, and finding innovative solutions to enhance efficiency. As a result, even more activities are being moved to developing countries, both from developed nations to India, and also from India to other developing countries, due to labor arbitrage (substituting cheaper workers for more expensive ones) and the search for talent. The structural changes that facilitated the initial development of the offshore services industry have accelerated during the economic crisis, and these changes will likely become entrenched in future years.

Substitution Effect Versus Demand Effect

During the recent global economic crisis, the offshore services industry suffered two conflicting effects.[6] The first is the "substitution effect" whereby activities are relocated to cheaper locations, leading to the growth in offshoring. The "demand effect" is a decrease in demand from the industry's clients that were affected by the recession and consequently reduced their offshoring services.

Substitution Effect

In a globally competitive environment, companies use different strategies to reduce costs. Unbundling activities and relocating them to countries that have lower labor costs has gained popularity in the past 10 years. In other words, there has been a substitution effect, moving activities from high-cost locations to lower-cost locations. This phenomenon has continued during the economic crisis. Indeed, some countries have seen acceleration in the offshore services industry.

According to *The 2009 A.T. Kearney Global Services Location Index*, the economic slowdown may increase the number of clients that use offshoring in their search for cost reductions. The report also notes that new offshore operations tend to be more efficient because they are not constrained by the bureaucracy in place in onshore facilities (A.T. Kearney 2009b).

A recent study on human resources (HR) outsourcing (Hewitt Associates 2009) says that HR departments will maintain their strategies aimed at outsourcing HR services despite the economic crisis. One-third of the companies surveyed indicated that they were more inclined to outsource compared to two years ago because of the cost reductions and improved efficiencies. In 2006, the same survey showed that the most important activity for HR managers was to "attract, retain, and grow talent," whereas the 2009 survey found that their number one impetus is to "reduce operating costs" (Hewitt Associates 2009). The U.S. consulting firm Deloitte, for example, is planning to hire 15,000 people in India over the next three years. The company's global chief executive Jim Quigley explains: "The global economic crisis is also an opportunity to expand and acquire assets at attractive valuations" (Current IT Market 2009a).

A country case example of the substitution effect is the Philippines, which has seen accelerated growth in offshore services in the past three years, despite the global financial crisis. According to the Business Processing Association–Philippines (BPAP), the offshore services industry in 2006 generated approximately US$3.3 billion in revenues and employed more than 235,000 people. Further, the association estimates that by the end of 2010, the industry will reach US$13 billion and will employ close to 1 million people (BPAP 2007).[7]

A key factor explaining this sustained growth is that the services being carried out in the Philippines are considered "nondiscretionary spending," that is, services essential to maintaining a company's business operations.[8] The country is now one of the leading destinations worldwide for call centers, as well as finance and accounting outsourcing. According to the Call Center Association of the Philippines, call centers generated US$5 billion in revenues in 2009 and employed more than 275,000 people (Villafania 2009). The capital Manila has already become the world's largest city destination for BPO activities (Vashistha and Nair 2010). Its large workforce, low costs, and significant English-speaking population make it a key destination for these services. A number of Indian providers have opened up call center operations in the Philippines during the past two years, to diversify their operations base and further lower costs.

The offshore services industry in the Philippines began less than 10 years ago and showed growth rates from 2004 to 2007 on the order of 50 percent annually (see table 9.5). During the crisis, the information technology–BPO services revenue growth rate declined to 24 percent in 2008 and 18 percent in 2009. However, comparing the same indicators in India (see table 9.6), the Philippines presents higher growth rates in both industry revenues and employment. In 2009, the growth rate for offshore services employment in the Philippines was 19 percent compared to India's 11 percent.

The past two years have confirmed the consistent rise of the Philippines as a leading BPO destination. In the opinion of some market experts, the crisis has accelerated the takeover of India's back office supremacy by the Philippines (SiliconIndia 2009). In 2007, India had more than 300,000 call agents, while the Philippines had just half of that. Today, India and the Philippines have equal strength with 350,000 employees each in call centers (Economic Times 2010).

According to a survey of BPO providers conducted by the Business Processing Association of the Philippines and Outsource2Philippines, 49 percent of executives said that in 2009–10 they would expand their headcount by at least 11 percent; 33 percent of the respondents confirmed that the crisis had accelerated their service

Table 9.5 Offshore Services Industry Indicators in the Philippines, 2004–09

Indicator	2004	2005	2006	2007	2008	2009
Philippines GDP (current US$, billions)	84.6	98.4	117.6	144.1	167.5	160.8
GDP growth (percent)	6.1	5.0	5.3	7.1	3.8	0.9
Revenues of offshore services industry: Philippines (US$, billions)	1.5	2.2	3.3	4.9	6.1	7.2
Growth rate of offshore services industry (percent)	46	47	50	48	24	18
Offshore services share of Philippines GDP (percent)	1.8	2.2	2.8	3.4	3.6	4.5
Offshore services employment	101,000	163,000	236,000	300,000	372,000	442,000
Growth rate of offshore services employment (percent)	61	61	45	27	24	19

Sources: National Statistical Coordination Board; Business Processing Association of the Philippines; Economist Intelligence Unit.

Note: Offshore services industry refers to information technology–business process outsourcing (IT-BPO).

Table 9.6 Offshore Services Industry Indicators in India, 2004–09

Indicator	2004	2005	2006	2007	2008	2009
India GDP (current US$, billions)	700.9	810.2	914.9	1,176.9	1,217.5	1,182.2
GDP growth (percent)	6.9	9.3	9.4	9.6	5.1	7.7
Revenues of offshore services industry: India (US$, billions)	12.9	17.7	23.6	31.3	40.4	47[a]
Growth rate of offshore services industry (percent)	37	37	33	33	29	16
Offshore services share of India GDP (percent)	1.8	2.2	2.6	2.7	3.3	4.0
Offshore services employment	830,000	1,058,000	1,293,000	1,621,000	2,010,000	2,236,614[a]
Growth rate of offshore services employment (percent)	27	27	22	25	24	11

Source: Center on Globalization, Governance and Competitiveness (CGGC), Duke University, Durham, NC; based on data from NASSCOM and the World Bank; Economist Intelligence Unit.
a. NASSCOM estimates.

expansion process; only 5 percent declared that the effect of the crisis was "very significant." Finally, the poll showed that some innovative firms were identifying new opportunities as a result of the downturn (Philippine Daily Inquirer 2009; TeamAsia 2009). Overall, it is estimated that the BPO industry in the Philippines will create 90.000 new jobs during 2010 (ABS-CBNnews.com 2010).

Many of the leading companies in the BPO industry, such as Genpact, Wipro BPO, Intelenet, Aegis BPO, and Firstsource, are scaling up their investments in the Philippines. Wipro BPO, one of the largest Indian service companies that specializes in IT and BPO, set up a new BPO center in Cebu City, Philippines, that hired 1,000 workers (SiliconIndia 2009). Similarly, Convergys opened three new call centers in the Philippines employing 3,000 workers in April 2009 (TeamAsia 2009).

Chile has also seen an increase in its offshore services operations during the economic crisis. Prior to 2000, the offshore services industry in Chile was insignificant. Yet by 2008, the country registered close to US$1 billion in service exports (IDC Latin America 2009). Today the Chilean offshore services industry includes companies in all areas of offshoring, ITO, BPO, and KPO, as well as industry-specific services that cannot be easily applied in other industries (Gereffi and Fernandez-Stark 2010).[9] ITO and BPO services have grown considerably, together accounting for over one-third of offshore exports and 12,300 jobs (IDC Latin America 2009).

The Chilean industry has not been severely affected by the economic crisis, and the sector continues to grow, with several new projects established in the country during 2009. Of particular importance was General Electric's announcement in September 2009 that it was opening a new IT center in Valparaiso, Chile, that would hire 1,000 workers (*El Mercurio* 2009). More offshore services providers are planning to set up new projects, including Tata Consulting Services, McAfee, UST Global, and Konecta.[10]

Demand Effect

A second, and in some ways contradictory, effect of the economic crisis is a general decline in the demand for offshore services by existing clients. This is the first time that the industry has faced a slowdown; however, it still presents positive growth rates. A key factor in the decline has been the slack demand from the financial services sector, which was severely affected by the economic crisis. The financial sector has consistently been the largest buyer of offshore services, representing 32 percent of demand in 2008 (Technology Partners International 2008). The slowdown in demand is the result of a number of factors, including frozen offshore service contracts, a reduction in the scope of the contracts, and pressure on pricing (NASSCOM Newsline 2009). The immediate consequences for providers have been the need to lay off workers, reduce salaries, and freeze hiring.

One of the most affected countries in terms of decreasing demand is India. The national characteristics that are key for offshore industry growth—low costs, strong technical and language skills, vendor maturity, supportive government policies, and an effective industry association—have made India the global leader of offshore services, with approximately 45 percent market share (NASSCOM 2008). The industry has evolved steadily, upgrading its activities from lower value-added activities to more advanced activities such as R&D services. Table 9.6 shows continuous positive growth rates for Indian offshore services, which grew fourfold in five years; in 2004, revenues were US$12.9 billion, while in 2009 revenues were estimated to reach US$47 billion. By 2008, offshore services employed over 2 million people, with an indirect job creation of about 8 million (NASSCOM 2009).

The offshore services industry's growth rates slowed down from around 30 percent during 2004–08 to 16 percent in 2009. This decrease also affected the industry's employment. While aggregate employment reached 2.3 million in 2009 (NASSCOM 2009), employment growth rates slowed from an average of 25 percent between 2004 and 2008 to 11 percent in 2009 (NASSCOM 2009). One of the groups in India most affected by this economic crisis is new IT graduates: more than half of the 300,000 graduates were left unemployed in 2009. The oversupply of workers has also affected entry-level salaries, which have declined up to 30 percent (Current IT Market 2009b).

During the crisis, Tata Consultancy Services, the largest Indian offshore services provider, announced 1,300 layoffs, approximately 1 percent of its total workforce. Additionally, the company increased working hours to 45 hours per week from 40 hours (Finance Trading Times 2009). Despite these effects, the company is already showing signs of recovery and is planning new hiring in 2010 (Current IT Market 2009b). This is also true for other Indian companies like Wipro and Cognizant, which have begun offering promotions and salary increases. Infosys is also experiencing a recovery, but its policy is to wait for greater stability before offering promotions and salary increases (Indiatimes Infotech 2009).

The Indian industry began to show signs of recovery in the last months of 2009. A recent report from NASSCOM (India's National Association of Software and Services Companies), the offshore services Indian association, explains that the first half of 2009 was extremely difficult, with business paralysis and clients requesting immediate cost reductions. In the second half of the year, clients appeared to be in a better situation. They were requesting longer-term cost reduction initiatives moving forward and demonstrating a willingness to analyze new projects and initiatives. The Indian offshore services industry is expecting this slowdown to end during 2010 (NASSCOM Newsline 2009).

Since the economic downturn, the industry is still adjusting to the new business environment. The most important changes in India's offshore services as a result of the crisis (NASSCOM Newsline 2009)[8] are as follows:

- Greater services specialization, with companies covering niche needs
- Industry consolidation
- New demand from vertical services
- Expansion into new locations
- Payment based on performance.

The Differential Impact of the Economic Crisis across Segments of the Offshore Services GVC

The economic crisis has impacted all segments of the offshore services GVC, especially vertical offshore activities, in different ways.[11] Sectors negatively impacted by the global recession generally faced lower demand for offshore services. In other cases, clients in industries less affected by the recession show similar demand patterns as before the financial downturn, and in some cases there is demand for even more services.

The impact of the crisis also depends on the maturity of the industry in different countries, making it difficult to generalize across the value chain. For example, India saw similar declines in both IT and BPO activities, while the Philippines IT services sector was more affected than the BPO segment in which the country has more experience. In this section, two case studies of India and the Philippines, the two leading countries in these segments, provide further analysis of the impact of the crisis on the value chain.

In general, KPO services have been more insulated from the economic downturn. Business intelligence and legal services continued to perform well during the crisis. According to Gartner's annual EXP Worldwide Survey 2009 (Gartner 2009), covering 1,500 chief information officers worldwide, the business intelligence sector was the top investment priority. It has been the top priority for four consecutive years, and companies in the sector continue to grow, taking advantage of new opportunities afforded by the crisis. For example, MAIA Intelligence, an Indian market intelligence provider, launched affordable reporting and analytics solutions for small and medium enterprises. In the past, this service had only been available for large enterprises, but MAIA Intelligence found this niche to be an opportunity to offer this innovative product (NASSCOM Newsline 2009).

Legal services, referred to as legal process outsourcing in the GVC, are still mostly limited to India. The annual growth rate slowed from 40 percent precrisis, still reached a promising growth of 28 percent in 2008, which in 2009 declined to 16 percent (India PRwire 2009). The two largest companies in the segment, Mindcrest and CPA, saw positive growth during the crisis, likely the result of early and rapid consolidation of the still infant industry segment, with 20 percent of the providers in India exiting the industry (BPOWatch India 2008). Leading companies expect the sector to expand significantly in 2010 as a result of the tremendous cost-saving opportunities afforded for law firms (Crain's Chicago Business 2010).

Impact of the Crisis on National Offshore Services GVCs

The Indian offshore services industry faced the crisis with an already mature industry that had strengths in several key areas: IT and BPO services, engineering services, R&D, and software products. Prior to the crisis, the industry presented a sound upgrading trajectory. The country entered the industry offering IT services, moving to BPO operations and later added KPO activities. Additionally, the Indian industry provides sophisticated services to vertical industry segments, including R&D services. India has offerings in the entire offshore services GVC shown in figure 9.2.

The IT sector accounts for 57 percent of the total services; BPO activities, 27 percent; and engineering services, R&D, and software products, 16 percent. These market shares have been constant since 2005, and the economic crisis did not impact the proportions (see table 9.7 and figure 9.7).

Figure 9.7 shows that almost every Indian segment of the offshore services industry saw a decline in demand in 2009. The IT services segment had growth rates equal to or higher than 30 percent during the period 2006–08, but during the economic downturn, the growth rate decreased to 16 percent. BPO activities followed a similar pattern, experiencing growth rates over 30 percent annually and decreasing to half of that rate in 2009. The third category, engineering services and R&D, and software products, based on discretionary spending projects, is subject to greater fluctuation in demand and saw its growth shrink slightly more than the other segments. This is a category that combines two completely different sets of activities, "engineering services and R&D" and "software products." Offshoring of engineering and R&D services has shown strong growth in the past two years, leading to the assumption that the fluctuations represent changing demand for new software products.

Table 9.7 India's Revenues from the Offshore Services Industry, FY2005–FY2009

Fiscal year/ indicator	IT services	BPO	Engineering services and R&D, software products	Total
2005				
Revenue (US$, billions)	10	4.6	3.1	17.7
Percentage of total revenue	56	26	18	100
2006				
Revenue (US$, billions)	13.3	6.3	4	23.6
Percentage of total revenue	56	27	17	100
2007				
Revenue (US$, billions)	17.8	8.4	4.9	31.1
Percentage of total revenue	57	27	16	100
2008				
Revenue (US$, billions)	23.1	10.9	6.4	40.4
Percentage of total revenue	57	27	16	100
2009 (estimate)				
Revenue (US$, billions)	26.9	12.8	7.3	47
Percentage of total revenue	57	27	16	100

Source: NASSCOM.
Note: BPO = business process outsourcing; IT = information technology; R&D = research and development.

Figure 9.7 India's Offshore Services Industry Growth Rate, 2006–09

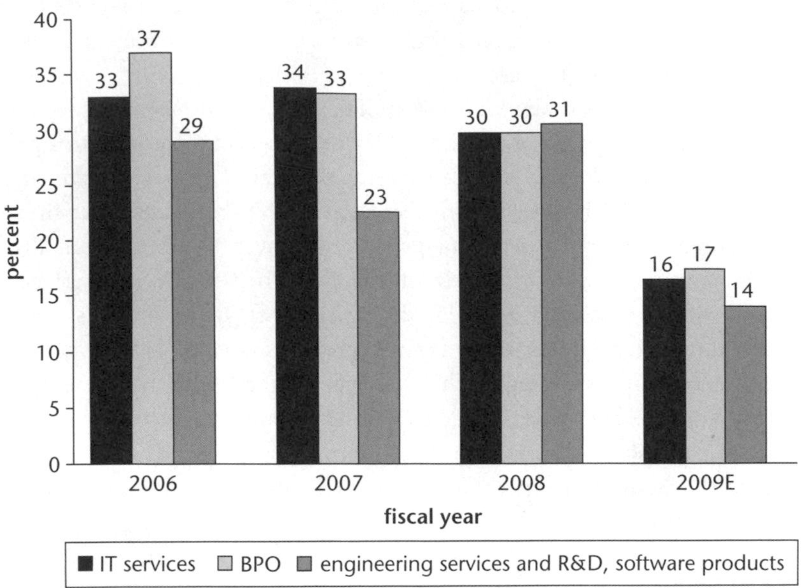

Source: NASSCOM.
Note: BPO = business process outsourcing; E = estimate; IT = information technology.

In the Philippines, the offshore services industry is concentrated in BPO activities. In 2009, revenues in this segment increased by 22 percent over the previous year. The KPO segment increased by 35 percent, and similar trends were expected for 2010 (BusinessMirror 2010). According to the Business Processing Association of the Philippines (BPAP), 70,000 jobs were created in 2009 in the BPO sector alone. The IT sector, on the other hand, declined by 5.5 percent, while revenues for other activities such as engineering services outsourcing and transcription were unaffected by the crisis (BusinessMirror 2010).

Impact of the Crisis on Industry-Specific Vertical Services

As mentioned earlier, banking, financial services and insurance (BFSI) was the economic sector most affected by the global recession. It is also the industry that uses the highest percentage of offshore services. In 2008, BFSI represented 41 percent of the total Indian offshore services market (NASSCOM 2009). The downturn of the mortgage market and related financial markets hit firms in the sector hard, shrinking demand for their services; as a result, BPO revenue from these sectors became exposed and vulnerable (Gartner 2009). At the same time, on top of a decline in demand for BPO services, these firms cut back on their IT spending. Financial institutions in Europe and the United States have reduced their outsourcing activities sharply in the wake of the financial crisis. By one account, they have cut the volume of newly awarded IT outsourcing contracts by nearly 30 percent in 2008 compared to the previous year, explained Deutsche Bank economist Thomas Meyer (Meyer 2009).

According to Gartner, the decrease in demand for offshore services in the BFSI sector is also the result of insourcing strategies. The consolidation of the banking industry as a consequence of the crisis has resulted in a negative impact on the offshore services sector. A number of financial services firms merged, with previously outsourced processing being absorbed by internal shared-service centers. This was an important strategy to employ existing internal human resources to avoid even more widespread layoffs (Gartner 2009).

Offshore services providers that serve the BFSI segment thus saw demand for their services decline, with clients asking to renegotiate contracts. In order to respond to client demand, providers reduced internal costs, reorganized production, and also cut wages. For example, TCS, India's largest exporter of financial services, reacted to the crisis by reducing salaries by 1.5 percent and cutting new hires from 35,000 to 30,000. Similarly, Infosys reduced hiring by 10,000, to just 25,000 new recruits, far below their precrisis hiring estimates (Business-In-Asia, 2008). However, this trend appears to be temporary; as soon as economic expectations improve, the companies are likely to increase salaries again. In early 2010, TCS, Infosys, and Wipro announced wage increases of 8 to 12 percent (Business Standard 2010).

A number of providers in the sector responded to the crisis with a different approach based on innovation and diversification of the product portfolio. FIS, for example, is one of the world's largest providers of banking and payments technology, with the U.S. banking industry accounting for 67 percent of its total client base (ABS-CBN news.com 2010). This American company consolidated its market position by acquiring a key competitor, Metavente, and diversifying its client base (CBR News 2009). It opened a facility in Manila with approximately 1,000 workers (ABS-CBN News 2010) and made new investments to provide innovative, high-quality services. One such innovation, HORIZON,[12] which was released during the crisis, was a best-seller in 2009, attracting many long-terms contracts with large financial institutions (FIS Press Release 2010) and contributing to the flat growth of overall revenues for 2008 despite the crisis.

Other sectors have not been affected significantly by the crisis, and some are even demanding more services. For example, the global health care industry is demanding more IT services from India as a result of the global increased focus on public health and attempts to make health care and health insurances affordable and universal (NASSCOM 2009). Medical transcription services have also expanded during the crisis period, especially in the Philippines. Myla Reyes, the president of the firm Total Transcription Services in the Philippines, explains that "as a cost-cutting measure, more clients tend to 'shop around' for medical transcript service providers outside the US. This gives us an advantage as one of the destinations of choice in providing this type of service" (TeamAsia 2009).

Conclusions

While the offshore services industry has grown tremendously over the past decade, it is still considered a nascent industry with vast potential remaining largely untapped. Companies looking to improve their competitiveness continue to externalize many of their activities, not only back-office operations, but their core activities like R&D as well. The recent demand for these higher value-added activities indicates that few services will be retained exclusively in the developed world and that the industry growth will continue to be strong in future years.

The 2008–09 economic crisis was the first event that has tested the industry, and it has demonstrated marked resilience. The recession forced providers to upgrade and improve their services, increasing both efficiency and competitiveness for clients. The economic downturn created only a small inflection in the industry. The two conflicting effects discussed in this chapter (the substitution effect and the demand effect) are finding a positive reconciliation in 2010. The demand for offshore services continues to increase and is soon expected to reach similar growth rates as in the years before the crisis. The substitution effect will be even stronger in the future, as new sources of demand emerge from industries with limited current participation in the sector and as suppliers gain a greater degree of specialization. Increased growth and industry consolidation will, in turn, drive expansion to new locations, creating further opportunities for developing countries.

Offshore services is one of the few global industries where some developing nations have a real competitive advantage over the developed world, owing to their low cost of service provision and their educated labor force. Developing countries with a strong educational infrastructure thus have an important opportunity to enhance their economic development with this industry. Looking ahead, there is still room for new economies to emerge as offshore destinations. More activities will be offshored and more talent will be sought. This presents a great opportunity for developing countries to continue upgrading their economies to offer higher value-added activities that in the past were reserved for developed nations.

Notes

1. While outsourcing contributes significantly to gross domestic product (GDP) in developed countries, it requires internal or domestic demand to drive it. Most developing countries do not have sufficient demand for these internal services for them to be major factors in economic development.
2. For a detailed description of governance of GVCs, see "Value Chain Governance" (Frederick and Gereffi 2009).
3. NASSCOM® is the chamber of commerce of the IT-BPO industries in India. NASSCOM is a global trade body with more than 1,200 members, which include both Indian and multinational companies that have a presence in India.
4. At the end of FY 2007, Capgemini's Indian operations added at least 8,000 new employees, taking the figure from the current 27,000 to a new high of 35,000, surpassing for the first time the number of employees in the United States (Shah 2007).
5. According to the report, "Solid utilities provide available and cost-effective infrastructure, trusted suppliers add product delivery capabilities, and partner players are tightly aligned with the business" (Andrews 2008, 4).
6. As mentioned previously, the offshore services industry is a recent global phenomenon and has been evolving rapidly. There are no official data available at a global level. The economic crisis analysis in this section is based on country and company cases that support the main findings.
7. These estimates were prepared before the economic crisis.
8. Nair, Ed. 2010. "The Impact of the Economic Crisis in the Offshore Services Industry." Personal communication with K. Fernandez-Stark. March 10.
9. For an in-depth description and analysis of the global offshore services value chain, as well as the evolution of each segment of the industry in Chile, see Gereffi and Fernandez-Stark (2010) and Fernandez-Stark, Bamber, and Gereffi (2010).
10. Castillo, Mario. 2010. "Offshore Services Industry—CORFO—Chile." Personal communication with CGGC research team, February 18.
11. See figure 9.2 for a diagram of the offshore services value chain.
12. HORIZON is a core account processing, solution for financial institutions. It offers financial reporting capabilities, transaction processing, and relationship management technology to help banks gain a more comprehensive view of their customers.

References

AbhiSays.com. 2009. "IT Attrition Rate Has Gone Down in India." January 31. Accessed March 3, 2010 from http://abhisays.com/sofware-companies/it-attrition-rate-has-gone-down-in-india.html.

ABS-CBN News. 2010. "Financial BPO Sets Up Shop in Philippines." February 17. Accessed March 2, 2010 from http://www.abs-cbnnews.com/business/02/17/10/financial-bpo-sets-shop-philippines.

ABS-CBN news.com. 2010. "BPO Targets 90,000 More Jobs in 2010." February 22. Accessed March 8, 2010 from http://www.abs-cbnnews.com/business/02/22/10/bpo-targets-90000-more-jobs-2010.

Andrews, Christopher. 2008. "Selling IT Services in an Economic Downturn: When Economic Conditions Are Poor, Segmentation and Positioning Matter More Than Ever." Cambridge, MA: Forrester Research, Inc.

A.T. Kearney. 2007. "Offshoring for Long-Term Advantage." In *The 2007 A.T. Kearney Global Services Location Index*. Chicago, IL: A.T. Kearney.

———. 2009a. "The Future of Outsourcing in Latin America: El Salvador," A.T. Kearney, April 23.

———. 2009b. "Geography of Offshoring Is Shifting: The 2009 A.T. Kearney Global Services Location Index." Retrieved March 3, 2010 from http://www.atkearney.com/index.php/News-media/geography-of-offshoring-is-shifting.html. http://www.atkearney.com/images/global/pdf/Global_Services_Location_Index_2009.pdf.

Bárcena, Alicia. 2009. *Competitividad: Visión de Organismos Regionales.Comisión Económica para América Latina (CEPAL).* Conference: Foro de Competitividad de las Américas III, Santiago, Chile. September 28–29.

BCG (Boston Consulting Group). 2007. *Estudios de Competitividad en Clusters de la Economía Chilena. Documento de Referencia Offshoring.* May 18.

BPOWatch India. 2008. "Best of 2008 and Challenges for 2009." Accessed March 5, 2010 from http://www.bpowatchindia.com/BPO_special_features.html.

Business-In-Asia. 2008. "Business Process Outsourcing (BPO) Hitting a Speed Bump in Asia as a Result of Financial Crisis." Accessed March 7, 2010 from http://www.business-in-asia.com/news/business_process_outsourcing.html.

BPAP (Business Processing Association of the Philippines). 2007. "Offshoring and Outsourcing Philippines: Roadmap 2010." Business Processing Association of the Philippines. http://www.bpap.org/bpap/ publications/bpap_roadmap.pdf.

Business Standard. 2010. "After Two-Year Lull, Top Indian IT Firms Plan 8–12% Salary Increases." March 4. Accessed March 8, 2010 from http://www.business-standard.com/india/news/after-two-year-lull-top-indian-it-firms-plan-8-12-salary-increases/387460/.

BusinessMirror. 2010. "RP's BPO Revenue Grows 19% in 2009." February 10. Accessed March 7, 2010, from http://www.businessmirror.com.ph/index.php?option=com_content&view=article&id=21636:rps-bpo-revenue-grows-19-in-2009&catid=23:topnews&Itemid=58.

CBR News. 2009. "FIS to Acquire Metavante: Competitive Dynamics and Implications." April 9. Accessed March 2, 2010 from http://enterpriseapplications.cbronline.com/comment/fis_to_acquire_metavante_competitive_dynamics_and_implications_090409.

Chakrabarty, Sujit K., Prashant Gandhi, and Noshir Kaka. 2006. "The Untapped Market for Offshore Services: McKinsey." http://www.mckinseyquarterly.com/Operations/Outsourcing/The_untapped_market_for_offshore_services_1772.

Crain's Chicago Business. 2010. "Legal Outsourcer Mindcrest Taps India for Talent." January 26. Accessed March 1, 2010 from http://www.chicagobusiness.com/cgi-bin/blogs/ecity.pl?plckController=Blog&plckScript=blogScript&plckElementId=blogDest&plckBlogPage=BlogViewPost&plckPostId=Blog%3a16ea2629-7e90-46f0-a706-dd6152764513Post%3a9a9aafb0-d460-464d-9126-12285381178 c&plckCommentSortOrder=TimeStampAscending&sid=sitelife.chicagobusiness.com.

Current IT Market. 2009a. "Deloitte to Hire 15,000 People in India." November 11. Accessed March 8, 2010 from http://www.currentitmarket.net/2009/11/deloitte-to-hire-15000-people-in-india.html.

———. 2009b. "IT's Not All That Hot for Fresh Recruits." November 4. Accessed March 4, 2010 from http://www.currentitmarket.net/2009/11/its-not-all-that-hot-for-fresh-recruits.html.

Datamonitor. 2009. *Global IT Services.* London: Datamonitor.

Dossani, Rafiq, and Martin Kenney. 2007. "The Evolving Indian Offshore Services Environment: Greater Scale, Scope and Sophistication." Sloan Industry Studies Working Papers. http://www.industry.sloan.org/industrystudies/workingpapers/.

Duke Offshoring Research Network & Booz&Co. 2007. "Offshoring 2.0: Contracting Knowledge and Innovation to Expand Global Capabilities." https://offshoring.fuqua.duke.edu/pdfs/DukeServiceProviderReport_web.pdf.

ECLAC (Economic Commission for Latin America and the Caribbean [of the United Nations]). 2009. "Foreign Direct Investment in Latin America and the Caribbean." Santiago, Chile: Economic Commission for Latin America and the Caribbean.

———. 2008. "Offshore Corporate Services in Latin America and the Caribbean." Seminar held in Santiago, Chile, October 13.

Economic Times. 2010. "India's Long-reigning Voice BPO Losing Out on Accent." *The Economic Times.* Accessed January 26, 2010 from http://economictimes.indiatimes.com/infotech/ites/Indias-long-reigning-voice-BPO-losing-out-on-accent/articleshow/5478861.cms.

El Mercurio. 2009. "Nuevo Centro de GE en Chile Generará US$50 mills. en Exportanciones y Mil Puestos de Empleo." *El Mercurio.* August 13, p. 4.

Everest Research Institute. 2009. *Market Vista Annual: Global Sourcing*. Dallas, TX: Everest.

Fernandez-Stark, Karina, Penny Bamber, and Gary Gereffi. 2010. "The Chilean Offshore Services Industry: A Global Value Chain Approach." Report for Chilean Agency for Economic Development. Center on Globalization Governance and Competitiveness, Duke University, Durham, NC.

Finance Trading Times. 2009. "TCS Layoffs Job Cut: To Fire 1300 Employees." March 8. Accessed March 4, 2010 from http://www.finance-trading-times.com/2009/03/tcs-job-cutstcs-layoff-layoff-tcs-job.html.

FIS Press Release. 2010. "FIS' HORIZON Increasing Deployment Momentum." January 13. Accessed March 8, 2010 from http://finance.yahoo.com/news/FIS-HORIZON-Increasing-bw-2083533586.html?x=0&.v=1.

Frederick, Stacy, and Gary Gereffi. 2009. "Value Chain Governance." USAID Briefing Paper, Center on Globalization, Governance, and Competitiveness, Duke University, Durham, NC. http://www.microlinks.org/ev.php?ID=35948_201&ID2=DO_TOPIC.

Gartner. 2009a. "Business Process Outsourcing Vendor Consolidations: Is Your Contract at Risk?" August 27.

———. 2009b. "Gartner EXP Worldwide Survey: 2009." Accessed January 8, 2010 from http://www.gartner.com/it/page.jsp?id=855612.

Gereffi, Gary, and Karina Fernandez-Stark. 2010. "The Offshore Services Industry: A Global Value Chain Approach." Report for the Chilean Agency for Economic Development. Center on Globalization Governance and Competitiveness, Duke University, Durham, NC.

Gereffi, Gary, John Humphrey, Raphael Kaplinsky, and Timothy J. Sturgeon. 2001. "Introduction: Globalisation, Value Chains and Development." *IDS Bulletin* 32 (3): 1–8.

Gospel, Howard, and Mari Sako. 2008. "The Unbundling of Corporate Functions: The Evolution of Shared Services and Outsourcing in Human Resource Management." Report for Society for the Advancement of Socio-Economics Conference, San Jose, Costa Rica.

Gupta, J. B. 2008. "Drug Discovery and India: A Force to Reckon With." *Pharma Focus Asia* 9. Accessed August 18, 2009 from http://www.pharmafocusasia.com/strategy/drug_discovery_india_force_to_reckon.htm.

Harris, Jason. 2009. "Outsourcing Forecast Assumptions, Worldwide, 2000–2013." Gartner. http://www.gartner.com/DisplayDocument?id=1106212.

Hewitt Associates. 2009. "HR Outsourcing Trends and Insights—Survey Findings." http://www.hewittassociates.com/_MetaBasicCMAssetCache_/Assets/Articles/2009/Hewitt_HR_Outsourcing_Study_2009_Results.pdf.

IDC Latin America. 2009. *La Industria dc Servicios Globales en Chile—Estudio Cluster de Servicios Globales*. Santiago: Chilean Agency for Economic Development.

India PRwire. 2009. "Negative Short Term Impact on Legal Process Outsourcing." November 17. Accessed March 7, 2010 from http://www.indiaprwire.com/pressrelease/other/2009111737681.htm.

Indiatimes Infotech. 2009. "No Hikes, Promotions at Infosys." September 14. Accessed March 4, 2010 from http://infotech.indiatimes.com/articleshow/5008359.cms.

Lewin, Arie, Silvia Massini, Nidthida Perm-Ajchariyawong, Derek Sappenfield, and Jeff Walker. 2009. "Getting Serious about Offshoring in a Struggling Economy." https://offshoring.fuqua.duke.edu/pdfs/Shared%20Services%20News_ORN.pdf.

Lopez, Andres, Daniela Ramos, and Ivan Torre. 2008. *Las Exportaciones de Servicios de América Latina y su Integración en las Cadenas de Valor*. Buenos Aires: CENIT: Documento realizado para la Comisión Económica para América Latina y el Caribe (CEPAL). March 2008.

McDougall, Paul. 2009. "IBM Offers to Move Laid Off Workers to India." *InformationWeek* February 2. Accessed January 12, 2010 from http://www.informationweek.com/news/global-cio/outsourcing/showArticle.jhtml?articleID=213000389.

McKinsey & Company. 2006. "The Untapped Market for Offshore Services." *McKinsey Quarterly*. http://www.mckinseyquarterly.com/The_untapped_market_for_offshore_services_1772.

McKinsey Global Institute. 2009. "The Emerging Global Labor Market." Accessed July 17, 2009 from http://www.mckinsey.com/mgi/publications/emerginggloballabormarket/Part2/supply.asp.

Meyer, Thomas. 2009. "Economic Crisis Complicates Offshoring of Services." February 9. *YaleGlobal*. Accessed January 12, 2010 from http://www.yaleglobal.yale.edu/content/economic-crisis-complicates-offshoring-services.

NASSCOM. 2008. "NASSCOM-Everest India BPO Study: Roadmap 2012—Capitalizing on the Expanding BPO Landscape." NASSCOM, New Delhi.

———. 2009. "Indian IT-BPO Industry Factsheet." Accessed July 17, 2009 from http://www.nasscom.in/upload/5216/IT_Industry_Factsheet-Mar_2009.pdf.

NASSCOM Newsline. 2009. "2009 Is Gone. 2010 Beckons: The IT-BPO Industry—Looking Back, Looking Ahead." December. Accessed March 3, 2010 from http://blog.nasscom.in/nasscom newsline/2009/12/2009-is-gone-2010-beckons-the-it-bpo-industry-looking-back-looking-ahead/.

OECD (Organisation for Economic Co-operation and Development). 2008. "Europe Regional Investment Strategy: Key Findings of the Sector Specific Study." Private Sector Development Division, Organisation for Economic Co-operation and Development, Sarajevo, BA.

Philippine Daily Inquirer. 2009. "BPOs Not Entirely Crisis-Proof, Study Says." May 28. Accessed March 1, 2010 from http://business.inquirer.net/money/topstories/view/20090528-207661/BPOs-not-entirely-crisis-proof-study-says.

Sako, Mari. 2005. "Outsourcing and Offshoring: Key Trends and Issues." Paper presented at the Emerging Markets Forum, Oxford, UK. Accessed July 6, 2009 from http://www.sbs.ox.ac.uk/NR/rdonlyres/99F135D4-E982-4580-9BF0-8515C7B1D40B/1752/EMFOutsourcingNov05.pdf.

Shah, Kalpana. 2007. "Accenture Shifts Growth to India." *Red Herring*. Accessed January 6, 2010 from http://www.redherring.com/Home/20989.

SiliconIndia. 2009. "India Fast Losing BPO Jobs to Philippines." December 27. Accessed March 8, 2010 from http://www.siliconindia.com/shownews/India_fast_losing_BPO_jobs_to_Philippines_-nid-64084-cid-1.html.

Sturgeon, Timothy, and Gary Gereffi. 2009. "Measuring Success in the Global Economy: International Trade, Industrial Upgrading, and Business Function Outsourcing in Global Value Chains." *Transnational Corporations* 18 (2): 1–35.

TeamAsia. 2009. "State of the BPO Industry: Well-Managed, Innovative Firms Are Growing." June 16. Accessed March 8, 2010 from http://www.teamasia.com/pr/PR_clientnews.asp?art_no=489.

Technology Partners International. 2008. "The TPI Index." http://www.tpi.net/knowledgecenter/tpiindex/

UNCTAD. 2009. "Information Economy Report 2009: Trends and Outlook in Turbulent Times." United Nations Conference on Trade and Development, New York and Geneva. http://www.unctad.org/en/docs/ier2009_en.pdf.

Vashistha, Avinash, and Ed Nair. 2010. "Location Assessment: Perception and Reality for Global Businesses." Webinar, January 15,Tholons Inc. & Global Services.

Villafania, Alexander. 2009. "Call Center Revenues Reach $5B in '09." Accessed January 11, 2010 from http://newsinfo.inquirer.net/breakingnews/infotech/view/20090720-216409/Call-center-revenues-reach-5B-in-09.

Wadhwa, Vivek, Ben Rissing, Gary Gereffi, John Trumpbour, and Pete Engardio. 2008. "The Globalization of Innovation: Pharmaceuticals; Can India and China Cure the Global Pharmaceutical Market." Kauffman Foundation. http://papers.ssrn.com/sol3/papers.cfm?abstract_id=1143472#PaperDownload.

Young, Allie, Dane S. Anderson, Kenneth F. Brant, Robert H. Brown, Linda R. Cohen, Susan Cournoyer, Claudio Da Rold, Matthew Goldman, Helen Huntley, Venecia K. Liu, Richard T. Matlus, William Maurer, Ben Pring, Cathy Tornbohm, Gianluca Tramacere, Jim Longwood, Ian Marriott, Dean Blackmore, T. J. Singh, Cassio Dreyfuss, and Rishi Sood. 2008. "Gartner on Outsourcing, 2008–2009." Gartner. http://www.gartner.com/DisplayDocument?doc_cd=164206.

INDEX

Boxes, figures, maps, notes, and tables are indicated by *b*, *f*, *m*, *n*, and *t*, respectively.

B

T

U

ECO-AUDIT

Environmental Benefits Statement

The World Bank is committed to preserving endangered forests and natural resources. The Office of the Publisher has chosen to print ***Global Value Chains in a Postcrisis World: A Development Perspective*** on recycled paper with 50 percent postconsumer fiber in accordance with the recommended standards for paper usage set by the Green Press Initiative, a nonprofit program supporting publishers in using fiber that is not sourced from endangered forests. For more information, visit www.greenpressinitiative.org.

Saved:

- 16 trees
- 5 million Btu of total energy
- 1,512 lb. of net greenhouse gases
- 7,280 gal. of waste water
- 442 lb. of solid waste